George Buchanan

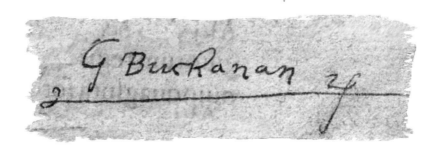

George Buchanan's signature from *Scotorum Historiæ a prima gentis origine, cum aliarum et rerum et gentium illustratione non vulgari, libri XIX. Hectore Boethio Deidonano auctore ... Accessit & huic editioni eiusdem Scotorum Historiae continuatio, per Ioannem Ferrerium Pedemontanum* (Paris, 1574), fol. 1r. Courtesy of St Andrews University Library (classmark TypSwL.B74LBA)

George Buchanan

Political Thought in Early Modern Britain and Europe

CAROLINE ERSKINE
University of Aberdeen, UK

and

ROGER A. MASON,
University of St Andrews, UK

ASHGATE

Published by
Ashgate Publishing Limited
Wey Court East
Union Road
Farnham
Surrey, GU9 7PT
England

Ashgate Publishing Company
Suite 420
101 Cherry Street
Burlington
VT 05401-4405
USA

www.ashgate.com

British Library Cataloguing in Publication Data
George Buchanan: Political Thought in Early Modern Britain and Europe. –
    (St Andrews Studies in Reformation History)
    1. Buchanan, George, 1506–1582 – Influence. 2. Buchanan, George,
    1506–1582 – Political and social views. 3. Political science – Great Britain –
    History – 16th century. 4. Political science – Great Britain – History –
    17th century. 5. Political science – Europe – History – 17th century.
    6. Scotland – Politics and government – 17th century – Philosophy.
    I. Series II. Mason, Roger A. III. Erskine, Caroline.
    320'.01'092–dc23

Library of Congress Cataloging-in-Publication Data
George Buchanan: Political Thought in Early Modern Britain and Europe /
    edited by Roger Mason and Caroline Erskine.
        p.   cm. – (St Andrews Studies in Reformation History)
    Includes bibliographical references and index.
    1. Buchanan, George, 1506-1582 – Political and social views. 2. Great Britain
    – Intellectual life – 16th century. 3. Europe – Intellectual life – 16th century.
    I. Mason, Roger A. II. Erskine, Caroline.
    DA787.B9G54 2012
    320.01–dc23   2011051254

ISBN 9780754662389 (hbk)
ISBN 9781409448648 (ebk)

Printed and bound in Great Britain by the
MPG Books Group, UK

Contents

List of Abbreviations

BL	British Library
Buchanan, *De Iure Regni*	*A Dialogue on the Law of Kingship among the Scots, a Critical Edition and Translation of George Buchanan's 'De Iure Regni apud Scotos Dialogus'*, ed. Roger A. Mason and Martin S. Smith (Aldershot, 2004)
Buchanan, *History*	George Buchanan, *History of Scotland*, ed. and trans. James Aikman (4 vols, Glasgow, 1827)
Buchanan, *Opera Omnia*	*Georgii Buchanani ... Opera Omnia*, ed. Thomas Ruddiman (2 vols, Edinburgh, 1714-15)
Buchanan, *Political Poetry*	George Buchanan, *The Political Poetry*, ed. and trans. Paul J. McGinnis and Arthur H. Williamson (Scottish History Society, 1995)
Buchanan, *Tragedies*	George Buchanan, *The Tragedies*, ed. and trans. P. Sharratt and P.G. Walsh (Edinburgh, 1983)
Buchanan, *Tyrannous Reign*	*The Tyrannous Reign of Mary Stewart: George Buchanan's Account*, ed. and trans. W.A. Gatherer (Edinburgh, 1958)
CSP Foreign	*Calendar of State Papers, Foreign: Edward VI, Mary, Elizabeth I* (25 vols, London, 1861-1950)
CSP Scot.	*Calendar of State Papers relating to Scotland and Mary Queen of Scots* (13 vols, Edinburgh, 1898–1969)
Durkan, *Buchanan Bibliography*	John Durkan (ed.), *A Bibliography of George Buchanan* (Glasgow, 1994)
EUL	Edinburgh University Library
McFarlane, *Buchanan*	I.D. McFarlane, *Buchanan* (London, 1981)
NAS	National Archives of Scotland
NLS	National Library of Scotland

ODNB	*Oxford Dictionary of National Biography*
STC	*A Short Title Catalogue of Books Printed in England, Scotland and Ireland and of English Books Printed Abroad, 1475–1640*, ed. A.W. Polland, G.R. Redgrave *et al.* (3 vols, London, 1976-91)

List of Figures

Notes on Contributors

John Coffey is Professor of Early Modern History at the University of Leicester. He is the author of several books, including *Politics, Religion and the British Revolutions: The Mind of Samuel Rutherford* (Cambridge, 1997). Most recently, he has co-edited *The Cambridge Companion to Puritanism* (Cambridge, 2008) and *Seeing Things Their Way: Intellectual History and the Return of Religion* (Notre Dame, 2009).

Martin Dzelzainis is Professor of Renaissance Literature and Thought at the University of Leicester. An acknowledged authority on Milton, he is the editor of John Milton, *Political Writings* (Cambridge, 1991) and has written extensively on political culture in seventeenth-century England. Among other current projects, he is completing *The Flower in the Panther: Print and Censorship in England, 1660–1690* for OUP, and editing Milton's historical writings for OUP's *Complete Works of Milton*.

Caroline Erskine is a Teaching Fellow in History at the University of Aberdeen. She is a co-editor of *Scotland: The Making and Unmaking of the Nation c.1100–1707* (Dundee, 2007), and her interests lie primarily in political traditions and historical narratives of resistance as an aspect of the Scottish Reformation, and the transmission and reception of these through the sixteenth and seventeenth centuries.

Andrew Hadfield is Professor of English at the University of Sussex. He is the author of a number of works on early modern literature, including *Shakespeare and Republicanism* (Cambridge, 2005, paperback, 2008); *Literature, Travel and Colonialism in the English Renaissance, 1540–1625* (Oxford, 1998, paperback, 2007); *Spenser's Irish Experience: Wilde Fruyt and Salvage Soyl* (Oxford, 1997); and *Literature, Politics and National Identity: Reformation to Renaissance* (Cambridge, 1994). He is the editor of *Renaissance Studies* and a regular reviewer for *The Times Literary Supplement*. He is currently working on a biography of Edmund Spenser for OUP, and is editing *The Oxford Handbook to English Prose, 1500–1640*.

Clare Jackson is Lecturer and Director of Studies in History at Trinity Hall, Cambridge. She has been co-editor of *The Historical Journal* and is the author of *Restoration Scotland. Royalist Politics, Religion and Ideas,*

1660–1689 (Woodbridge, 2003), together with numerous articles on early modern British political, legal and intellectual history. She is currently researching a biography of Sir George Mackenzie of Rosehaugh (1636–91), and is also editing the volume of *Later English political writings* for *The Cambridge Edition of the Works of Jonathan Swift*.

Colin Kidd is Professor of Modern British History at the University of St Andrews. He was elected a Fellow of the British Academy in 2010. His most recent book is *Union and Unionisms: Political Thought in Scotland 1500–2000* (Cambridge, 2008).

Tricia A. McElroy is Assistant Professor of English at the University of Alabama and on faculty for the Hudson Strode Program in Renaissance Studies. She has published articles on Scottish satire and the memoirs of Sir James Melville of Halhill. Her current projects include a book about Mary Queen of Scots and a new edition of Reformation satirical literature for the Scottish Text Society.

Allan I. Macinnes is Professor of Early Modern History, University of Strathclyde. He has written extensively on British state formation, Scottish Jacobitism and Highland Clans. His latest monograph is *The British Confederate: Archibald Campbell, Marquess of Argyll, c.1607–1661* (Edinburgh, 2011).

Roger A. Mason is Professor of Scottish History and Director of the Institute of Scottish Historical Research, University of St Andrews. He has written extensively on early modern Scottish political thought and culture, including the ideas of John Knox and George Buchanan. He is the editor (with Martin Smith) of *A Dialogue on the Law of Kingship among the Scots, a critical edition and translation of George Buchanan's 'De Iure Regni apud Scotos Dialogus'* (Aldershot, 2004).

Esther Mijers is a lecturer in History at the University of Reading. She has worked extensively on Scottish commercial, educational and cultural links with the Low Countries and is the author of a monograph on Charles Mackie and the Republic of Letters published by Brill as well as several articles on Scotland and the Netherlands.

Astrid Stilma is Senior Lecturer in English Literature at Canterbury Christ Church University in Kent, where she teaches early modern drama. She is particularly interested in the interplay between literature, religion and politics, and has published on the writings of King James VI & I, George Buchanan, and representations of kingship and resistance in Jacobean drama.

Robert von Friedeburg is Professor of Modern History and Director of the Erasmus Centre for Early Modern Studies at Erasmus University Rotterdam. His recent publications include *Self-Defence and Religious Strife in Early Modern Europe: England and Germany, 1530–1680* (Aldershot, 2002); 'The Roots of Modern Germany', in Helmut Walter Smith (ed.), *Compendium of Modern German History* (Oxford, 2011); 'Ecclesiology and the English state. Luther and Melanchthon on the Independence of the Church in English Translations of the 1570s', *Archiv für Reformationsgeschichte*, 101 (2010): pp. 137–161; and 'The Holy Roman Empire of the German Nation' (sections I–III), in Howell Lloyd *et al.* (ed.), *European Political Thought, 1450–1700* (New Haven, 2007), pp. 102–166.

Arthur Williamson is Professor of History at California State University, Sacramento. His most recent books include: *Apocalypse Then: Prophecy and the Making of the Modern World* (Westport, CT, 2008); *The British Union: a critical edition and translation of David Hume of Godscroft's 'De Unione Insulae Britannicae'* (with Paul McGinnis; Edinburgh, 2002); *George Buchanan: the Political Poetry* (with Paul McGinnis; Edinburgh, 2000). His 'The Nation Epidemicall: From Scoto-Britannus to Scoto-Polonus' appeared in *Britain and Poland-Lithuania* edited by Richard Unger (Leiden, 2008). Most recent is his 'The Rise and Decline of the British "Patriot": Civic Britain, *c.* 1545–1605', *International Review of Scottish Studies* 36 (2011): pp. 7–32. He is currently working on a volume under the title, *Scotland and the European Social Imagination: from radical nominalism to political economy*.

Preface

This volume has grown out of a conference held at the University of St Andrews in 2006 to mark the 500th anniversary of George Buchanan's birth. Papers delivered at the conference appear here in revised and expanded form, while others were written, primarily by the editors, to fill perceived gaps in the book's coverage of Buchanan's thought and legacy. That the gestation period between the conference itself and the publication of its proceedings has been so appallingly protracted is entirely my responsibility. The contributors to the volume have been models of patience and forbearance as a combination of illness, incompetence and indolence has made the business of pulling the collection together a far longer and more sporadic one than I could ever have envisaged or than they should ever have been asked to tolerate. I am grateful to them all, but especially to my co-editor, Caroline Erskine, who has borne the brunt of the project's stop-start 'progress' and without whose sterling work on the introduction its publication might have been still further delayed.

The book's eventual appearance, however, does give me a very belated opportunity to thank those institutions and individuals who helped make the conference a hugely enjoyable and stimulating event. These include the British Academy and the School of History at the University of St Andrews for financial support; the staff of the University Library's Special Collections Department for making it possible to mount an exhibition on the theme of the conference; and Dr Jamie Reid Baxter and the Director of 'Sang Scule', James Hutchinson, for an extraordinary performance in St Salvator's Chapel of the musical settings by Jean Servin and Statius Olthoff of Buchanan's Psalm Paraphrases. Particular thanks are also due to 'Team GB' – John McCallum, Steven Reid, Claire Webb (now Gregory) and Isla Woodman – who have all now moved on to better things, with doctorates in hand, but without whose good humour and practical help the conference would have been much the poorer.

Roger A. Mason
St Andrews
November 2011

George Buchanan: Influence, Legacy, Reputation

Caroline Erskine and Roger A. Mason

George Buchanan (1506–82) was the most distinguished Scottish humanist of the sixteenth century with an unparalleled reputation as a Latin poet, playwright, polemicist, historian and political theorist. Aspects of his political thought have received considerable attention from historians, not least his espousal of a remarkably radical theory of popular sovereignty, and he is generally recognized as a thinker whose importance extends well beyond the confines of Scottish history to the broader fields of British and Continental Renaissance and Reformation studies.[1] Recent years have seen important steps in the production of modern editions of his writings, with the publication of English translations of his political poetry and of his short but incendiary political tract, *De Iure Regni apud Scotos*.[2] Yet, while Buchanan's significance in the ideological battles of the sixteenth century has long been recognized, little attempt has been made to explore the subsequent influence of his writings. The purpose of this volume, therefore, is to explore Buchanan's legacy in the two centuries following his death, focusing primarily on his political, historical and polemical output.

Of Buchanan's life, we need only provide a brief sketch.[3] Born into the Gaelic-speaking community of Killearn, in Stirlingshire, in 1506, Buchanan acquired mastery of Latin at an early age, facilitating the cosmopolitan leanings and extensive travel that would mark his career. Of the seventy-six years of his life, he spent more than thirty abroad. He studied and taught in St Andrews and Paris universities in the 1520s and 1530s, where he encountered the respected Scottish scholastic theologian John Mair (or Major), but, more significantly, was exposed to the 'new learning' of the

---

[1]   Hence the inclusion of Buchanan in standard general studies of early modern political thought: e.g., Quentin Skinner, *The Foundations of Modern Political Thought* (2 vols, Cambridge, 1978), esp. vol. 2; and J.H. Burns and Mark Goldie (eds), *The Cambridge History of Political Thought, 1450–1700* (Cambridge, 1991).

[2]   Buchanan, *Political Poetry*; Buchanan, *De Iure Regni*. Buchanan's longest work, the 20-book *Historia*, remains the least studied of his works, and is in need of a modern translation.

[3]   The standard biography is McFarlane, *Buchanan*; but see also P. Hume Brown, *George Buchanan: Humanist and Reformer* (Edinburgh, 1890).

humanists. It was primarily as a humanist educator and man of letters that Buchanan built his reputation in the succeeding decades, acting as tutor to an illegitimate son of James V of Scotland before a flirtation with Protestantism forced him into exile. From Scotland he fled first to England, then to a teaching post at the Collège de Guyenne in Bordeaux and subsequently to a professorship of Greek at the new University of Coimbra in Portugal, where further allegations of heresy led to a period of imprisonment by the Lisbon Inquisition. By the time of his release in 1552 Buchanan had authored a number of didactic plays, including *Jephthes* and *Baptistes*, a profusion of Latin poems on subjects ranging from royalty to Reformation, and the Psalm Paraphrases produced during his imprisonment. These Latin literary works, often with a sharp political as well as spiritual edge, would be published and republished throughout the early modern period and beyond.[4]

Buchanan spent the remainder of the 1550s in France and Italy, cultivating the patronage of the French monarchy and the related and influential Guise family. His brushes with Protestantism apparently behind him (he entered the Catholic priesthood in 1557), his prospects for a life as a Valois court poet appeared secure. But the years from 1559 to 1561 brought about a number of significant reverses for Buchanan and the woman with whom his prospects were becoming ever more closely linked: Mary Queen of Scots. Her marriage to the French Dauphin in 1558 had promised an alliance of the families of Stuart, Guise and Valois, and a union of the Scottish and French crowns, which Buchanan duly celebrated in stylish Latin verse. But the death of Mary's husband Francis in 1560 left her with little option but to return to her own kingdom. Buchanan also decided to make his way home, and he and his Queen returned to Scotland, probably at around the same time, in 1561. They arrived in a Scotland that was much changed since their enforced departures, not least as a result of the Protestant Reformation, which the previous year had severed the country's links with its Catholic past and shifted its diplomatic alliances away from France and towards England. In contrast to Mary, by the time of his return to Scotland, Buchanan had switched confessional allegiances (under circumstances that remain obscure) and was a declared and committed Protestant.

For a time Buchanan was on very good terms with Mary, her continued adherence to the Catholic faith notwithstanding. He acted as her unofficial court poet and classical tutor, for which he received a pension in 1564. But by the mid-1560s Buchanan was cultivating relations with a new potential patron, the Queen's half-brother, James Stewart, Earl of Moray, the

---

[4]   For the full range of his works and their publication history down to 1715, see Durkan's invaluable *Buchanan Bibliography*.

unofficial leader of the Protestant cause in Scotland. Following the murder of Mary's second husband, Lord Darnley, in 1567, Buchanan turned against her and became the Queen's most violent detractor. He acted as Moderator of the General Assembly in the pivotal summer of 1567, the time of Mary's deposition; and in 1570, he was appointed tutor to James VI, the son in whose favour Mary had been forced to abdicate. Buchanan was instrumental in preparing the 'case for the prosecution' against Mary, narrating her misdeeds and attempting to justify her deposition in the polemical *De Maria Scotorum Regina* (better known as the *Detectio*) first published in 1571. His political theory had the same aim, justifying rights of resistance against tyrannical monarchs, and the *De Iure Regni apud Scotos*, although published in 1579, was probably written as early as 1567. In his *Rerum Scoticarum Historia*, published in 1582, the last year of his life, Buchanan sought to demonstrate that his principles of resistance were embedded in the grand sweep of Scottish history.

These three texts – the *Detectio*, the *De Iure Regni* and the *Historia* – were not Buchanan's bestselling works, either during his lifetime or after his death in 1582. They were consistently outsold by collections of his poetry and editions of his Psalm Paraphrases.[5] However, they were his most controversial works, and therefore those which were most contested in his life and afterlife. All were responses to the deposition of Mary Queen of Scots. The *Detectio* is a polemical smear of the Queen as an adulteress and a murderess and included some of the text of the infamous Casket Letters that implicated Mary in an affair with Bothwell and the plot to murder Darnley. The *De Iure Regni* is a more abstract essay in political theory that contends that, if a monarch degenerates to rule as a tyrant, he or she can be legitimately resisted by the people, or even murdered by an individual citizen. And the *Historia* recounts the history of Scotland from long before the time of Christ through to the reign of Mary herself in order to demonstrate that such principles of resistance were consistently practised in Scotland, although more often by virtuous members of the nobility than by a lowly or lone assassin. It is primarily these three key works, and how they were received and interpreted, used and abused, in the two centuries following Buchanan's death, that are the subject of the following chapters.

The essays in Part One consider their impact among Buchanan's contemporaries and their immediate successors in England as well as Scotland. Roger Mason's opening chapter reminds us that, despite the radicalism of his political ideas, Buchanan's stature as a cultural icon in early modern Scotland made his *Historia* in particular a text that even

---

[5]   For a major recent reassessment of his literary output, see Philip Ford and Roger P.H. Green (eds), *George Buchanan: Poet and Dramatist* (Swansea, 2009).

those unsympathetic to his politics appealed to as an authoritative source. Thus it is argued that, in the face of English hostility, both his endorsement of the antiquity of the Scottish royal line and the pioneering description of Scotland that opens the *Historia* played a critical role in Scottish self-fashioning in the decades immediately before and after the union of the crowns in 1603. This is followed by Tricia McElroy's unpicking of the *Detectioun of the duinges of Marie Quene of Scots*, the Scots and English version of the 1571 *Detectio*, examining in fine detail the polemical strategies of Buchanan's writing in tension with those of Elizabeth's government in England and its wish to smear Mary without being seen to debase monarchy. Next Andrew Hadfield considers Edmund Spenser's reading of Buchanan's writings on ancient and recent history in *A View of the Present State of Ireland*, and *The Faerie Queene*, written in the 1590s, to argue that, while Buchanan's radicalism did not entirely rub off on Spenser, the latter's comments on the responsibilities of monarchs had a radical character that did not go unnoticed by either Elizabeth in England or James VI in Scotland. Finally, Arthur Williamson links British to European concerns by exploring the international character of the rhetoric of patriotism in the 1570s and 1580s, when Wars of Religion traumatized France and Revolt against Spain shattered the Netherlands, and examines Buchanan's critical significance in the development of civic discourse in Britain and beyond.

As Part Two on Buchanan in Europe highlights, the international applications and connections of Buchanan's writings were not confined to his own lifetime or to the period immediately after his death, but persisted well into the seventeenth century. Astrid Stilma highlights early translations of Buchanan's *De Iure Regni* and his politically resonant play *Baptistes* into the vernacular, in this case Dutch, illustrating differing receptions in the context of the Dutch Revolt in the 1590s, and the consolidation of the Dutch Republic in the 1650s, to show how translation for different contexts could entail a shifting of Buchanan's texts and emphases. Robert von Friedeburg questions how Buchanan was read in Germany, where those who sought to use his resistance theory – approvingly or disapprovingly – had to struggle to situate it amid multiple and overlapping layers of authority, municipal, civil and ecclesiastical, and where the language of citizenship and patriotism was embedded in a complex legal frame of reference. And Allan Macinnes considers the reception of Buchanan's writings – most particularly the *Historia* – in northern Europe in the seventeenth century, from Denmark–Norway, where the Oldenburg dynasty had pretensions towards absolutism, to the commonwealth of Poland–Lithuania, where the tradition of *rokosz* or aristocratic rebellion appealed to ideas of resistance and elective kingship through sources that included Buchanan's writings – ideas that *mutatis mutandis* might find application in Britain in the debates surrounding the Revolution of 1688–89 and the Anglo-Scottish parliamentary union of 1707.

As this suggests, the reception of Buchanan's ideas on resistance was also highly significant in the British Isles in the seventeenth century. Yet that reception was by no means straightforward, as the chapters in Part Three on Buchanan and Revolutionary Britain clearly illustrate. For example, while John Milton may have shared Buchanan's view on the right of an individual to kill a tyrant, it is far from certain that he derived the idea from reading the *De Iure Regni*. Indeed, as Martin Dzelzainis argues, while both Buchanan and Milton might draw on a rich and much-debated heritage of Calvinist and neo-scholastic resistance theory, their explosive endorsement of single-handed tyrannicide can be derived more simply from a passage in Cicero's *De Officiis*. In similar revisionist vein, John Coffey questions Buchanan's influence on the Scottish Covenanters in their disputes with the Stuart monarchy, from Samuel Rutherford in the 1640s to Alexander Shields in the 1680s, and argues that, while his *Historia* supplied the Covenanters with a usable Protestant past, the influence of the *De Iure Regni* was patchy and shaped by shifting contexts as the Covenanting movement progressed from the political mainstream led by aristocrats to a persecuted plebeian remnant. In contrast, Clare Jackson considers the private writings of the remarkable former mercenary and royalist officer James Turner, which range from fanciful fictions demonizing Buchanan to reasoned critiques of his political thought and history, but which ultimately attribute to Buchanan's pernicious influence much of the blame for the mid seventeenth-century disorders in the three kingdoms. Finally, Caroline Erskine compares the reception of Buchanan's writings in seventeenth-century England to those of the more celebrated and canonical contemporary resistance theorists John Locke and Algernon Sidney, to argue that the bestowal of celebrity and canonicity upon political theories is dependent on contingency as much as on merit.

While the infernos of regicide, revolution and resistance had largely burned out by the end of the seventeenth century, the embers of these issues continued to glow well into the eighteenth century, and Part Four considers the influence of Buchanan in the age of Enlightenment, an age that was very distant from that in which he himself had lived. Esther Mijers offers a re-evaluation of Charles Mackie, the first professor of 'Universal History' at the University of Edinburgh, looking through the lens of his engagement with Buchanan's historical writings to argue that he was both a more sophisticated historian and a less vulgar Whig than has been supposed. Mackie's critique of Father Thomas Innes's attempted demolition of Buchanan's ancient kings, and involvement in an abortive attempt to provide a Whig alternative to the Jacobite Thomas Ruddiman's edition of Buchanan's *Opera Omnia*, offer important reflections on the continuing vitality of Buchanan's legacy. This emerges too from Colin Kidd's survey of the vigorous contestation of theories and examples of assassination from the sixteenth to the nineteenth centuries, tracing the changing currents of denominational and intellectual controversy over this issue, rooted in the theories of George Buchanan and the actions of the Restoration Covenanters – not least the murder of Archbishop James Sharp – and still resonating in the novels of John Galt and James Hogg in the 1820s. Finally, in the concluding chapter of the collection, Caroline Erskine assesses the reputation of George Buchanan down to 1788, two centuries after his death, when a monument to him was erected in his birthplace of Killearn, arguing that the firebrand theorist of resistance was rehabilitated in eighteenth-century Scotland as a moderate Protestant hero in line with the 'Revolution Principles' that celebrated the Revolution of 1688. Buchanan thus took his place in a pantheon of Scottish heroes that stretched from William Wallace to Robert Burns.

From this wide range of contributions, a number of common themes emerge, but also a number of methodological difficulties concerning how one demonstrates or quantifies such an elusive concept as the 'influence' of a thinker upon his contemporaries or upon later generations. 'Influence' is a term used by many of the contributors to this volume, although often with caution. Andrew Hadfield gives examples of what Spenser 'may have taken from Buchanan', but he notes that observations of this type made by historians can be 'no more than speculative, shadowy possible resemblances'. Colin Kidd detects Buchanan's 'shadowy presence' behind the controversies over the righteousness of assassination. Arthur Williamson allows that Buchanan had 'intellectual heirs' or 'successors', but emphasizes their re-evaluation of his legacy in their own times. And Martin Dzelzainis and Caroline Erskine grapple with the question of whether it can be verified that giants of political theory in seventeenth-century England such as John Milton, John Locke and Algernon Sidney read the works of George Buchanan. Even where Buchanan's name is cited, it is by no means certain that his texts have been read accurately, or even read at all.

These issues arise in many forms in the following chapters, but are most directly confronted and problematized by Caroline Erskine in her chapter on Buchanan, Sidney and Locke. She argues that anxiety about 'influence' among historians arises from Quentin Skinner's methodological warnings on the risk of creating 'mythologies' in the analysis of political texts. He has argued that, to attempt to chart the influence of one theorist upon another, or the extent to which an earlier theorist 'anticipated' later ideas, is effectively to debase the history of ideas to a 'search for approximations to the ideal type'.[6] To avoid the vocabulary of influence, Conal Condren suggests that historians take up an alternative vocabulary of 'usage'. Users can be acknowledged for their creative appropriations from older texts, and not merely treated as passive receivers of influence.[7] The terminology of 'usage' is gaining ground among historians of political thought, and even more so among historians working in the emerging field of the study of reputations. Such an approach is exemplified by Blair Worden's *Roundhead Reputations*, an analysis of how the afterlives of English radicals and regicides, such as Edmund Ludlow and Oliver Cromwell, were shaped.[8] In such studies, the users, far from being passive receivers of wisdom from the recent or distant past, hold all the power.

Users can be considered as exploiters and even creators of texts, ideas and symbols from the past. Worden identifies editors and biographers as influential shapers of alternative versions of the past, and the contributors to this volume reach similar conclusions, treating the timing and context of the publication or republication of Buchanan's writings as significant. Roger Mason shows how sections of Buchanan's *Historia* were selected and repackaged – with and without acknowledgement – to serve a variety of political and patriotic ends. Tricia McElroy explains that the 1571 English edition of the *Detectioun* should properly be seen as a distant collaboration between George Buchanan and Elizabeth's government, a 'trump card' that was held back for some years until the Ridolfi plot of 1571 made the discrediting of Mary Queen of Scots desirable. Astrid Stilma analyses a Dutch translation of the *De Iure Regni* in 1598 as a contribution to the propaganda of the Dutch Revolt, which altered the title of the work to remove the 'apud Scotos' reference and replace it with a Dutch one. Indeed, Allan Macinnes identifies Dutch publishers as instrumental in the transmission of Buchanan's writings throughout Europe. Caroline Erskine considers the context of the first published English translations of the *De Iure Regni* and the *Historia* in the decade between 1680 and 1690. And Esther Mijers notes the controversy over the publication of Buchanan's *Opera Omnia* in 1715, and the formation of a pressure group by those

---

[6]   Quentin Skinner, 'Meaning and Understanding in the History of Ideas', in *Visions of Politics: Regarding Method* (Cambridge, 2002), p. 63.

[7]   Conal Condren, *The Status and Appraisal of Classic Texts* (Princeton, NJ, 1985). Francis Oakley has endorsed Condren's suggestion that the concept of 'usage' is preferable to 'influence', but nonetheless argues that it is an inescapable fact that thinkers have influence upon one another. 'The influence concept,' he declares, has 'an important and probably indispensable role to play in the history of ideas. It should be permitted to play it.' Francis Oakley, 'Anxieties of Influence: Skinner, Figgis, Conciliarism and Early Modern Constitutionalism', *Past and Present*, 151 (1996): pp. 60–110, at p. 110.

[8]   Blair Worden, *Roundhead Reputations: The English Civil Wars and the Passions of Posterity* (London, 2001).

who considered themselves the proper Whig presbyterian custodians of Buchanan's reputation.

The examples raised above highlight the flexibility of the politics of language in early modern Europe. Buchanan's Latinity might be posited as an explanation for the decline of his celebrity in the twentieth and twenty-first centuries. But in the early modern world, Buchanan's Latin was key to exporting his ideas to Europe, where they might thereafter be translated into vernacular languages. In the British Isles too, publication in Latin appears not to have hindered the transmission of his ideas, probably because the standard of Latin among the educated classes was sufficiently high to facilitate the reading of his texts, and secondly because of other means by which Buchanan's message was disseminated in vernacular languages, albeit in diluted and not necessarily accurate forms. Through citations in English language – seventeenth-century theorists from the Covenanter Samuel Rutherford to the regicide John Milton read Buchanan in Latin but cited his ideas in English – Buchanan's name became known and associated with the radical principles of resistance and tyrannicide.

In such instances, editorial treatments of Buchanan – translations, abridgements, additions, and paratextual material such as prefaces – are to be understood not as disrespectful tamperings with Buchanan's sacred texts, but as opportunities to gain insights into the minds of the users, their contexts, their priorities, their moulding of the Buchanan that they wanted. Of course, attempts to enlist Buchanan in support of new causes were not confined to editions of his writings, but can be sought in texts that cited his name and works. The contributors to this volume have sought to draw attention to important citations, and repeatedly emphasize the value of misunderstood or manipulated readings of Buchanan in revealing the preoccupations of his readers and users in early modern Europe. If the contributors, then, are reluctant to call attention to Buchanan's influence on the political and intellectual debates of the seventeenth and eighteenth centuries, the contemporary participants in these debates had no such compunctions.

Studies of reputations tend to trace either a positive or a negative trajectory. For example, Worden's study of the regicides and republicans focuses on those of later generations who treated them as allies, while Jon Parkin's study of the reception of the political thought of Thomas Hobbes focuses mainly on those who opposed his ideas.[9] What emerges from the contributions to this volume is a picture of Buchanan's reputation that is more richly textured, idiosyncratic and even contradictory. Buchanan

---

    [9]   Worden, *Roundhead Reputations*; Jon Parkin, *Taming the Leviathan: The Reception of the Political and Religious Ideas of Thomas Hobbes in England, 1640–1700* (Cambridge, 2007).

was an asset to users who identified with him positively, *and* to those who identified with him negatively. Indeed, in some contexts the protean Buchanan was more useful as a villain than as a hero.

It might be expected that Buchanan would be viewed and shaped positively by Whigs and presbyterians in the British Isles, by those who were most naturally sympathetic to checks upon over-mighty authority. To a considerable extent this was the case, although the following chapters throw up a number of caveats to this observation. John Coffey notes that the Covenanters were the natural heirs of those who shaped the first Scottish Reformation and that, while they did make use of Buchanan's history and political theory, their preoccupation with biblical examples made Buchanan's preference for classical authorities less appealing to them than the more conventionally orthodox writings of John Knox. Colin Kidd notes that following the re-establishment of the kirk in 1690, the presbyterian mainstream was reluctant to acknowledge or celebrate radical heroes such as Buchanan or the Covenanters. And Caroline Erskine argues that the lionization of Buchanan as a Protestant and Whig hero in the eighteenth century required considerable creativity to tame his radicalism. In short, those who might appear to be the intellectual and political successors to Buchanan did not always identify positively with his legacy, and at times displayed downright discomfort over his radical reputation.

Such discomfort was a polemical gift to the enemies of resistance and aggressive reformed Protestantism, and the professors of such views were among the most enthusiastic exploiters of Buchanan's reputation. Robert von Friedeburg emphasizes the significance of negative labels such as 'monarchomach' that were attached to resistance theorists from the more moderate Huguenots to the highly radical Buchanan, and allowed the conflation of Protestant and Jesuit extremes. Clare Jackson's study of the royalist James Turner highlights the extent to which he believed that the Covenanters, regicides and republicans who shaped the three kingdoms in the mid-seventeenth century were acting under the influence of Buchanan's ideas. And Caroline Erskine suggests that royalists during the Restoration, while highly vocal in their denunciations of Buchanan, were among his most careful and penetrating readers.

The well read and the well educated of early modern Europe could choose from many texts to read, and many sources to cite, in their political and polemical battles. In making these choices they weighed up not just the intellectual and ideological value of what they had read, but also the associations – positive or negative – that accompanied the authors' names. While the chapters in this volume demonstrate the extent to which Buchanan was read, admired, used and commemorated in positive senses, many also highlight Buchanan's place as a totemic villain, a symbol of anarchy. Both Robert von Friedeburg and Caroline Erskine notice, while considering quite different contexts, that the negative connotations of Buchanan's name that had developed by the seventeenth century were comparable to those of the Jesuit resistance theorists who advocated the papal power to depose heretical monarchs or sanction their assassination.

These studies reveal that Buchanan had multiple reputations in early modern Europe. There was the Buchanan that was read, the Buchanan that provided a resource for those who wanted to justify or oppose resistance against tyranny or who saw him as a promoter of Scotland's historic integrity. There was the Buchanan that was created; the Buchanan that was not a writer, but a symbol; the Buchanan that was not quite presbyterian enough to stand as a representative of the Covenanting ethos; and the Buchanan that was too radical, too heavily associated with regicide and assassination principles, for the presbyterian mainstream in Scotland after the Glorious Revolution – the Buchanan that had to be shorn of these negative attributes to be celebrated as a hero compatible in 1788 with the Glorious Revolution of a century earlier.

The chapters that follow, then, seek to explore contexts in which Buchanan's name and his works were used, discussed and contested. For the purposes of political theory or polemic Buchanan could serve as a representative of the Calvinism that shaped the Scottish Reformation and deposed a Catholic Queen, as a radical theorist of resistance or 'monarchomach', as a hero or a villain. The vocabulary of 'influence' would do a disservice to the readers of Buchanan and the shapers of his image in early modern Europe and the British Isles, because they were not merely passive receivers of the great man's wisdom, but creative agents using Buchanan to fight their own battles. And so if the terminology of 'usage' is to be preferred to that of 'influence', then the language of 'legacy' might also be considered. 'Legacy' articulates the possibility of a posthumous gift from Buchanan, ideological currency that could be invested or spent according to the needs of later generations. This volume is as much a celebration of Buchanan's readers and their responses to his texts as it is of the man and his writings. The reputation of George Buchanan was wrought not only by the writings he left to posterity, but by the creative and exploitative choices that posterity made and continues to make.

PART ONE
Buchanan in Reformation Britain

CHAPTER 1

From Buchanan to Blaeu: The Politics of Scottish Chorography, 1582–1654[*]

Roger A. Mason

The importance of the appearance in Amsterdam in 1654 of Volume 5 of Joan Blaeu's *Atlas Novus*, with its forty-nine engraved maps of Scotland and its regions, can hardly be exaggerated.[1] This was by any standards a landmark publication. For the first time Scots had to hand a detailed visual representation of their country – its geographical shape and extent and main topographical features – accompanied by verbal descriptions that combined history and geography in a way, known to contemporaries as chorography, that firmly anchored Scotland in time as well as space. The role played by George Buchanan in this project, albeit from well beyond the grave, has not received the recognition it deserves. Yet Buchanan has the unique distinction of being the only Scot, either past or present, to have his birthplace explicitly identified in the *Atlas*, on the map of Lennox where the Moss on the River Blane near Killearn is described as 'G. Buchanani patria'.[2]

At one level, there is a perfectly simple explanation for why Buchanan should have been honoured in this way: he was a cultural icon for early modern Scots, the most distinguished literary figure the country had produced in generations, whose Latin poetry was widely read, revered and imitated throughout contemporary Europe, and who had inspired in Scotland a vogue for neo-Latin poetry of which the makers of the *Atlas*,

---

[*]   This chapter was prompted by work on the exhibition on Buchanan's legacy that accompanied the 2006 conference when my attention was first drawn to the extent to which Buchanan featured in Blaeu's famous *Atlas*. I am grateful to Alison Cathcart, Caroline Erskine, Steven Reid, Jacqueline Rose and Grant Tapsell for their helpful comments on various drafts as it has evolved since the conference took place.

[1]   Joannes Blaeu, *Theatrum Orbis Terrarum, sive Atlas Novus. Pars Quinta* (Amsterdam, 1654). The volume also contains six maps of Ireland.

[2]   A complete facsimile of all the original maps, together with translations of the textual material (by Ian Cunningham), is now available in an excellent modern edition: *The Blaeu Atlas of Scotland* (Edinburgh, 2006), where Buchanan's birthplace will be found marked on map 27: 'The Province of Lennox, called the Shyre of Dun-Britton'.

not least Sir John Scot of Scotstarvit, were very well aware.[3] But Buchanan was also, of course, though much more controversially, a historian and political theorist; and it is not without interest that some copies of the *Atlas* include the entire text of the *De Iure Regni apud Scotos Dialogus* among the range of other information on Scotland that its creators thought it was important to know.[4] More integral to the *Atlas* as such, however, was the description of Scotland that comprised Book I of Buchanan's *Rerum Scoticarum Historia* and that was heavily exploited in providing the textual material that accompanied the regional maps. For in true chorographical fashion, Blaeu's *Atlas* is much more than just a book of maps: it is also an encyclopaedia of Scotland, deliberately intended to make a firm statement about the country's past, present and future status. Buchanan played a critical – if often unacknowledged – role in the development of this cultural project. However, it is one that can only be properly understood by exploring the purposes that his own *Historia* was meant to serve and the continuing significance of its early books in defining who and what the Scots were in the decades following its publication – and its author's death – in 1582.[5]

Buchanan's *Historia*, Books I–IV

Among modern scholars Buchanan's reputation as a historian has never fully recovered from the onslaught on his motives and method launched by Hugh Trevor-Roper as long ago as 1966.[6] It was Trevor-Roper's contention that, by the time he wrote the *Historia* in the 1570s, Buchanan was nothing more than an ageing party hack, justifying the revolutionary events of the 1560s and the theory of revolution he had developed in his *De Iure Regni* by continuing to lend his authority to a view of the Scottish past that he knew to be false. Indeed, according to Trevor-Roper, Buchanan's vanity and deceit are all too apparent in the opening Books I

---

[3]   Scotstarvit was responsible for orchestrating the publication, also by Joan Blaeu, of the great treasury of Scottish neo-Latin verse, *Delitiae Poetarum Scotorum*, edited by Arthur Johnston (Amsterdam, 1637).

[4]   I am grateful to Ian Cunningham for pointing out that the *Atlas* could be customized to suit the purchaser's requirements, so not all copies include the *De Iure Regni*. One in St Andrews University Library (classmark r17ff G1015.B6) has the text (without the dedication to James VI or the concluding lines of verse 'Rex Stoicus ex Seneca') printed in double columns over fifteen leaves with separate foliation and signatures.

[5]   On chorography and national 'self-fashioning' in Scotland, see the pioneering work of Charles Withers, *Geography, Science and National Identity: Scotland since 1520* (Cambridge, 2001).

[6]   H.R. Trevor-Roper, 'George Buchanan and the Ancient Scottish Constitution', *English Historical Review* (1966), supplement 3.

and II of the *Historia* where he attacked in disproportionately angry terms the reputation of an obscure Welsh antiquary, Humphrey Lhuyd or Llwyd (1527–68), whose *Commentarioli Descriptionis Britannicae Fragmentum* had been published posthumously in Cologne in 1572.[7] What lay behind Buchanan's intemperate outbursts against the unfortunate Lhuyd was, according to Trevor-Roper, nothing more but nothing less than the fact that the Welshman had exposed as a fabrication the first seven centuries of the Scottish kingdom's existence as chronicled in immensely colourful detail by Hector Boece in his *Scotorum Historia* of 1527. In other words, Lhuyd had dismissed as entirely fanciful both Boece's story of the Scottish kingdom's foundation by Fergus I in 330 BCE and his subsequent highly elaborate account of some forty Scottish kings who were said to have reigned over an independent Scottish kingship until the fourth century CE. More pertinent for Trevor-Roper's argument, however, was that, in doing so, Lhuyd had also destroyed the historical basis of Buchanan's ancient Scottish constitution, which allegedly rested foursquare on the precedents set by those early Scottish monarchs, so many of whom had degenerated into tyranny and been legitimately held to account by their subjects, but all of whom were now exposed as imaginative fictions. It was, therefore, or so Trevor-Roper gleefully concluded, only with reluctant embarrassment that a discredited Buchanan finally published the *Historia* in the last year of his life.[8]

As we shall see, Trevor-Roper's argument does have some merit, but his contemptuous attitude to the *Historia* is wholly undiscriminating and takes no account of some of the positive – indeed pioneering – aspects of Buchanan's work on the early history of Scotland. As William Ferguson has argued, in Book II of the *Historia*, Buchanan exploited his knowledge of the Gaelic tongue to offer a highly sophisticated analysis of the linguistic communities inhabiting early Britain that adds up to a startlingly original account of the origins of the Celtic peoples, including the hitherto mysterious Picts.[9] In addition, as Ferguson also notes, Book I is the most comprehensive region-by-region survey of Scotland to be written in the sixteenth century and Buchanan deserves much more credit than he is generally accorded for penning what proved to be a remarkably influential

---

[7] The Latin edition was published by Lhuyd's friend, Abraham Ortelius, who had encouraged both his map-making and chorographical studies. It was published in London in 1573, translated by Thomas Twyne, as *The Breviary of Britayne*.

[8] The tone of Trevor-Roper's attack on Buchanan is less hostile in his posthumously published *The Invention of Scotland: Myth and History* (New Haven, CT, and London, 2008), chs. 2–3, but the substance of his case remains the same.

[9] For this and what follows, see William Ferguson, *The Identity of the Scottish Nation: An Historic Quest* (Edinburgh, 1998), ch. 5; see also William Ferguson, 'George Buchanan and the Picts', *Scottish Tradition*, 16 (1990–91): pp. 18–32.

description of the country. Unfortunately, however, Ferguson was so intent on demonstrating that it was Trevor-Roper rather than Buchanan who deserved the epithet 'vain old fraud' that the broader cultural significance of Buchanan's achievement in the *Historia* eluded him. Admittedly, in contrast to Trevor-Roper, he recognized that Lhuyd's demolition of Boece was itself part of an enthusiastic restatement of the historical lore about the ancient Britons, deriving ultimately from Geoffrey of Monmouth, that put the legendary accounts of Brutus and Arthur to work in substantiating English claims to feudal superiority over the British Isles. Despite the scepticism of the likes of Polydore Vergil (still more reviled than Boece by Lhuyd), the so-called 'British History' was still very much alive in the later sixteenth century, shaping English self-perceptions just as it continued to fuel Anglo-British imperial aspirations.[10] As a result, just as Buchanan responded vigorously to the negative view of Scotland's status embedded in this English historiographical tradition, so his compatriots continued to cling to the Fergusian line of kings as proof of the kingdom's antiquity and autonomy throughout the seventeenth century and beyond. Yet, while Buchanan's role in perpetuating this mythology has long been recognized, the ways in which the early books of his *Historia* work together to assert Scotland's unique topographical as well as historical identity have not received the attention they deserve.

It is worth recalling in this respect Trevor-Roper's detailed reconstruction of when Buchanan wrote the *Historia* and particularly his argument, based on a detailed examination of a surviving manuscript of the *Historia*, that its first two books were originally written as a separate work. The manuscript predates the published version of the *Historia* and Trevor-Roper presents a series of convincing arguments in support of his contention that Books I and II comprised a separate composition subsequently pressed into service as an introduction to the seventeen books of the *Historia* proper (with Book III containing extracts from classical and other sources sandwiched between them).[11] The evidence of the manuscript is compelling, and Trevor-Roper may well be correct in arguing that Buchanan wrote Books I and II in a fit of pique following his reading of Humphrey Lhuyd. It is equally possible, however, that the attacks on Lhuyd were worked into an essay on

---

[10]   T.D. Kendrick, *British Antiquity* (London, 1950) is still a useful introduction to Lhuyd's scholarly context and the traditions within which he was working. For a Scottish perspective, see Roger A. Mason, 'Scotching the Brut: Politics, History and National Myth in Sixteenth-century Britain', in Mason (ed.), *Scotland and England, 1286–1815* (Edinburgh, 1987), pp. 60–84. For a more recent treatment, see Philip Schwyzer, *Literature, Nationalism and Memory in Early Modern England and Wales* (Cambridge, 2004), where Lhuyd is discussed in ch. 3.

[11]   The manuscript is in EUL MS Dc 4. 60, and is described in detail in Trevor-Roper, 'Buchanan and the Ancient Constitution', pp. 51–3. My own examination of the MS confirms the accuracy of Trevor-Roper's very full and helpful description.

early Britain that Buchanan had already drafted. Buchanan tells us himself in the dedication to the *Historia* that, when he returned to Scotland from France in 1561, he was entreated by his friends to take up his pen and write a history of his native land – presumably to replace or update Boece's work, which must have seemed increasingly jejune to more sophisticated humanist sensibilities.[12] Indeed, Buchanan may have already embarked on such a project, for we know that a decade earlier in 1552 Giovanni Ferrerio (1502–79), who in 1574 published an edition and continuation of Boece's *Scotorum Historia*, was inquiring after a work of a similar title – 'historiam Scoticam' – that he believed Buchanan to have written.[13] It is certainly conceivable that the young Buchanan, who probably met Boece when the latter travelled from Aberdeen to Paris in 1526 to see his work through the press, should seek subsequently to demonstrate his superior humanist skills by undertaking a linguistic analysis of the peoples of pre-historic Britain that would render tales of the Scots-alleged progenitors, Gaythelos and Scota, as absurdly obsolescent as those of Brutus and Arthur. This is no more than speculation, but further weight may perhaps be added to it by the fact that Buchanan's attacks on Lhuyd occur at the very beginning of Book I, before the description of Scotland gets underway, and at the very end of Book II, where it is more obviously tacked on as an after-thought to Buchanan's essay on the peopling of Britain.[14] Inference aside, however, what we know for certain is that, in the early 1570s, a decade before the

---

[12] See Buchanan, *History*, vol. 1, p. ciii, where he recounts how he was implored to concern himself less with publishing new and accurate editions of his poetry and turn his attention instead to writing the history of Scotland, 'for this was an employment becoming my age, and the expectations of my countrymen; nor was there any other subject more praiseworthy or more likely to confer a lasting reputation'.

[13] McFarlane, *Buchanan*, pp. 416–17. A Piedmontese humanist, Ferrerio was educated at Paris in the mid-1520s where he met both Buchanan and Boece. He spent the years 1528–37 in Scotland, initially at the court of James V and then at the abbey of Kinloss (to which he returned for a second spell between 1541 and 1545). He knew Buchanan well enough to testify against him to the Lisbon Inquisition. For details of his career, see Nicola Royan in *ODNB*, and John Durkan, 'Giovanni Ferrerio, Humanist', in K. Robbins (ed.), *Religion and Humanism* (Oxford, 1981), pp. 181–94.

[14] Buchanan's initial attack on Lhuyd is launched almost immediately in Book I, sparked by Lhuyd's attempt to give the name of Britain a Welsh derivation, and continues for several pages thereafter (*History*, vol. 1, pp. 2–19). It is not clear that Buchanan includes Lhuyd among the unnamed 'recent writers' mentioned at the beginning of Book II who have pronounced so confidently on the obscure subject of the origins of the Britons (ibid., vol. 1, pp. 67–8) or that he can be identified as the writer 'of no mean name' who claimed that 'the Trojans spoke British' (ibid., vol. 1, p. 75), though it is certainly he whose 'stupidity' led him to identify the Attocotti as Scots and the Caledonians as Britons rather than Picts (ibid., vol. 1, p. 93). Buchanan's lengthy attack on Lhuyd, however, and his defence of Boece, comprises the last part of Book II (ibid., vol. 1, pp. 116–29), beginning: 'I had resolved here to finish the dispute respecting the origin of the British nations, had not Lhuyd drawn me unwillingly back, by contending that the Scots and Picts came only lately into Scotland'.

publication of the *Historia*, and possibly in reaction to his reading of Lhuyd, Buchanan wrote or rewrote an essay described in a contemporary source as 'De origine gentium Britanicarum libri duo'.[15] Although Book I of the published *Historia* (the description of Scotland) does contain material relevant to Book II (the linguistic analysis of the peopling of Britain), the 'libri duo' that this refers to may well be the latter together with the extracts from classical and other sources published as Book III.

Trevor-Roper was undoubtedly correct to argue that, in finally preparing the *Historia* for publication, Buchanan was driven by a partisan agenda aimed at legitimizing the Reformation-rebellion of 1560 and the overthrow of a queen regnant in 1567. However, we must also be sensitive to the broader ideological functions served by its early books, up to and including the account of Fergus's foundation of the kingdom and the reigns of his immediate successors in Book IV. For here Buchanan's agenda is not simply to provide precedents for the deposition of kings or even to demonstrate the antiquity of the kingdom, but also to explain the origins of the Scots and describe the physical boundaries and unique topography of the land they inhabited. In both respects, Buchanan improved markedly on what his predecessors had achieved. Before proceeding further, therefore, it is worth glancing at these earlier Scottish efforts to delineate the country and describe its inhabitants to themselves and others.

Descriptions of Scotland before Buchanan

The late medieval Scots' view of themselves as a distinct people with a unique history is most conveniently summed up by the monastic chronicler, Walter Bower, whose *Scotichronicon* was compiled in the 1440s on the basis of the narrative first systematically set down by John of Fordun in the 1380s.[16] This account described the Scots' original descent from Gaythelos and Scota, their descendants' settlement of Spain and Ireland, and the eventual migration of Fergus I, a scion of the Scotic royal house,

---

[15]   An undated list of works written by Buchanan in the BL refers to 'De origine gentium Britanicarum libri duo', but as the next item on the list is 'De coniuratione Reginae Mariae cum Bothuelio' (presumably some version of the *Detectio*), it cannot pre-date the York–Westminster Conference of 1568 or more likely the actual publication of the *Detectio* in 1571. Similarly, Buchanan's friend Daniel Rogers wrote to him in September 1576 saying that three years earlier Buchanan had held out hope that Rogers would shortly see a book 'de origine gentium Britannicarum'. However, while these references confirm that the early books of the *Historia* were conceived and written as a separate work, they do not provide conclusive evidence that Buchanan had drafted them before the appearance of Lhuyd's book in 1572. See McFarlane, *Buchanan*, pp. 302, 420.

[16]   See Walter Bower, *Scotichronicon*, gen. ed. D.E.R. Watt (9 vols, Aberdeen and Edinburgh, 1987–98); vol. 9 contains copious commentary on Bower himself and his sources.

from Ireland to the northern British mainland and his establishment there of a separate kingship in 330 BCE. The main theme of the history that follows was the extraordinary success of Fergus' descendants, numbering in total over 100 kings, in defending the integrity of their kingdom against subsequent attempts at conquest by alien invaders – Romans, Anglo-Saxons, Vikings and Normans – culminating in the triumphant vindication of the kingdom's freedom in the face of Edward I's imperial ambitions in the late thirteenth and early fourteenth centuries. And it was this narrative, developed in part to counter the Galfridian claims to English feudal superiority over Scotland, on which Boece was to build his own much more elaborate chronicle. However, while Bower said much about the origins of the Scots and their heroic defence of their independent kingship, he had a good deal less to say about the extent and shape of the kingdom itself. His description of Scotland's physical boundaries was sketchy, becoming still hazier the further west and north he looked, while as far as the western and northern isles were concerned, he was able to supply a fairly extensive list of names, but not much else.[17] He did note that two languages were spoken in the kingdom, 'Scotica' and 'Theutonica', and that two different lifestyles had developed that distinguished the Scots of the Lowlands from those of the Highlands and Islands. But if this linguistic and cultural fissure caused him concern, it did not lessen his over-riding commitment to an independent Scottish kingship to which all the crown's subjects owed common allegiance.

Bower's view of Scotland as culturally divided but politically united was picked up and developed by the earliest of the sixteenth-century Scottish historians, John Mair or Major (*c*.1467–1550), whose *Historia Maioris Britanniae tam Angliae quam Scotiae* (Paris, 1521) is best known today for arguing the case for Anglo-Scottish union. In pursuit of that agenda Mair devoted a number of chapters of Book I of his text to ridiculing the origin myths of the Scots as well as the Britons and to describing the situation and extent of the British Isles and Scotland's place within it.[18] This combines ethnographic observations on the customs and manners of the Scots and other peoples – very much in the tradition of Gerald of Wales – with remarks on Scotland's basic topographical features such as its rivers, towns, harbours, churches and universities. Overall, although patchy and unsystematic in its geographical coverage, Mair provided a rather fuller and more balanced introduction to the country and its peoples

---

[17] Ibid., vol. 1, pp. 181–95.

[18] John Major, *A History of Greater Britain as well England as Scotland* [Paris, 1521], ed. and trans. A. Constable, Scottish History Society (Edinburgh, 1892), pp. 5–54. On Mair and his *History*, see Roger A. Mason, *Kingship and the Commonweal: Political Thought in Renaissance and Reformation Scotland* (East Linton, 1998), ch. 2; see also J.H. Burns, 'The Scotland of John Major', *Innes Review*, 2 (1951): pp. 65–76.

than did Bower, while also setting Scotland in a comparative British frame of reference that tended to reflect negatively on the northern realm. At the same time, of course, and more famously, Mair followed Bower in commenting on the linguistic and cultural divisions between the Scots of the Lowlands and those of the Highlands. As with Bower, however, the difference is not seen as a racial one: although it might have suited his unionist argument to do so, Mair did not suggest that 'civilized' Lowland Scots were of Anglo-Saxon origin as opposed to the 'wild' Gaelic-speakers of the north and west whose ancestry was Irish. Rather, he insisted that, though the inhabitants of Scotland spoke two languages and led two different ways of life, they were nevertheless all Scots whose identity was defined by their allegiance to the same royal dynasty. Indeed, recognition of Scotland's ancient monarchy and continuing integrity were crucial to the kind of Anglo-Scottish union – based on parity of status and esteem – that Mair thought achievable through such dynastic inter-marriages as that of James IV to Margaret Tudor.[19]

Mair's work has the distinction of being the first history of Scotland to appear in print. It was not long, however, before Hector Boece's *Scotorum Historiae a prima gentis origine* was published by the same Parisian printer, Jodocus Badius, in 1527.[20] In stark contrast to Mair, and presumably quite deliberately, Boece (*c.*1465–1536) not only reinstated the legendary material about the Scots' original descent from Gaythelos and Scota on which Mair had poured scorn, but went on to provide an astonishingly circumstantial account of the foundation of the Scottish kingdom by Fergus I and – still more remarkably – to endow some forty of his immediate successors with detailed biographies that had been completely unknown to Mair and Bower.[21] It was this line of kings to which Lhuyd took such exception and which Buchanan sought to defend, partly (as Trevor-Roper argued) because it could be manipulated to provide evidence of the elective nature of the Scottish monarchy, but equally because it provided evidence of the antiquity and autonomy of the Scottish kingdom. It was primarily the latter that Boece himself had set out to celebrate, and

---

[19] On the Highlands, see Major, *History*, esp. pp. 48–50; for his broader unionist agenda, see Mason, *Kingship and the Commonweal*, pp. 42–52.

[20] *Scotorum Historiae a prima gentis origine, cum aliarum & rerum & gentium illustratione non vulgari* (Paris, 1527).

[21] For more detailed treatment of Boece as a historian, see Roger A. Mason, 'From Chronicle to History: Recovering the Past in Renaissance Scotland', in Rudolf Suntrup and Jan Veenstra (eds), *Building the Past / Konstruktion der eigen Vergangenheit*, Medieval to Early Modern Culture, vol. 7 (Frankfurt, 2006), pp. 53–66; and the same author's 'Civil Society and the Celts: Hector Boece, George Buchanan and the Ancient Scottish Past', in E.J. Cowan and Richard Finlay (eds), *Scottish History: The Power of the Past* (Edinburgh, 2002), pp. 95–120. For a lucid discussion of the vexed issue of his sources, see N. Royan, 'Hector Boece and the Question of Veremund', *Innes Review*, 52 (2001): pp. 42–62.

which ensured that the *Scotorum Historia* proved much more influential than Mair's less flattering view of Scotland and its past. This applied also to Boece's 'Descriptio regni Scotiae', which precedes the main body of his narrative, and which is both much more positive in its appraisal of Scotland's people and its resources and more systematic in its exposition of the kingdom's geography. Admittedly, Boece regales his readers with a whole series of natural wonders – some more credible than others – that Scotland uniquely had to offer. But he also took them on what was the first region-by-region tour of the Scottish kingdom, beginning with the borders, working up the west coast from Galloway to Argyll and Lochaber and beyond to Ross and Strathnaver before heading south again through Cromarty to Moray, Aberdeenshire and the Mearns, Fife, Lothian and the Forth Valley.[22] In the course of this whistle-stop tour, Boece touched on local customs as well as unusual natural features, while also taking note of towns, castles and religious houses, and commenting on such issues as the fertility of the soil and the quality of the fishing. Notably absent from his account, however, is any reference to wild Highlanders speaking an alien language and threatening the civilized Lowlands. On the contrary, according to Boece, it was precisely in the Gaelic-speaking north and west of the kingdom, untainted by intercourse with England, that the pristine virtue of the original Scots still animated their direct descendants.[23]

There is certainly a degree of naivety as well as credulity in Boece's description of the country, which is further accentuated by the way he views history in terms of a cyclical pattern of declension from and recovery of the primitive virtue displayed by the Scots' remote ancestors.[24] It is nonetheless a pioneering attempt to provide an account of both the physical geography of the kingdom and, in proto-chorographical form, its social and political landscape. It was perfectly fitting, therefore, that both the *Scotorum Historia* and the Scots vernacular translation done of it by John Bellenden in the 1530s, should be dedicated to King James V.[25] For here was a monarch acutely conscious of his own, and his kingdom's, imperial status, and intent on defining the territorial boundaries of the realm while

---

[22]   For the description of Scotland, see Boece, *Historia*, fols 3r–17r.

[23]   Boece avoids any suggestion of colonization or miscegenation in explaining Lowland Scots' adoption of the English tongue, preferring instead to refer more obliquely to the influence exerted through long and close association; see Mason, 'Civil Society and the Celts', p. 102.

[24]   Boece's view of the Scots' primitive virtue is conveniently epitomized in the last section of the 'Descriptio' entitled 'Scotorum prisci & recentes mores' where the manners of the ancients are favourably compared to those of his contemporaries: ibid., sigs cci^v–cciiii^v.

[25]   Boece, *Historia*, dedication ('praefatio'), sigs aiii^r–av^v; [Hector Boece], *The Hystory and Croniklis of Scotland* (Edinburgh, [?1540]), 'The proheme of the history', sigs Eiiii^r–Evi^v; see also the printer's colophon on sig. Evi^v, where it is made clear that the translation was done at the king's command.

ensuring the primacy of royal authority within them. The mapping of
the kingdom, albeit verbal rather than visual, was an essential element
of the extension of royal power just as it was of the promotion among
its inhabitants of a powerful sense of identity, not just with the crown
and an ancient royal dynasty, but with the kingdom's varied landscape
and distinctive flora and fauna.[26] In fact, it was James V's well-known
seaborne expedition to Orkney and the western isles in 1540 to impress
royal authority on the outlying regions of his kingdom that generated one
of the earliest and most accomplished maps of the Scottish coastline.[27]
And it is surely no coincidence that the northern and western islands –
where the ancient Scottish discipline had allegedly remained uncorrupted
through the centuries – were also the areas of the kingdom about which
Boece had least information to hand. Indeed, the Orkney and Shetland
islands, only ceded to Scotland by the Danish crown in 1469, are dealt with
in very summary fashion, descriptive substance giving way to moralizing
observations such as that the Orcadians were given to excessive drinking
but lived nevertheless to a wondrous old age.[28] If anything, the western
isles, historically semi-autonomous and still beyond the effective reach
of royal authority, fared even less well, with only a brief and inaccurate
listing from Man in the south to Hirta or St Kilda in the north (Boece
evidently believing that St Kilda lay to the north rather than the west of
the Hebrides).

Whatever its inaccuracies and inadequacies, however, Boece's
description of Scotland – what Bellenden called his 'Cosmographie and
discription of Albion' – proved extremely influential. In addition to
Bellenden's vernacular version, the original Latin was reproduced verbatim
in the edition and continuation of the *Scotorum Historia* that (as was
noted earlier) Giovanni Ferrerio published in Paris in 1574.[29] Moreover, it
was Englished – using both Boece's Latin and Bellenden's Scots translation

---

[26]   See Roger A. Mason, 'This Realm of Scotland is an Empire? Imperial Ideas and
Iconography in Early Renaissance Scotland', in Barbara Crawford (ed.), *Church, Chronicle
and Learning in Medieval and Early Renaissance Scotland* (Edinburgh, 1999), pp. 73–91.

[27]   Known as the 'Rutter of the Scottish Seas', and attributed to Alexander Lindsay,
James V's pilot on the naval expedition of 1540, it was first published in French in *Vraye &
exacte descriptio Hydrographique des costes Maritimes d'Escoss, Isles Hebrides & Orchades
servat a la Navigation, Par Nicolay d'Arfeuille Daulphinois, premier Cosmographe du Roy*
(Paris, 1583). For further details, see D.G. Moir *et al.*, *The Early Maps of Scotland*, Royal
Scottish Geographical Society (2 vols, 3rd edn, Edinburgh, 1973), vol. 1, pp. 19–23; I.H.
Adams and G. Fortune (eds), *Alexander Lindsay; A Rutter of the Scottish Seas, c. 1540*,
National Maritime Museum Monographs and Reports 44 (HMSO, 1980).

[28]   Boece, *Historia*, fols xv^r–xvi^r.

[29]   *Scotorum Historiæ a prima gentis origine, cum aliarum et rerum et gentium
illustratione non vulgari, libri XIX. Hectore Boethio Deidonano auctore. Accessit & huic
editioni eiusdem Scotorum Historiae continuatio, per Ioannem Ferrerium Pedemontanum*
(Paris, 1574).

– by William Harrison for the Scottish volume of Raphael Holinshed's chronicles of 1577, and was reprinted a decade later in the 1587 version of the same work.[30] Meanwhile, John Leslie, the exiled Catholic Bishop of Ross (1527–96), made extensive use of it in his version of Scottish history, published in Rome in 1578. As a whole, Leslie's *De Origine Moribus, et Rebus Gestis Scotorum* is heavily indebted to Boece for its basic outline and chronology. Although Boece's early narrative books are greatly condensed, Leslie accepts more or less uncritically his account of the Fergusian line of kings and their totemic significance down to and beyond the accession of the Stewarts, though unlike Boece or Ferrerio he takes the story forward to the 1560s, ending in Book X with an extended apologia for Mary Queen of Scots and the Catholic religion.[31] As for his description of Scotland, though Leslie's work is the first of its kind actually to include a full-scale map, the latter is highly inaccurate and the former is largely a reworking of Boece (though some use is also made of Mair) with additional local information particularly on the north-east of Scotland based on personal observation. Leslie follows a different itinerary to Boece, dividing the country north and south of a line from Argyll to the Tay, but in a way that is territorial and physical rather than linguistic and cultural.[32] That aside, his approach is very similar to Boece in terms of noting a mixture of topographical features, distinct regional flora and fauna, and prominent local towns, religious houses and the castles of the nobility. Like Boece too, Leslie is woefully ill informed about the northern and western isles and has disappointingly little to add to what his predecessor had said about these regions.[33]

Yet, for all that, there are aspects of the early books of his history that do break new ground. Leaving the unprecedented provision of a map aside, he adds to what is a fairly conventional account of the peopling of Scotland and the manners of its inhabitants a much more specific and innovative discussion of the three estates, the clergy, nobility and 'status

---

[30]   See William Harrison's dedicatory remarks in Raphael Holinshed, *Chronicles of England, Scotland, and Ireland* ... (4 vols, London, 1577), vol. 2, sig. *bii*ʳ; reprinted in ibid. (6 vols, London, 1587), vol. 4, pp. 3–4.

[31]   *De Origine Moribus, et Rebus Gestis Scotorum libri decem ... Accessit noua & accurata regionum & insularum Scotiae, cum vera eiusdem tabula topographica, descriptio. Authore Ioanne Leslaeo* (Rome, 1578).

[32]   He does, however, dwell on the wildness of the borderers and the tendency of observers to tar all Scots with the same brush of lawlessness and ungovernability. For his 'Regionum et Insularum Scotia Descriptio', see *De Origine*, pp. 1–41. The double-page map is inserted immediately before the description, its odd shape accentuated by its west–east axis. Leslie evidently became aware of its inadequacies and had a new one engraved (now extremely rare) on the basis of a far superior one published by Abraham Ortelius in his *Theatrum Orbis Terrarum* (Antwerp, 1573); see further Moir, *Early Maps*, vol. 1, pp. 14–18.

[33]   *De Origine*, pp. 39–41.

plebeiorum'.[34] This comprises a vigorous defence of the Catholic church against the charges levelled against it by blasphemous heretics, but also an account of the changing role of the nobility as the ancient form of elective monarchy gave way to hereditary right. Although a stout defender of monarchical authority, Leslie was by no means anti-aristocratic, presenting the nobility as essential to the crown in offering counsel as well as military service and portraying them as distinguished by their loyalty. He also gives a breakdown of the various categories of nobility, from the peerage to landed gentlemen, and this unusually analytical approach to social status is followed by an equally detailed breakdown of the 'plebian estate', by which he means the urban elite, the merchants and craftsmen who represented the burghs in parliament. Already, in providing this kind of social analysis, Leslie was going far beyond anything previous histories had offered. But he went still further. Himself a doctor of both civil and canon law, who was instrumental in compiling and publishing in 1566 the first codification of Scottish statute law, he not unexpectedly saw law and legal administration as essential to the good ordering of politics and society. It was entirely appropriate, therefore, that he should end the preliminaries to his narrative proper with an explanation of the founding of the College of Justice and a brief description of Scotland's legal and other officers of state.[35]

Buchanan on Scotland and the Scots

If Buchanan knew of Leslie's work, he chose to ignore it. As we have seen, he had probably written the early books of his *Historia* some time before *De Origine* was published in 1578, so it is perhaps not surprising that in writing his own description of Scotland he took no account of the latter's more innovative features. However, while he was more indebted to his earlier predecessors, Mair and particularly Boece, he also went far beyond them in terms of the scope and precision of his topographical survey and his linguistic analysis of the peopling of Britain.[36] Book I, in fact, opens with the first of his virulent attacks on Lhuyd, in this instance over the

---

[34] 'Tres Regni Ordines': ibid., pp. 66–74.

[35] 'De Magistratibus': ibid., pp. 78–80. Leslie was a graduate of King's College Aberdeen, subsequently studying theology and law at Paris and Poitiers respectively. In the 1560s he was among Mary's most trusted advisers, serving on her privy council as well as being made Bishop of Ross and a Senator of the College of Justice. He chaired the commission that finally produced the *Actis and Constitutionis of the Realm of Scotland* (Edinburgh, 1566), the first successful codification of Scots statute law, beginning in 1424 and continuing through to Mary's personal rule.

[36] Buchanan's own copy of Ferrerio's edition of Boece is in St Andrews University Library (classmark TypSwL.B74LBA). Appropriately enough, Buchanan's signature appears

etymology of the name 'Britain', and it is some way into the text before he remarks that Boece in his description of Scotland 'has inserted some things not strictly correct' and announces his intention to provide a more succinct and accurate version.[37] This he proceeds to do, beginning as Boece had done by traversing the borders from east to west, but then doubling back to Lothian before heading west again through Clydesdale, Lanark and Glasgow, and on to the south-western regions of Carrick, Kyle and Cunningham. Buchanan's descriptions of these areas are precise and spare, confined to major topographical features – rivers, lakes, mountain ranges, towns – and largely ignore the anecdotes and tall tales that enlivened Boece's description. Only occasionally, as when he turns east again to Stirlingshire, does he pause to consider local antiquities in more detail, in this instance at Dunipace on the River Carron, notable for an ancient round building (popularly known as Arthur's Oven or O'on) that Buchanan speculates might have been a temple dedicated to the Roman God Terminus. This in turn leads him to discuss the Antonine Wall (attributed to Emperor Severus) and to argue that it was this wall rather than Hadrian's earlier one to the south that marked the limits of Roman Britain as well as the boundary between the Scots and Britons.[38]

While this shows a willingness to look at archaeological remains with a more historically refined sense of time and place than was evident in his predecessors, Buchanan does not pursue further his reference to the engraved stones and classical inscriptions that the remains of the wall still yielded. Instead he continues his itinerary, taking in his own *patria* of Lennox before heading west and north to Argyll, Kintyre and Lochaber. Again, in contrast to Boece, Buchanan's principal concern is to locate these regions in relation to each other and to delineate their natural boundaries and (less consistently) their length and breadth or the distances between them. He says little or nothing about the tower-houses, castles and kirks that featured in the contemporary landscape and that Boece and others were so keen to point out. Indeed, in criss-crossing the country, first eastward through Breadalbane to Strathearn and Fife, then west again via Abernethy to Loch Tay, and then back east through Dunkeld to Perth and Dundee, he says nothing of the landed elite who dominated these regions. It is tempting to see Buchanan's lack of interest in the landscape and hierarchy of power as a reflection of his populist politics, but given the role he assigns to the nobility in the *Historia* as guardians of the commonwealth this is hardly convincing. In any event, where in Book I he does pause for reflection, it is not usually to comment on the seats of the local elite but to exercise

---

on fol. 1r, next to the section title 'Scotorum Regni Descriptio, Hectore Boethio auctore'. Regrettably, there are no further annotations.

[37] For Book I, see *History*, vol. 1, pp. 1–63; the description proper begins on p. 20.

[38] Ibid., vol. 1, pp. 23–8.

his linguistic skills in questioning received etymological wisdom. Thus Dunkeld is said to be a corruption of the ancient Pictish name Caledonia, while he prefers to derive Dundee from the Gaelic 'Taodunum, that is, a hill near the Tay', rather than Boece's fanciful Latin 'Deidonum' ('the gift of God').[39] Yet otherwise Buchanan's landscape is largely unpopulated and the built environment largely undescribed. Moving north again through the Mearns to Aberdeen, there is an uncharacteristic mention of the Earl Marischal's castle at Dunnottar, but that barely interrupts Buchanan's steady march through Mar, and then west by Badenoch to Lochaber – a name he thinks absurdly tautological as Aber 'in the language of the country' means a kind of gulf or loch; nevertheless, he praises the area in the highest terms as 'remarkably rich in the products both of the water and of the land'.[40]

Returning to Mar, Buchanan heads north again through Buchan to Loch Ness and the northernmost regions of Ross, Strathnaver and Caithness. Here, perhaps appropriately, he ends his survey of the mainland with a final speculative passage, prompted by Ptolemy's geography, on the possible kinship between the ancient Cornavii of Caithness and of Cornwall, before turning his attention to Scotland's three island groups, the Hebrides, Orkney and Shetland.[41] It is here above all that Buchanan's description far excels that of any of his predecessors, particularly as regards the Gaelic-speaking western isles, where he openly acknowledges that he has benefited from the work of Donald Monro, 'a pious and diligent man, who went over the whole of them himself, and minutely inspected them in person'.[42] Monro was a Catholic clergyman from near Cromarty but with extensive family connections in the west where he was made Archdeacon of the Isles in 1549.[43] This appointment prompted him to undertake a fact-finding tour of the islands within the diocese and his now famous 'Description of the Western Isles' was the result of this expedition. After the Reformation in 1560, Monro conformed to the new Protestant dispensation, becoming minister of his native parish of Kiltearn in Cromarty, and playing an active part in the deliberations of the early General Assemblies of the Kirk. It was probably through such meetings of the Assembly that Buchanan became acquainted with him and gained access to the detailed topographical material about the islands that his predecessors had lacked. As a result he was able to add a wholly

---

[39]   For Dunkeld and Dundee, see ibid., vol. 1, pp. 30–31.

[40]   Ibid., vol. 1, p. 32.

[41]   Ibid, vol. 1, pp. 37–8.

[42]   Ibid., vol. 1, p. 39.

[43]   For full details of Monro's career and the text of the Description, see R.W. Munro (ed.), *Monro's Western Isles of Scotland and Genealogies of the Clans* (Edinburgh and London, 1961).

new dimension to existing descriptions of Scotland, giving much clearer definition to the *terra incognita* of its western seaboard. At the same time, however, he followed Boece's lead in creating an image of primitive austerity that turned the islanders into the surviving exemplars of ancient Scottish discipline and virtue.

Buchanan follows Monro's itinerary very closely, faithfully mentioning by name almost all 250 of the islands of which his source had recorded details, from Man, Ailsa and Arran in the south to Harris, Lewis and Rona in the north (more correctly locating Hirta some sixty miles to the west). However, Buchanan strips out much of the material that had been of interest to the archdeacon – the churches and religious houses, the castles and tower-houses, the produce of the land and sea – confining himself rather to basic topographical features, the dimensions of the islands, and the distances between them. Where he does remark on an island's arable or pastoral farming or on its woods, rivers and fisheries, his descriptions are much less full than those of Monro and, as with those of the mainland, devoid of references to the heads of the kin-groups who dominated them. Perhaps surprisingly, given the nature of his political ideas, while he remarks on the fourteen-man Council of the Isles that Monro described as traditionally meeting on Islay to advise the 'king' of the Isles, Buchanan does not pause to consider the broader constitutional significance of this practice.[44] Similarly, he is more than usually expansive about Iona, but does not go beyond Monro in noting the significance of the Abbey of St Columba and the 'Tumulus Regum Scotiae' where forty-eight kings of Scots were said to be buried alongside the tombs of four Irish and eight Norwegian kings.[45] For the most part, in other words, he is content simply to recast Monro's detailed vernacular notes in suitably literary Latin.

One of the few occasions when Buchanan does depart from his source is in his account of Rona where, after following Monro in describing its remoteness and the poverty of its inhabitants, he then adds his own reflections on how the islanders, unfamiliar with avarice and luxury, have found 'in their ignorance of vice that innocence and tranquility of mind which others laboriously search for in the discipline and precepts of wisdom'.[46] This view of untutored virtue is of a piece with Buchanan's introductory remarks on the western isles – which owe more to Boece's imaginative account of the Scots' ancient manners than to Monro's personal observations of their descendants – where he commends the simplicity and austerity of their lifestyle.[47] But the same theme is pursued in considering Orkney and Shetland. Buchanan's source of information on the northern

---

[44] Ibid., pp. 56–7; Buchanan, *History*, vol. 1, p. 44.
[45] Monro, *Western Isles*, pp. 62–3; Buchanan, *History*, vol. 1, pp. 46–7.
[46] Monro, *Western Isles*, pp. 87–8; Buchanan, *History*, vol. 1, p. 55.
[47] Ibid., vol. 1, pp. 40–41.

island groups is not known, but using classical authors, some linguistic expertise, and presumably some more direct source of local knowledge, he is able to piece together a much more detailed 'map' of them than his predecessors had achieved.[48] Yet here again his geographical observations are embellished with reflections on the exemplary virtue of primitive islanders who have remained uncorrupted by commerce and luxury and whose abstemious lifestyle ensures 'uninterrupted health both of body and mind'.[49] Although Buchanan believed the people of Orkney and Shetland to be of Gothic origin, they seem nonetheless to function in the same way as the Gaelic-speaking natives of the western isles as exemplars of an ancient virtue that his contemporaries would do well to emulate. Thus, in the closing sentences of Book I, on one of the very few occasions when Buchanan turns to the kind of anecdotal evidence so frequently invoked by Boece, he recounts a tale of Lawrence the Shetlander, who, exemplifying the rude good health of a people 'unacquainted with inebriety', took a wife when he was 100 years old and was still fishing in the roughest of seas at the ripe old age of 140.[50]

The last uncharacteristically credulous moment aside, Buchanan's description is notable for being remarkably matter of fact as well as more comprehensive than those of his predecessors. That said, however, it has little of the richly textured chorographical detail that the young William Camden (1551–1623) was to provide in the first edition of his *Britannia*, published only four years after Buchanan's *Historia* in 1586.[51] Camden combined extensive fieldwork and personal observation with a keen interest in Roman remains to produce an unprecedentedly detailed study of ancient Britain that was expanded over successive editions to recover the English people's Anglo-Saxon roots as well as their classical heritage.[52] As we shall see, the first edition had only a short chorographical section on Scotland – substantial new material was only added to the final post-union edition of

---

[48]   The more detailed description of the Orkney Islands by the otherwise unidentified 'Jo. Ben.', dating from 1529, was not known to Buchanan; see A. Mitchell (ed.), *Geographical Collections relating to Scotland*, 3 vols (Scottish History Society, 1904–1908), vol. 2, pp. 302–24.

[49]   Buchanan, *History*, vol. 1, p. 57.

[50]   Ibid., vol. 1, p. 63: 'He died but lately,' Buchanan concludes, 'not cut off by the stroke of any painful disease, but dismissed gently by the gradual decay of old age.' There is no equivalent of this in Boece's chronicle.

[51]   William Camden, *Britannia sive Florentissimorum regnorum, Angliae, Scotiae, Hiberniae, et insularum adjacentium ex intima antiquitate chorographica descriptio* (London, 1586).

[52]   Enlarged editions of *Britannia* appeared in 1587, 1590, 1594, 1600 and 1607. On the increasing importance of the Anglo-Saxons in his thinking, partly prompted by the research of his disciple, Robert Cotton, see the useful brief overview of Camden's achievements in Graham Parry, *The Trophies of Time: English Antiquarians of the Seventeenth Century* (Oxford, 1995), pp. 22–48.

1607 – but it did include in its account of the peopling of Britain a section on the 'Scoti' in which Camden lent his support to Humphrey Lhuyd's attack on Boece and dismissed Buchanan as a much better poet than he was an antiquary.[53] As a result, ignoring the innovative linguistic analysis that features in Book II of the *Historia* (alongside Buchanan's scornful dismissal of those like Lhuyd who had too readily accepted the authority of the monkish fabler Geoffrey of Monmouth), Camden insisted instead that, though the Picts were aboriginal Britons, the Scots were of Scythian and hence Gothic origin. Camden simply remained oblivious to Buchanan's knowledge of Gaelic and the innovative use of place-name evidence that enabled him to differentiate between the various linguistic communities in Britain – pioneering the distinction between what became known as P- and Q-Celts – and trace their origins to the tribes of ancient Gaul.[54] This part of the *Historia* was wholly overshadowed in Camden's eyes by his endorsement of Boece's account of Fergus I's foundation of the kingdom in 330 BCE and, still worse, his argument that the Scottish monarchy was from its foundation an elective rather than a hereditary one. Elsewhere, abandoning his customary circumlocutions, Camden perhaps revealed his true attitude to Buchanan when he described him simply as a 'Spite-king'.[55] In addition, however, as would become clearer in later editions of *Britannia*, Camden was intent on correcting the impression, first created by Boece but lent greater substance and credibility by Buchanan, that the Scottish people as a whole – English-speaking Lowlanders as well as Gaelic-speaking Highlanders – were of Celtic rather than Germanic descent.[56]

This is a matter to which we shall return. Meanwhile, it will suffice to note that Buchanan's own doubts about the veracity of Boece's account of the early centuries of the kingdom's existence may well be reflected in his drastic reduction of the six books that Boece had devoted to the first seven centuries of its existence to a single one. This process of condensation, however, had the effect of highlighting the emphasis that Buchanan placed on the *ius regni*, first established in the reign of Fergus's successor, Feritharus, and continuing to regulate the royal succession for

---

[53]   Camden, *Britannia* (1586), p. 39.

[54]   For a recent (positive) appraisal of Buchanan's achievement, see John Collis, 'George Buchanan and the Celts in Britain', in Ronald Black *et al.* (eds), *Celtic Connections, Proceedings of the 10th International Congress of Celtic Studies I* (East Linton, 1999), pp. 91–107.

[55]   William Camden, *Remains Concerning Britain*, ed. R.D. Dunn (Toronto, 1984), p. 130.

[56]   For Buchanan's less than positive view of the Anglo-Saxons, see *History*, vol. 1, pp. 113–15. While there had been a time in the later middle ages when there was considerable interest in exploiting Scottish royal and aristocratic associations with the Anglo-Saxon monarchy through St Margaret's marriage to Malcolm Canmore, this does not seem to have survived the Reformation. See Steve Boardman, 'Late Medieval Scotland and the Matter of Britain', in Cowan and Finlay (eds), *Scottish History*, pp. 47–52.

over a thousand years, that excluded minors and allowed the kingship to
alternate between adult representatives of different branches of the royal
family.[57] Interestingly, Boece had argued that this was a pernicious custom
that had proved damaging to the Scottish commonwealth, leading all too
frequently to internecine struggles between rivals for the throne. Buchanan,
on the other hand, saw it as a fundamental law that established the elective
nature of the Scottish monarchy and vested in the nobility the right not
only to regulate the succession but also to hold errant rulers to account. In
this respect, as Trevor-Roper believed, the *Historia* certainly does bear out
the theoretical arguments for 'popular' sovereignty and the legitimacy of
resistance to tyranny that Buchanan developed in his *De Iure Regni*. Nor,
given their incendiary nature, is it altogether surprising that in the anti-
presbyterian 'Black Acts' of 1584, the Scottish parliament should have
sought to censor both works, demanding on pain of a fine of £200 that all
copies be handed in to the privy council so that they could be 'purgit of the
offensive and extraordinare materis'.[58] If he did not actually prompt the
legislation of 1584, the young James VI certainly shared this attitude to his
former tutor's writings, and subsequently, in his *Basilikon Doron* of 1599,
expressly warned his son, Prince Henry, against such 'infamous invectives'
as Buchanan's *Historia*. Yet he was careful not to throw the royalist baby
out with the republican bathwater. After all, as he had argued in his *Trew
Lawe of Free Monarchies* the previous year, not only had Fergus I claimed
– indeed created – the Scottish kingdom through force of arms, but he had
founded a line of kings as old as any in Europe of which Charles James
Stewart was the direct lineal descendant.[59]

In other words, despite Buchanan having tainted the Fergusian line
with the stain of election and accountability, it remained for James a
symbol of that indefeasible hereditary right that was crucial to his claim
to the English throne. Many of James's Scottish subjects no doubt shared
this conviction. But whether or not they were sympathetic to the king's
claim to England (or his divine right to rule), they were at one in seeing
Fergus and his successors as symbolizing the antiquity and autonomy of
their kingdom. While the increasing likelihood of union with England gave
rise to some excited speculation about the future of Britain, it also induced
anxiety about Scotland's future status within such an enlarged imperial
monarchy. In this context, the Fergusian line became for Scots a totem of
their distinctiveness within a potentially threatening Anglocentric imperial
system and, in the course of the seventeenth century, was repeatedly
invoked as a means of creating – or maintaining – a 'space' for Scotland

---

[57]   Buchanan, *History*, vol. 1, pp. 159–60. For further discussion of this, and Boece's
negative attitude to it, see Mason, 'Civil Society and the Celts', pp. 107–9.
[58]   This is discussed further in Mason, *Kingship and the Commonweal*, pp. 201–2.
[59]   Ibid., pp. 229–30.

within the new British *imperium*. As a result, despite the government's attempts at censorship, Buchanan's *Historia* became a critical – if often unacknowledged – source of reassurance, locating the kingdom's ancient monarchy within a comprehensive 'map' of Scotland that could be populated with a rich mix of chorographical detail substantiating the community's distinct social and political identity. The union of the crowns, however, and the avowedly British agenda that the new king subsequently pursued, was not just threatening to Scotland. It was also profoundly unsettling for an English governing elite that in the course of Elizabeth's reign had become ever more aware of the Englishness of England, embracing an image of the unique political, legal and ecclesiastical character of their kingdom that differentiated it from (and ensured its superiority to) other realms and peoples.[60] This process of self-fashioning, and the increasingly patriotic self-awareness that accompanied it, had a powerful chorographical dimension that, as we shall see, the Scots not only found hard to match but that was profoundly subversive of their own distinctive identity.

1603: Scotland and the Englishing of Britain

Two works stand out as particularly crucial in revolutionizing English self-understanding in the late sixteenth century. One is Camden's *Britannia*, which, while initially enabling England's educated elite to celebrate their classical Roman heritage, increasingly in its successive editions also made it possible for them to connect meaningfully with their Anglo-Saxon past – and, in the process, to abandon Galfridian history altogether. The other is the cartographical research of Christopher Saxton, who by 1579 was able to bring together in published form his pioneering series of county maps in a single atlas encompassing the whole of England and Wales.[61] Saxton's efforts were facilitated by the crown and fully supported by William Cecil for governmental purposes, but his mapping of the shires also reinforced identification with a local *patria* among the landed elite whose country seats were identified on the maps. As well as being able to imagine England

---

[60]   On this generally, see in particular Richard Helgerson, *Forms of Nationhood: The Elizabethan Writing of England* (Chicago, IL, 1992).

[61]   STC 21805.1–2: [Christopher Saxton, *Atlas of the Counties of England and Wales* (London, 1579)]. The publication has no title page (only two variant frontispieces featuring images of Elizabeth) and no indication of authorship or publisher. A second edition of 1590 (STC 21805.5) includes the map of Scotland (based on Ortelius) and five maps of Ireland and its four provinces that were subsequently used by Camden and Speed. On Saxton, and governmental interest in map-making, see Peter Barber, 'England II: Monarchs, Ministers and Maps, 1550–1625', in David Buisseret (ed.), *Monarchs, Ministers and Maps: The Emergence of Cartography as a Tool of Government in Early Modern Europe* (Chicago, IL, and London, 1992), pp. 57–98.

as a historically rooted complex of legal, ecclesiastical and political structures, therefore, they could equally now visualize the country as a well-defined territorial unit within which their own local communities were visibly inscribed on richly delineated landscapes of power. Richard Helgerson has plausibly argued that this chorographical emphasis on place and particularity gave the gentry a sense of ownership of the land, and the laws and liberties that at once enshrined and legitimized their authority over it, that was antithetical to royal power and would return to haunt the governmental authorities who had first sponsored it.[62] This is a point to which – with reference to Scotland – we shall return by way of conclusion. Meanwhile, it is easy enough to understand how the idea of a Scottish king un-Englishing England in the name of Britain was profoundly unsettling to a landed elite that had already invested so heavily in refashioning their own and their country's identity.

Not surprisingly, therefore, James's grandiose plans for closer union were effectively neutered by an English parliament that, while prepared to rejoice in the Stuart succession as a happy alternative to dynastic conflict, was reluctant to countenance any measure that threatened to erode what was conceived of as the Englishness of England. As a result, whatever visionary British schemes James or his Scottish subjects conjured up, they were unlikely to find favour in the southern kingdom unless they amounted to a recognition that Britain was to all intents and purposes England writ large. The elision of any distinction between the two had a long pedigree in English historical writing that works like Camden's *Britannia* served only to reinforce: 'Britannia', after all, might mean the whole island or just the Roman province that extended no further north than Hadrian's or at most the Antonine Wall. Camden was primarily interested in Roman Britain and, despite the apparent inclusiveness signalled by the subtitle of *Britannia* (*sive florentissimorum regnorum Angliae, Scotiae, Hiberniae, et Insularum adiacentium*), he had little interest in the peoples who inhabited the northern fringes of Rome's (and subsequently England's) *imperium*.[63] In the five editions of *Britannia* that appeared in Elizabeth's reign, Scotland was in fact treated little differently from an English county, following on directly from the description of Northumberland, and never occupying more than ten pages of a work that never totalled less than 550. It was only in the final 1607 edition – dedicated to James VI & I – that Camden felt obliged to add substantially to the chorographical description of Scotland. Here the northern kingdom is allotted some thirty-five pages, with the

---

[62]   Helgerson, *Forms of Nationhood*, esp. ch. 3.

[63]   Although Ireland was even less touched by Rome than Scotland, it was of much more interest to Camden, as well as much better known and mapped, because of contemporary English policies of conquest and colonization. Hence, all editions of *Britannia*, from 1586 to 1607, contain much more substantial sections on Hibernia than on Scotia.

addition of new material on Roman inscriptions found at the Antonine Wall and notices of such antique remains as the curiously constructed Roman temple at Dunipace that Camden described in terms that are clearly borrowed (without acknowledgement) from Buchanan.[64] Yet Camden's geographical coverage of Scotland is highly restricted – he did not avail himself of Buchanan's description of the north and west of the mainland and ignored his account of the western isles entirely – presumably on the grounds that these regions were beyond the boundaries of both the Roman Empire and the later influence of the Anglo-Saxon kingdoms. Instead he fleshed out his Scottish chorography with a long series of Latin poems on Scottish towns kindly supplied by the St Andrews professor John Johnston, together with his own genealogical remarks, drawing on his experience as Clarenceux herald, on families with close connections to the king, such as his father's kin, the Lennox Stewarts, and his Scottish Lord Chancellor, Alexander Seton, first Earl of Dunfermline.[65]

In one respect, however, Camden did at least give the impression of treating Scotland more seriously than in earlier editions, prefacing the chorography proper not only with a map and separate title page, but with a range of preliminary materials that recognized the kingdom's sovereign status by detailing its regional, ecclesiastical and civil divisions, the nature of its three estates, and its judicial institutions from parliament to sheriff and burgh courts.[66] This information, reminiscent of the kind of material John Leslie had thought worth recording, was supplied (we are told in Philemon Holland's English translation of *Britannia*) by the king's justice clerk in Scotland, Sir Alexander Hay. Whatever the source, however, James VI was no doubt pleased to hear that, like the king of England, the king of Scots 'directus est totius dominii Dominus', possessing authority and jurisdiction over both the ecclesiastical and the temporal estates of his kingdom. Likewise, Camden judiciously noted that the union with England had eliminated the 'borderers', who were now – as James himself had similarly boasted – at the very heart of the British Empire ('in Britannici imperii vmbilico'). At the same time, however, Camden pointed out –

---

64   Compare Camden, *Britannia* (1607), p. 700, with Buchanan, *History*, vol. 1, pp. 23–4, for strong verbal echoes. On the same page Camden actually quotes some lines of verse from 'optimus ille poeta G. Buchananus' on the Roman Empire reaching its limits at the River Carron, but he does not credit him for the description of the temple. Later (p. 713) Camden does make reference to Buchanan noting the existence of a stalactite in a cave in Buchan, but he carefully prefaces his use of Buchanan's *Historia* as an authority with an exculpatory reference to the book having been banned by the Scottish parliament in 1584.

65   Johnston contributed poems on *inter alia* Haddington, Edinburgh, Ayr, Glasgow, Stirling, St Andrews, Perth, Dundee, Aberdeen, Inverness and the Fife coastal burghs. On the Lennox Stewarts and Dunfermline, see *Britannia* (1607), pp. 697–8 and 702–3 respectively.

66   Camden, *Britannia* (1607), pp. 667–85 (for the map and preliminaries), 685–718 (the description itself).

again echoing the king – that there remained in Scotland a deep division between the civil English-speaking Lowlanders and the primitive Irish of the Highlands and Islands.[67] Moreover, to the discussion of the 'Scoti' that occurs early in *Britannia*, he added in 1607 a paragraph emphasizing that what he had to say there applied only to the Scots of Irish descent and not to the more civil Lowlanders who shared the same Germanic origins as 'we English'.[68] Whether intended or otherwise, the effect of this was to highlight how little southern Scots differed from their English neighbours while marginalizing the alien people and culture of the north and west. Yet, as he made clear in an apologetic opening to the Scottish chorography (present in all editions of *Britannia*), he had no real interest in or knowledge of Scotland – 'willingly, I assure you, will I enter into it, but withall lightly passe over it' – but he had felt it appropriate to include details of 'some places of ancient note and memorie'. In 1607, these prefatory remarks were considerably expanded, not least to include reference to the happy conjunction of the two kingdoms now providentially realized in the person of the king's sacred majesty. Nonetheless, Camden still preferred to treat Scotland with such 'compendious brevity that I will not prevent their curious diligence, who are in hand to set out these matters with a fuller pensill, and to polish the same with more lively and lasting collours'.[69]

This indicates that Camden knew of someone with a 'fuller pensill' who was already engaged in a more extensive chorographical study of Scotland. And this is borne out by a further attempt to add a post-union British dimension to an essentially English – or perhaps greater English – imperial project: that is, John Speed's *The Theatre of the Empire of Great Britaine*, published in 1612 to celebrate the new Britain in both cartographic and chorographic terms. The politically correct title, however, is instantly subverted by the imposing frontispiece in which it is set, featuring an elaborate triumphal arch housing stylized figures representing the peoples who had shaped the island's history: Britons, Romans, Saxons, Danes and Normans.[70] There was no room here for the Scots. Moreover, while in

---

[67]   Ibid., pp. 684, 682.
[68]   Ibid., p. 85: '... ex eadem qua nos Angli Germanica origine'.
[69]   Camden, *Britannia* (1586), p. 477; cf. Camden, *Britannia* (1607), pp. 680–81 (Holland's translation); see also ibid., p. 718, for a similar though still vaguer reference to someone else wielding 'a more flourishing pensill'. Camden also prefaced his earlier discussion of the Scoti with a disclaimer of his ignorance and desire not to meddle (ibid., p. 85).
[70]   *The Theatre of the Empire of Great Britaine presenting an exact geography of the kingdomes of England, Scotland, Ireland, and the iles adioyning: with the shires, hundreds, cities and shire-townes, within ye kingdome of England, divided and described by Iohn Speed* (London, 1612). There follows, however, a dedication to James – 'Inlarger and Uniter of the British Empire; Restorer of the British Name' – opposite which is an engraving with an elaborate version of the new British royal coat of arms surrounded by no less than twenty-four armorial shields representing 'the severall kings that have aunciently raigned within his

Books I and II Speed could draw on a combination of Saxton's county maps and Camden's *Britannia* to provide an exhaustive anatomy of England and Wales (extending to roughly ninety and thirty pages respectively), Book III on Scotland consists of one map and two pages of text.[71] It is true that Speed goes out of his way to compliment 'the second Kingdom of *Great Britaine*', which he describes as 'faire and spacious' and whose nobility and gentry are 'verie studious of learning and of all ciuil knowledge'. But this positive attitude was not applicable to the whole country, for Speed followed Camden in emphasizing the distinction between civilized Lowlanders who shared the same Saxon origins as the English and the rude Highlanders who were of Irish descent. While never spelled out, the implication is that, while Lowland Scotland could be readily assimilated to a greater England, the Highlands and Islands required the same civilizing policy of colonization and plantation that the king himself had advocated in *Basilikon Doron* and that he was currently encouraging in Ulster as well as Scotland.[72] Rather than pursue this further, however, Speed excused himself by saying that he would have described Scotland in more detail 'had I not beene happily prevented by a learned Gentleman of that Nation, who hath most exactly begunne, and gone through the greatest difficulties thereof'. A marginal note identifies this learned gentleman as 'M. Timothy Pont'.[73]

As we shall see, Pont had begun his pioneering fieldwork in the 1580s, drafting the maps that would eventually, long after his death, bear fruit in Blaeu's *Atlas*. In 1612, however, none of this material had been published, and though Speed was evidently aware of Pont's work he contented himself with a map of Scotland based on that produced by Ortelius in 1573 but given a more up-to-date gloss by decorating the margins with figures representing 'James King of Great Britain, Fraunce and Ireland', his wife Anna, and their two male heirs, 'Henry Prince of Wales and Ireland' and 'Charles Duke of York and Albany'.[74] For further details of the ancient Scottish kingdom, however, contemporaries would have had to look elsewhere – or the distinct identity of the Scottish realm would simply be overwhelmed by what Allan Macinnes has described as a 'Britannic'

---

nowe Dominions'; these include kings of Scotland and Ireland along with the kings of the Heptarchy (Christian and Heathen) and those of Man, Cornwall, Wales, and so on.

[71]   Ibid., pp. 128–32.

[72]   On this Irish dimension, see Christopher Ivic, 'Mapping British Identities: Speed's *Theatre of the Empire of Great Britaine*', in D.J. Baker and W. Maley (eds), *British Identities and English Renaissance Literature* (Cambridge, 2002), pp. 135–55.

[73]   Speed, *Theatre of Great Britaine*, p. 131.

[74]   Ibid., pp. 132–3. Tellingly, later editions replace the royal family with less than flattering figures representing 'A Scotch Man' and 'A Scotch Woman' and 'A Highland Man' and 'A Highland Woman'.

perspective that was unashamedly Anglocentric.[75] It was perhaps with this
in mind that in 1612 the otherwise obscure John Monipennie published
in London *The Abridgement or Summarie of the Scots Chronicles*, which
sought to present, albeit only verbally, a concise portrait of the northern
kingdom's unique history and topography.[76] Dedicated to James as King
of Great Britain, France and Ireland, Monipennie's *Abridgement of the
Chronicles* was intended as a celebration of 'your Highnesse ancient
kingdome of Scotland, unconquered under the Empire and government
of one hundred and six kings, your Maiesties royall progenitors'.[77] In
fact, Monipennie went on to summarize the reigns of 107 rather than 106
of James's predecessors, drawing on a king-list, ultimately deriving from
Buchanan, that had achieved wide currency in Scotland in the decade prior
to 1603.[78] Here, however, any residual influence exerted by Buchanan is
extinguished altogether by Monipennie's clear preference for the more
romantic and less subversive narrative of Boece. For he not only rehearses
the myth of the Scots' descent from Gaythelos and Scota, recounting
in some detail their voyage from Egypt to Spain and their descendants'
subsequent migration to Ireland and the final establishment of Fergus I's
kingship in Scotland, but he goes on to follow Boece in condemning the
custom of tanistry – Buchanan's *ius regni* – because it 'raised much discord
in this Realme of Scotland' through 'the killing of Kings and Nobles
to the great damage of the Realme and Common wealth'.[79] The 'True
Chronology' of the kings that follows is in effect an epitome of Boece with

---

[75]   See Allan I. Macinnes, *The British Revolution, 1629–1660* (Basingstoke, 2005),
pp. 8–13, and his Chapter 7 below, where Camden and Speed are similarly identified as
influential exponents and disseminators of this view of Britain.

[76]   STC 18014: *The Abridgement or Summarie of the Scots Chronicles, with a short
description of their originall, from the comming of Gathelus their first progenitor out of
Græcia into Egypt. And their comming into Portingall and Spaine, and of their kings and
gouernours in Spaine, Ireland and Albion, now called Scotland, (howbeit the whole number
are not extant) with a true chronologie of all their kings. Their reignes, deaths and burials,
from Fergusius the first king of Scotland, vntill his Royall Maiestie, now happily raigning
ouer all Great Brittaine and Ireland, and all the isles to them appertaining. With a true
description and diuision of the whole realme of Scotland, and of the principall cities, townes,
abbies, fortes, castles, towers and riuers, and of the commodities in euery part thereof, and
of the isles in generall, with a memoriall of the most rare and wonderfull things in Scotland.*
By Iohn Monipennie. (London, 1612).

[77]   Ibid., sig. A2[r–v]; Monipennie follows the Scottish chronicle tradition in making a
virtue of necessity by celebrating the fact that Scotland, unlike England and much of 'civilized'
Europe, remained unconquered 'in speciall when almost the whole world was brought under
the Roman Empire by the Sword'.

[78]   The source of this king-list is discussed more fully in Roger A. Mason, '*Certaine
Matters Concerning the Realme of Scotland*: George Buchanan and Scottish Self-fashioning
at the Union of the Crowns' (forthcoming).

[79]   Monipennie, *Abridgement*, pp. 13–14.

the addition of a series of more circumspect pen portraits of James VI and his immediate predecessors.

Clearly, Monipennie was no original historian, but by reverting to Boethian fable in order to reassert the Scottish kingdom's separate identity within Britain he was able to portray the Scots as a single racial as well as regnal community, and thus to skate over the ethnic and linguistic divisions between Highlands and Lowlands, Gaels and Saxons, that Camden and Speed – and the king himself – seemed intent on exposing. Ironically, Buchanan's linguistic analysis in Book II of the *Historia* both explained and, in the process, deepened awareness of these fissures, while his solution – the adoption of Latin as the language of all Scots – was no more realistic than Monipennie's atavistic appeals to a common Scotic ancestress.[80] When Monipennie leaves the summary of the chronicles, however, and turns his attention to a chorographical description of Scotland, his approach is somewhat more innovative – though paradoxically also increasingly indebted to Buchanan. For Monipennie takes Buchanan's spare topographical survey of the regions of Scotland and grafts onto it a catalogue of the nobility and lairds whose 'special residences' he locates on the landscape along with other notable features, such as towns and ecclesiastical buildings, and occasional remarks on agricultural and other natural resources. Now and again, Monipennie is forced to admit that the sheer number of noblemen makes it 'tedious' to list all their castles and tower-houses. But it is of course precisely in situating the landed elite in their particular localities, in effect giving them ownership of the landscapes that they dominated, that Monipennie's work both builds on and distinguishes itself from Buchanan's. At least initially, Monipennie's description is very much his own, and he is able to add a wealth of detail – albeit often in the form of a catalogue of names – to the topography of the regions south of the Tay. The further north and west he goes, however, the less additional detail he is able to supply, and the more obviously reliant on Buchanan he becomes. Thus in describing Lennox and Argyll, the east coast up to Aberdeen and beyond, and further north still to Ross, Strathnaver and Caithness, Buchanan's original description becomes ever more clearly evident as Monipennie's ability to people the landscape diminishes. As for the isles, here Monipennie falls back entirely on Buchanan, including his general description of the western isles and their inhabitants (though omitting Buchanan's acknowledgement of his debt to Monro), before

---

[80]   See Buchanan, *History*, vol. 1, p. 9, where he famously envisaged the 'gradual extinction of the ancient Scottish language' and its replacement by 'the softer and more harmonious tones of Latin', in the process transforming 'rusticity and barbarism' into 'culture and civilisation'.

adding as a separate section in black letter type 'The Description of the Isles of Scotland', translated more or less verbatim from Buchanan.[81]

Needless to say, just as the evidence of Buchanan's debt to Monro is suppressed, so Monipennie's debt to Buchanan is wholly unacknowledged. This remains the case in subsequent editions of Monipennie's work, which was republished with minor revisions on at least four occasions in the seventeenth century (1633, 1650, 1662 and 1671). Notably, all these editions were printed in Edinburgh or Glasgow rather than London, strongly suggesting that English interest in Scotland rapidly waned after 1603 and that summaries of Boethian legend had much more purchase in north Britain than they did in the south. It is equally notable, however, that there was no attempt in the seventeenth century to challenge or replace the Boethian master narrative as rehearsed by Monipennie: the Fergusian kings remained the backbone of Scottish historical self-understanding across the political and religious spectrum well into the eighteenth century.[82] Instead, interest in the Scottish past among Scotland's educated elite was increasingly focused on family history and genealogical research. As David Allan has argued, while preoccupation with pedigree was characteristic of early modern noble culture in general, and sprang from a variety of social anxieties as well as cultural proclivities, it may well be that following 1603 the political insecurities of the Scottish elite led them to cleave to 'their family identities, their impressive lineages, their noble ancestries, with renewed tenacity'.[83] Alongside this obsessive interest in lineage, however, there ran an equally striking fascination with locality. Indeed, in the minds of the armigerous gentry of early seventeenth-century Scotland, genealogy and chorography were two sides of the same coin. Together they provided the cultural dynamic that lay behind the creation of Blaeu's *Atlas*, securely embedding the landed elite in place as well as time.

---

[81]   In fact, most copies of the 1612 edition do not include either the 'Description of the Isles' or 'A Memorial of the most rare and wonderfull things in Scotland', a brief compendium of Scotland's more exotic flora and fauna largely culled from Boece, both of which had first been printed in Edinburgh in 1594: for full details, see Mason, '*Certaine Matters*'.

[82]   The publication in 1729 of Father Thomas Innes's *Critical Essay on the Ancient Inhabitants of the Northern Parts of Britain, or Scotland* marks the beginning of the end of the Fergusian kings' cultural significance. For different perspectives on the controversies surrounding Innes's work, see Ferguson, *Identity of the Scottish Nation*, esp. chs. 9–10, and Colin Kidd, *Subverting Scotland's Past: Scottish Whig Historians and the Creation of an Anglo-British Identity, 1689–c.1830* (Cambridge, 1993), ch. 6.

[83]   David Allan, '"What's in a Name?" Pedigree and Propaganda in Seventeenth-century Scotland', in Cowan and Finlay (eds), *Scottish History*, pp. 147–67 (quote from p. 167).

The Making of Blaeu's *Atlas*

In the light of this, it is perhaps not surprising that among those who took a keen interest in the *Atlas* project was not just the cultural entrepreneur, Sir John Scot of Scotstarvit, but also his Fife neighbour, Sir James Balfour of Denmilne (*c.*1600–1657), Scotland's senior heraldic officer, whose voluminous surviving manuscripts attest to his lifelong interest in chorography as well as his professional interest in genealogy.[84] Among his manuscript volumes, for example, is a hefty folio catalogued as 'Balfour's Topographical Notes', but in reality an embryonic Scottish chorography. Divided into twenty-nine separate sections, interspersed with blank leaves where additional material might be added, Denmilne amassed topographical, historical and genealogical information about the different regions of Scotland culled from a wide range of sources that included substantial passages extracted verbatim from both Camden's *Britannia* and Monipennie's *Abridgement* as well as the fruits of his own research in medieval charters and monastic cartularies.[85] Interestingly, although Balfour paraphrased passages from Buchanan in the sections devoted to Ross, Caithness, Lennox and Kintyre, he never acknowledged his debt to him.[86] Indeed, his 'A Shorte Survay of the Westerne Iyllands of Scotland' is essentially a transcription of Buchanan's description of the Hebrides as it had appeared in Monipennie, though without acknowledging either of them (let alone Donald Munro).[87] Elsewhere, like Monipennie, Denmilne displays a preference for a Boethian version of Scotland's history over Buchanan's ideologically more highly charged account.[88] Yet Monipennie's appeal lay not just in his political conservatism: as we have seen, he had begun the process of peopling Buchanan's bare Scottish landscape in a manner that intimately connected the local elite with the regions they inhabited. 'Balfour's Topographical Notes' builds on Monipennie's example, bringing together local genealogical, historical and geographical information in a rich chorographical mix. Not untypical of the information he gathered was a transcription of 'Cunningham Topographized' by none other than Scotland's pioneering map-maker, Timothy Pont. As one might expect of a cartographer, and as the title indicates, this begins with a detailed topographical survey of the region. Yet Pont's interests

---

[84]   On Denmilne, see the entry by Alexander Du Toit in *ODNB*. Neither his career nor his surviving papers have received the attention they deserve.

[85]   'Balfour's Topographical Notes', NLS Adv MS 33.2.27.

[86]   Ibid., fols 158v (Ross), 17r (Caithness), 240r (Lennox), 247r–v (Kintyre).

[87]   Ibid., fols 355r–363r.

[88]   See for example his 'Abbreviat of Scottish History', NLS Adv MS 33.2.29, an epitome of Boece – or possibly Monipennie – detailing the reigns of each king from Fergus I to James VI.

were evidently much more wide-ranging, for this is followed by a full chorographical description systematically arranged in the form of 'Ane Alphabett of the touns, parishes, Towers, Villages, Hamletts & houses of Name ... with Necessarey Remembrancess of diuerss of them'.[89]

Despite much valuable recent research, Pont's career remains remarkably shadowy. The son of the distinguished Protestant minister, Robert Pont, and a graduate of St Andrews University, little is known for certain about how, why or even when he undertook the extensive fieldwork on which his maps were based.[90] It seems likely, however, that it was carried out in the 1580s and 1590s and that chorographical description, such as 'Cunningham Topographized', was part and parcel of the process. There is evidence of Pont petitioning James VI & I for financial aid towards publishing a chorographical atlas in the early 1610s, at a time when Speed and Camden were clearly aware of his work, but Pont was dead by 1615 and nothing came of the project. Indeed, his maps and descriptions were almost entirely lost to view until they were rescued by Denmilne in the late 1620s and subsequently passed on to Scotstarvit. Coincidentally, Joan Blaeu was already, as early as 1626, corresponding with Scotstarvit about supplying the Amsterdam press with maps of Scotland for a projected *Novus Atlas* that would encompass the entire known world, a new and ambitious *Theatrum Orbis Terrarum*.[91] Thanks to Denmilne, by the early 1630s, Scotstarvit was able to oblige, and Blaeu subsequently engraved some 35 of the 48 regional maps that appeared in 1654 directly from Pont's manuscripts. The remaining maps were the work primarily of Robert Gordon of Straloch (1580–1661) and his son James Gordon (1617–86), also known as the parson of Rothiemay, though Scotstarvit may have advised Blaeu in clarifying some of Pont's less legible drawings. It is unclear what became of Pont's chorographical descriptions. Like many of the manuscript maps, some of them (or at least transcriptions of the originals) ended up in the collections of the later seventeenth-century antiquary, Sir Robert Sibbald.[92] However, they did not accompany

---

[89]   'Cunningham Topographized by Mr. T. Pont', in 'Balfour's Topographical Notes', NLS Adv MS 33.2.27, fols 205r–215r. For a printed version, see J.S. Dobie (ed.), *Cunningham Topographized by Timothy Pont* (Glasgow, 1876).

[90]   The fullest exploration is Ian C. Cunningham (ed.), *The Nation Survey'd: Essays on late Sixteenth-century Scotland as Depicted by Timothy Pont* (East Linton, 2001), on which what follows is largely based.

[91]   For the genesis and development of this vast project, resulting in 1662 in the eleven volumes of the Latin *Atlas Maior*, see the overview in C. Koeman, *Joan Blaeu and his Grand Atlas* (London, 1970).

[92]   On Sibbald's place in this story, see Withers, *Geography, Science and National Identity*, ch. 3; and his 'Geography, Science and National Identity in Early Modern Britain: The Case of Scotland and the Work of Sir Robert Sibbald (1641–1722)', *Annals of Science*, 53 (1996): pp. 29–73.

the maps to Amsterdam and were not used by Blaeu to flesh out Pont's cartographical work. Rather, the texts that accompany the regional maps in the printed *Atlas* are by a wide assortment of different hands.

Such a miscellany of contributors was probably not what Blaeu had in mind when he first mooted a Scottish atlas – and the complex history of the texts as well as the maps may also help explain why it took more than two decades for the project to come to fruition.[93] When Blaeu published his *Atlas of England* in 1645 – volume 4 of the *Atlas Novus* – he was able simply to interleave new engravings of Speed's maps with Camden's descriptions of the English and Welsh counties without any further additions or editorial interventions. Indeed, the only parts of *Britannia* that do not appear verbatim in volume 4 are the sections on Scotia and Hibernia that Blaeu avowedly intended to use in dealing with those kingdoms in volume 5.[94] Compiling the Scottish *Atlas*, however, proved a good deal less straightforward. Extensive use is indeed made of Camden in the textual material that accompanies the regional maps, and it may well be that Blaeu used Camden's regional divisions of Scotia as a means of organizing the cartographical material. At least for Lowland Scotland, the *Atlas* closely follows Camden's ordering of the Scottish regions as listed in *Britannia*, though for the north and north-west there are increasing divergences from Camden, and the islands (not covered by Camden) necessarily required separate treatment. Nonetheless, Blaeu exploited Camden's *Britannia* to the full: the only sections of the 1607 description of Scotia that do not appear in the *Atlas* are those on the Merse and Lothian, which are entirely replaced by new descriptions, and a brief section on Caledonia, which is omitted altogether. Yet otherwise there is not a scrap of Camden's text (including John Johnston's poems) that does not also appear in the *Atlas*, invariably with the acknowledgement 'Ex Camdeno'.

That said, and crucially, Camden's words are never left to stand alone: invariably there is additional chorographical material added by the likes of Scot of Scotstarvit and Gordon of Straloch, while with the express encouragement of the kirk a number of ministers also contributed material on their localities (and a series of poems by the distinguished neo-Latinist Arthur Johnston supplemented those by his earlier namesake).[95]

---

[93] The gestation of the Scottish volume is surprisingly well documented compared with others in the *Atlas* series: see Koeman, *Blaeu and his Grand Atlas*, pp. 70–76.

[94] The English *Atlas* is the longest in the series; for Blaeu's approach to putting it together, and his promise that the next volume would cover Scotland and Ireland, see his note to the reader ('Joannes Blaeu lectori SPD'), dated September 1645, at the beginning of the preliminary matter.

[95] The role of the church in the project is discussed in David Stevenson, 'Cartography and the Kirk: Aspects of the Making of the First Atlas of Scotland', *Scottish Studies*, 26 (1982): pp. 1–12; for a full analysis of the contributors, see Ian C. Cunningham, 'Blaeu's

The Scots were clearly not content to leave Camden's thin and patchy treatment as the sole authority on the northern kingdom, and the result is a much richer and more extensive chorographical survey of the country than the Englishman alone provided. This applies equally to the prefatory material. The introductory section on Scotland's government and civil and ecclesiastical divisions that Camden belatedly added to the 1607 edition of *Britannia* is faithfully reproduced by Blaeu, but here it is substantially – though silently – expanded, probably by Scotstarvit or Straloch, to give a very much fuller account of the working of Scotland's separate parliament, privy council and judicial system, both civil and criminal. Despite the profound contemporary tensions over issues of ecclesiastical polity, even Camden's notice of Scotland's episcopal hierarchy is included, though a note is added that 'the government of the church [now] proceeds differently' and a short concluding section is appended outlining the basics of the presbyterian system.[96] All of these additions may be seen simply as fleshing out Camden's cursory coverage of Scotia in *Britannia*. But there is a strong sense too of an ideological agenda aimed at countering the Anglocentricity of Camden's work and asserting the integrity of the Scottish kingdom. It is surely no coincidence that Scotstarvit's brother-in-law, the poet, genealogist and historian William Drummond of Hawthornden, had in his extensive library a manuscript with the tantalizing title 'Nuntius Scoto-Britanus, or, a paire of Spectacles for W. Camden, to look upon North-Britain'.[97] Regrettably the manuscript is lost, but it suggests a common Scottish concern that Camden's description of Scotland was not just incomplete, but that 'Britannia' could too readily be construed simply as greater England.

This patriotic agenda – one that cut across political and religious divisions – becomes still clearer when one turns to consider the voluminous additional material that precedes the *Atlas* proper. Leaving aside the possibility that Buchanan's *De Iure Regni* might be bound into the volume, readers on opening the *Atlas* would encounter first of all a lengthy Latin poem of some 1300 lines entitled *Scotiae Topographia* by Andrew Melville (1545–1622), the doyen of Scottish presbyterian intellectuals who had been incarcerated in the Tower of London by James VI & I in 1607 and only released in 1611 on condition that he went into exile in France. Melville is best known for his uncompromising religious convictions – and the confrontations with the king over ecclesiastical polity to which they gave rise. Yet, as Arthur Williamson reminds us elsewhere in this

---

Atlas Novus, Volume V: The Texts and their Authors', *Scottish Geographical Journal*, 121 (2005): pp. 269–87.

   [96]   See *The Blaeu Atlas of Scotland* (above, note 2), pp. 56–9.

   [97]   R.H. MacDonald (ed.), *The Library of Drummond of Hawthornden* (Edinburgh, 1971), p. 224 (no. 1339).

volume, he was also an accomplished neo-Latin poet, a friend and admirer of Buchanan, who had already in an unfinished epic poem *Gathelus*, published in 1602, used the Scots origins' legend as a means of exploring the apocalyptic implications of the anticipated clash between the Britannic and Hispanic empires.[98] Here, however, his mind and muse are working in a very different vein and the *Topographia*, written in the years just following the union of 1603 and dedicated to Prince Henry Frederick, turns out on closer inspection to be nothing other than a faithful rendition into Latin verse of the entire text of Buchanan's description of Scotland as found in Book I of the *Historia*.[99] If the inclusion of Melville's poem (its only known printing) signals clearly enough the importance of Buchanan to the cultural project embodied in the *Atlas*, it is made still clearer at the end of the prefatory material where the original prose description is also included in its entirety, beginning with Buchanan's onslaught on the unfortunate Lhuyd (omitted by Melville) and continuing verbatim through to his comments on the Cornavii of Caithness and Cornwall. At this point, the text is cut short, but only to assure the reader that Buchanan's full description of the isles (including his acknowledgement of his debt to Donald Munro) is printed later in the *Atlas* where it appears *in extenso* up to and including his remarks on the longevity of Lawrence the Shetlander.[100] Here, then, far from there being any reluctance to acknowledge Buchanan as a source, there is a sense of him being celebrated as a champion of Scottish integrity who well deserved the unique privilege of having his place of birth identified on the map of Lennox. But just as important as these invocations of Buchanan's authority, and reinforcing his importance in underwriting Scottish identity, is what is sandwiched between the verse and prose versions of his description. For here we find a series of shorter essays by Gordon of Straloch that negotiate between Buchanan and Camden in a way that is clearly intended to counter the Anglo-British imperialism of *Britannia*.

Straloch is perhaps the least celebrated of those who participated in the *Atlas* project, yet his contribution was not only substantial but critical in giving it ideological shape and bite. Educated at Marischal College Aberdeen and the University of Paris, he was by the 1630s an established figure in the political and cultural landscape of north-east Scotland, his moderate views and close connections with the Gordon Earls of Huntly – whose family history he wrote – making him an ideal negotiator between

---

[98]   See Buchanan, *Political Poetry*, pp. 284–97, for the full text and translation; see also Arthur Williamson, Chapter 4 below.
[99]   *The Blaeu Atlas of Scotland*, pp. 35–41, for full English prose translation.
[100]   Ibid., pp. 49–53, 110–14; the section on Shetland is separated from the rest on p. 120.

royalists and covenanters.[101] It was during the tumultuous years between 1641 and 1648, following a commission from Charles I himself, that he undertook the bulk of his work for the *Atlas*, including the pioneering chorographical surveys of much of the far north of Scotland that fleshed out with a wealth of topographical and historical detail the bare descriptions offered by Buchanan and the patchy comments of Camden.[102] In this context, however, it is the preliminary essays that he contributed to the *Atlas* that are especially worthy of note. For immediately following Melville's *Scotiae Topographia*, we find Straloch's *Adnotata ad Scotorum Antiquitatem*, beginning with an essay on the first settlement of the Scots in Britain that confronts directly the view of Lhuyd and Camden that the early history of Scotland as told by Boece and Buchanan was no more than a patriotic fiction.[103] According to Straloch, his essay was necessary not only because English historians persisted in placing the arrival of the Scots in Scotland at the same time as the arrival of the Anglo-Saxons in England (i.e., *c.*440 CE), but also because with Scots and English now joined 'in one empire' it was more important than ever that those who argued 'partially, impudently, and against the factual evidence', and whose Latin writings were being read in many countries, should not go unchallenged: 'our case must be presented,' he concluded, 'or our recognisance forfeited'. In other words, in post-union Britain, where Scots and Englishmen had 'a reasonably good agreement in language, religion and customs', Straloch thought it imperative that the Scottish kingdom's distinct identity not be lost by default.

Chief among the English writers whom he had in his sights was Camden. Though 'an erudite man and skilled in every aspect of antiquity', Straloch insisted that the great antiquarian was by no means beyond reproach. On the contrary, in his views on the Scots' origins, the 'dictator of the antiquarian world', as Straloch mockingly described him, was demonstrably both prejudiced and disingenuous. In countering Camden's view of the late settlement of the Scots in Britain, however, Straloch is careful not to follow Buchanan in simply mounting a vituperative defence of Fergus I and Boece's ancient line of forty kings. Rather, and much more ingeniously, he argues that Camden (and Lhuyd) had wilfully ignored the

---

[101]   There is a bare sketch of Straloch's career by Shona MacLean Vance in *ODNB*, where he is described as a cartographer, but this hardly does justice to the range of his intellectual interests. Like Balfour of Denmilne's, his life would undoubtedly repay more thorough and systematic research.

[102]   For precise details of Straloch's chorographical contribution, see Cunningham, 'Blaeu's *Atlas*: The Texts and their Authors', pp. 271, 277–83.

[103]   'Notes on the Antiquity of the Scots, And their second crossing into Britain from Ireland under the leadership of Reuther, whom Bede calls Reuda', in *The Blaeu Atlas of Scotland*, pp. 42–3.

Venerable Bede's testimony that the Scots had settled in Scotland 'before the first arrival of Caesar' in 60 BCE and had thus deliberately truncated the Scottish kingdom's history by some 500 years. Moreover, they had similarly omitted to mention that the Scottish king Reuther, referred to by Bede as Reuda, led a settlement into Scotland that predated Caesar's invasions of the island by 144 years.[104] At this point, the origins of the Scottish kingdom having been pushed as far back as 204 BCE, Straloch neatly sidestepped any explicit defence of Fergus I's foundation of the kingdom more than a century earlier by concluding simply that it was unnecessary to inquire further into the matter as Camden's case – the 'impartial reader' would no doubt agree – was already clearly lost.

Straloch was too good a historian to swallow Boece's early history whole, but too good a patriot to allow Camden to go unchallenged. Similarly, as was the case with many of those involved in the *Atlas* project, he was too conservative to accept Buchanan's radical politics, but too conscious of Buchanan's importance to Scotland's cultural identity to reject his work out of hand. Indeed, having briefly disposed of the hoary old jibe that the early Scots were cannibals, Straloch proceeds to upbraid 'our dictator' (Camden) who 'reviled [Buchanan] for ignorance or negligence' in tracing the origins of the Scottish people to the tribes of ancient Gaul, while he himself 'sends us off to Scythia, although there was never any contact by our ancestors with these regions or peoples'.[105] There follows an erudite if less highly charged critique of Camden's understanding of when and why the Roman walls were constructed before Straloch finally embarks on a more detailed explanation of why English has replaced Gaelic as the language of the Scots. Here, in much less polemical mode, he treads a delicate line that distinguishes between accepting that the Scots had abandoned Gaelic – a language he admits is barbarous – in favour of English and rejecting that this was the result of conquest, subjugation or even assimilation. It was true that, except on the western seaboard, 'where deep barbarity retains the old language among the common people', English was now the language of the Scots. Yet this was not the result of Edward I's invasions any more than of Malcolm Canmore's marriage to St Margaret and the influx of Saxons to Scotland that followed the Norman Conquest of England. It

---

[104] Straloch's argument here is reminiscent of the more sceptical approach to Scotland's early history adopted by John Mair but eclipsed by Boece's more fanciful and engaging account: Mair similarly appealed to Bede's reference to Reuda to demonstrate the early foundation of the kingdom and was similarly concerned to uphold Scottish identity within the context of British union: see Mason, *Kingship and the Commonweal*, p. 46.

[105] *The Blaeu Atlas of Scotland*, p. 43. The reference to Scots as cannibals, allegedly based on the authority of St Jerome, was popularized by William Harrison in the Scotophobic 'Description of Britain' that he wrote for Raphael Holinshed's *Chronicles* of 1577. Camden also mentions it, but denies that it was the Scots to whom Jerome was referring; see *Britannia* (1607), p. 91.

was rather a much more lasting consequence of the far earlier creation of the English-speaking kingdom of Northumbria that had encompassed eastern Scotland south of the Forth and involved the settlement of Anglo-Saxons at the expense of the Picts who were forced back beyond the Forth, and the Roman wall that had protected Britannia from Picts and Scots alike. Subsequently, with the collapse of the Northumbrian kingdom, the Picts had reclaimed these territories, but rather than displacing the English-speaking farmers who had long settled the countryside, they lorded over them and in time adopted their language. By far the richest region of Scotland, the centre of 'law, power, business, in a word whatever is avidly sought by mortals for a good and happy life', it was the language of south-eastern Scotland, with its English-speaking farmers and Pictish lords, that became the common language of the Scots.[106]

Conclusion

In 1683, in a manifesto for a new chorographical study of Scotland, Robert Sibbald claimed that Blaeu's *Atlas* 'containeth little more than what *Buchanan* wrote, and some few scrapes out of *Cambden*, who is no friend to us in what he writeth'.[107] While partly correct, Sibbald should have known better than to dismiss so casually the work of Straloch, to whose papers he had after all fallen heir. For Straloch's understanding of the settlement of northern Britain was clearly a good deal more sophisticated than that of most of his contemporaries – or any of his predecessors. Yet his work on the *Atlas* was equally clearly inflected by the patriotic agenda that drove the project as a whole. His defence of Scotland's antiquity maintained the critical space for Fergus I and his hundred royal successors to continue to symbolize Scottish integrity, while his cartography as well as his chorography effectively detailed the kingdom's unique history and geography. With the publication of the *Atlas* in 1654, Scotland was as well mapped and as thoroughly 'topographized' as any region then known to man. Scotia's unique place on the world map was, quite literally, there for all to see.[108]

The significance of George Buchanan in this assertion of Scotland's distinct geographical and historical identity was clearly immense. Not only did his own pioneering description of Scotland provide a template

---

[106]   *The Blaeu Atlas of Scotland*, pp. 44–5.

[107]   Quoted in Withers, 'Geography, Science and National Identity', pp. 49–50.

[108]   In fact, the five volumes of the *Atlas Novus* published in 1654 were issued in French, German and Dutch as well as Latin (though not English), and subsequent ever more comprehensive editions of the *Atlas* in 1655 and 1662 were similarly published in a range of languages: see Koeman, *Blaeu and his Grand Atlas*, pp. 104–5.

for subsequent topographical and chorographical self-fashioning, but his stature as an iconic figure in the Latinate culture of contemporary Europe made it hard to resist invoking his authority. Yet Buchanan's legacy was profoundly ambiguous. His republican politics had little appeal to the network of cultured country gentlemen who were largely responsible for compiling the *Atlas*. It is both true and instructive that in 1635 Drummond of Hawthornden advised Charles I that he should read Buchanan's *De Iure Regni* 'for his own private and the publick Good'.[109] But this unlikely remark was not intended as a ringing endorsement of the principles of election and accountability with which Buchanan had invested Scotland's ancient line of kings. Rather it was an expression of a Stuart loyalism, shared by almost all Hawthornden's Scottish contemporaries, that was being stretched to breaking point by an aloof, absentee and unresponsive monarch. We are perhaps too often inclined to characterize mid-seventeenth-century Scotland in terms of a dour and intellectually arid clerisy that appropriated Buchanan for the radical presbyterian cause. We would do well to remember that there was also an educated and inquiring landed gentry, often closely linked to regional magnates as well as local clergy, who espoused an ideology of moderate constitutional royalism that owed much to the baronial conciliarism exemplified in Buchanan's *Historia* if not to the radical principles that underlay it. Deeply versed in the minutiae of lineage and locality, comfortable in the landscapes of power that they both dominated and delineated, they were increasingly affronted by Charles I's assaults on noble privilege and the structures of authority – the laws and liberties – that underpinned them. Whether or not their own copies of Blaeu's *Atlas* included the text of *De Iure Regni* – and the roll-call of 110 kings of Scots from Fergus I to Charles II that appears on the verso of its last page – there is no denying Buchanan's critical role in the process by which such early modern Scots had come to know and define themselves and their kingdom.

---

[109] The remark occurs in *An Apologetical Letter* protesting against the trial of Balmerino for treason: see *The Works of William Drummond of Hawthornden*, ed. Thomas Ruddiman and John Sage (Edinburgh, 1711), p. 134; see also Roger A. Mason, 'The Aristocracy, Episcopacy and the Revolution of 1638', in Terry Brotherstone (ed.), *Covenant, Charter and Party: Traditions of Revolt and Protest in Modern Scottish History* (Aberdeen, 1989), pp. 7–24, esp. pp. 16–17.

CHAPTER 2

Performance, Print and Politics in George Buchanan's *Ane Detectioun of the duinges of Marie Quene of Scottes*

Tricia A. McElroy

This chapter begins with a familiar story: the downfall of Mary Queen of Scots in 1567. After the murder of her husband Darnley and her rash marriage to the Earl of Bothwell, Mary was forced to abdicate by a group of Scottish nobles; her half-brother James Stewart, Earl of Moray, assumed the regency of Scotland. A year later, Mary escaped from her prison at Lochleven and mustered her supporters. Defeated at Langside, she fled to England, convinced she would receive aid from Elizabeth. Although the allegations of conspiracy, murder and adultery against her had begun circulating in early 1567, Mary's flight to England in 1568 precipitated the first formal anti-Marian tracts, documents designed to portray her as morally corrupt and politically incompetent. The most important of these is George Buchanan's *De Maria Scotorum Regina*, known in the vernacular as *Ane Detectioun of the duinges of Marie Quene of Scottes*. Though printed later in 1571, the *Detectioun* originated with Elizabeth's request in 1568 that the Earl of Moray justify the rebellion against Mary with proof of her misconduct. Recruited by Moray to shape his party's case against the Queen and supplied with the necessary documentation, Buchanan crafted what would become the standard narrative about her descent into criminality. As one of Europe's most accomplished humanists, Buchanan was an excellent choice: his intellectual interests and political theories pervade the summary of Mary's misdeeds and give force to the evidence against her.

The *Detectioun* emerges from the same period of energetic production as Buchanan's more influential works – the *De Iure Regni apud Scotos Dialogus* (1579) and the *Rerum Scoticarum Historia* (1582). Indeed, the three texts contribute to the shared goal of justifying Mary's deposition: the *De Iure* sketches his political theories about limited monarchy; the *Detectioun* details Mary's specific tyranny; and the *Historia* contextualizes the entire episode in the patterns of Scottish history. Yet the *Detectioun* occasions the least scholarly study, lacking the proto-democratic appeal of the *De Iure* and the monumental sweep of the *Historia*. Jenny Wormald cleverly captures the quality of the *Detectioun*, calling it 'copy for the *Sun* in the style of *The Times*'.[1] Its shameless inaccuracies and polemical distortions, which rely on a predictable tale of female passion and treachery, would hardly seem to merit serious critical attention. Still, Buchanan's indictment should not be dismissed as empty sensationalism. As sophisticated propaganda, it enacts the political theories advocated by his more respectable works and reveals how literary and political discourses could be strategic partners in the sixteenth century.

This essay takes as its focus the 1571 English version of the *Detectioun*, in which Buchanan's indictment precedes the elaborate presentation of Moray's documentary evidence against Mary. The literal binding together of criminal narrative with corroborating evidence results in rhetorical and bibliographical complexity, creating the illusion of an open legal hearing in which the reading audience assumes an adjudicatory role. This effect is generated largely through specialized discourses – political, literary and legal – that both structure and unify the elements of the *Detectioun*. John Pocock has argued that a historical work can be reconstituted according to the 'languages' or 'specialized idioms' by which that text 'performs'. Complex texts, he says,

> may be seen as performing polyvalently: not only will there be several continuities of discourse (another term is levels of meaning) within which it may be read and seen to have acted but it may be seen as performing all manner of cunning games as it moves from one level to another.[2]

The languages or idioms of the *Detectioun* 'perform' in a number of ways. Buchanan uses theatrical tropes, as we shall see, to characterize Mary's tyrannical behaviour, and the result is a narrative that puts his ideas about kingship and popular sovereignty into action. Taking its cue from Buchanan's indictment, the printed form of the *Detectioun* presents all the documents and voices of a criminal trial. Working together, the theatrical and legal idioms challenge the reader to respond actively, to become an observer and a participant in Mary's trial. The *Detectioun* suggests that the reader, to quote Pocock again, is 'an actor in the sense that he is one in a historical process'.[3] In this volume, the reader seems as palpable as the

---

[1]   Jenny Wormald, *Mary Queen of Scots: A Study in Failure* (London, 1991), p. 14.

[2]   J.G.A. Pocock, 'Texts as Events: Reflections on the History of Political Thought', in Kevin Sharpe and Steven N. Zwicker (eds), *Politics of Discourse: The Literature and History of Seventeenth-century England* (Berkeley, CA, 1987), pp. 27 and 28.

[3]   Ibid., p. 29.

prosecutorial voice that bellows from its pages. And the fiction that he can fairly judge the Queen using the evidence provided makes the *Detectioun* a pivotal contribution not only to the Marian controversy but to late sixteenth-century debates about the sources of political power – to which, of course, Buchanan was a key contributor.

Using legal and theatrical discourses as guides, the following discussion will clarify how political circumstances dictate the design of the *Detectioun*; consider how theatrical idiom articulates the political distinction between good kingship and tyranny; and examine how the controlling metaphors of Buchanan's narrative define Mary's character and suggest the common people as a source for truth. Buchanan's classical tragedy, *Baptistes sive calumnia tragœdia* (1577) – another text pertinent to his political thought in the 1570s – serves as a case study, both for understanding how Buchanan's dramatic tastes contribute to the argument of the *Detectioun* and, more importantly, for exposing how his political ideals become ideological tools in the service of anti-Marian propaganda.

The Politics of Design

The composition, printing and distribution of the *Detectioun* comprise several complicated stories, all of which cannot be recounted here. Two aspects of the *Detectioun*'s bibliographical history deserve emphasis, however, because they explain both its content and material form. First, the *Detectioun* began as a Latin summary of Mary's crimes written by Buchanan and presented by Moray in 1568 to an Elizabethan commission charged with the task of determining Mary's fate. That commission met first at York, then at Westminster, in closed hearings; though represented by a small group of adherents, the Queen of Scots was not permitted to attend or to see the evidence against her. In addition to Buchanan's indictment, Moray and his party presented documentary evidence of Mary's guilt: marriage contracts; court records and correspondence; criminal confessions; and the notorious Casket Letters and Sonnets. When the English commission adjourned in stalemate in early 1569 and the Scottish commissioners returned north, copies of Buchanan's indictment and its supporting evidence remained behind in London, carefully catalogued by William Cecil, Elizabeth's principal secretary. There this material remained for almost three years, an unpublished trump card.

This leads to the second point about the genesis of the printed book: the *Detectioun* was sponsored by Elizabeth's government in response to a crisis of its own. The published *Detectioun* is, in other words, a volume of Scottish material, designed and assembled by the English. The discovery in 1571 of the Ridolfi conspiracy – a plot for a Spanish invasion and Catholic uprising; a marriage between Mary and the Duke of Norfolk; and the English crown for Mary – altered English policy towards the Scottish Queen. Although Elizabeth had discouraged anti-Marian material since 1568, at least publicly, she now needed to advertise Mary's duplicity. Deciding it was time to initiate an 'elaborate series of bibliographical deceptions',[4] the English government dusted off the Scottish documents left behind in 1568.

Tracing the evolution of the printed volume exposes the Elizabethan propaganda machine at work as it builds an argument with text, print and covert sponsorship. Buchanan's indictment was first printed as *De Maria Scotorum Regina* in October 1571 by John Day in London; the volume indicated no author, date or place of publication.[5] Almost immediately thereafter, Day printed *Ane Detectioun of the duinges of Marie Quene of Scottes*, an English translation of the Latin *De Maria*, which orthographically imitates Scots: the palimpsest effect betrays a translator either struggling with native Scots or aiming to make the text seem Scottish for an English audience.[6] The title page to this version first acknowledges Buchanan's authorship in print ('Translatit out of the Latine quhilke was written by G.B.'), but like the Latin *De Maria* it provides no publication details.[7] In 1572, Robert Lekpreuik printed a genuine Scots version at St Andrews,[8] and in that same year a French version appeared, the *Histoire de Marie Royne d'Escosse*, most likely printed in La Rochelle though the title page claims Edinburgh.[9] These multiple translations, with their deceptive imprints and orthographies, were designed to serve distinct

---

[4]   James E. Phillips, *Images of a Queen: Mary Stuart in Sixteenth-century Literature* (Berkeley, CA, 1964), p. 63.

[5]   STC 3978. For a review of all editions, see J. Scott, 'A Bibliography of Works Relating to Mary Queen of Scots: 1544–1700', *Edinburgh Bibliographical Society*, 2 (1896): pp. 1–96. See also Durkan, *Buchanan Bibliography*.

[6]   The man usually thought to be the translator is Thomas Wilson, eminent scholar and Master of the Court of Requests during this period. Wilson sent a letter to Cecil on 8 November 1571, enclosing 'so much as his [sic] translated into handsome *Scottishe*'. William Murdin, *A Collection of State Papers relating to Affairs in the Reign of Queen Elizabeth, from the Year 1571 to 1596* (London, 1759), p. 57.

[7]   All quotes are taken from the 1571 *Detectioun* and noted parenthetically. John Day printed a second edition in 1572. He held royal privileges and was the first to print John Foxe's *Book of Martyrs* (W.W. Greg, *Some Aspects and Problems of London Publishing Between 1550 and 1650* [Oxford, 1956], pp. 99–100). In 1571, 'accordyng to the Scotish copie Printed at Strivilyng by Robert Lekpreuik', Day also printed Buchanan's *Ane Admonitioun direct to the trew Lordis mantenaris of the Kingis Grace Authoritie* (STC 3967).

[8]   STC 3982.

[9]   STC 3979. McFarlane speculates about the *Histoire*'s translation and publication history (*Buchanan*, pp. 348–50). English sponsorship is likely. For even greater detail about its uses for foreign policy, see Robert M. Kingdon, 'The Use of Clandestine Printings by the Government of Elizabeth I in its French Policy, 1570–1590', in Frank McGregor and Nicholas Wright (eds), *European History and Its Historians* (Adelaide, 1977), pp. 49–52.

purposes and to reach specific audiences. The English strategy generally speaking was to suggest that this text not only issued from a Scottish pen but was printed on a Scottish press. England need not look guilty of character assassination: no imprint, false imprint, inauthentic vernacular – all contribute to the pretence that this book originated with Mary's own nobles, making the case against her all the more convincing.[10]

The contents are wide-ranging. All versions include two principal sections: Buchanan's detailed account (or 'detection') of Mary's misconduct and an accompanying oration. In the oration, the narrator uses the preceding 'detection' as the source text for a legal argument that emphasizes and embellishes certain aspects of the prosecution's case.[11] The *De Maria* also includes three of the Casket Letters translated into Latin and two poems. The next three vernacular versions – beginning with the 1571 English *Detectioun* – append all of the corroborating evidence provided by Moray's party in 1568.[12] To these items, the French *Histoire* adds an essay that reviews Mary's conspiracies to attain Elizabeth's throne. Finally, only the English *Detectioun* concludes with a scurrilous meditation on the danger of replacing Elizabeth with Mary. Four stanzas of 'versified, gnomic reflections' ask 'Englischmen if / it be gud to change Quenis':[13] 'Quhen rude Scotland hes vomited up ane poisoun, must fine England lick it up for a restorative?' No such meditation finds its way into the *Histoire* or Lekpreuik's St Andrews version, for obvious reasons in the latter case: its sentiment hardly caters to a Scottish readership. Directed demonstrably towards an English audience, the 1571 *Detectioun* demands that the

---

Phillips (*Images of a Queen*, p. 63 and corresponding note) suggests the possibility of German editions, which McFarlane (*Buchanan*, p. 348) is not inclined to credit.

[10]   Phillips, *Images of a Queen*, p. 63.

[11]   Although Buchanan's authorship of the first section seems certain, the oration cannot be as firmly attributed to him and, in fact, may have been written by Thomas Wilson working under Cecil's direction. McFarlane gives a balanced view of this debate (*Buchanan*, pp. 344–8). Even if Buchanan did not write the oration, the structure, argument and *topoi* of his narrative crucially inform the 'oration' and the rest of the volume.

[12]   The order in which these documents are printed corresponds exactly to the records of their presentation at Westminster. The *Detectioun*'s 'Memorandum' is literally lifted from the commissioners' minutes (7 and 8 December 1568), and symbols code each item to its summary in the minutes. (See The National Archives, London, SP 53/2/60, for the minutes from 7 December; SP 52/2/62 and 52/2/65, for example, are two Casket Letters coded with corresponding symbols.) Previously unnoticed, this correspondence conclusively proves English sponsorship of the published *Detectioun* and links Cecil specifically to its conception and production. For the minutes from 6 and 8 December 1568, see Walter Goodall, *Examination of the Casket Letters said to be written by Mary, Queen of Scots to James, Earl of Bothwell* (Edinburgh, 1754), pp. 227–38. Minutes from 7 December are printed in John Hosack, *Mary Queen of Scots and her Accusers* (2 vols, Edinburgh, 1869), vol. 1, pp. 549–53.

[13]   McFarlane, *Buchanan*, p. 340.

reader be wary of continued plots to steal Elizabeth's throne, especially those that involve Scotland's 'poisoun'.

How do we make sense of this complex volume, attached to Buchanan's name but brought to fruition by other hands and other motives? Critically, the *Detectioun* has fallen victim to the standard approach to Marian propaganda, one preoccupied with the Queen's guilt or innocence and often neglectful of argumentative strategy.[14] Readers tend to worry over the details of Buchanan's narrative, to collate items of evidence, to quibble over which letter tallies with this or that document. And, of course, the most celebrated items, the Casket Letters, have trapped generations of historians, both professional and dilettante, in an interpretative either-or. Such myopia can be excused. Those responsible for writing and publishing the *Detectioun* riveted our attention on scandal and trained us to look for answers in the minutiae of date, time and diction: the reader is encouraged to retrace Mary's movements, to sort through her possible actions, and even to carry out an exegesis of selected passages from the Casket Letters. An unfamiliar *Detectioun* emerges, however, if we confront the volume *as a whole*, made up of interlocking pieces that collaborate to produce an implicit political argument. Such a perspective requires attending to form as well as content, both the discursive strategies of Buchanan's narrative and the bibliographical features of the printed volume.

The 1571 English *Detectioun* sets the precedent of supplementing the two principal sections with copious evidence – an editorial decision that radically transforms its meaning.[15] By ostensibly providing detailed textual and material support for the indictment of Mary, the *Detectioun* is transformed into a pre-packaged legal proceeding, one that slyly professes fairness by claiming to give 'Mary's' side of the story through the Casket Letters and Sonnets: 'Let us bring forth a royall witnesse', the oration bellows. 'Read her awin letter, her letter (I say) written with her awin hand' (sig. Hiii[r]). This trick of bibliography results in the most compelling

---

[14]   This is not meant to detract from Gordon Donaldson's and W.A. Gatherer's valuable appraisals of Buchanan's narrative; nor McFarlane's detailed attention to authorship and publication issues. Gordon Donaldson, *The First Trial of Mary, Queen of Scots* (London, 1969); W.A. Gatherer (ed.), *The Tyrannous Reign of Mary Stewart* (Edinburgh, 1958). Also see Anne McLaren, 'Gender, Religion, and Early Modern Nationalism: Elizabeth I, Mary Queen of Scots, and the Genesis of English Anti-Catholicism', *American Historical Review*, 107/3 (2002): pp. 739–68; and John Guy, '*My Heart is my Own': The Life of Mary Queen of Scots* (London and New York, 2004), ch. 28.

[15]   R.H. Mahon does not believe the supplementary material was originally included in the *Detectioun* (*The Indictment of Mary Queen of Scots* [Cambridge, 1923], pp. 24–5). His evidence is scanty, and his hypothesis unnecessarily complicates an already difficult textual history. In any case, the only surviving versions of these books include this material, and the contemporary *Copie of a Letter* (cited below) confirms that the second part of the *Detectioun* is devoted to the other 'Parties" testimony.

fiction of the *Detectioun*, that the reader observes an impartial trial in which he can rule justly and competently. 'Ech man may plainely perceive' Mary's guilt, the text claims repeatedly, by listening to the oration and perusing the evidence (sig. Ciiiiʳ). A contemporary pamphlet, *The Copie of a Letter, written by one in London to his Frend*, confirms this design. Of the *Detectioun*, the anonymous author writes:

> in the same one Booke, are both Parties to be heard, the one in the former Parte, both in the Declaration and Oration of Evidence; the other in the latter Parte, in the Parties owne Contractes, Songes, Letters, Judiciall Procedynges, Protestations, Examinations, and Confessions.[16]

When the reader reaches the end of the book, those odd stanzas exhort him to study the evidence and judge whether it would be wise to replace Elizabeth with the poisonous Scottish queen. The exhortation is politically suggestive, placing trust in the reader's judgement. The strategy may reflect a Protestant conviction in individual understanding; but, even more interestingly, Buchanan's republican ideals support the injunction for 'eche man' to play a role in determining Mary's guilt. As one sees repeatedly in anti-Marian propaganda, the suggestion of individual engagement in the political life of the state – however illusory or potentially subversive – can be a convincing argument of its own, creating a powerful sense of popular consensus.

The structure of a legal hearing is enhanced by a sense of performance in which many voices are 'heard': the prosecutorial voice, Scottish nobles, legal officers, Darnley's father, Bothwell's co-conspirators, Mary, even the Scottish people – all contribute in different ways throughout the narrative and supplementary evidence. This performative quality derives in part from the strategic use of typography and language, a 'marking' of the text to give it 'order and meaning' and to help the reader distinguish voices as well as important information.[17] In a passage from the oration, for example, where the prosecutorial voice argues that Mary poisoned Darnley, excerpts from the second Casket letter are quoted as evidence and printed in Roman type; the narrator's words appear in black letter (see sig. Hiiiʳ⁻ᵛ; Figs 2.1 and 2.2).

Isolated by the clean lines of Roman type and surrounded by the stodgy black letter voice of the prosecution, Mary's alleged words leap from the page, making the case against her seem self-evident. The full reproduction

---

16   *The Copie of a Letter, written by one in London to his Frend, concernying the Credit of the late published Detection of the Doynges of the Ladie Marie of Scotland* [London: John Day, 1572], sig. Aiiᵛ. STC 17565.

17   Julie Stone Peters, *The Theatre of the Book, 1480–1880: Print, Text, and Performance in Europe* (Oxford, 2000), p. 17.

thingis doutfull ſa oft preuaylen ? Loe
here a man of ſingular vprightnes, and
of maiſt notable faythfulnes and credite
beareth witneſſe, agayuſt a womã bur=
nyng in hatrit of hir huſband, & in loue
of ane adulter, and in baith theis diſea=
ſis of corrupt affectiounis vnbridelit,
vntemperable by her eſtayt, raging by
hyr power, and indulgently following
the wantonnes of hyr wealth. But let
vs omit auld and diſſuſed thingis, and
let vs ſeuer the credite of inconſtaunt
multitude from the caſe of Princes. Let
vs in ſa greit a mater admit no witneſſe
in quhom eyther hys eſtait may be ſuſ=
pectit, or his manners may be blamit.
Quhat witneſſis than ſchall we vſe? for
by thys conditioun, we may bring forth
none vnder the royall degree of a King
or a Quene. But ſic vile actis are nat
wont to be committit by noble and gud
men, but by leud and wickit miniſteris.
Howbeit that herin alſwa the maiſt pre
ciſe may be ſatiſfyit, go to, let vs bring
forth a royall witneſſe. Read her awin
letter, her letter (I ſay) written with
her awin hand. what mean theis wor=
des, He is nat mikle deformit, and yit he
hes receiuit mikle. Quairof baith he receauit mikle? The thing it ſelfe, the di=
ſeaſe, t he pimples, the ſauour do tel you.
Euin that perdy he reccauit, that broght
deformitie, forſoth veray poyſon. But
           H. iij.   her

Figure 2.1   *Ane Detectioun of the duinges of Marie Quene of Scottes* (London, 1571), sig. Hiii^r. Courtesy of the Bodleian Library, University of Oxford.

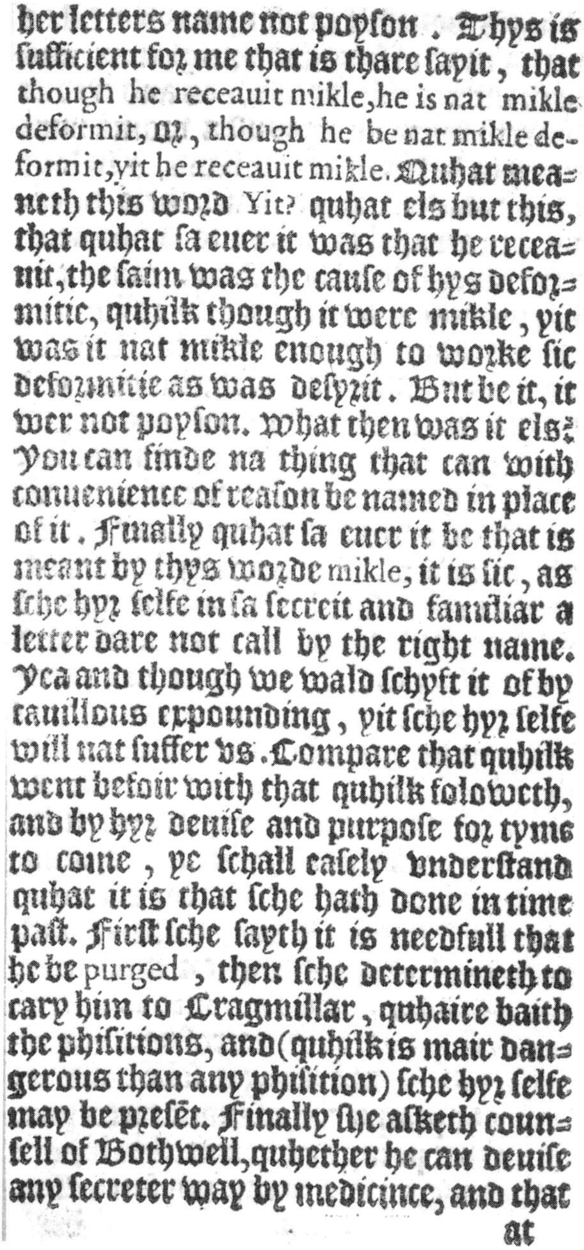

her letters name not poyson . Thys is
sufficient for me that is thare sayit , that
though he receauit mikle, he is nat mikle
deformit, or , though he be nat mikle deformit, yit he receauit mikle. Quhat mea-
neth this word Yit? quhat els but this,
that quhat sa euer it was that he receauit, the saim was the cause of hys deformitie, quhilk though it were mikle , yit
was it nat mikle enough to worke sic
deformitie as was desyrit . But be it, it
wer not poyson. what then was it els?
You can finde na thing that can with
conuenience of reason be named in place
of it . Finally quhat sa euer it be that is
meant by thys worde mikle, it is sic, as
sche hyr selfe in sa secreit and familiar a
letter dare not call by the right name.
Yea and though we wald schyft it of by
cauillous expounding , yit sche hyr selfe
will nat suffer vs .Compare that quhilk
went befoir with that quhilk foloweth,
and by hyr deuise and purpose for tyme
to come , ye schall easely vnderstand
quhat it is that sche hath done in time
past. First sche sayth it is needfull that
he be purged , then sche determineth to
cary him to Cragmillar , quhaire baith
the phisitions, and (quhilk is mair dangerous than any phisition) sche hyr selfe
may be preset. Finally she asketh coun-
sell of Bothwell, quhether he can deuise
any secreter way by medicine, and that
                                        at

Figure 2.2   *Ane Detectioun of the duinges of Marie Quene of Scottes*
(London, 1571), sig. Hiii[v]. Courtesy of the Bodleian Library,
University of Oxford.

and tharfoyz in respect that they deliuerit ac=
cozding to thayz knawlege , pzotestis that
thay should incur na wilfull erroz in any wise
heirafter . Quhilk instrument and pzotesta=
tioun immediatly after the reentry of the sayd
Erle of Caythnes Chaunceloz,and ane pairt
of the named of the sayd persons of assyise in
the sayd court of iusticiarie,befoyz the pzonunz
ciatioun of thayz deliueraunce fozesayd at the
desire of the sayd Erle of Caythnes was o=
penly read in iugement. And thayzupon he of
new askeit actis and instrumentis , and pzote=
steth in manner aboue exzzemit.

Extractum de libro Actorum Adiornalis
S. D. N. Reginæ. Per me Ioannem Bellenden
de Auchnoule militem, elericum iusticiaria
eiusdem generalem. Sub meis signo & subscri-
ptione mannalibus.

Ioannes Bellenden
Clericus Iusticiariæ.

Note that at the same tyme pzote=
statioun was made by Geozge Erle of
Catnes Chanceller of the sayd Assise
that the said dittay oz enditement was
nat in this point true,vz . in allegyng
the murder to be committit the ix . day
of Febzuarie foz that in dede the mur=
der was committed the next day be=
yng ther . day in the moznyng at twa
houres after midnight whiche in law
was and ought to be truely accomptit
the x. day and so the acquitall that way
but cauillously defendit.
                                        The

The writynges and letters
found in the sayd casket,which
are auowit to be written with
the Scottishe Quenis awne
hand.

Certaine French Sonnettes writ=
ten by the quene of Scottes to Both=
well,befoir hir mariage with him,and
(as it is sayd)quhile hir husband lyuit,
But certainly befoir his diuozce from
hys wife as the wozdes tham selues
shew , befoir quhom she here prefer=
reth hir selfe in deseruing to be belo=
ued of Bothwell.

O *Dieux ayez de moy compassion,*
Et m'enseignez quelle preuue certain
Ie puis donner qui ne luy semble Vain
De mon amour & ferme affection.
Las n'est il pas ia en possession
Du corps,du cœur qui ne refuse paine
Ny deshonneur,en la Vie incertaine,
Offense de parentz, ne pire affliction?
Pour luy tous mes amis i'estime moins que
Et de mes ennemis ie Veux esperer bien. (rien,
I'ay hazardé pour luy & nom & conscience:
Ie Veux pour luy au monde renoncer :
Ie Veux mourir pour luy auancer.
Que reste il plus pour prouuer ma constance?
                Q.iiij.   *Entre*

Figure 2.3   *Ane Detectioun of the duinges of Marie Quene of Scottes*
              (London, 1571), sigs Qiii^v–Qiiii^r. Courtesy of the Bodleian
              Library, University of Oxford.

of the Casket Letters and Sonnets similarly demonstrates the marking of
voice. The entire section is introduced in Roman type: 'The writynges and
letters found in the sayd casket, which are avowit to be written with the
Scottishe Quenis awne hand' (sig. Qiiii^r; Fig. 2.3). Then, after a black-
letter preface, which verifies a timeframe for adultery, the French sonnets
appear in italic, followed by their Scots translation in black letter (see sigs
Rii^v–Riii^r; Fig. 2.4). The contrast in both language and typeface is striking.
Although Mary's authorship is only conjectural, presenting the sonnets in
French forges a strong associative link with the Queen. Juxtaposed with
the italic French, the Scots version of the sonnets, with its grave return to
black letter, wrenches the words away from 'Mary': the voice becomes

Sans aymer rien que vous, soubz la subiection
De qui ie veux sans nulle fiction
Viure & mourir & a ce i'obtempere.

Mon cœur, mon sang, mon ame, & mon soucy,
Las, vous m'auez promis qu'aurons ce plaisir
De deuiser auecques vous a loysir,
Toute la nuict, ou ie languis icy,
Ayant le cœur d'extreme paour transy,
Pour voir absent le but de mon desir
Crainte d'oublir vn coup me vient a saisir:
Et l'autre fois ie crains que rendurcie
Soit contre moy vostre amiable cœur
Par quelque dit d'vn meschant rapporteur.
Vn autre fois ie crains quelque auenture
Qui par chemin detourne mon amant,
Par vn fuscheux & nouueau accident.
Dieu detourne toute malheureux augure

Ne vous voyant selon qu'auez promis
I'ay mis la main au papier pour escrire
D'vn different que ie voulu transcrire.
Ie ne scay pas quel sera vostre aduis
Mais ie scay bien qui mieux aymer scaura,
Vous diriez bien que plus y gaignera.

O Goddis haue of me compassioun,
And schew quhat certaine proofe
I may geif, quhich shall nat seem to him vaine,
Of my loue and feruent affectioun.
Helas, is he nat alredy in possessioun
Of my bodie, of hart, that refusis no payne,
Nor dishonour in the life vncertaine,
Offence of frendes, nor worse afflictioun,
For

For him I esteme al my fredes les the nathing,
And I will haue gude hope of my enemeis.
I haue put in hasard for him both fame & con-
I will for his sake renounce ye world, (science,
I will die to set him forwart.
Quhat remayneth to gief proofe of my con-
stancie?

In his handis and in his full power,
I put my sonne, my honour, and my lyif,
My contry, my subiectis, my soule al subdewit,
To him, and has none vther will
For my scope, quhilk without deceit,
I will folow in spite of all enuie
That may ensue: for I haif na vther desire,
But to make him perceiue my faythfulnes,
For storme or sayre wedder that may come,
Neuer will it change dwelling, or place.
Schortly I sall geif of my trueth sic proofe,
That he sall know my constancie about fiction,
Not by my weping, or faynit obedience,
As other haue done: but by vther experience.

Sche for hyr honour oweth you obedience:
I in obaying you may receiue dishonour,
Nat being (to my displesure) your wife as she.
And yit in this poynt she shall haue na prehe-
minence.
Sche vseth constancy for hyr awin profite:
For it is na litle honour to be maistres of your
goodes,
And I for luifing of you may receiue blame,
And will nat be ouercumme by hyr in loyall
obseruaunce.
Sche has no apprehension of your euyll,
I feare so all appearing euill that I can haue
na rest.
Sche had your acquaintance by consent of hyr
freindes,

B.iij. I

Figure 2.4 *Ane Detectioun of the duinges of Marie Quene of Scottes* (London, 1571), sigs Riiv–Riiir. Courtesy of the Bodleian Library, University of Oxford.

that of the prosecution, reading her words publicly and emphasizing each incriminating parallel between the poetry and her actions.[18]

The strategic effects of these bibliographical decisions should be clear. The calculated bringing together of criminal narrative, prosecutorial oration and documentary evidence creates the sense of a trial in progress or, more interestingly, of a trial that has happened. Of course, Mary had not been legally tried – the 1568 conferences at York and Westminster had no real judicial power – but the *Detectioun* seems to present an official transcript, a justification after the fact. Printed in this way, Mary's alleged

---

[18] Restored to their original printed context, the Casket documents do not function as expected, in fact, but begin to expose the central and futile debate between the opposing parties. For this argument, see my 'Executing Mary Queen of Scots: Strategies of Representation in Early Modern Scotland' (unpublished DPhil thesis, University of Oxford, 2005), ch. 2.

words are shifted into a public realm, where they can be scrutinized and interpreted. Distinguished with language and typography, her 'testimony' becomes available for the author's analysis, which in turn models for the reader the proper way to read the evidence. The form of the *Detectioun* constructs the competent reader it needs, one able to decipher evidence and to cast judgement. All of these elements of presentation point to conscious decisions in service of specific political agendas – in the case of the 1571 *Detectioun*, of ensuring that an English-reading public can distinguish the 'truth' about Mary.

Buchanan's *Baptistes* and the Theatre of Politics

The truth about Mary, argued vigorously by Buchanan, is her political and moral tyranny, for which she was necessarily deprived of her crown by the nobles of Scotland. As a proponent of elective and limited monarchy, the 'herald of popular sovereignty and modern constitutionalism',[19] Buchanan contended that the people could legitimately resist a monarch who failed to govern according to the law. In contrast to a just and virtuous prince, the tyrannical monarch was cruel, bestial, hypocritical and wracked with passion – self-serving behaviour that warranted, even demanded, action against him. Mary's brand of tyranny as characterized by Buchanan grows out of her fickle affections and overpowering lust for Bothwell, which not only turn her into a murderer but also – and crucially – make her willing to sacrifice the public good for the sake of her private desires.[20]

As a humanist, Buchanan inherited his characterization of tyranny from classical sources and the tradition of *speculum principis*. But these ideas also travelled through classical and native theatre, where the hypocrisy and passion of tyrants were presented on stage. Tragedy showed the tyrant behaving badly like the tyrannical figures of history and legend; in turn, the qualities of the stage tyrant began to epitomize what one could expect from a real-world tyrant. As Rebecca Bushnell argues, this shared symbolic system fostered the characterization of the tyrant as hypocrite

---

[19]   Roger A. Mason, '*Rex Stoicus*: George Buchanan, James VI and the Scottish Polity', in John Dwyer, Mason and Alexander Murdoch (eds), *New Perspectives on the Politics and Culture of Early Modern Scotland* (Edinburgh, 1982), p. 9. On Buchanan's political theory, also see Quentin Skinner, *The Foundations of Modern Political Thought* (2 vols, Cambridge, 1978); and J.H. Burns, *The True Law of Kingship: Concepts of Monarchy in Early Modern Scotland* (Oxford, 1996).

[20]   For Mary's failure to fit Buchanan's model of civic values, see Roger A. Mason, 'George Buchanan and Mary Queen of Scots', *Records of the Scottish Church History Society*, 30 (2000): pp. 1–27; see also his introduction to Buchanan, *De Iure Regni*, esp. pp. lxvii–lxix.

and actor.[21] Buchanan's writings both recognize and take advantage of the link between politics and drama. In the *Detectioun*, he turns his austere political philosophy against Mary by using the theatrical trope and casting her in the role of tyrant. But he also wrote tragedy proper, and Buchanan's original Latin drama *Baptistes sive calumnia tragœdia* (1577), published during the same period as his political prose, explores his conception of tyranny and of politics in dramatic form.[22]

Buchanan composed *Baptistes* early in his career, probably during his teaching days at Bordeaux in the early 1540s. Like his other early plays – *Medea*, *Alcestis* and *Jephtha* – *Baptistes* was designed as a teaching tool. It demonstrates his (and his contemporaries') interests in rhetoric, Latin drama and the reworking of classical tragic models.[23] Here can be found humanism's deliberate turning away from the more popular medieval forms of morality plays and interludes, which are also filled with tyrants but marked by a taste for spectacle and violence. As David Norbrook reminds us, 'Many Renaissance humanists were somewhat suspicious of the popular theatre of their day, complaining that it appealed to the emotions rather than to the intellect'.[24] Emphasis, then, shifts from spectacle to language in neoclassical plays, putting the tyrant 'in debate with others and himself' and introducing 'the rhetoric of debate about tyranny'.[25] When he writes about *Baptistes* to his pupil James VI in 1576, Buchanan signals his approval of this cultural shift as well as the didactic benefits of this play for the young king:

> for, although abortive, it is none the less my first production and calls young persons away from the popular taste for theatrical allegories towards the imitation of antiquity as well as endeavouring vigorously to incite in them a zeal for true religion, which at that time was everywhere persecuted. But what can be seen to be of particular concern to you, is its clear portrayal of the sufferings of tyrants and of their miseries even when they seem to prosper most.[26]

---

[21]   Rebecca Bushnell, *Tragedies of Tyrants: Political Thought and Theater in the English Renaissance* (Ithaca, NY, 1990), p. xiv.

[22]   *Baptistes* was printed by Thomas Vautrollier at London in 1577. For its editions, see Durkan, *Buchanan Bibliography*. Citations from the play are from Buchanan, *Tragedies*.

[23]   Ibid., p. 9; Timothy J. Reiss, *Tragedy and Truth: Studies in the Development of a Renaissance and Neoclassical Discourse* (New Haven, CT, 1980), p. 49.

[24]   David Norbrook, '*Macbeth* and the Politics of Historiography', in Sharpe and Zwicker (eds), *Politics of Discourse*, p. 112.

[25]   Bushnell, *Tragedies of Tyrants*, p. 103.

[26]   Quoted in McFarlane, *Buchanan*, p. 386. See Plato's *Republic*, Book IX for the idea that tyrants are the unhappiest of men (especially 576a–579e).

As James's tutor, Buchanan stresses the pedagogical function of this play as moral exemplum; as political theorist, Buchanan explores in *Baptistes* the implications of theatricality in public life.[27] Although humanist drama commonly dealt with biblical matter, Buchanan takes the subject of *Baptistes* – the conflict between John the Baptist and Herod – 'in a rather different direction, in that he laicises and politicises it'.[28] The play is animated by Buchanan's argument about the distinction between kingship and tyranny; his loathing for hypocrisy and political actors; and his distrust of the feminine faculty in political life. Although we do not know whether Buchanan revised *Baptistes* for its first publication in 1577, the themes of the play are germane to his political thought at that time; indeed, it has been regarded as 'part of the pattern that leads to the appearance of the *De Jure Regni* and the *Historia*' just a few years later.[29] For that reason, *Baptistes* gives insight into Buchanan's political imagination and his conception of how literary and political elements, when combined, can have considerable argumentative force. It opens up surprising perspectives on the strategy of the *Detectioun*.

Baptistes begins with a debate about the religious and political threat posed by John the Baptist. The rabbis attack John for questioning their authority and argue that his 'appearance of stern sanctity' has duped the common people into taking him for a new prophet. The Chorus develops this theme of false appearances, lamenting how men, especially tyrants, conceal their monstrousness with feigned modesty and piety (p. 141). No one is who he seems, and the prevalence of calumny and gossip makes it impossible to distinguish between what seems to be true and what is true.[30] Enter Herod, the tyrant, publicly speaking the lines of a wise and prudent king. In soliloquy, however, he describes how kings merely 'don the mask of respectability' (p. 145), and he secretly resolves to kill John the Baptist. During their confrontation, Herod once again plays the consummate politician. And he offers John an escape: 'I pray that you may dissolve the … charges against you in such a way that your innocence leaves me no occasion to exercise harshness' (p. 144). John refuses to play Herod's game of prevarication by revising the representation of his character. He claims that he speaks the 'naked truth', that his words, even when abusive, are uttered in public, subject to the scrutiny of the people, and this grants them

---

[27]   McFarlane discusses the pedagogical role of *Baptistes* but also emphasizes its political uses for 'militant humanists' (*Buchanan*, p. 386).

[28]   Ibid., p. 385. Bushnell, *Tragedies of Tyrants*, p. 113, makes a similar point.

[29]   McFarlane, *Buchanan*, p. 387.

[30]   Ibid., p. 389. Despite our awareness that the Baptist will be martyred by Herod's tyranny, the play first raises the possibility that even John feigns holiness. Malchus defines him as an ambitious demagogue; the queen warns Herod that 'deceit is to be feared from stern-faced hypocrites' (Buchanan, *Tragedies*, p. 141).

authority: 'I am a voice crying on the distant ridges of the mountains', he exclaims (p. 151). Yet, John is no match for the hypocrisy and calumny practised by Herod's court; and Buchanan's drama highlights his inability (or unwillingness) to equivocate in the political realm, which will silence him by the play's end. This is a familiar story: John is certain to lose his head, and Herod's shrewdness does not exactly occasion surprise. But when political actors in the real world challenge the authenticity of one another's words, the play seems to ask, who will sort the hypocrites from the sincere?

On the truth about John's character, one rabbi resolves, 'each man can draw his conclusion as his mind dictates' (p. 140). His suggestion that the individual must bear the burden (or right) of determining the authenticity of language elevates the opinion of that individual as a member of the political community. Ian McFarlane has noted the play's theme that 'truth is more likely to be discovered in or through the people'.[31] While not wishing to dispute this entirely, the play's attitude towards the crowd is arguably more subtle than that. Nearly all of the characters in the play criticize the common people for their ignorance and fickleness. Even John refers to the 'fickle crowd', although he excuses them for the faults of 'the Levite shining afar with gleaming robe' (p. 150): the people seem foolish because they become the prey of hypocritical priests and kings. At the same time, political contenders – even John – recognize the power of the crowd and seek to absorb that power for themselves. Herod himself boasts to John that the people approve of and follow him. It matters little whether the people can actually discern truth from fiction; what counts is the claim that they recognize and applaud your truth as the authentic one. *Baptistes* thus connects political success with the ability to co-opt the common voice. Discovering truth 'in or through the people' is just a politic fiction.

Baptistes, as critics have noted, becomes a war of words in which both sides struggle to label the other as hypocritical.[32] As a political instrument, language can define and deceive, whether to shape public opinion about an opponent or to disguise one's own secret motivations. Political hypocrisy and prevarication come in for severe criticism, especially as the audience hears Herod speaking like the proper king and witnesses his actions to the contrary. Yet Buchanan's loathing for hypocrisy involves an acute perception of how to survive in the world of politics. The most powerful and destructive propaganda, according to the play, can be calumny, specifically as an act of defining and naming your opponent's character

---

[31]   McFarlane, *Buchanan*, p. 407. For a thorough assessment of the role Buchanan envisioned for the common people, see Roger A. Mason, 'People Power? George Buchanan on Resistance and the Common Man', in Robert von Friedeburg (ed.), *Widerstandsrecht in der frühen Neuzeit: Erträge und Perspektiven der Forschung im deutsch-britischen Vergleich* (Berlin, 2001), pp. 163–81.

[32]   Both Bushnell, *Tragedies of Tyrants*, and Reiss, *Tragedy and Truth*, explore this theme in their readings of the play.

according to your terms, of staking out your rhetorical territory.[33] The point is that in *Baptistes* Buchanan reveals his attentiveness to the tricks – calumny, rumour, propaganda – through which political figures may rise or fall. And his portrayal of how propaganda works threatens to undermine his brash criticism of political deceit in other contexts – in the *Detectioun*, that is. The play's observations about politics and propaganda, in other words, reveal more about Buchanan's rhetorical strategy for condemning Mary – and that of his supporters among the Scottish nobility – than about her actual political behaviour.

'Ane enterlude upon a stage': The Drama of the *Detectioun*

Buchanan may have found drama a fitting literary form in which to work out his ideas about kingship and tyranny, hypocrisy and theatricality, but in the *Detectioun* the presentation of those ideas has real political consequences. No longer aimed at theoretical or educational debate, the literary deployment of his political ideas now targets with deadly seriousness the specific goal of justifying the deposition of Mary Queen of Scots. While the material features of the printed *Detectioun* stage Mary's trial, Buchanan's narrative relies even more complexly on the collaboration of theatrical, moral and political discourses to condemn the Queen. Although biased and inaccurate, his indictment seizes for itself all claims to truth. Its assertion of openness becomes the basis for its argument, particularly as contrasted with the secrecy of Mary's court. Ironically, the *Detectioun* sheds its 'light of treuth' through shrewd fictions (sig. Ki^v). Embellished with colourful detail, Buchanan's narrative banks on the convincing qualities of a good story. The reader is meant to be gripped by the spectacle and intrigue of Mary's tragic descent into immorality.

The *Detectioun*'s basic agenda is to label her as a tyrant, and it explains her brand of political deceit largely through theatrical metaphor. The preparation for and execution of Darnley's murder, for example, occasions the more theatrical moments of the story. Once Darnley arrives in Edinburgh, Mary 'finely … play[s] hir part' with him (sig. Diii^v): she visits him daily, torturing him with fair promises and fostering quarrels between him and other nobles. Bothwell, meanwhile, prepares 'the tragical stage for the murder' (sig. Lii^r). Mary enjoys her starring role in this murderous drama. Rather than allow Darnley's enemies to participate, she allows them to be 'but lukers on, and nat pairtplayers in this tragedie: but the glorie of the fact sche reservit to hyr self and Bothwell' (Liii^r). Mary reacts calmly to the

---

[33]   For more on the significance of this as a political act, see Bushnell, *Tragedies of Tyrants*, pp. 42–7.

news of Darnley's death – in fact, she lies in until noon the following day – but quickly realizes that she must 'counterfeit[eth] a mourning' in order 'to appease the hartes of the grudgying pepill' and, thereby, avoid 'marring the play' (sigs Miii^r, Eii^v). All is nearly lost when Sir Henry Killigrew visits the Queen to offer official condolences on behalf of Elizabeth. He arrives suddenly and unmasks Mary's disguised mourning: 'yet he came in sa unseasonably ere the stage wer prepared and furnished, that he found the windowes open, the candeles nat yet lighted, and all the provision for the play out of order' (sig. Eiii^r). The trial of Bothwell is a travesty of legal procedure, compared to 'ane enterlude upon a stage'; similarly, his divorce from Lady Jean Gordon fails 'to observe the ceremonies of lawful order, but (as thay use to do in enterludes) thay providit a certain shew or disguisit counterfayting of commoun usage' (sig. Ni^v). In the end, Mary becomes the *deus ex machina* of her own play. When Bothwell quails at the prospect of combat at Carberry Hill, she rescues his valour by giving an 'honest colour' to his refusal to fight: 'the Quene, as it weir some God out of a ginne in a tragedie, had by hir auchoritie taken up the mattir, and forbidden hir prety venereous pigioun to do battaile' (sig. Iii^r). These examples should leave no doubt that the theatrical idiom (expressed in references to stage, actor, tragedy, play, interlude, disguise, even props) provides a metaphorical framework for the *Detectioun*. Presenting this story through the language and conventions of drama makes it more intelligible. Whether through classical or native tradition, this language was familiar: the reader would know what to expect from tragedy and what was expected of him as a spectator. Moreover, by creating the sense of a performance, the *Detectioun* cleverly adopts the perspective of theatre: all viewpoints may be presented. The reader not only observes activity behind the scenes but is meant to feel a more impartial judge for doing so.

The entertainment of the *Detectioun* can be described as of the lower sort, bawdy and raucous. Sexual escapades and adventure abound: Mary seeks another lover for her husband; sails with pirates; summons half-naked men to her room; sneaks through gardens at night; carouses at Seton; and is abducted by Bothwell. Her brief sojourn at the Exchequer house provides the most colourful action of the narrative. Here, she has convenient access to Bothwell, for he temporarily resides at David Chalmers's house, whose back door abuts the garden of the Exchequer. The encounter between Mary and Bothwell is engineered by Lady Reres, described by Buchanan as 'a woman of maist vile unchastitie wha had sometime been one of Bothwels harlots', and who has now changed careers, from 'horedome' to 'bawderie'. First, Lady Reres brings Bothwell through the garden to Mary's chamber, where the Queen is 'forced agaynst hir will' (sig. Bii^r). An enthusiastic convert to adulterous pleasure, Mary seeks out Bothwell's company a few days later. The ensuing comedy is worth quoting at length:

> The Quene with Margaret Carwod, a woman privie of all her secretes, dyd let her [Lady Reres] downe by a stryng over an auld wall into the next garden. But in sic weirlike affaires, all thynges can not ever be so well foreseen, but that some incommodious chaunce may overthwartly happen. Behald, the stryng sodenly brake, and downe with a great noyse fell Dame Rerese, a woman very heavy baith by unweldy age and massy substance. But sche an auld beaten soldiar, nothyng dismayed with the darkenes of the night, the heighth of the wall nor with the sodennesse of the fall, up sche getteth, & winneth into Bothwels chamber, sche gyt the dore open, and out of his bed, even out of his wives armes, halfe a slepe, halfe naked, sche forceably brings the man to the Queen. (sig. Bii^v)

As rhetorical strategy, the moment in which the rope breaks and the hefty Lady Reres falls to the ground, regaining her senses quickly enough to yank Bothwell out of his bed, is far more sophisticated than its slapstick comedy might suggest. Its garden wall, successfully penetrated to reach the desired and unattainable woman within, recalls a literary motif common to medieval and Renaissance romance. The motif is then comically – and threateningly – inverted, with the women tumbling over the wall to retrieve the man. The description of the women's 'weirlike affaires', with the Lady Reres an 'auld beaten soldiar', satirizes their tactics of scaling a wall for an illicit sexual encounter. The garden chaos draws attention not only to the frivolous and immoral matters with which women concern themselves, but also to their transgressive behaviour.

The women's nocturnal adventure conjures the *fabliau* comedy of stories like Chaucer's 'Miller's Tale'. In terms of a theatrical trope, it might also recall the unruly forces of 'lively and realistic farces'.[34] Whether an allusion to the popular stage or literary farce, the moment's melodrama will surely rouse the reader's imagination. Because Buchanan privileged humanist drama over the 'popular taste for theatrical allegories', he likely invents this, like other raucous moments in the *Detectioun*, to underscore Mary's common indecency. 'Language over enactment' in drama suits the grave and learned Buchanan. Yet in a text imbued with theatrical metaphor, he explains Mary's immorality and duplicity by casting her in scenes of coarse comedy.[35] Both form and content contribute to the insulting implication: her tyranny does not even merit the linguistic restraint of neo-classical

---

[34]   David Bevington, *From Mankind to Marlowe* (Cambridge, MA, 1962), p. 9.

[35]   See Bushnell, *Tragedies of Tyrants*, pp. 82–3; and Norbrook, '*Macbeth* and the Politics of Historiography', p. 112.

tyrant tragedy. She is too common for that genre, too common to be that kind of tragic figure.

Mary is also an actor, the embodiment of deceit, the instigator of conspiracy. Rather than govern her country, she devises illicit sexual encounters; worries with her lover's wardrobe; plots her husband's death; and still manages to attend a 'masking daunce' on the night of the murder (sig. Mii^r). Such intrigue and licentiousness must keep a monarch busy! The *Detectioun* shares with *Baptistes* a concern with deceptive appearances. Entirely preoccupied with feigned behaviour, the *Detectioun* asserts that nothing about Mary is authentic – hence, its goal of uncloaking her treachery. Specific instances of intrigue form the backbone of Buchanan's narrative: adultery, secret plans, murder plots, fake mourning, phoney trials, sham rapes. And language reinforces Mary's deceptiveness, returning obsessively to the discrepancy between what is seen and unseen: as Buchanan variously describes it, she feigns, devises, pretends, dissembles, invents and 'shifts'. Behind her title and appearance of nobility lurks a woman willing to sacrifice the weal of her country to the success of her private desires.

Mary's role as a 'trope of duplicity'[36] not only gives thematic unity to the narrative but also serves as political strategy: her hypocrisy – like her female passion – specifically recalls the definition of a bad ruler. As a woman, she is the feminized tyrant, rash and histrionic. As a queen, she is an actor, manipulating her nobles, delivering the lines of the good wife, engineering schemes to promote her interests. Her tyranny also receives more open declaration. Buchanan accuses her of intending 'to set up a tyrannicall regiment' (sig. Di^v), though her desire for 'untemperit authoritie' will be withstood, of course, by the political safeguards he cherishes: 'the custome of the contrey, the lawes and statutes, and principally the consent of the nobilitie' (sigs Iiii^{r-v}). If the purpose of the *Detectioun* is to justify the rebellion against Mary, its strategy is to expose and describe her tyranny, to let her strut and fret her way across its pages. As Bushnell notes, the naming of a tyrant is itself a 'political act': 'the point [is] to be able to call your enemy a tyrant and on that ground to claim that he or she [has] forfeited a subject's respect due to a monarch in the natural order'.[37] Quite simply, to make Mary into a tyrant justifies her overthrow. Just as *Baptistes* dramatizes how calumny can be used against political rivals,[38] the *Detectioun* uses propaganda to define and demonize an opponent in very specific terms. In both works, the victors are those who can manipulate language.

---

[36] Sarah Dunnigan's phrase, surprisingly apt in this context: *Eros and Poetry at the Courts of Mary Queen of Scots and James VI* (London, 2002), p. 21.
[37] Bushnell, *Tragedies of Tyrants*, p. 46.
[38] Ibid., p. 113.

All parties responsible for the *Detectioun* – the Scottish nobles, Buchanan, the English government – recognized the importance of controlling the terms of the debate. Like John in *Baptistes*, they proclaim the 'naked truth' of their words in contrast to Mary's hypocrisy. Yet the success of her hypocrisy – whence the need for their words – is arguable. The narrator frequently admits that describing her misbehaviour in print is unnecessary, as she was flagrantly licentious: why reiterate her wickedness when it 'was openly done in all mens sight, & continueth emprint in all mens memorie' (sig. Bi^v). With its firm insistence on Mary's duplicity, the *Detectioun* gets caught between rival claims: was she a master of deception, or can 'all men' easily recognize and recall her malice? In this narrative, even Mary often seems unsure about just how secretive she wants to be. Buchanan characterizes her adultery with Bothwell as so blatant that 'thay semed to feare nathing mair than least thair wickednes should be unknawen' (sig. Biiii^v). As if to underscore this dilemma, in several copies of the *Detectioun* a sixteenth-century hand has emended a similar statement by the insertion of 'not': 'baith she and her company so framed thair speche & countenance, as if thay semed to feare nothing mair than that the king should ^not^ perceaue that thay lothed him' (sig. Aiiii^v).[39] These contradictions do not suggest a very accomplished hypocrite – she is either stupid or arrogant – and the narrative seems unable to decide between Mary's duplicity and her laughably obvious schemes. The *Detectioun* gets caught in this bind because it needs Mary to be both an expert and a failed dissembler: the expert unquestionably tyrannous, the failure exposed and shamed. This distinction – one of the more important aspects of the *Detectioun* – is largely gendered. Herod's queen in *Baptistes* displays the tyrannical qualities of rage and passion, but she is not quite up to the political acting of Herod. In fact, in *Baptistes* Buchanan does not really ask the audience to consider Herod's queen: she is simply female, and politically less interesting and less instructive. The real tyrant in the play is Herod, more calculating, the one who can manipulate language. Women, in other words, simply cannot be politicians because they are weak and incompetent. For his political argument in the *Detectioun*, however, Buchanan needs a cruel tyrant, worthy of deposition. He works through this dilemma by presenting a conniving queen, who stupidly flaunts her deceit. Not only is Mary a dissembling tyrant, but her female nature also makes her an inept one.

Should any doubt remain about Mary's tyrannical behaviour, one need only consult the 'commoun pepill', for in the *Detectioun* they discover her

---

[39]   Of the ten copies I have consulted, seven have this emendation: Bodleian Library, Buchanan f.128 and Wood 255(1); University of Michigan, DA787.A1 B93; and all four copies held by the Folger Shakespeare Library (HH37/22; ac5286; HH37/22a; HH37/23.2). This consistency suggests a workshop change.

tyranny and become the benchmark for her condemnation. At first, Mary's secrecy ensures that neither her subjects nor those 'right familiar and present' can be sure of her intentions. Soon, however, she and Bothwell become 'infamous amang the pepill' (sig. Biiii^r). Her cruelty to Darnley raises 'the pepils suspicioun, utherwise of it selfe alredy enough inclined to that judgement, of the unchast companiyng of the Quene with Bothwell' (sig. Cii^{r–v}). The common people recognize the 'disguising of the court' after Darnley's murder, and finally the 'indignatioun of the pepill' prevails: by rumours, 'by bukes ... & by pictures', the 'hale multitude in generall' can no longer be restrained (sigs Ei^r, Eii^v). With regard to *Baptistes*, it has been argued here that, while the play suggests that truth will be discovered 'in and through the people', it more readily appreciates that assuming the common voice as your own, having the people claim your 'truth', can be a political argument of great force. It hardly matters whether you put stock in their opinion or not; it is the illusion of their support that counts. In the *Detectioun*, this tactic, embraced by Buchanan, confirms the authenticity of the narrative, for the common people do not just applaud its truth – they are the first to perceive it.

After 1568, Buchanan probably had no more involvement with the *Detectioun*, but his theatrical tastes and radical political ideas continue to influence its design and effect. While congenial to Buchanan, the political argument of the *Detectioun* – that 'eche man' can and should judge a queen – seems surprising, both risky and threatening to Elizabeth's own authority. Desperate measures must have been in order: worried about Mary's persistent ability to stir up plots against Elizabeth, the English government orchestrated this covert publication. Yet we should be wary of too quickly reading the *Detectioun* as evidence of a demonstrably new faith in the opinion of the ordinary reader. Like the common people who supposedly recognize Mary's criminality, and whose force and consequence at this historical moment we should rightly question, the informed and judicious audience of the *Detectioun* is itself a rhetorical construction, another politic fiction meant to convince us of the public consensus about Mary's duplicity and immorality.[40] Despite the shrewd manipulation of content and form, the trial of the *Detectioun* is imaginary, its outcome a foregone conclusion, its adjudicator not really necessary. Indeed, as 'participants' in this textual space, the reader and the 'commoun pepill' serve less as sources of reliable political truth than as the versatile instruments of political persuasion. Even if Buchanan's theories about limited monarchy and popular sovereignty presage

---

[40]   This is not to suggest that the politically aware and influential did not read the *Detectioun*. We know that Gabriel Harvey owned both the Latin and English editions, for example (see McFarlane, *Buchanan*, p. 348).

later democratic thought, the *Detectioun* should temper an impulse to romanticize, demonstrating, as it does, the deeply ideological ends that could be served by his humanist and political ideals.

CHAPTER 3

Spenser and Buchanan

Andrew Hadfield

Buchanan's work was well known to a literate English audience and it is clear that he exercised a significant influence on the development of English politics, religion and literature. Buchanan's hostile attack on Mary Stuart may even have been sponsored by the English authorities as a means of discrediting her and marginalizing support for her as a deposed queen soon after she fled south of the border in 1568.[1] Buchanan's representation of Mary as the faithless, murdering Queen, who betrayed both husband and country to satisfy her selfish whims, determined how Mary was seen by an English audience.[2] Given that Buchanan was also known in Elizabethan England as the main advocate of monarchomach resistance theory in the British Isles, and that he advocated the moral need for godly subjects to assassinate ungodly monarchs, there was something of an irony in such official English sponsorship.[3] And, of course, Buchanan was also known as the most significant humanist theorist of poetics in the British Isles.[4]

Nevertheless, the extent of Buchanan's influence has been under-estimated by scholars, principally because his works were not translated

---

[1]   See Tricia A. McElroy's chapter above, and her 'Executing Mary Queen of Scots: Strategies of Representation in Early Modern Scotland' (unpublished DPhil thesis, University of Oxford, 2005), ch. 2.

[2]   Kristen Post Walton, *Catholic Queen, Protestant Patriarchy: Mary, Queen of Scots, and the Politics of Gender and Religion* (Basingstoke, 2007), pp. 159–64; Rosalind Smith, *Sonnets and the English Woman Writer, 1560–1621: The Politics of Absence* (Basingstoke, 2005), pp. 2, 9; Sarah Dunnigan, *Eros and Poetry at the Courts of Mary Queen of Scots and James VI* (Basingstoke, 2002), pp. 16–17, *passim*; Howard Erskine-Hill, *Poetry and the Realm of Politics: Shakespeare to Dryden* (Oxford, 1996), pp. 29–30.

[3]   Buchanan's political theories are extensively analysed in many works: see, for example, Robert M. Kingdon, 'Calvinism and Resistance Theory, 1550–1580', in J.H. Burns and Mark Goldie (eds), *The Cambridge History of Political Thought, 1450–1700* (Cambridge, 1991), pp. 193–218, at pp. 215–18; J.H. Burns, 'George Buchanan and the Anti-monarchomachs', in Roger A. Mason (ed.), *Scots and Britons: Scottish Political Thought and the Union of 1603* (Cambridge, 1994), pp. 138–58; J.H. Burns, *The True Law of Kingship: Concepts of Monarchy in Early-modern Scotland* (Oxford, 1996), ch. 6; Buchanan, *De Iure Regni*, introduction, pp. xlv–lxxi (subsequent references to this edition in parentheses in the text).

[4]   David Norbrook, *Poetry and Politics in the English Renaissance* (rev. edn, Oxford, 2002), p. 84, *passim*; Buchanan, *Political Poetry*, p. 1; James E. Phillips, *Images of a Queen: Mary Stuart in Sixteenth-century Literature* (Berkeley, CA, 1964).

and produced in editions in England. Given his support for radical Calvinist political theory, and the understandable hostility of his former pupil, James VI of Scotland, whose own theories of kingship were undoubtedly formulated in opposition to those of his stern and violent tutor, a folio set of Buchanan's collected works was never really likely to appear in the decades after his death.[5] In *Basilikon Doron* (1598), James publicly advised his son, Prince Henry, to suppress the works of John Knox and Buchanan.[6] We know that Buchanan's works were avidly read by the Sidney circle, who were especially fascinated by monarchomach theories of government, as Blair Worden has demonstrated in his extensive study of the *Arcadia*. Not only did Sir Philip Sidney and his familiars read Buchanan, but they were also influenced by the most important work of Huguenot resistance theory, *Vindiciae, Contra Tyrannos* (1579), a work that openly acknowledged its debt to Scottish political theory, principally the work of Buchanan (both the *Vindiciae* and Buchanan's works were attacked as identical delusions in William Barclay's *De Regno et Regali Potestate* (1600)).[7] It is also evident that large numbers of English readers had access to sections of Buchanan's *Rerum Scoticarum Historia*, even if they could not read the Latin edition of 1582, through the – admittedly hostile – translation/adaptation of Francis Thynne published in Holinshed's *Chronicles* when it was revised in 1587, one of whom was William Shakespeare.[8] As it was likely – but hardly inevitable – that James VI of Scotland would succeed Elizabeth, there was an understandably widespread interest in the violent and rocky course of Scottish history in England in the late 1580s and early 1590s.[9]

Buchanan, through his access to radical French and Scottish political thought, developed what many would isolate as a strain of English

---

[5]   On Buchanan's relationship to James, see Roger A. Mason, 'James I, George Buchanan and the *Trew Lawe of Free Monarchies*', in *Kingship and the Commonweal: Political Thought in Renaissance and Reformation Scotland* (East Linton, 1998), pp. 215–41; Roger A. Mason, '*Rex Stoicus*: George Buchanan, James VI and the Scottish Polity', in John Dwyer, Mason and Alexander Murdoch (eds), *New Perspectives on the Politics and Culture of Early Modern Scotland* (Edinburgh, 1982), pp. 9–33.

[6]   James VI & I, *Basilikon Doron*, in *Selected Writings*, ed. Neil Rhodes, Jennifer Richards and Joseph Marshall (Aldershot, 2003), pp. 199–258, at p. 243.

[7]   James E. Phillips, 'George Buchanan and the Sidney Circle', *Huntington Library Quarterly*, 12 (1948–49): pp. 23–55; Blair Worden, *The Sound of Virtue: Philip Sidney's Arcadia and Elizabethan Politics* (New Haven, CT, 1996), *passim*; Brutus, Stephanus Junius, the Celt, *Vindiciae, Contra Tyrannos, or, concerning the legitimate power of a prince over the people, and of the people over a prince* (1579), ed. George Garnett (Cambridge, 1994), introduction, pp. xx, liii; Burns, *True Law of Kingship*, p. 228.

[8]   See Annabel Patterson, *Reading Holinshed's Chronicles* (New Haven, CT, 1994), p. 57, *passim*.

[9]   Susan Doran, 'Revenge Her Foul and Most Unnatural Murder? The Impact of Mary Stewart's Execution on Anglo-Scottish Relations', *History* 85 (2000): pp. 589–612; Andrew Hadfield, *Shakespeare and Republicanism* (Cambridge, 2005), pp. 35–40.

republicanism before the 1640s. He emphasized the responsibility and duty of the monarch towards the people, the need for the people to control and limit the power of the monarch, as well as the right of the people to overthrow the monarch if he or she violated their wishes, provided these were in line with the will of God. For many commentators Buchanan developed the most extreme case of resistance theory available in Europe at the time.[10] Buchanan also played the key role in the British Isles in disseminating a hostile portrait of Mary Stuart, one that was either imitated or, in the case of John Leslie, Bishop of Ross, Mary's most important champion, vigorously opposed.[11] Buchanan represented Mary as an English nightmare: a wanton Franco-Scottish Catholic who was a slave to her passions, and so lacked the ability to govern like a rational man, unlike her sister Queen Elizabeth, who had gone out of her way to stress her male qualities, making her an exception to the general rule of her sex.[12] If Elizabeth was an honorary man, Mary was represented as just a woman, weak and foolish, her life dominated by amorous intrigue.[13] And, if the vices of the vain and silly French and Scottish courts did not provide enough damning evidence of her inabilities, she had allowed herself to be drawn into the plot to murder her second husband, Henry, Lord Darnley, and had foolish, tyrannical ambitions. As James Phillips points out, no other historian had anything positive to say about Darnley, but Buchanan, as a means of damning Mary still further, transforms him into 'the noble and innocent victim of a designing woman, the Sampson of Mary's Delilah and the Agamemnon of her Clytemnestra'.[14] Buchanan's representation of Mary's character is worth quoting at some length, as it emphasizes how a weak nature degenerates and hardens into perversity and evil without proper education and guidance:

---

[10]   David Norbrook, 'Macbeth and the Politics of Historiography', in Kevin Sharpe and Steven N. Zwicker (eds), Politics of Discourse: The Literature and History of Seventeenth-century England (Berkeley, CA, 1987), pp. 78–116; David Norbrook, Writing the English Republic: Poetry, Rhetoric and Politics, 1627–1660 (Cambridge, 1999), pp. 21, 150, 172, passim; Buchanan, De Iure Regni, introduction, pp. li, lxiv.

[11]   McElroy, 'Executing Mary Queen of Scots', ch. 3; Walton, Catholic Queen, Protestant Patriarchy, pp. 9–81, passim.

[12]   Carole Levin, The Heart and Stomach of a King: Elizabeth I and the Politics of Sex and Power (Philadelphia, PA, 1994).

[13]   A trenchant case against her is made in Jenny Wormald, Mary Queen of Scots: A Study in Failure (London, 1991). More sympathetic is John Guy, 'My Heart is My Own': The Life of Mary Queen of Scots (London, 2004).

[14]   Phillips, Images of a Queen, p. 66. Buchanan's praise of Darnley was probably also motivated by his connections to the Lennox-Stewart family; see Buchanan, De Iure Regni, pp. lxviii–lxix.

Born amid the bitter storms of war, she lost her father within six days. She was taught diligently, indeed, by her mother, an accomplished lady, but she was abandoned amid domestic rebellions and foreign wars, a prey to the strongest, and exposed to all the dangers of outrageous fortune, before she was of age to understand her evil case ... apart from the fascination of her varied and perilous history, she was graced with surpassing loveliness of form, the vigour of maturing youth, and fine qualities of mind, which a court education had increased, or at least made more attractive by a surface gloss of virtue. This, far from being genuine, was a mere shadowy representation of virtue; so that her natural goodness would be weakened by an earnest desire to please; and the seeds of virtue, wizened by the allurements of luxury, would be prevented from reaching ripeness and fruition.[15]

From such roots developed the tyrannical murderess of low cunning. In his most influential representation of Mary, the popular and polemical, *Ane Detectioun of the duinges of Marie Quene of Scottes* (1571), Buchanan portrays Mary as scheming and devious. Immediately after she has given birth to James she plans 'to dispacche away the King be ane way or other howesauever, and to Mary with Bothwell.'[16] So 'that hir self suld not be tuchit with suspicioun of the Murther', Mary deliberately begins to 'saw seedis of dissentioun between the King and the Lordis that wer than in Court' (sig. A2v). Only God's will saves the innocent from her treacherous plans (sig. A3r). When not plotting Darnley's murder by means of subtle statecraft, Mary tries more feminine wiles, urging her husband while she is pregnant to consort with the Earl of Moray's wife, and so be revenged on all three and 'thair with all to win a collour & thus of divorce to mak emptie bedrowme for Bothwell' (sig. A2v).

Buchanan's political thought is consistent and lucid, though hardly subtle, as he makes the case time and again that monarchs are responsible for the welfare of the subjects they represent, and that evil monarchs who fail in their duties can be overthrown by the loyal and dutiful subject. Buchanan does not spend a great deal of time defining how we might be able to know when a monarch can be deposed, or in telling readers how to sort the loyal crusader for freedom from the deranged assassin, a task carried out by later writers.[17] Given the use he made of his political plays and poetry to propagate his ideas, and his reputation as a major humanist scholar and literary theorist, it is not surprising that Buchanan appealed to Protestant English writers impressed by his learning, receptive to his

---

[15]   Buchanan, *Tyrannous Reign*, pp. 53–4. All subsequent references to this edition in parentheses in the text.

[16]   George Buchanan, *Ane Detectioun of the duinges of Marie Quene of Scottes* (1571), sig. A2v. All subsequent references to this edition in parentheses in the text.

[17]   Hadfield, *Shakespeare and Republicanism*, p. 34.

Protestant ideas, and hopeful that they might eventually enjoy a similar European profile.

Perhaps the writer most obviously influenced by Buchanan was Edmund Spenser (1553?–1599), an avid reader of Buchanan's works – as he acknowledges in his own writings. Even if we take what Spenser himself tells us, Buchanan clearly played an important role in Spenser's reading matter and helped him to formulate ideas and substantiate key points in his arguments. However, even though the notes to the Variorum Edition of Spenser's works make numerous acknowledgements of passages that owe a debt to the Scottish writer, there has been little serious thought about how and why Spenser might have used Buchanan.[18] The edition acknowledges the debt of *A View of the Present State of Ireland* to Buchanan's *Rerum Scoticarum Historia*, and the index to the poetry points out that historically informed passages in *The Faerie Queene*, such as the chronicle of the British kings in Book 2, canto 10, probably make use of the same work. A long passage from H.S.V. Jones's pioneering work further acknowledges that Spenser was interested in the story of Mary's life and execution and that he would undoubtedly have consulted Buchanan's writings when writing Book 5 of *The Faerie Queene*.[19] Neither A.C. Hamilton's extensively annotated edition of *The Faerie Queene*, nor Bart Van Es's excellent monograph, *Spenser's Forms of History*, makes any reference to Buchanan.[20] With the honourable exception of Willy Maley and Richard McCabe, Spenser scholars and commentators on English Renaissance verse in general, have been remarkably silent about the influence of one of the major European figures well known to English writers.[21] My own sense is that not only was Buchanan a major source who helped Spenser substantiate his ideas, but he was also a crucial influence on Spenser's thinking. It might even be argued that reading Buchanan helped to shape the political form and substance of *The Faerie Queene*.

Spenser made extensive use of Buchanan's *Rerum Scoticarum Historia* when he was composing *A View of the Present State of Ireland* in c.1596, suggesting that he probably had a copy of the work in his library in Ireland.

---

[18]   See *The Works of Edmund Spenser: A Variorum Edition*, ed. Edwin Greenlaw *et al.* (Baltimore, MD, 1932–49).

[19]   H.S.V. Jones, *A Spenser Handbook* (New York, 1947), p. 377.

[20]   Edmund Spenser, *The Faerie Queene*, ed. A.C. Hamilton (London, rev. edn, 2001); Bart Van Es, *Spenser's Forms of History* (Oxford, 2002).

[21]   Willy Maley, *Salvaging Spenser: Colonialism, Culture and Identity* (Basingstoke, 1997), *passim*; Richard A. McCabe, *Spenser's Monstrous Regiment: Elizabethan Ireland and the Poetics of Difference* (Oxford, 2002). Maley does not develop an argument about Spenser's use of Buchanan, but does provide a series of scattered and insightful comments, e.g., 'My own feeling is that Spenser is something of an incipient republican. Influenced by Bodin, Buchanan and Machiavelli' (p. 115), *passim*. Richard McCabe's references to Buchanan are confined to his influence on the Irish material.

Spenser follows the early sections of Buchanan's *Historia* in a number of key passages, notably when he establishes a link between the Scots and the Irish, establishing the Irish as the original Scots, and their island as 'Scotia Major', Scotland itself being 'Scotia Minor': 'Neverthemore are theare two Scottlandes, but twoe kinde of Scotts theare weare indeede as ye maye gather out of *Buckhanan* the one Irin or Irishe Scottes the other Albin Scottes.'[22] The effect is to demonstrate the mutually dependent and interlinked character of the British Isles, a major theme in Spenser's poetry and prose, in which he frequently argues that the fates of England, Ireland and Scotland cannot be prised apart.[23] A few lines later, when attacking the authenticity of Irish historians, Spenser cites a long list of scholars who have accurately represented Ireland, giving pride of place to Buchanan:

> of all of which I give most Credite unto *Buckhanan*, for that he himselfe being an Irishe Scott or Pict by nacion and beinge verye excelentlye learned and Industrious to seke out the truethe of these thinges Concernynge the Originall of his owne people hath bothe set downe the Testimonies of the Ancientes trulye, and his owne opinion withall verye reasonablye, thoughe in some things he doe somewhat folter (p. 86).

This is a fulsome, but nevertheless intriguing reference. What are the faults of Buchanan? They might be his attacks on Humphrey Lhuyd (or Llwyd), who Spenser has just cited and whose *Breviary of Britain* (1573) is used elsewhere in a *View*, and who was taken seriously by Spenser's friend and ally, Gabriel Harvey, as well as Sir Philip Sidney.[24] Such comments indicate that Spenser was a careful reader of Buchanan, as well as a critical one. The reference to Buchanan as a Pict, or Irish Scot, would appear to be designed to confer on him an extra layer of authenticity, separating him out from a Scottish hierarchy or Catholic nobility, and so establishing him as truly knowledgeable about Scottish traditions and histories. Immediately afterwards, Spenser performs the same intellectual manoeuvre when making use of the Irish chronicles as a means of establishing their credentials to support his arguments about Irish history (p. 87).

---

[22] Spenser, *Prose Works*, ed. Edwin Greenlaw *et al.* (Baltimore, MD, 1949), p. 83. All subsequent references to this edition in parentheses in the text. I have silently modernized u/v and i/j.

[23] Maley, *Salvaging Spenser*; Andrew Hadfield, *Shakespeare, Spenser and the Matter of Britain* (Basingstoke, 2003).

[24] On Buchanan's attacks on Lhuyd, see McFarlane, *Buchanan*, pp. 419–27; on Harvey and Lhuyd, see Virginia F. Stern, *Gabriel Harvey: His Life, Marginalia and Library* (Oxford, 1979), pp. 224–5; on Sidney and Lhuyd, see Philip Schwyzer, *Literature, Nationalism and Memory in Early Modern England and Wales* (Cambridge, 2004), pp. 76–9.

Buchanan is later cited as an authority on the use of names derived from the Gauls in Scotland, and so increasing the plausibility of a Gaulish presence in Ireland. In establishing that the battle cry of the Irish, 'Faragh Farragh', was really Scottish, Spenser refers to Buchanan as the authority who noted that Fergus was one of the first Scottish kings who fought against the Picts (pp. 103–4). Buchanan is then cited alongside Hector Boethius (Boece) as testifying to the fact that the Scots (i.e., the Irish) used broad swords that were of distinctly Scythian style, further illustrating the barbarian Scythian culture of Ireland, a case Irenius is determined to make (p. 106).[25] And finally Buchanan is cited to make the same case of genealogical origin, showing that the ancient Scots/Irish drank blood from bowls together, 'vowinge thearby to spende theire laste blodd in that quarrell' (p. 108), exactly as the barbarous Scythians did.

Such parallels have been noted and have often received excellent commentary in Spenser criticism, notably in Richard McCabe's *Spenser's Monstrous Regiment*, which has a splendid analysis of Spenser's representation of racial categories and distinctions. But the possibility that Buchanan had a more central and pervasive influence on Spenser has not been considered, principally because Spenser is still generally regarded as an apologist for the status quo of Elizabethan England, holding the monarchy up to a searching critique but never going beyond accepted paradigms.[26] McCabe suggests that Spenser may well have used Buchanan and John Knox's arguments about the unsuitability of female rule, but concludes, 'Dissatisfaction with the policies of an individual monarch does not constitute a rejection of monarchy, and disillusionment with female regiment may even serve to strengthen the desire for a stronger male succession.'[27] This is true and is a sensible warning against those who see oppositional sentiment every time the monarchy is criticized in early modern Britain.[28] However, what we have to believe is that a writer who extensively cites and acknowledges the importance of Buchanan, more so than any other English writer at this time, remained unaffected by Buchanan's political vision, taking the opposite political position, yet never actually argued with him.

---

[25] Andrew Hadfield, 'Briton and Scythian: Tudor Representations of Irish Origins', *Irish Historical Studies*, 112 (1993): pp. 390–408.

[26] For recent versions of this familiar argument, see Paul Suttie, 'Edmund Spenser's Political Pragmatism', *Studies in Philology*, 95 (1998): pp. 56–76; J.B. Lethbridge, 'Introduction: Recuperating the Return to History', in Lethbridge (ed.), *Edmund Spenser: New and Renewed Directions* (Madison, 2006), pp. 15–57.

[27] McCabe, *Spenser's Monstrous Regiment*, p. 5.

[28] For a similar warning, see Blair Worden, 'English Republicanism', in Burns and Goldie (eds), *Cambridge History of Political Thought*, pp. 443–75.

It is perhaps also worth noting that there are many fine studies of the relationship between a *View* and the tradition of dialogue in Europe, yet none mentions, even in passing, Buchanan's dialogue on kingship, *De Iure Regni apud Scotos*.[29] There may indeed be some parallels between the style and structure of this dialogue and a *View*. A *View* is a dialogue between the rational but ignorant Eudoxus, a reasonable humanist, and Irenius, an Englishman who has just returned from Ireland. Irenius wants to persuade Eudoxus that the pacification of Ireland can only occur if drastic action is taken and a huge army sent over to extirpate rebellion, a solution that horrifies Eudoxus, who wants to believe that Ireland can be transformed through the spread of law and order.[30] Irenius is, of course, right, and Eudoxus has to admit time and again that his faith in the due process of law simply will not work in Ireland. Irenius's solution to the Irish question suggests that a reform tradition is at an end and that the only way of making Ireland loyal to the English crown is to abandon the long-held hope that Irish lord deputies can be used to control and reform Ireland.[31] The resemblance to the progress of the debate between Thomas Maitland and George Buchanan in *De Iure Regni* is striking. In Buchanan's dialogue, Maitland continually has to admit that his faith in the good will of kings to treat their subjects properly is misplaced and that Buchanan's more radical solution that sovereignty is located in the people is, in fact, correct, as Maitland confirms at the end of the dialogue. Maitland concludes Buchanan's text with the words 'As far as I am concerned you have fully satisfied me, and if I can likewise satisfy others I shall feel that I have profited greatly from this discussion and gained relief from an extreme irritation' (p. 163), indicating that the reader should also be persuaded and follow his lead in converting others to the political doctrine of limited sovereignty that Buchanan expounds. Spenser's *View* contains a similar balance between the roles of the two interlocutors, Irenius speaking for most of the text, challenged and asked to explain his meaning at greater length by Eudoxus, placing the reader in a similar position. The dialogue concludes with the two speakers agreeing that an army needs to be sent over to crush rebellion in Ireland, as Irenius had proposed, and Irenius outlining exactly how this should be done. Maitland starts Buchanan's dialogue sceptical that evil monarchs should be deposed, even killed, but

---

[29]   See, for example, Patricia Coughlan, '"Some Scourge which shall by her come unto England": Ireland and Incivility in Spenser', in Coughlan (ed.), *Spenser and Ireland: An Interdisciplinary Perspective* (Cork, 1989), pp. 46–74.

[30]   Andrew Hadfield, *Spenser's Irish Experience: Wilde Fruyt and Salvage Soyl* (Oxford, 1997), ch. 2.

[31]   See Ciaran Brady, *The Chief Governors: The Rise and Fall of Reform Government in Tudor Ireland, 1536–1588* (Cambridge, 1994), p. 300; Ciaran Brady, 'Spenser's Irish Crisis: Humanism and Experience in the 1590s', *Past and Present*, 111 (1986): pp. 17–49.

ends it agreeing that Buchanan is right to advocate such apparently extreme measures. Eudoxus starts Spenser's dialogue believing that English law can be made to work in Ireland and sceptical that violence is as obviously required as Irenius claims, but ends a *View* convinced that Ireland breaks all the rules of rational, humanist government. Reaching one of the most controversial passages of a *View*, Irenius has to persuade Eudoxus that violence must precede religious conversion, a case he eventually accepts. Eudoxus still asks for points of clarification, but the ways in which he phrases his objections signals to the reader that the dispute is effectively over and all that remains is to take the very last steps: 'Surelye I ame of your minde, that nothinge will bring them from theire uncivile life soner then learninge and discipline nexte after the knowledge and feare of god' (p. 218); 'This was a good ordinananuce' (p. 220); 'I doe now perceave your reasone well' (p. 221); 'Surelye these ordinaunces seme verie expedient' (p. 226). We move towards an agreed conclusion in each text, a process of arguing that Spenser may have taken from Buchanan.

Such parallels are worth pointing out, given the emphasis placed on Buchanan's work in Spenser's writings, but they remain no more than speculative, shadowy possible resemblances. Far more significant is Buchanan's generally unacknowledged influence on the politics of *The Faerie Queene*, given that Buchanan's most widely read work in England was *Ane Detectioun*, which represented Mary Stuart in such an unflattering light. James, eager to become king of England, even if he had little affection for a mother he never knew, was acutely sensitive to what he read as slanderous attacks on Mary, comments that might damage his path to the English crown.[32] He reacted with great hostility to criticism of Mary, one of the most high profile offenders being Spenser himself.

Spenser aroused James VI's wrath through his portrait of the trial of Duessa in *The Faerie Queene*, Book V, canto 9, a transparent allegory of the trial and execution of Mary Queen of Scots on 8 February 1587.[33] The English ambassador in Scotland, Robert Bowes, wrote to Lord Burghley on 1 November 1596 that James refused to allow the second edition of *The Faerie Queene* to be sold in Scotland and 'further he will complain to Her Majesty of the author as you will understand at more

---

[32]   D. Harris Willson, *King James VI and I* (London, 1956), ch. 5; Alan Stewart, *The Cradle King: A Life of James VI and I* (London, 2003), pp. 88–93; Phillips, *Images of a Queen*, pp. 196–208, *passim*.

[33]   For analysis, see Richard A. McCabe, 'The Masks of Duessa: Spenser, Mary Queen of Scots, and James VI', *English Literary Renaissance*, 17 (1987): pp. 224–42; Andrew Hadfield, 'Spenser and the Stuart Succession', *Literature and History*, 13/1 (Spring, 2004): pp. 9–24.

length by himself'.[34] On 12 November, Bowes wrote again explaining that the problem stemmed from 'som dishonourable effects (as the King deems thereof) against himself and his mother deceased'. Although Bowes claimed that he had persuaded James that the book had not been 'passed with privilege of Her Majesty's Commissioners', James 'still desire[d] that Edward [sic] Spenser for his fault be duly tried and punished'.[35] But the affair was still not over. On 5 March 1598, George Nicolson, a servant of Robert Bowes, wrote to Sir Robert Cecil that Walter Quinn, a poet later to enjoy a successful career at the courts of James and Charles I, was 'answering Spenser's book, whereat the king is offended' (p. 747).[36] The work, assuming it was ever completed, has not survived.

This was an extensive and serious diplomatic incident, and not the first time that Spenser had got himself into serious hot water. Spenser had managed seriously to offend William Cecil, Lord Burghley, when his satirical beast fable, *Mother Hubberds Tale*, which represented Burghley as a crafty fox, was published as part of the volume of *Complaints* in 1591, and all unsold copies of the poem were called in.[37] Had Spenser lived to greet the new monarch in 1603, it was quite possible that he would have suffered the same fate as his friend, Sir Walter Raleigh, who was imprisoned in the Tower of London for a number of years after his supposed involvement in the Bye Plot.[38] Moreover, Spenser had publicly defended Raleigh in the second edition of *The Faerie Queene* (1596) – in which the slight to Mary took place – when he had alienated the Queen for his marriage to Elizabeth Throckmorton, one of her maids of honour, and advertised their friendship in the preface to the poem, *Clouts come home againe* (1595), which would not have escaped James's notice.[39]

The evidence would suggest that James saw Spenser's representation of his mother as one that ultimately derived from Buchanan, who stood for everything that James despised, which would explain his furious and prolonged reaction to *The Faerie Queene*. For James, not only did

---

[34]   Cited in Willy Maley, *A Spenser Chronology* (Basingstoke, 1994), p. 678. On Bowes, see *ODNB* entry.

[35]   Maley, *Spenser Chronology*, p. 68; *Calendar of State Papers, relating to Scotland, 1589–1603* (London, 1858), p. 723. Subsequent references to this edition in parentheses in the text.

[36]   On Quinn, see *ODNB* entry.

[37]   Richard S. Peterson, 'Laurel Crown and Ape's Tail: New Light on Spenser's Career from Sir Thomas Tresham', *Spenser Studies*, 12 (1998): pp. 1–35.

[38]   Robert Lacey, *Sir Walter Ralegh* (London, 1975), chs. 37–8.

[39]   Ibid., pp. 155–9; James P. Bednarz, 'Ralegh in Spenser's Historical Allegory', *Spenser Studies*, 4 (1983): pp. 49–70. See also Andrew Hadfield, '"Bruited Abroad": John White and Thomas Harriot's Colonial Representations of Ancient Britain', in David Baker and Willy Maley (eds), *British Identities and English Renaissance Literature* (Cambridge, 2002), pp. 159–77.

Buchanan's ideas undermine his ability to govern and lead to anarchy, but they threatened to prevent him becoming king of England.[40] James was surely right. It appears counter-intuitive to imagine that Spenser, who clearly and frequently acknowledges the influence of Buchanan in his work – and in a work that was designed to be read by numerous government officials – had somehow missed Buchanan's writings on Mary.[41] It is well attested that Renaissance readers did not always read complete books, often taking from volumes what they needed, but it is hard to imagine that Spenser had no idea of the extensive attacks on Mary in the last books of Buchanan's *Historia*, even had he failed to read *Ane Detectioun*.[42]

In *The Faerie Queene*, Book V, canto 9, the passage that so offended James, Mercilla (Elizabeth) has to be forced to agree to the execution of Duessa (Mary), through the vigorous pleading of her loyal subjects who clearly see the threat that Duessa poses to her rule.[43] Zele, who functions as an alter ego of Artegall, the Knight of Justice, and who clearly bears an allegorical relationship to Spenser's patron Arthur Lord Grey de Wilton, as he took a prominent role in arguing for the execution of Mary after the discovery of the Babington plot, makes the case against Duessa:

> First gan he tell, how this that seem'd so faire
> And royally arrayd, *Duessa* hight
> That false *Duessa*, which had wrought great care,
> And mickle mischiefe vnto many a knight,
> By her beguyled, and confounded quight:
> But not for those she now in question came,
> Though also those mote question'd be aright,
> But for vyld treasons, and outrageous shame,
> Which she against the dred *Mercilla* oft did frame.
>
> For she whylome (as ye mote right wel
> Remember) had her counsels false conspyred,
> With faithlesse *Blandamour* and *Paridell*,
> (Both two her paramours, both of her hyred,
> And both with hope of shadowes vaine inspyred,)
> And with them practiz'd, how for to depryue

---

[40] See above, note 5.

[41] On the audience and readership of a *View*, see Nicholas P. Canny, 'Edmund Spenser and the Development of an Anglo-Irish Identity', *The Yearbook of English Studies*, 13 (1983): pp. 1–19; Brady, 'Spenser's Irish Crisis'; McCabe, *Spenser's Monstrous Regiment*, ch. 14.

[42] See Eugene R. Kintgen, *Reading in Tudor England* (Pittsburgh, 1996), ch. 2; Lisa Jardine and Anthony Grafton, '"Studied for Action": How Gabriel Harvey Read His Livy', *Past and Present*, 129 (1990): pp. 30–78; Kevin Sharpe, *Reading Revolutions: The Politics of Reading in Early Modern England* (New Haven, 2000).

[43] For comment, see McCabe, 'Masks of Duessa'; Douglas A. Northrop, 'Spenser's Defence of Elizabeth', *University of Toronto Quarterly*, 38 (1969): pp. 277–94.

Mercilla of her crowne, by her aspyred,
That she might it vnto her selfe deryue,
And trymph in their blood, whom she to death did dryue. (V. ix. 40–41).[44]

Although the specific crime mentioned here is treason against Mercilla, Spenser is careful to link Duessa's transgressions with earlier crimes, creating a mixture of political intrigue with murder and sexual sin. The link with Blandamour and Paridell is especially interesting, as the three figures formed a disruptive and unstable love triangle in Book 4. Paridell has already played a significant role in the poem at the end of Book 3, seducing Hellenore, in a parody of the events of the *Iliad*, using the tales of his Trojan ancestry to win her over and persuade her to leave her husband, Malbecco.[45] Paridell's use of his heroic past to gain short-term sexual satisfaction is contrasted to Britomart, who is descended from the Trojan Aeneas, and tells stories of her country's heroic genealogy to counteract Paridell's use of history for very different purposes. Paridell abandons Hellenore to a troop of satyrs, and, when they crown her with laurel (III. x. 44), she becomes their quean (prostitute), not their queen (ruler).

Trying to establish precise and sustained historical allegory in Spenser is not always rewarding and risks collapsing the subtle and varied allegorical nature of the poem.[46] What is important for our understanding of the ramifications of the representation of the execution of Mary and its relationship to Buchanan is how carefully Spenser has placed this episode within the development of the plot and its more general allegorical significance. Duessa is guilty of treason, and this is the crime for which she must be tried; but she has already committed a number of reprehensible acts, shaming knights and spilling blood, just like Mary. She is already associated with the abuse of sovereignty and the prostitution of her sexuality before she is tried and then executed. Mercilla, in fact, shows pity for her rival queen, and has to be persuaded, forced even, to have her executed. Spenser's point is that this is all false pity, because we see Mercilla's court assaulted by serious threats to her power in the form of Malengin the shape-shifter (V. ix. 5–19), dangers that are not recognized

---

[44]   All references to Hamilton's edition of the poem. On Grey as Zele, see Richard A. McCabe, 'The Fate of Irena: Spenser and Political Violence', in Coughlan (ed.), *Spenser and Ireland*, pp. 109–25.

[45]   On Paridell and Hellenore, see Harry Berger, Jr., 'The Discarding of Malbecco: Conspicuous Allusion and Cultural Exhaustion in *The Faerie Queene* III. xi–xii', in *Revisionary Play: Studies in the Spenserian Dynamics* (Berkeley, CA, 1988), pp. 154–71; Andrew Hadfield, *Literature, Politics and National Identity: Reformation to Renaissance* (Cambridge, 1994), pp. 198–200.

[46]   On the nature of Spenser's allegory, see Isabel G. MacCaffrey, *Spenser's Allegory: The Anatomy of Imagination* (Princeton, NJ, 1976); Paul Suttie, *Self-interpretation in The Faerie Queene* (Woodbridge, 2006).

by those in power.[47] Furthermore, this is the very canto in which we witness the sight of the poet Bon-Font with his tongue nailed to a post and his name changed to Mal-Font for the crime of producing evil words and blaspheming against the queen.[48] The allegory suggests that Spenser's Mercilla, like Elizabeth, is prepared to tolerate the dangerous treason of her rival while punishing those who transgress through producing words that are not well received, perhaps poorly interpreted, a claim Spenser suggests as his own fate in the final stanza of the second edition of the poem (VI. xii. 41).[49] The fact that Spenser was actually nearly punished for offending a sovereign for writing this very passage, makes his words either ironic or prescient.

In this episode Spenser is very careful to link murder, sex and bad government, precisely the case that Buchanan launched against Mary in his *Historia* and *Ane Detectioun*. Like Buchanan he sees Duessa/Mary as the culmination of generations of bad princely behaviour and focuses on her as the principal threat to the liberty and well-being of the people. Buchanan's narrative of Mary's disastrous reign ends with her fleeing to England, so he does not have any comment on her behaviour in exile and captivity.[50] But he makes it clear that Mary is already guilty of all the crimes that Spenser accuses her of having committed, before she became involved in the plots that led to her execution. Having banished the noble Lord James Stewart, Earl of Moray from court, Mary seeks to establish a tyranny in Scotland, setting aside all feelings of pity and affection for her own family to satisfy her own base desires:

> Now that she was rid of this honest and popular man, the Queen tried to remove the other obstacles to her tyranny. These were the lords who had been unwilling to subscribe to her crime [i.e., removing Moray], and seemed reluctant to accept the actions she had planned. She hated those especially who, seeing that her mind was not more favourable towards her son than it had been towards her husband, had banded together at Stirling – intending no treason, but determined to protect the child. For his mother wanted to hand him over to the keeping of his stepfather. No one doubted that Bothwell would have the child removed at the first opportunity, that he might not live to be the

---

[47] Hadfield, *Spenser's Irish Experience*, pp. 160–64.

[48] For comment, see M. Lindsay Kaplan, *The Culture of Slander in Early Modern England* (Cambridge, 1997), ch. 2; Norbrook, *Poetry and Politics*, p. 118.

[49] For comment, see Andrew Hadfield, 'Duessa's Trial and Elizabeth's Error: Judging Elizabeth in Spenser's *Faerie Queene*', in Susan Doran and Tom Freeman (eds), *The Myth of Elizabeth* (London, 2003), pp. 56–76.

[50] For analysis of the political ramifications of the existence of two queens within the realm, see A.N. McLaren, *Political Culture in the Reign of Elizabeth I: Queen and Commonwealth, 1558–1585* (Cambridge, 1999).

avenger of his father's death, or an obstacle to Bothwell's children's inheriting the throne (Buchanan, *Tyrannous Reign*, p. 138).[51]

Mary's political crimes cannot be separated from her personal ones. She chooses her unsuitable lover over both the people and her son. No pity can possibly be shown to such a monarch, a point that has to be impressed upon Mercilla in *The Faerie Queene*, just as Spenser clearly felt it had to be impressed upon Elizabeth (in reality, Elizabeth had been rather less feeble-minded than Spenser alleged, but he was not party to the complex machinations of court politics).[52] Throughout Buchanan's writings on Mary the same links between political and personal behaviour are made: Mary is a bad queen because she is a bad person and, for failing to put the safety and happiness of her subjects above her personal wishes, and for her inability to distinguish between *rex* and *lex*, she has forfeited the right to life. The same case is made by Spenser's representation of Duessa, whose progress throughout *The Faerie Queene* links sexual and political crime.[53] Duessa's character is established in terms of the description of her produced by Buchanan. Only by acting firmly and demanding Duessa's execution can Mercilla/Elizabeth demonstrate that she is able to make the proper distinctions between true and false pity that are required of a resolute ruler. Instead, she vacillates and allows herself to be swayed by 'self-feeling of her feeble sexe' (III. i. 54, line 2), a sign that she has not overcome the limitations of her gender and is in danger of becoming as bad a queen as her supposed nemesis.[54]

Spenser developed his sense of the political significance of Mary/Duessa in 'Two Cantos of Mutabilitie'.[55] Mutabilitie's challenge to Cynthia for control of the universe is framed explicitly in terms of Mary's challenge to Elizabeth for the right to govern England, showing how Mary's legacy after her death would be chaos and destruction, the future Spenser feared if James became king of England. Mutabilitie is seen to be another legacy of Mary. Spenser was wrong in his judgement, as, whatever criticism might have been made of James, he was hardly the agent of the apocalypse that Spenser feared.[56] Nevertheless, Spenser was not the only observer who

---

[51]   On Buchanan's championing of Moray, see McFarlane, *Buchanan*.

[52]   Wallace T. MacCaffrey, *Elizabeth I* (London, 1993), pp. 350–53.

[53]   On Duessa, see Anthea Hume, 'Duessa', in A.C. Hamilton (ed.), *The Spenser Encyclopaedia* (London and Toronto, 1990), pp. 229–30.

[54]   For analysis, see Claire McEachern, *The Poetics of English Nationhood, 1590–1612* (Cambridge, 1996), ch. 2. On female rule, see Amanda Shephard, *Gender and Authority in Sixteenth-century England* (Keele, 1994); Constance Jordan, 'Woman's Rule in Sixteenth Century British Political Thought', *Renaissance Quarterly*, 40/3 (1987): pp. 421–51.

[55]   For discussion, see Hadfield, 'Spenser and the Stuart Succession'.

[56]   For comments on James, which concentrate on his unpleasant behaviour and personal corruption, see Robert Ashton (ed.), *James I by his Contemporaries: An Account of*

was nervous at the prospect of the son of an executed traitor inheriting the English throne, many influenced by what they had read at first or second hand from Buchanan.[57] And he more than anyone, probably even Raleigh, had good reason to fear the wrath of James.[58]

The writings of Buchanan exerted a particular influence on Spenser in a number of ways. The importance of *Rerum Scoticarum Historia* for the genealogy of the Irish is clear enough, especially as the dialogue ends with Eudoxus urging Irenius to keep his promise that they 'mete againe upon the like good occacion', when he 'will declare unto us [his] observacions which [he] have gathered of the Antiquities of Ireland' (*Prose Works*, pp. 230–31), which must involve revisiting Buchanan's *Historia*. But the impact of Buchanan's representation of Mary Stuart on Spenser's images of female rulers has not really been acknowledged, an oversight given the central importance of Mary in Spenser's understanding of the political workings of the British Isles. Furthermore, Spenser was clearly interested in and, arguably, influenced by republican thought and it is hard to imagine that he did not take account of Buchanan's political ideas, especially given his associations with those who were keen to use and promote Buchanan's writings.[59] Spenser has been seen as 'Elizabeth's arse-kissing poet' for too long, a view that is still dominant whatever evidence is presented to the contrary.[60] The representation of sovereignty in *The Faerie Queene* needs to be read in terms of a long tradition of 'mirrors for princes' literature, and, just as importantly, its offshoot, 'mirrors for magistrates' literature.[61] If the poem makes any one point it is surely that the monarch is responsible to those whom he or she governs, the central political creed of the period, and one that could be inflected with a radical or a conservative slant.[62] Reminding the monarch of their duties towards the people in the late

---

his Career and Character as seen by some of his Contemporaries (London, 1969).

[57]   See Doran, 'Revenge Her Foul and Most Unnatural Murder?'; McCaffrey, *Elizabeth*, ch. 34.

[58]   Raleigh's troubles with James began rather later: see Lacey, *Raleigh*, pp. 304–6.

[59]   Andrew Hadfield, 'Was Spenser a Republican?', *English*, 47 (1998): pp. 169–82; David Scott Wilson-Okamura, 'Republicanism, Nostalgia, and the Crowd', *Spenser Studies*, 17 (2003): pp. 253–73; Andrew Hadfield, 'Was Spenser a Republican After All? A Response to David Scott Okamura-Wilson', *Spenser Studies*, 17 (2003): pp. 275–90.

[60]   The quotation is from Karl Marx: see Editors and Anthony W. Riley, 'Marx & Spenser', in Hamilton (ed.), *Spenser Encyclopaedia*, pp. 457–8.

[61]   Hadfield, *Literature, Politics and National Identity*, ch. 6; Lester K. Born, 'The Perfect Prince: A Study in Thirteenth and Fourteenth Century Ideals', *Speculum*, III (1928): pp. 470–504.

[62]   For discussion, see for example, J.P. Sommerville, *Politics and Ideology in England, 1603–1640* (Harlow, 1986); Kevin Sharpe, *Remapping Early Modern England: The Culture of Seventeenth-century Politics* (Cambridge, 2000), pt. 1; Glenn Burgess, *The Politics of the Ancient Constitution: An Introduction to English Political Thought, 1603–1642* (Basingstoke, 1992).

1590s could not but have taken a radical slant, even if any such utterance did not commit the author to Buchanan's oppositional stance.[63] The failure of justice that we witness in Book 5 leads directly to the besieged pastoral landscape of Book 6, the Book of Courtesy, in which no one is safe from marauding brigands and savages, a direct result of the monarch's inability to govern properly and effectively.[64] As the trial of Duessa in Book 5, canto 9 indicates, subjects have rights to tell the monarch how to govern for the good of everyone, something that was perhaps already enshrined in the Bond of Association of 1584, designed to protect the crown and constitution from assassination attempts, principally inspired by the threat of Mary.[65] Similar sentiments were articulated throughout the work of George Buchanan, one of the most obvious sources for anyone looking for arguments about the rights of subjects in the 1590s. It is hard to imagine that Spenser was unaware of Buchanan's political arguments when he wrote *The Faerie Queene*, a work that examines the role and purpose of the monarchy, and the behaviour of the monarch, precisely the focus of Buchanan's political thought in *Ane Detectioun*, the *Historia* and *De Iure Regni*.[66] Buchanan evidently influenced the passages that discuss the role of Mary Stuart, as her son (or his advisers) spotted, but he may have had a much wider influence on the politics of the poem that should be explored in future studies.

[63]   John Guy, 'Introduction: The 1590s: The Second Reign of Elizabeth I?', in Guy (ed.), *The Reign of Elizabeth I: Court and Culture in the Last Decade* (Cambridge, 1995), pp. 1–19.

[64]   Hadfield, *Spenser's Irish Experience*, ch. 5.

[65]   On the 'Bond of Association', see John Guy, *Tudor England* (Oxford, 1988), pp. 331–2.

[66]   On Spenser's judging the queen, see Michael O'Connell, *Mirror and Veil: The Historical Dimension of Spenser's Faerie Queene* (Chapel Hill, NC, 1977), pp. 52–4.

CHAPTER 4

George Buchanan and the Patriot Cause[*]

Arthur Williamson

'Secularization was an evangelical pursuit.'

Mark Goldie

'Le patriote de 1580 a déjà quelques traits du patriote de 1789.'

Henri Hauser, 1916[1]

Reformation, the Three Kingdoms, and the Advent of 'un Évangélisme Civil'

In 1575 the Huguenot jurist Pierre Fabre made an impassioned appeal to 'every good citizen and patriot' (*tout bon citoyen et patriote*) to take up arms and preserve France from impending destruction. In the wake of the great massacres and the seizure of power by the Catholic League and their Spanish allies, religion ceased to be the point, confessional difference had become irrelevant; rather, the issue concerned the survival of French society:

Bref, il est maintenant question du droit public, et de la laisser perdre, ou de le retenir, et non pas de la verité de nostre foy et doctrine. Or c'est chose qu'il nous faut et tous autres bon patriotes defender, non pas par une simple patience et complainte, mais en resistant par armes ...

[In sum, it is today a question of the public law, and whether we shall let it be lost or whether we shall retain it, and not about the truth of our faith and doctrine. Now this is a thing that is incumbent on us and all other good patriots to defend, not by mere suffering and protestation, but by resisting in arms.]

[*]   My thanks to Paulina Kewes, Paul McGinnis and Malcolm Smuts, whose comments, criticism and linguistic insight have significantly strengthened this paper.
[1]   Mark Goldie, 'The Civil Religion of James Harrington', in A. Pagden (ed.), *The Language of Political Theory in Early Modern Europe* (Cambridge, 1987), p. 200; Henri Hauser, *Le Principe des Nationalités* (Paris, 1916), p. 18.

'Un bon patriot' needed to take action, learning from Roman history and the examples of such activists as Ahala Servilius, Scipio Nascia Serapio, 'et autres bons citoyenes' who are greatly and universally praised for their virtuous resistance to tyranny. To save 'nostre patrie', which was dearer to us than life and in which it pleased God to have us born as citizens, was a sacred obligation.[2] In the previous year the anonymous author of *Discours politiques des diverses puissances establies de Dieu au monde* similarly insisted:

> Or est il impossible qu'entre bons & fidelles citoyens & patriottes, & gens qui ont conspire pour leur particulier contre l'utilité publicque, y ait iamais concorede asseuree

> [Now it is impossible for there ever to be secure agreement between good and faithful citizens and patriots, and those who have conspired for their own interest against the public welfare.][3]

The author also urged that his countrymen look beyond particular religious doctrines to the social ties that ultimately drew together French citizens. All human intercourse was founded in 'l'amitié Politique'.[4] Again as with Fabre, these bonds were spiritual rather than a secular alternative to religion.

Fabre and the author of the *Discours* provide some of the earliest instances of the terms 'patriot' and 'citizen' used in the modern sense. The civic vocabulary, however, had become a signal feature in French political culture long before, and acquired urgent cogency and immediacy with

---

²   Pierre Fabre, *Traitte duquel on peut apprendre en quel cas il est permis à l'homme Chrestien de porter les armes, et par lequel est respondu à Pierre Charpentier ...* ['Treatise from which we learn the circumstances in which a Christian man may bear arms, and through which Pierre Charpentier is answered'] (n.p., 1576), pp. 21, 36–7: '... nostre patrie, qui nous est plus chere que la vie, en laquelle il a pleu à Dieu nous faire naistre citoyens.' Originally published in Latin, *Ad Petri Carpentrii ... Petri Fabri responsio* (Newstadii, 1575). Two expanded translations subsequently appeared in that year and the following. There exist no direct counterpart passages between the Latin text and the passages cited here. Ahala, a legendary figure from the fifth century BCE, preserved the republic through tyrannicide. Serapio (*c.*133 BCE) preserved republican 'liberty' by leading the senatorial charge against Tiberius Gracchus. Pierre Fabre has proven difficult to trace, and the name may be a pseudonym – possibly for the jurist and cleric Lambert Daneau.
³   *Discours politiques des diverses puissances establies de Dieu* ['Political discourses on the various forms of power established by God'], in Simon Goulart (ed.), *Mémoires de l'estat de France sous Charles IX* (3 vols, Middleburg [Geneva], 1578), vol. 3, p. 244b. Cf. Sarah Hanley, 'The French Constitution Revised: Representative Assemblies and Resistance Right in the Sixteenth Century', in M.P. Holt (ed.), *Society and Institution in Renaissance and Early Modern France* (Athens, GA, 1991), pp. 36–50.
⁴   *Discours politiques*, p. 231b.

the outbreak of the Wars of Religion. As Charlotte Wells has described, civil war compelled Frenchmen in growing numbers to imagine their country as 'one great city', and to declare that, under all the vast, intricate patchwork of hierarchies, orders, ranks, constituted bodies, privileges, and immunities that legally comprised the French kingdom, there lay a shared civic connection. From beneath these massive and extended structures of feudal and ecclesiastical law emerged a common cause, the public good, the self-created world that truly was France. As early as 1562 the chancellor Michel de l'Hôpital declared, 'many can be citizens who are not Christians, even the excommunicant does not cease to be a citizen' ('plusierus peuvent ester *cives qui non erunt christiani*, mesme l'excommunité ne laisse pas d'estre citoyen').[5] The great Huguenot scholar Henri Lancelot de Voisin, sieur de la Popelinère, maintained that

> A good citizen always measures his passions to fit the welfare of the state where he was born or in which he is settled. Thus if you love your country well, the satisfaction it will receive as the fruit of your labours will be the sole point of your thinking.

The Huguenot leader Phillippe Duplessis-Mornay and even Henri of Navarre made similar civic appeals. The 'tu ciuis' of the Huguenot *Vindiciae, Contra Tyrannos* (1579) becomes 'mon patriotte' in its 1581 French translation.[6] Following Fabre, in the later 1570s and 1580s both Huguenots and Politiques increasingly refer to themselves as 'patriots'. In 1581 Nicolas Froumenteau insisted that his work on finance would be of service 'à tous bons patriotes'. In the same year the anonymous author of *La supreme restauration du Royaume de France* urged that

> Each person have regard to others as good and native Frenchmen, enjoying the same or similar privileges, carrying out all the other duties of good patriots and fellow citizens, so that the bond of human society, which has been broken and

---

[5]   Charlotte Wells, *Law and Citizenship in Early Modern France* (Baltimore, MD, 1995), pp. 91, 173, n. 154; Charlotte Wells, 'The Language of Citizenship in the French Religious Wars', *Sixteenth Century Journal*, 30 (1999): pp. 441–56, at pp. 441, 449. Also see Hanley, 'French Constitution Revised', pp. 36–7.

[6]   Wells, *Law and Citizenship*, p. 172, n. 149, quoting La Popelinère, *L'Amiral de France et par occasion, celuy des autres nations, tant vieilles que nouvelle* (Paris, 1585): 'Un bon citoyen mesure toujours ses passions au bien de l'estat auquel il est né ou habitué. Donques si vous aymez bien vostre pais le contentement qu'il recevra du fruit de vos labours sera pour le seul but à vos conceptions'; Wells, *Law and Citizenship*, pp. 171, nn. 138, 141; Ronald Knowles, '"The All-Attoning Name": The Word *Patriot* in Seventeenth-century England', *Modern Language Review*, 96 (2001): pp. 624–43, at p. 637, n. 71.

torn apart by the burning torches of civil war, may be taken up and retied with a knot that cannot be undone.[7]

Such appeals to the 'public good' and the duties of 'bons patriottes et concitoyens [fellow citizens]', became ever more prominent in the language of the Huguenots and the Politiques, peaking in the 1580s.

Although by the late 1580s the Liguers too could speak of citizenship as embracing the public good, the term carried very different meanings for them. As one could be French and a citizen only by also being Catholic, their 'public' was severely narrower than that of the Huguenots and Politiques. The inclusive Protestants and the exclusive Catholics created two quite different conceptions; the latter was inherently confessionalized, the former just the opposite. In the end the rights granted the Huguenots by the Edict of Nantes (1598), as Wells points out, comprised a form of naturalization, thereby making Huguenots aliens in their own land. Even so, the fundamental thrust of Counter-Reform was not a competing notion of citizenship but a rejection of such language altogether – perhaps most prominently with Michel de Montaigne.[8]

Civic values could reach deeply into reformed regions, and even at the community level there appeared analogous appeals. In Lyons the printers' society, the Society of the Giffarins, was overwhelmingly Protestant, but invented a classically derived mythology for their trade based on Minerva, 'the mother of printing and the goddess of knowledge', in part to accommodate the small Catholic minority.[9]

---

[7]   Froumenteau, *Le Secret des finances de France* (n.p., 1581), p. 38, cited by G. Dupont Ferrier, 'Le Sens des mots "patria" et "patrie" en France au moyen age et jusqu'au début de XVIIe siécle', *Revue Historique*, 188 (1940): p. 97; cited earlier by Henri Hauser, *Le principe des nationalités*, p. 18. On Froumenteau, see also Henry Heller, *Anti-Italianism in Sixteenth-century France* (Toronto, 2003), pp. 167–8, 172, 174. *La supreme restauration du Royaume de France* (Paris, 1581), p. 3; cited by Myriam Yardeni, *La Conscience Nationale en France pendant les Guerres de Religion (1559–1598)* (Paris, 1971), pp. 172–3; translated by Wells, 'The Language of Citizenship', pp. 449–50.

[8]   Ibid., pp. 452, 455; Wells, *Law and Citizenship*, p. 91; Luc Racault, *Hatred in Print: Catholic Propaganda and Protestant Identity during the French Wars of Religion* (Aldershot, 2002). See P.J. McGinnis and A.H. Williamson, *The British Union: A Critical Edition and Translation of David Hume of Godscroft's 'De Unione Insulae Britannicae'* (Aldershot, 2002), pp. 32–3, and the discussion below. Ferrier was troubled by the identification of patriotism with Protestantism and the elision from reform to reformation. Citing Catholic usage of the term, he expostulated: 'Le *patriotisme* n'etait donc pas, aux yeux de tous, le monopole de protestantisme' ('Le Sens', p. 97). Yet in a very real sense it was. The term had Huguenot origins, and by the last decade of the century, when Ferrier takes his examples, the restoration of monarchical authority increasingly made the term simply the equivalent of 'subject'. Moreover, Counter-Reformation thought enjoined hierarchy, both clerical and social, and decisively rejected the relative equality inherent in the civic ideal.

[9]   N.Z. Davis, 'Strikes and Salvation at Lyon', in *Society and Culture in Early Modern France* (Stanford, CA, 1965), pp. 1–16.

By the end of the decade the new French vocabulary would be taken up in the Dutch revolt, and we encounter a *Lettre d'un gentilhomme, bon patriot*, published in Flanders.[10] In 1578 the militant Calvinist Dr Pieter Beutterich published *Le vray Patriot aux bons Patriots* that urged no compromise with the invaders or with the Roman Antichrist. Beutterich saw a republican future for the Netherlands on the model of the Swiss confederation – 'qu'ilz se liguent vraiement à la Suisse'. Beutterich's tract made something of a splash and appeared in German translation in the following year under the title, *Le Vray Patriot &c. Das ist: Getreues Ermanen und Auszschreiben deren inn den Niederlanden umb gemeyn Heyl des Vatterlands sorgetragenden und Eiferigen ... Stände.* The German translation simply retained the French neologism. By 1580 that had changed, and Dutch pamphlets warned against 'valsche Patriotten'.[11]

The same vocabularies, if not Beutterich's extraordinary radicalism, appeared also in contemporaneous England and Scotland. In 1559 John Aylmer insisted that, *pace* John Knox, female rulers need not inevitably turn out to be catastrophes like Mary Tudor. If Englishmen had stood by their laws and taken an active part in protecting their society, no calamity would have occurred. Aylmer's assumptions subsequently played out in practical politics on the council, in parliament, in the streets – manifesting themselves perhaps most dramatically with the Bond of Association of 1584. From the outset, William Cecil and other members of the council regarded governance consistently in conciliar, collegial, and broadly republican terms. The prospect of an interim republican regime

---

[10] Ferrier, 'Le Sens', p. 97. Ferrier and Hauser observe that, although the word 'patriot' appears as early as the fifteenth century, its meaning was 'compatriot', the fellow inhabitant of a localized *pays* or *patria*. The earlier usage carried no sense of civic duty or love of country, while the notion of country itself gradually expanded during the sixteenth century, ultimately to mean the whole of France (Ferrier, 'Le Sens', pp. 92, 95; Hauser, *Le Principe des Nationalités*, p. 18). Hauser saw the term indicating the emergence of ideas that would triumph with the French Revolution: 'N'est-il pas intéressant de constater que la revolution qui a pour la première fois détaché complètement l'idée de nation de celle de monarchie, le sentiment national de la fidélité dynastique, soit aussi celle qui a donné son nom à ce sentiment nouveau?'

[11] *Vray Patriot*, sig. C2v. Translation by Johann Fischart, *Afgheworpene Brieven van sommighe vermommede ende valsche Patriotten ...*, in W.P.C. Knuttel (ed.), *Catalogus van de Pamfletten-Verzameling* (9 vols, 1890–1920; reprinted Utrecht, 1978), vol. 1.1, pp. 77, 79, 104 (nos. 392, 402, 531, 532); A.A. van Schelven, 'De Staatsvorm van het Zwitsersche Eedgenootschap den Nederlanden ter navolging aanbevolen', in Léon van der Essen (ed.), *Miscellanea Historica* (Brussels, 1947), pp. 747–56, at 748, 754–56. Dutch scholars have long recognized that the term 'patriot' and republican politics arose with the most determined opponents of the Spanish reconquest (ibid., p. 754). See also Laura Cruz, 'Turning Dutch: Historical Myths in Early Modern Netherlands', *Sixteenth Century Journal*, 39 (2008): pp. 1–22; K.H. Kossmann and A.F. Mellink (eds), *Texts concerning the Revolt of the Netherlands* (Cambridge, 1974), pp. 159–63; W.G. Naphy (ed.), *Documents of the Continental Reformation* (Houndmills, 1996), pp. 88–9.

was real enough at moments of crisis, notably in 1563 and 1584–85. Patrick Collinson's description of England in the Elizabethan period as a 'monarchical republic' (in which citizens were concealed within subjects) turns out to be surprisingly apt, and 'the Elizabethan Exclusion Crisis', as he terms it, may make Knox more relevant to both realms than conservative historians have ever allowed. As in France local communities and societies in England also adopted civic and at times recognizably republican vocabularies.[12] Shared governance, initially enjoined in the sixteenth century by the instability resulting from religious upheaval and compounded by a female ruler, became an ongoing norm that found fruition in the mid-seventeenth-century republic.[13]

For much of this period Scotland was a *de facto* republic. The absentee monarch, Mary Stuart, was very nearly deposed in 1560, seven years before the actual event.[14] High levels of direct action occurred during the 1559–60 revolution in the shires, with the Lords of the Congregation, at the Reformation Parliament – all understood by sympathizers and participants, not unreasonably, as manifestations of civic virtue. These values continued to suffuse Scottish politics after Mary's unexpected return in 1561 and became altogether central in the 1567–68 upheaval that overthrew her. Perhaps for these reasons the neologism 'patriot' entered English by the mid-1580s, well before the Armada crisis, via the Scots. Or so it seems. For, like Fabre and other French writers a decade earlier, when David Hume of Godscroft spoke of the 'good patriot' in his 1585–86 dialogue with the Earl of Angus, he was clearly using a familiar term.[15]

The rise of this political culture in England, Scotland and France (as well as in the Netherlands) – and we need to remember that these are the real three kingdoms – relied heavily on George Buchanan. No other contemporary intellect more thoroughly penetrated the thinking of all four

---

[12]   Patrick Collinson, 'The Monarchical Republic of Queen Elizabeth I', *Bulletin of the John Rylands Library*, 69 (1986–87): pp. 394–424, esp. pp. 407–8; Patrick Collinson, 'The Elizabethan Exclusion Crisis and the Elizabethan Polity', in *Proceedings of the British Academy* (Oxford, 1994), pp. 51–92. Also S. Alford, *The Early Elizabethan Polity: William Cecil and the British Succession Crisis, 1558–1569* (Cambridge, 1998), pp. 2, 7, and *passim*; Patrick Collinson, '*De republica Anglorum*, or history with the politics put back', in *Elizabethan Essays* (London, 1994), p. 19; M. Peltonen, *Classical Republicanism and English Political Thought, 1570–1640* (Cambridge, 1995), pp. 58ff., and *passim*. Conservative historians (see notes 33 and 47) discount the advent of civic culture and the role of the Reformation in its creation.

[13]   Sean Kelsey, *Inventing a Republic: The Political Culture of the English Commonwealth, 1649–1653* (Manchester, 1997).

[14]   Gordon Donaldson, *The Scottish Reformation* (Cambridge, 1960), p. 138; C. Kellar, *Scotland, England, and the Reformation, 1534–1561* (Oxford, 2003), p. 199; Collinson, 'Monarchical Republic', p. 403.

[15]   David Hume of Godscroft, *History of the House of Douglas* (London, 1644), p. 417.

societies. No other contemporary intellect, not even Beutterich, developed these lines of thought more radically, more uncompromisingly, or more comprehensively. Buchanan wrote all but exclusively in Latin and may never have used the vernacular word, employing instead the classical term for devotion to country, *pietas*. Nevertheless he undoubtedly knew the French literature (along with its authors), and, much more than they, emerges as a founder of what we may call 'the patriot cause' – thereafter becoming a pillar in the Atlantic republican tradition.

It is now a commonplace to observe that the tumultuous and remarkable decade 1558–68 saw the Reformation unleash a revolutionary upheaval that challenged authority throughout north-western Europe. Authority became destabilized in England, was twice overthrown in Scotland, radically contested in France, and violently rejected in the Low Countries. What is less well recognized today is that the civic voice, appeals to the public good, the 'patriot' and the 'citizen', did not simply arise in response to religious crisis and social breakdown. The language of crisis comprised no more than a deepened version of the language of reform itself. L'Hôpital's bold words in 1562 disconnected excommunication (and religious affiliation) from citizenship. But they did not comprise a desperate appeal to the 'practical' or attempt to get religion out of politics. Instead they mandated what the historian Loris Petris has recently called 'un évangélisme civil'.[16] As Henri Hauser observed long ago, the early modern 'patriote est le partisan des réformes populaires, l'ennemi des abus', and that almost reflexively extended to reform of the church. Increasingly, reformed religion *became* civil religion. The association of the 'vray patriote' with the 'vray huguenot' ('en bon François') long remained a commonplace. Irrespective of formal doctrine, Fabre and other such writers saw service to society and pursuit of the public good as genuinely religious undertakings.[17]

Similar lines of thought spread through French, English, Scottish and Dutch societies. However, as George Buchanan's career highlights, their similarities comprised more than simply a response to parallel problems and analogous opportunities. Figures like Buchanan, Philip Sidney, Edmund Spenser, Andrew Melville and Hume of Godscroft, along with a

---

[16]   Loris Petris, *La Plume et la Tribune: Michel de l'Hôpital et ses discours (1559–1562)* (Geneva, 2002), pp. 93, 94: 'l'exercice de la politique est inséparable de la pragmatique qui oeuvre à la séparation du politique et du religieux et à la laicisation de l'Etat. Sa conception monarchique est tout entière conditionnée par un idéal évangélique engagé dans la vie civile: un évangélisme civil.' See also Petris, '"Toutes passions laissees et depossees": Hatred in Michel de l'Hospital's Poetry and Policy', *Renaissance Studies*, 17 (2003): pp. 674–94, esp. pp. 691–3.

[17]   Hauser, *Le Principe des Nationalités*, p. 18; Ferrier, 'Le Sens', p. 97; Wells, 'Language of Citizenship', p. 449.

great many others, participated in what they perceived as a great common cause, the 'patriot' cause. At or near its intellectual centre stood Scotland's great humanist poet.

Consequently, we shall find ourselves ill served by focusing on narrow theological categories, simple confessional conflict, or, still less, the ecclesiological controversies that later exercised nineteenth-century church historiography. Nor shall we be well advised to adopt today's regnant preoccupation with identity – what Richard Wolin has called 'the anti-politics of cultural self-affirmation'.[18] Quite the reverse. Early modern 'patriots' were consistently internationalists. Their purposes, strategies, activism, all normally had a pan-regional orientation – and extended from there to all of Europe and throughout the globe. Rarely did 'patriots' become apologists for their home government, and normally they were at odds with it. Their civic world pointed to confederation and the most intimate collaboration in the struggle against the Counter-Reformation – and, outstandingly, the eschatological Last World Empire of the Habsburgs.[19] They bear no resemblance to modern post-Romantic nationalists. Mission defined self, rather than the other way around.

For Fabre and for Buchanan, for early modern 'patriots', politics and civic action, the pursuit of the public good, comprised spiritual, potentially redeeming acts. This confluence of the sacred and civic, this fusion of classical *pietas* with Christian piety is characteristic throughout the region, but especially so in Buchanan's Scotland. From the beginning, Protestant services in Scotland were structured as corporate and communal events, designed to create public space. One could easily celebrate a private mass; a private communion could only constitute a contradiction in terms.[20] The very simplicity, even austerity of the service emphatically implied the priesthood of all believers. The preoccupation with 'discipline', with Stoic self-restraint of private interest and corrupting passions, was prerequisite for public decision-taking and the exercise of virtue. It enjoined, ideally, self-imposed law, the world of Cato along with that of Calvin.[21] In this

---

[18]   Richard Wolin, *The Seduction of Unreason: The Intellectual Romance with Fascism, from Nietzsche to Post-modernism* (Princeton, NJ, 2004), p. xii.

[19]   A.H. Williamson, 'Scotland and the Rise of Civil Culture, 1550–1650', *History Compass*, 4/1 (2006): pp. 91–123. Conrad Russell long ago recognized that the term was adopted by opponents of the crown: *Crisis of Parliaments: English History, 1509–1660* (Oxford, 1971), p. 209. Also see Blair Worden, *The Sound of Virtue: Philip Sidney's 'Arcadia' and Elizabethan Politics* (New Haven, CT, 1996), ch. 3; Roger Kuin, 'Querre-Muhau: Sir Philip Sidney and the New World', *Renaissance Quarterly*, 51 (1998): pp. 549–83; A.H. Williamson, *Apocalypse Then: Prophecy and the Making of the Modern World* (Westport, CT, 2008), ch. 3.

[20]   Donaldson, *Scottish Reformation*, pp. 82–3, 180.

[21]   Cf. M. Todd, 'Seneca and the Protestant Mind: The Influence of Stoicism on Puritan Ethics', *Archiv für Reformationsgeschichte*, 74 (1983): pp. 182–200, esp. p. 189.

church Buchanan, a putative layman, would serve as the Moderator of its General Assembly. We can have little doubt that Buchanan saw the Church of Scotland as a civil church, an institution ruled not only by clergy but also by the laymen elders who comprised the political nation. Similarly, this new non-hierarchical church structure, imported from France and promoted by 'patriots', further reinforced the perception of spiritual life as concomitantly political life.

That perception became highly visible with the 1559–60 revolution, led by Scottish forces calling themselves the 'Lords of the Congregation'. The term 'congregation' carried strongly non-hierarchical and anti-clerical connotations, and thereby strongly communitarian ones. The term meant of course church or kirk; William Tyndale had used it in this way. But the term additionally carried the meaning of *ekklesia*, the assembly of adult male citizens that had the ultimate decision-making power in the Greek state, and archetypally for Buchanan, Athens. Scotland, even more dramatically than France, had become 'one great city', a dispersed polis, where virtuous citizens realized themselves as they determined the public good, created social value, and worked their redemption. This line of thought achieved its fullest expression, famously, in Buchanan's *De Iure Regni apud Scotos Dialogus* (1567, published 1579). Scholars have often puzzled over the frustratingly vague constitutional mechanisms apparently endorsed in the *Dialogus*. The 'mechanisms' are vague because Buchanan, despite extensive knowledge of civil law, is thinking in terms of morality rather than juridical structure, virtue rather than institutional arrangements, direct action rather than legal procedure. Free assemblies, public debate and *ad hoc* open gatherings, rather than any rules prescribing and thereby restricting venues, are his central concern.

Italy, Brutus and Tyrannicide

Buchanan spoke simultaneously in multiple registers, and his words at once carried a range of resonances. Perhaps we will encounter no more dramatic illustration of his polyphonic fusion of politics and religion than in his doctrine of tyrannicide. In a passage of the *Dialogus*, no less distressing to the early twenty-first century than to the late sixteenth-, Buchanan declared the duty of every citizen personally to strike down a tyrant. That obligation was unconditional. It was also spiritual. Caesar's assassination provided the model. As Buchanan made clear in his liminary verses to Marc-Antoine de Muret's Latin tragedy, *Julius Caesar*, Brutus was both a republican hero and a righteous man, at once an agent of liberty and of piety:

Such great virtue as there was deep-seated in the heroic soul of Brutus,
When the pious daggers were given him on behalf of his country,
A virtue, equally his, inspired your lofty voice, Muret,
When you sang of his pious deeds.
And even though Fortune, oftentimes envious of bright beginnings,
Scattered his bones in Phillippi's field,
He comes to life again, greater after death, by you.
And his honour restored grows by your artistry,
And rejoices more enshrined in the glorious monument [of your drama]
Than if the labour of the pyramids were covering his bones.[22]

It is as a citizen rather than as a senator, an office-holder or a patrician that Brutus has brought down Caesar. The assassination is an act of 'virtue', indeed civic virtue, and so his action (and even his daggers) are 'pious'.

Buchanan draws heavily on classical sources, as we might well expect from a sometime professor of Greek. But his thinking is also mediated powerfully and at times decisively by the Italian Renaissance. With these verses and others like them, we encounter the re-evaluation of Brutus that took place in *quattrocento* and *cinquecento* Italy, the republican voices of Coluccio Salutati, Leonardo Bruni, most prominently Niccolò Machiavelli – and even the republican movement spawned by the career of Girolamo Savonarola. Buchanan's contemporaries also adopted this assessment of Brutus, perhaps most notably Andrew Melville in his poetry of 1574.[23]

---

[22]   Buchanan, *Political Poetry*, pp. 5, 86–7. Cf. Gordon Braden, *Renaissance Tragedy: Anger's Privilege* (New Haven, CT, 1985), p. 126. The author of the *Discours politiques* (pp. 245b–246a) also entered into 'the dispute about the deed of Brutus' and found for the assassin: Brutus and his associates 'ont hazardé leur vie à faire vne guerre sommaire pour establir la paix publicque & la liberté des citoyens'; 'C'est ce que les amis de la societé ciuil doient procurer.' The contrast was with the image of Caesar as the father of his country, which would make his death an act of unnatural parricide. The author clearly saw the issue as involving two competing visions of society. Quentin Skinner gives 'the prize' for being the most radical Huguenot tract to the *Discours politiques*. He sees it as offering 'a more anarchic theory of resistance than any other work of Huguenot political thought': Skinner, *The Foundations of Modern Political Thought* (2 vols, Cambridge, 1978), vol. 2, p. 305 and n. 1. Like Buchanan, the author of the *Discours politiques* seems to have envisioned a high level of direct action. The Scottish connection is reinforced when he cites Hector Boece's *Scotorum Historia* (Paris, 1527) as a source for the public trial of malfeasant kings (*Discours politiques*, p. 294b). However, Sarah Hanley has identified the work's institutional and political context as far from 'anarchic' ('The French Constitution Revised').

[23]   Lorenzo Polizzotto, *The Elect Nation: The Savonarolan Movement in Florence, 1494–1545* (Oxford, 1994); Steven Reid, 'Early Polemic by Andrew Melville: The *Carmen Mosis* (1573/4) and the St Bartholomew's Day Massacre', *Renaissance et Réforme*, 30 (2008): pp. 63–82, at 70–72. Buchanan may well have had a specific event and illustration in mind with his arresting image of Brutus' 'pious daggers'. Lorensino de Medici, the assassin of the restored prince Alessandro in 1537, portrayed himself as a latter-day Brutus defending republican liberty. A medal presenting him in this way (and modelled on an antique coin

More specifically, we are encountering a late Renaissance Italian tradition that reached into practical politics. The figure of Brutus had acquired what can only be described as a cult status within late Italian republicanism. The assassination of Alessandro de' Medici in 1537 by the 'new Brutus', Lorensino de' Medici, found celebration in the statuary of no less than Michelangelo Buonarroti. Brutus' tyrannicide became a model for action, repeated throughout the period, and needs to be seen as part of what Manfredi Piccolomini has called 'a kind of collective mania' for classical, indeed, pre-imperial, Rome.[24] More than fashionable posture was involved, however, for these actions comprised urgent, even desperate acts to preserve classical civilization – i.e., civilization – before the emergent authoritarian world of Habsburg and papal universal empire.

Buchanan was in Italy during the 1550s, the years immediately following the final demise of the Florentine republican tradition. His vision of the Valois–Habsburg rivalry as a clash of civilizations, one in which the French monarchy served as the protector of civil societies, was widespread, if not altogether well founded. It is surely telling that his poems decorated the walls of the French military headquarters in Italy.[25] We do not know which ones. But the witty and angry poems denouncing Alexander, Xerxes, Caesar, and the other enemies of the *polis*, Buchanan's great villains of antiquity – rather than his *bon mots* about Helen of Troy – seem the most likely candidates. The French expedition into Italy and elsewhere could portray itself as a struggle for liberation, and France as the protector of culture and civilization. Buchanan's hugely popular verses spoke eloquently to this purpose. At the same time, Buchanan also insisted that the Italian humanist scholar Lorenzo Valla had achieved even more than the heroes of the Roman republic. They had defended civic culture, but the Herculean Valla restored it.[26] Buchanan's purposes were nothing less.

---

celebrating the original event) had on its obverse two daggers flanking the Phrygian cap of liberty. See D.J. Gordon, 'Gionnotti, Michelangelo, and the Cult of Brutus', in D.J. Gordon (ed.), *Fritz Saxl (1890–1948)* (London, 1957), p. 292. As we might expect, by the 1560s Buchanan had become thoroughly hostile to Catherine de Medici and to the entire dynasty. In his poem *De Nicotiana Falso Nomine Medicaea Appellata*, written after 1561 and before 1572, Buchanan linked the French acquisition of tobacco from Portugal with Medician corruption. French writers, who regarded tobacco as a new wonder drug, wanted to name the newly discovered plant after Catherine. But nothing could be a panacea under the label 'Medici': Catherine and catarrh, the Medici meant bad medicine. The text of the poem appears in Robert Crawford (ed.), *Apollos of the North: Selected Poems of George Buchanan and Arthur Johnston* (Edinburgh, 2006), p. 34. Cf. Buchanan, *Political Poetry*, pp. 276–7.

[24]   Manfredi Piccolomini, *The Brutus Revival: Parricide and Tyrannicide during the Renaissance* (Carbondale, IL, 1991), pp. 38, 63, 64–5, and *passim*.

[25]   McFarlane, *Buchanan*, pp. 177–8.

[26]   Buchanan, *Political Poetry*, pp. 84–7, 90–91, 122–5, 272–3. During the Italian campaign Buchanan served as tutor to Timoléon de Cossé-Brissac, the son of the French

It is through this Italianate context that we need to read not only the *Dialogus*, but also Buchanan's contemporaneous poem, his bitter attack on the Cardinal Charles of Guise, the *Satyra in Carolum Lotharingum Cardinalem* ('Satire against Charles, Cardinal of Lorraine'). Undoubtedly written after his trip to France in 1565 and before 1570, Buchanan's verses portray the reactionary Cardinal as a fomenter of civil war: his militant obstruction of the Colloquy at Poissy in 1561 foreclosed a broad-gauged religious accommodation, and thereby deliberately launched the unspeakable horrors of religious conflagration. The effects of this marked Charles in the most grotesque way as the ultimate barbarian. The poem does more. It also celebrates the assassination of the head of the Guise faction, Charles's brother Francis, by the Huguenot Jean Poltrot de Méré in 1563.[27] The *Satyra* unmistakably points to the same fate for Charles himself. Similarly, the *Dialogus*, the poem's companion piece, surely calls for a Scottish Brutus to dispatch the would-be tyrant Mary Stuart.

Both Fabre and Buchanan looked to a Ciceronian *respublica*, but Fabre's state, unlike Buchanan's, would be guided by genuine Ciceronians, by *optimates* like Ahala Servilius and Scipio Serapio – all of whom feared and resisted the *populus*. Not so Buchanan, who in 1567 imagined much wider participation in politics. As Roger Mason and others have pointed out, in the *Dialogus* Buchanan developed a notion of citizenship and the potential for civic capacity in terms more radical than any other sixteenth-century theorist.[28] Neither the autonomy provided by property nor the status provided by blood and birth made one a citizen. Citizens were simply individuals capable of perceiving the public good and acting accordingly – that is, capable of exercising civic virtue. This rational capability to see beyond one's particular interest and self-serving passions was at once natural and divine. Many, even most, could use it. That did not mean everyone (*universus populus*). Buchanan was acutely aware

---

commander-in-chief. The young man's name itself is telling. In antiquity Timoleon ousted the tyrant Dionysius II of Syracuse and still other tyrants in Sicily. Machiavelli would celebrate Timoleon as a liberator, and an anti-type to Julius Caesar in the *Discourses* (1.10); this and subsequent citations are to book and chapter as in Max Lerner (ed.), *The Prince and the Discourses* (New York, 1950). That Timoleon was a foreigner, a Corinthian, similarly suited French purposes. It was only appropriate that Buchanan would undertake his great poem on the cosmos at this time – with its anti-imperial, anti-Iberian message of Stoic restraint – as a lesson for Timoléon. In the event Timoléon turned out a blood-thirsty, utterly brutal Liguer – neither the first nor the last of Buchanan's students to go 'wrong'.

27   Buchanan, *Political Poetry*, pp. 92–101 (ll. 20, 110–17, 138). It is inconceivable that Buchanan would celebrate assassination after the murder of his friend and patron James, Earl of Moray, in January 1570. Buchanan portrayed Charles as an especially grotesque form of cannibal, and thereby uniquely barbaric (ll. 104–17). Implicitly, Charles's religious fanaticism destroyed the prospect of common cause and thereby the public good – and made him a traitor.

28   Buchanan, *De Iure Regni*, pp. lxi–lxiii.

that the mere struggle for existence could prevent people from seeing beyond their most immediate needs. The threat, however, lay not in their unbridled radicalism but in their blinkered conservatism, and Buchanan, a true revolutionary, always feared the dangerous tyranny of custom. Yet such individuals were basically well meaning, more concerned to avoid tyranny than to tyrannize – quite unlike the rapacious aristocrat or the corrupt king. In the end, a virtuous aristocracy might propose policy, but policy could only become law through public debate and the approbation of, quite literally, the *ekklesia*. All law needed to be self-imposed law in order to be legitimate.

We shall find broadly similar sentiments about the strengths of the 'multitude' (*moltitudine*) in Machiavelli's famous chapter of the *Discourses*. But, as Mason has noted, unlike Machiavelli, Buchanan had nothing to say about the 'balance' of the one, the few and the many. There is no legislator– poet–prophet to politicize the people, to bring them off their farms and into the *polis*, to institute 'one great city'.[29] None of this commonplace classical apparatus surfaces in the *Dialogus*. The consequences prove remarkably radical. At one point Buchanan briefly mentions Numa, the king who brought religion and civilization to Rome, as an example of the ideal prince. By being a mirror for citizens, an exemplar of civic virtue, a model of culture, Numa like any legitimate prince needed no power beyond his own righteous adherence to the law. Buchanan's discussion of Numa then elides into a discussion of Moses, and concludes that through a true prince – that is, through civic society – shines the image of God.[30] Neither force nor well-crafted oratory was required.

Machiavelli agreed, citing the maxim, 'The voice of the people is the voice of God'. Yet the contrast between the two thinkers is revealing. For Machiavelli, Numa became the ideal legislator because he instituted religion; that is, civil religion. To do so, he needed to fool people into thinking that he acquired his laws from a nymph. Moses, presumably with the 'true' law, faced a similar problem of persuasion.[31] Buchanan's society,

---

[29]   Niccolò Machiavelli, 'The Multitude are Wiser and More Constant than Princes', *Discourses*, 1.58. Buchanan, *De Iure Regni*, pp. li, lxi.

[30]   Ibid., pp. 75–7. Buchanan had made the same observation in the previous year with his *Genethliacon* celebrating the birth of the future James VI – where the link is again made with Numa (and, this time, with Solomon): Buchanan, *Political Poetry*, pp. 158–9 (ll. 64–77, esp. 76–7), and p. 318, n. 11.

[31]   Machiavelli, 'The Religion of the Romans', *Discourses*, 1.58, 1.11: 'Numa, finding a very savage people, and wishing to reduce them to civil obedience by the arts of peace, has recourse to religion as the most necessary and assured support for any civil society; and he established it upon such foundations that for many centuries there was nowhere more fear of the gods than in that republic ...', '... if the question were discussed whether Rome was more indebted to Romulus than to Numa, I believe the highest merit could be conceded to Numa' (Lerner edn, pp. 147, 263). Machiavelli's comments on Girolamo Savonarola have

however, required no legislator because of the divine reason in the minds of all men. Society becomes self-created, the work of the future citizens. Buchanan's thinking would manifest itself in his intellectual heirs, notably Hume of Godscroft, in 1603, at the creation of Britain. King James VI & I would prove a founding legislator according to Hume, only in the sense that he needed to give his 'nod'. Britain would be constructed by the prospective Britons themselves.[32] Hume did propose a constitution for patriot Britain whereby it might emerge as a society of citizens. But in so doing, it inherently attenuated the super-charged energies of the aristocratically led yet popularly mandated direct action that dominated Buchanan's thought and made it so resolutely republican.

Crucially for Buchanan and for Hume (as well as for Fabre and probably Machiavelli) society was at once civic *and* spiritual, political *and* soteriological. It will not do to describe Buchanan, in a way that is now all but commonplace, as essentially secular in his outlook. For such a bifurcation between secular and sacred, reflexive since the Enlightenment, simply did not obtain in Buchanan's mental world. Consequently, the distance separating him from his friend and associate, Andrew Melville, is not nearly as great as often imagined – and certainly no one would call Melville 'essentially secular'.

Buchanan and his Scottish Successors

Andrew Melville has received an exceedingly bad press since at least the 1970s from revisionist and Catholic historians, recently being dismissed as merely a bully and a thug. In fact, Melville was a great Scottish 'patriot', one of enormous stature to contemporaries, and an individual totally immersed in the Patriot Cause.[33] Poet, church moderator, and professor, Melville is in each respect the collaborator and successor to Buchanan.

---

traditionally been taken as ironic and cynical. Increasingly, they are now read as seriously intended.

[32]   McGinnis and Williamson, *The British Union*, pp. 39–40.

[33]   Jenny Wormald, 'Godly Reformer, Godless Monarch: John Knox and Mary Queen of Scots', in Roger A. Mason (ed.), *John Knox and the British Reformations* (Aldershot, 1998), p. 223. More subtle and yet no less egregious is Michael Lynch's dismissal of Scottish patriotic poetry in Latin and specifically Andrew Melville. Most recently, Lynch, 'Patronage, Propaganda, and Princely Power ... in the Personal Reign of James VI (1585–1603)', paper presented at the University of Reading, 2003. More serious assessments of Melville have only occurred recently. Among them are James Doelman, *King James I and the Religious Culture of England* (Cambridge, 2000), ch. 4; the editors introduction to Buchanan, *Political Poetry*, pp. 31–5; McGinnis and Williamson, *The British Union*, pp. 9–19; A.H. Williamson, 'Scotland: International Politics, International Press', in S.A. Baron *et al.* (eds), *Agent of Change: Print Culture Studies after Elizabeth L. Eisenstein* (Amherst, 2007), pp. 193–215.

His Latin poetry thrilled contemporaries and would continually find itself recycled into new contexts and new conflicts during the early seventeenth century. His longest surviving poem is the *Scotiae Topographia* (*c*.1604, though undoubtedly drafted earlier), a verse rendering of Buchanan's chorography of Scotland, in the first book of his history of the realm, the *Rerum Scoticarum Historia* (1582). Melville had seen the great history through the press during the final year of Buchanan's life. The *Topographia* forms part of the dense intellectual tissue at St Andrews in the 1590s that involved such major intellects as William Welwood, Robert and Timothy Pont, and, intellectually if not physically, John Napier of Merchiston. They comprised elements within a cultural flowering that Buchanan had predicted in the *Dialogus*, and that, he claimed, would result directly from the creation of a civic society. Civil religion, civilization, civic society comprised a single package and, especially following Buchanan, a commonplace of the Patriot Cause.[34]

Melville's state poetry – the *Stephaniskion* of 1590, celebrating the coronation of James's bride, Anne of Denmark; and the *Principis Scoti-Britannorum natalia* of 1594, celebrating the birth of Prince Henry – was of international stature. The latter formalized, if it did not invent, the phrase 'Scoto-Britannic' as a term for understanding the British future. At some point by the early 1590s Melville began a Scottish national epic, today known as the *Gathelus*, a poem roughly contemporaneous with and in some ways similar to Edmund Spenser's *Faerie Queene*. If Melville's poem exists today only in tiny Latin fragments, and Spenser's is one of the longest and greatest ever produced in the Anglophone world, the broadly parallel character of their projects remains unassailable.

Like Spenser, Melville offered an apocalyptic vision of the British future and, for Melville though not Spenser, of Scotland's central place within it. It is in this regard that Buchanan's friends and successors departed from the great scholar and poet. They would integrate Buchanan's humanist republicanism into a Judaic and eschatological framework. Where Buchanan rejected prophecy, his successors made it their organizing principle, the mechanism through which the Patriot Cause would become intelligible as the thrust of European history, the locus of human experience. Buchanan broke with the ferocious medieval anti-Judaism of his mentor John Mair and lived happily with New Christians and crypto-Jews. But he adopted the Iberian anti-Judaic vocabulary to attack the Iberians. His successors went further and created early modern philo-Semitism. Where

---

[34]   See Hume's two poems to Francis Walsingham, in A.H. Williamson, 'Education, Culture, and the Scottish Civic Tradition', in A.I. Macinnes and Williamson (eds), *Shaping the Stuart World, 1603–1714: The Atlantic Connection* (Leiden, 2006), pp. 33–54.

Buchanan inverted Iberian racial claims, his successors challenged 'blood' as a category.

Buchanan, again the professor of Greek, was intimate with Erasmus' edition of the New Testament (1516) and its historical methods outlined in the *Paraclesis* and the *Method of Study* (*Ratio seu Methodus*). Adopting these techniques, he so severely historicized the text as to limit (if not eliminate) its relevance to politics – and potentially altogether. When Buchanan claims that Paul's famous lines to the Romans about obeying superior powers addressed a context far different from today, he seems almost to paraphrase Erasmus' preface. We needed to visualize the circumstances: 'Would you like me to put a clear picture of this before your eyes? Imagine that one of our teachers was writing to Christians under the Turks'. Erasmus had developed this approach: 'If we are familiar with the country, we can in thought follow the history and picture it in our minds, so that we not only read it, but also see it'. Buchanan consequently insisted that, in order to understand Paul, we had 'to consider not only his words, but also when he wrote them, to whom, and why'. This was no less true of all the apostles, as Erasmus had pointed out: 'we [had to] know from the study of history not only the position of those nations ... to whom the Apostles wrote, but also their origins, manners, institutions, religion, and character':

> To get at the real meaning, it is not enough to take four or five isolated words; you must look where they came from, what was said, by whom it was said, to whom it was said, at what time, on what occasion, in what words, what preceded, what followed.[35]

Erasmus had intended to make the New Testament not only accurate, but also real, alive, relevant – to 'even the weakest woman'. Buchanan's agenda led elsewhere, for context could inform against itself. The techniques that made the text supremely relevant for Erasmus would make it supremely irrelevant for Buchanan.

If the New Testament became drastically marginalized, so too did the Old. The Hebrew commonwealth, especially before Saul, offered no guidance to other societies precisely because of its unique sacred character. The Jewish kings and judges had been appointed by God through a divinely instituted formula, unlike all other societies that were sustained through popular will. Because God ruled in Israel by establishing their rulers, when the ancient Jews eventually rejected these procedures, the Lord declared

---

[35]   Buchanan, *De Iure Regni*, pp. xlviii, 121; Desiderius Erasmus, *Paraclesis to the New Testament*, in P. Riesenberg *et al.* (eds), *The Traditions of the Western World* (Chicago, IL, 1967), pp. 300–301; F. Seebohm, *The Oxford Reformers* (3rd edn, London, 1887), pp. 329–31.

that they had thereby rejected Him. As all other governments derived their legitimacy from the governed and could be legitimately overthrown, the two forms of political authority were not only completely different, 'but precisely the opposite'. Mason is surely right when he comments that Buchanan's biblical exegesis 'was little short of devastating to the religious culture of sixteenth-century Europe'.[36] His spiritualized politics, nevertheless, precludes his being 'essentially secular'.

By marginalizing scripture, he subverted scriptural impediments to the right of revolution. He also aimed at much more. No less important, he thereby sought to foreclose the Iberian claim to be the heir to the Children of Israel in receiving the 'grace of election'.[37] Through his treatment of Scripture, he attacked the notion of the Habsburg super-state as being Daniel's fifth empire, the universal empire arising immediately prior to the eschaton. In contrast, Buchanan's successors totally re-evaluated the Hebrew commonwealth: rather than being irrelevant, it comprised a promise or sign of the authentic religion now being achieved.

Further, where Buchanan saw commerce as an imperial phenomenon that subverted civic life (and so human destiny), his successors accommodated commerce and even promoted it. At its most fundamental, where Buchanan struck at the eschatological–racial ideology undergirding the Habsburg global empire, his successors developed a counter-eschatology, a civic apocalypse. Buchanan's Graeco-Italian radicalism and anti-imperialism became encompassed within a Jewish vocabulary, a Hebraic perspective. In so doing, they sacralized his vision and cast it within a linear form.[38]

---

[36] A.H. Williamson, 'British Israel and Roman Britain: The Jews and Scottish Models of Polity from George Buchanan to Samuel Rutherford', in R.H. Popkin and G.M. Weiner (eds), *Jewish Christians and Christian Jews* (Dordrecht, 1994), pp. 98–9. If the laws and procedures of the Hebrew commonwealth were unique and exclusive to the Jewish polity, would that also extend to the laws of Moses, specifically the moral law? Were they too a local (if special) phenomenon, relevant only for the ancient Jews? Did morality, like politics, derive instead from some Stoically conceived universal nature? Buchanan's abiding hostility to legislators and orator lawgivers would lend credence to the idea. So, too, might his apparently happy sojourn in the world of New Christian and crypto-Jewish refugees who perforce felt deep ambivalence about all religious authority, whether Christian or Jewish. In that case Buchanan could perhaps anticipate the views of Isaac La Peyrère (*Prae-Adamitae* [1655]) and, more plausibly, Baruch Spinoza (*Tractatus Theologico-Politicus* [1670]). However, rather than La Peyrère's Calvinist millenarianism or Spinoza's post-Cartesianism, we might best seek Buchanan's extraordinary spiritual naturalism in Italian Neo-Platonism, along with his better-known classical Stoicism. His beautiful *Morning Hymn to Christ* links Christ to the sun in language that may look back to Marsilio Ficino and forward to the Leveller Richard Overton. See Buchanan, *Political Poetry*, pp. 164–7, also B. Rekkers, *Benito Arias Montano (1527–1598)* (London, 1972), pp. 101–4; Williamson, *Apocalypse Then*, ch. 7.

[37] Yosef Kaplan, 'Political Concepts in the World of the Portuguese Jews of Amsterdam', in Kaplan *et al.* (eds), *Menasseh ben Israel and his World* (Leiden, 1989), p. 53.

[38] Shifting circumstances – notably the emergence of an adult king – necessarily qualified the earlier republicanism. At the same time there occurred an increasing accommodation to

To be sure, the Reformation apocalyptic long penetrated deeply into Scottish religio-political culture. The rise of the papal Antichrist, seen as an historical institution rather than as the medieval atemporal individual, had become the great European narrative leading up to the present crisis in the 'latter days'. Here lay the intellectual bedrock of the Reformation. The Reformation's historical vision had become evident in Scotland by the late 1530s when the Earl of Glencairn denounced the Catholic clergy as 'monsters with Beast's marke'. In 1550 John Knox outlined the apocalyptic programme underlying human experience in what would be his most remembered sermon. By the 1560s it featured in the university curriculum. By the 1570s it had become a political commonplace within popular culture: 'the quhilk thai preve be the buke of pocalippis', comments one of the wives in the *Diallog of the Twa Wyfeis*. By the 1580s with the prospect of counter-revolution, Catholics had no choice but to confront the Protestant apocalyptic and try to deflect it. Ending the mass showed the real Antichrist: 'And sacrifice of the Altar eik [also] aboleist; / Thus is zour Antichrist by S. Johne descryuit.' Antichrist resided in Geneva, not Rome. By the 1590s Calvinist merchants in Edinburgh would have highly politicized readings of the apocalypse done as murals on the walls of their homes.[39] The Protestant apocalypse was hardly news. But a specifically Scoto-Britannic apocalypse – a British-focused apocalypse – was new and characteristic of the 1590s, and the work of 'patriots': most visibly Edmund Spenser, Thomas Brightman and Andrew Melville.

In Melville's reading, the sacred drama retold the story of the struggle of commonwealth against empire, citizen against subject, culture against barbarism, civil religion against clerical idolatry. Melville undertook to tell this story in his *Gathelus* epic, the modern world anchored poetically in a vast analogue to the Hebrew experience. Although Melville celebrated history and, we now know, intended to draw heavily on Buchanan's *Rerum Scoticarum Historia*, his medium needed to be poetry.[40] Only

---

commerce and trade as a source of power and rectitude in addition to more traditional forms of virtue. Buchanan himself had departed from his full-throttled radicalism of the 1560s in the *Rerum Scoticarum Historia* (1582). Yet the fundamental assumptions had not changed at all. For a different view, see Richard Tuck, *Philosophy and Government, 1572–1651* (Cambridge, 1993), pp. 203–4, 233–4.

[39]   Williamson, 'Scotland and the Rise of Civil Culture', pp. 7–8. Knox's apocalyptic preoccupations have been underscored by his later correspondence, recently discovered by Jane Dawson: 'Some Unpublished Letters from John Knox to Christopher Goodman', *Scottish Historical Review*, 84 (2005): pp. 166–201 at pp. 195, 199; The National Archives, SP 52/17/70, f. 289; Michael Bath, 'A Guise Palace in Edinburgh?' in Robert Gowing and Robyn Pender (eds), *All Manner of Murals: The History, Techniques and Conservation of Secular Wall Paintings* (London, 2007), pp. 11–21.

[40]   Andrew Melville, *Historiae vera laus* ('The True Praise of History'), in Buchanan, *Political Poetry*, pp. 282–3; Roger A. Mason, *Kingship and the Commonweal: Political*

poetry could capture these underlying, conflicting spirits that competed for the destiny of man. Only poetry looked beyond the vast particulars of human experience to the logic behind the course of events, not to immediate (often ambivalent) causes, but to the fundamental dynamic. Poetry, far more than the sixteenth-century practice of history, could look to the future with confidence.

Melville visualized Gathelus, the eponymous founder of the Gaels, as the gentile equivalent to Abraham. Gathelus' two sons, counterparts to Isaac and Ishmael, embodied two different characters, two contrasting streams springing from the same fountain. The elder Hiber, founder of the Iberian Gaels, was utterly ambitious and knew no restraint. He sought to conquer the world and reach to the high heavens themselves. The younger, Hemecus, founder of the British Gaels, knew moderation, ruled through shared governance, adhered to the laws and, not incidentally, preserved the wisdom of Egypt and the culture of Greece. These two 'streams' culminated in civic Britain and imperial Spain, locked in final conflict to determine the destiny of mankind. These, Melville argued, were humanity's great cultural choices, the very spine of the human experience. Most emphatically, Britain and Spain were not two competing empires, but utterly contrasting ideals. Britain struggled 'in company with' the other civic societies; it led a great confederation of 'free' states against universal empire.[41] The story is apocalyptic and the conflict eschatological because the issues are at once political *and* spiritual. At stake lay nothing less than the historical redemption. Salvation required the virtuous citizen who turned out to be simultaneously the illumined saint.

Buchanan's citizen, Hume's 'patriot' and Melville's historical trajectory would have a long history before them. In significant ways their heirs are Thomas Jefferson and Maximilien Robespierre. We can almost hear Melville's voice in Robespierre's famous *Report on the Principles of Political Morality* (5 February 1794):

> One could say that the two contrary spirits [*genii*] that have been depicting competing for control of the realm of nature, are fighting in this great epoch of human history to shape irrevocably the destiny of the world, and that France is the theatre of this mighty struggle.[42]

To be sure, Jefferson's departed deist God and Robespierre's remote 'supreme being' put them in a secular world quite removed from Melville's

---

Thought in Renaissance and Reformation Scotland (East Linton, 1998), p. 184.

[41]   Andrew Melville, *Natalia*, in Buchanan, *Political Poetry*, pp. 278–9 (ll. 56–7 et seq.); discussed in McGinnis and Williamson, *The British Union*, pp. 13–19.

[42]   Maximilien Robespierre, *Report on the Principles of Political Morality*, in K.M. Baker (ed.), *The Old Regime and the French Revolution* (Chicago, IL, 1987), p. 374.

universe of Calvinist contingency and divine providence. Yet they are at one in their understanding of civic virtue and 'political morality'. They are at one in seeing history as its story and struggle. They are at one in seeing themselves in a climactic moment, involving choices of the most fundamental sort. They are at one in the Patriot Cause.

The Judaic dimension of the Scottish civic tradition reached its apogee with Hume of Godscroft and the prospect of a British society after 1603. Hume would meld the Scottish lion rampant with the lion of Judah to create the latter-day British lion that would fulfil the promise of ancient Israel. What the Hebrews had hoped for, the British would realize. What Israel had seen in the distance, Britain would walk. The new Britain would certainly prove militant and aggressive, manifestly the work for Prince Henry, not King James.

> See how the lion rears up roaring,
> How he darts his fiery eyes till all acknowledge him,
> Until he has overcome all things. Tremble ye people![43]

Certainly fierce. Britain would lead the world. Conquests lay in the future. As Melville had put it just over a decade before, Prince Henry, 'dear to heaven and dear to his fellow citizens, under God', will rejoice 'to have buried the insolent spirit of empire in its tomb'.[44] Yet at the same moment Britain would also be 'mindful of treaties'. The realm would be part of a great Protestant confederation – 'for who by himself is sufficient?' (*Quis enim per se suffecerit?*)[45] Hume's line is a direct riposte to the famous (or infamous) Spanish motto of the 1580s, 'The world is not enough' (*Non Suffecit Orbis*).[46] We have here, quite palpably, the tradition of Buchanan and Melville.

These values would be realized with the democratic revolutions and underwrite central elements within modernity. With Buchanan these values have been assailed by reactionaries from Adam Blackwood to John

---

[43]   *Daphn-Amaryllis* (London, 1605), p. 12. 'Aspice, ut assurgat generosum pectus; et ora / Quantus hiet, vibretque oculus ferus, omnia donec / Edomuit. Treme gens'. Cf. McGinnis and Williamson, *The British Union*, pp. 164–5.

[44]   Melville, *Natalia*, pp. 280–81. Cf. Robespierre, 'Letter to his Constituents, no. 4' (February 1793).

[45]   *Daphn-Amaryllis*, p. 10.

[46]   See Geoffrey Parker, *The World is Not Enough: The Imperial Vision of Philip II of Spain* (Wako, TX, 2001); M. Tanner, *The Last Descendant of Aeneas: The Habsburgs and the Mythic Image of the Emperor* (New Haven, CT, 1993), esp. ch. 12; A.H. Williamson, 'An Empire to End Empire: The Dynamic of Early Modern British Expansion', *Huntington Library Quarterly*, 68 (2005): pp. 227–56.

Guy.[47] With Melville they have been dismissed, with Hume ignored. Such ideals and their progenitors lose historical interest when civic society itself loses persuasiveness. Public culture today is in serious decline. The Patriot Cause has become our cause.

[47] For the ferocious reaction to the *Dialogus*, long before its publication, see J.H. Burns, 'George Buchanan and the Anti-monarchomachs', in Roger A. Mason (ed.), *Scots and Britons: Scottish Political Thought and the Union of 1603* (Cambridge, 1994), pp. 139–58; John Guy, *Queen of Scots: The True Life of Mary Stuart* (Boston, MA, 2003).

PART TWO
Buchanan in Europe

Tyrants and Translations: Dutch Interpretations of George Buchanan's Political Thought

Astrid Stilma

The dominant image of George Buchanan today is probably that of the rather dour pedagogue who attempted to educate the young James VI by, as an ode composed for the 1906 Buchanan quatercentenary puts it, '[w]ith voice and hand correcting kingly pride'.[1] Although he was much more than a proponent of resistance theory, many sixteenth- and seventeenth-century readers, too, were interested in Buchanan's work primarily for its insistence on the limits of royal power, and nowhere was this more clearly the case than in the Netherlands. Not surprisingly, the Dutch found the writings of this celebrated scholar entirely relevant to their own Revolt against Spain: his was an authoritative voice – and an impeccably Protestant one at that – defending the removal of tyrants for the greater good of the commonwealth. In addition to a number of Latin editions of Buchanan's works printed in the Netherlands, two texts were also published in Dutch: a translation of his political treatise *De Iure Regni apud Scotos Dialogus* (1579) appeared in 1598 and was reprinted in 1610, and his early play *Baptistes* (written in the 1540s, but first printed in 1577) was published in a Dutch version in 1652. The focus of this essay will be on these two translations – both in their own way investigations of kingship, tyranny and resistance – as illustrations of the particular contexts in which Buchanan's ideas were interpreted in the Dutch Republic.

The introduction of Buchanan's work to the Netherlands can be traced back to his friend Daniel Rogers, whose close connections with the Leiden poets Janus Dousa and Jan van Hout enabled the latter to make Dutch translations, unfortunately now lost, of the *Franciscanus* and *De Sphaera* as early as the mid-1570s.[2] Buchanan's popularity quickly spread beyond the Leiden circle, however. Numerous Latin editions of his works

---

[1] *George Buchanan: Glasgow Quatercentenary Studies 1906* (Glasgow, 1907), p. xiv.

[2] This episode is discussed in J.A. van Dorsten, *Poets, Patrons, and Professors: An Outline of Some Literary Connexions between England and the University of Leiden, 1575–1586* (Leiden, 1962), pp. 42–4.

were printed in the Low Countries throughout the seventeenth century; particular favourites were the Psalm Paraphrases and the *Poemata Quae Extant*, a collection that includes most of Buchanan's poetry and drama.[3] Appreciation for Buchanan as a literary figure is also witnessed by the fact that he is mentioned in Dutch poetry anthologies, such as *The Netherdutch Helicon* (1610), as a contemporary poet worthy of comparison with the ancients.[4]

It is Buchanan's political writings, however, that attracted particular attention in the United Provinces. The two works that were translated into Dutch and thus became available to a wider and not exclusively learned readership, *De Iure Regni* and *Baptistes*,[5] both engage with political issues. The affinity between the two texts has often been pointed out; *Baptistes* has been called a 'dramatic counterpart' to, or even 'the poetical draft' of, *De Iure Regni*.[6] Of course, there are at least as many differences as there are similarities between the political message of the play and that of the treatise – in *Baptistes*, for instance, the emphasis is on John the Baptist's stoical acceptance of suffering and death in the face of tyranny, but the play does not address the issue of active resistance that becomes Buchanan's main concern in *De Iure Regni*. However, it is clear that the themes of the two texts are closely related. Both investigate the behaviour of a tyrant, contrasting it to that of a good king, and both consider the position of subjects faced with the dilemma of what to do when royal commands are incompatible with God's laws or one's own conscience. Buchanan himself employed both texts as part of his education of James VI, dedicating them in similar terms to his royal pupil as 'manuals of political guidance and instruction'.[7] By studying in *Baptistes* 'the torments of tyrants and their miseries when most they seem to flourish', James would learn what to

---

[3]   The *Poemata* includes *inter alia* the *Vita*, the Psalm Paraphrases, *Jephthes*, *Baptistes*, *Franciscanus*, *De Sphaera*, translations of Euripides' *Medea* and *Alcestis*, and miscellaneous poetry. Editions were printed in the Netherlands in 1621, 1628, 1641, 1665, 1676 and 1687. Separate editions of the Psalm Paraphrases appeared in 1590, 1597, 1603, 1609, 1618, 1621 and 1650; some of these also included the tragedies *Jephthes* and *Baptistes*, which in addition appeared together in a separate volume in 1600. Several editions of *Rerum Scoticarum Historia* appeared between 1643 and 1697, and finally Buchanan's *Opera Omnia* was printed in 1725.

[4]   *Den Nederduytschen Helicon* (Alkmaar, 1610), p. 72. Buchanan is ranked here as one of the great French poets, alongside, among others, Ronsard, du Bellay and du Bartas.

[5]   McFarlane, *Buchanan*, p. 204, mentions an additional Dutch translation of *Jephthes* by Jeremias de Decker, but the volume to which his note refers contains only De Decker's *Baptistes*, the two plays have probably been confused.

[6]   Buchanan, *Tragedies*, p. 13; P. Hume Brown, *George Buchanan: Humanist and Reformer* (Edinburgh, 1890), p. 124.

[7]   Roger A. Mason, '*Rex Stoicus*: George Buchanan, James VI and the Scottish Polity', in John Dwyer, Mason and Alexander Murdoch (eds), *New Perspectives on the Politics and Culture of Early Modern Scotland* (Edinburgh, 1982), pp. 9–33, at p. 11.

avoid; and, as Buchanan added in a cautious disclaimer, if 'the license of royal power' should ever overcome the king's 'right education', it would not be his teacher's fault.[8] *De Iure Regni* in turn was to make James aware of the extensive duties and limited rights of kings, as well as the dire consequences of failure: bad kingship might (and indeed should) result in the loss of the crown. Although the language of these dedications struck some of Buchanan's contemporaries as 'a little harsh', it was generally hoped that the effect of such stern admonitions would be to give Scotland 'a most Christian king'.[9] Buchanan recognized that his books were 'harsh and sometimes insolent critic[s]' to his pupil, but he considered this a necessary measure to counteract the ubiquitous flattery that royal courts inevitably attract.[10] However promising James might seem to be, he could be corrupted at any moment unless he was constantly reminded of the weight of his responsibilities as a king and his own weakness as a man.

Buchanan's preoccupation with the danger of kings turning into tyrants was shared by the Dutch. The issue of tyranny as opposed to good kingship had been a mainstay of Dutch political thinking and popular propaganda since the early stages of the Revolt against Spanish rule. Few people in the sixteenth century would have objected in principle to monarchy as a system of government, or have disputed the idea that rebellion against a good and lawful king equals rebellion against God. In cases of tyranny, however, one could appeal to resistance theories that held it a duty to protect the commonwealth by opposing and ultimately deposing the tyrant. In order to take action against the King of Spain without being universally condemned as rebels, it was therefore of paramount importance for the Dutch to show that Philip II could be considered tyrannical.

In order to strengthen the case against Spain, defences of the Revolt tend to assert that Philip's behaviour fits into both categories of tyranny: he is a tyrant by oppression as well as usurpation. Oppressors, the most common type of tyrant, are relatively easy to recognize: as King James later put it in his kingship manual *Basilikon Doron*, which despite some fundamental differences echoes a great deal of Buchanan's teaching, a good king will subject 'his owne private affections and appetites to the weale and standing of his Subjects', whereas a tyrant will 'frame the common-weale ever to advance his particular: building his suretie upon his peoples

---

[8]   In Steven Berkowitz (ed.), *A Critical Edition of George Buchanan's 'Baptistes' and of Its Anonymous Seventeenth-century Translation 'Tyrannicall-Government Anatomized'* (New York, 1992), p. 351.

[9]   Pierre l'Oyseleur de Villiers to Walsingham, *CSP Foreign, 1584*, no. 710, p. 577; Daniel Rogers to Buchanan, letter of February 1577, as quoted in Berkowitz, *Baptistes*, p. 46.

[10]   Buchanan, *De Iure Regni*, p. 3.

miserie'.[11] In Philip's case, the oppression manifested itself in extortion (by means of the infamous 'Tenth Penny' tax) and in encouraging the persecution of Dutch Protestants at the hands of the Spanish Inquisition. It was tyranny by usurpation, however, that constituted the main thrust of the Dutch case against Spain. Even originally legitimate rulers can become usurpers if they exceed their authority, and this is precisely what Philip was accused of doing. The King of Spain, the Dutch claimed, ruled over the Netherlands not as a divinely ordained monarch but under certain conditions determined by their ancient privileges; after all, Philip's authority over the Low Countries derived from his father's titles of count, duke and lord – and *not* king – over the various provinces. Philip, however, behaved as though he were a king in the Netherlands just as he was in Spain, and had thereby technically turned into a usurper. Some even claimed that Philip had deliberately oppressed the Dutch in order to provoke a rebellion and thus provide himself with an excuse to abolish the provinces' ancient liberties by force: a calculated use of both types of tyranny in a move towards achieving Spain's ultimate goal, world domination. Having been exposed as a tyrant by oppression as well as usurpation, Philip II could now legally be disposed of. Citing mainly French monarchomach tracts, the Dutch attempted to show that they had had no other choice but to terminate Philip's contract, so to speak, in defence of their rights and their lives. Their actions did not make them rebels: on the contrary, it was Philip who had been criminally irresponsible in abusing his power, whereas his subjects had acted within the law.[12] Buchanan's assertion in *De Iure Regni* that a king enters into a 'mutual pact' with his people, who grant him the right to rule and ultimately 'dictate to him the extent of his authority', chimed extremely well with this Dutch defence.[13] When the Dutch translation of *De Iure Regni* appeared, theories very similar to Buchanan's notion of contract-based kingship had already been assimilated into popular anti-Spanish propaganda and had quickly become widespread. It is no wonder that this treatise found an audience in the Netherlands: here

---

[11]   King James VI, *Basilikon Doron*, in Neil Rhodes, Jennifer Richards and Joseph Marshall (eds), *King James VI and I: Selected Writings* (Aldershot, 2003), pp. 218–19.

[12]   For a discussion of various treatises in justification of the Dutch Revolt, see Martin van Gelderen, *The Political Thought of the Dutch Revolt, 1555–1590* (Cambridge, 1992). Translations of the original texts can be found in Martin van Gelderen (ed.), *The Dutch Revolt* (Cambridge, 1993).

[13]   Buchanan, *De Iure Regni*, p. 55. The Dutch were arguably less radical in their thinking than Buchanan: Buchanan argued that *any* king is limited by a mutual pact with his people, whereas King Philip's claim on the Netherlands was recognizably limited under law. In addition, the Dutch appear to have been less convinced than Buchanan of the legality of single-handed tyrannicide. They tended to follow Huguenot theory in its emphasis on the importance of magistrates, confining the right of resistance to 'the people as a collectivity' (Van Gelderen, *Political Thought of the Dutch Revolt*, p. 271).

was an internationally admired scholar confirming a theory that formed the cornerstone of the Dutch effort to legitimate the Revolt.

Dutch interest in *De Iure Regni* started quite early. In August 1576, Daniel Rogers wrote to Buchanan that he had 'very eagerly read your dialogue *De jure Regni*, which is not irrelevant to the conditions of this time', and had given the manuscript 'to Dutch men of letters' who would 'print it if they were informed of your willingness'.[14] This early edition of *De Iure* never materialized, but the book was apparently considered important enough for a Dutch translation to be published in 1598.[15]

The translator of *De Iure Regni*, Ellert de Veer (1540–99), is most widely remembered today for a series of histories of Holland and Zeeland known as the 'Division Chronicles', which focus on the Revolt and predictably reveal a strong anti-Spanish bias. A similar lack of subtlety can be found in De Veer's treatment of *De Iure Regni*. The translation itself is faithful and straightforward, presenting the Dutch public with what is essentially Buchanan's text. The paratext of the translation, however, offers a revealing insight into De Veer's interpretation of the argument and his intentions in selecting this treatise for publication in Dutch. His title, for one thing, translates into English as:

> Dialogue of the right of kings or authorities over their subjects, and of the subjects' duty to them, by mutual bond. From which one may judge: if the further-united Netherlands have been rebels against the king, or the king a tyrant to them, who has thereby lost, according to the laws of God, nature and all peoples, all rights of high government he had over them, and they are once more restored to their old freedom.[16]

De Veer's translation, then, is advertised on its title page, not as a discussion of the rights of Scottish kings (*apud Scotos*), but as a general text about kingship and authority with a particular application to the Low Countries. There was apparently a market for such recontextualized translated material on resistance theory: a Dutch version of the famous Huguenot monarchomach tract *Vindiciae, Contra Tyrannos* (1579) was published

---

[14]   As quoted in Berkowitz, *Baptistes*, p. 30.

[15]   I have discussed this translation in a different context in 'Justifying War: Dutch Translations of Scottish Books around 1600', in Andrew Hiscock (ed.), *The Mistress-court of Mighty Europe* (Bern, 2007).

[16]   Ellert de Veer (ed. and trans.), *Tsamenspreeckinghe Vant recht der Coninghen ofte Ouerheyt ouer haer Onderdanen, ende der Onderdanen plicht tegens haer, deur onderlinge verbindinge. Daer wt men oordeelen mach: Oft de nader-vereenichde Nederlanden, Rebellen des Conincx zijn geweest, oft de Coninck een Tyran ouer haer, ende daer door na Gods, der natuyren, ende aller volckeren wetten, verloren heeft, alle t'Recht der hooger Ouerheyt, dat hy ouer haer gehadt heeft, ende sy wederom ghestelt zijn, in haer oude vrijheyt. door GEORGIVM BVCHANANVM* (Amsterdam, 1598).

in 1586 under the similarly explicit title *A short instruction by one who loves the well-being of these Netherlands, wherein it is clearly proven to all christians, good communities and patriots, that it is permitted to resist a king.*[17]

In addition to pointing out its general relevance to Dutch concerns, De Veer also linked *De Iure Regni* to specific current affairs. In the year his translation appeared, 1598, the Dutch were hotly debating whether or not to follow the example of France, which had recently made peace with Spain in the Treaty of Vervins. While pamphleteers in the Catholic south argued in favour of a peace treaty (an idea not entirely unwelcome to certain factions within the Dutch government), supporters of the military leader Maurits of Orange in the north retorted that negotiating with Spanish wolves would most likely result in being eaten.[18] De Veer's title page, supported by his introduction, places his Buchanan translation in the context of this propaganda battle.

The engraving on the title page of the Dutch *De Iure Regni* shows four main figures, two grouped together on the left and two on the right (see Fig. 5.1). In each case, one figure offers the other an olive branch while holding a sword in his other hand. To the left, 'Arragonius' accepts the olive branch, dropping his own sword and shield in the process. De Veer is referring here, as he explains in his dedicatory letter to the States General, to the invasion of Aragon in the early 1590s by Castilian troops in pursuit of the disgraced secretary of Philip II, Antonio Perez. This was a breach of Aragon's ancient laws (*fueros*), which according to De Veer corresponded almost exactly to the Dutch privileges that had been similarly violated by King Philip; in both cases, moreover, Philip had engineered a pretext in order to carry out a deliberate act of usurpation. The technical details of the comparison may not be entirely correct, but these are not De Veer's main concern. His aim is to establish a pattern: Castilians have a history of invading other people's territories and are therefore not to be trusted. To the right of the misguided Arragonius a similar scenario is played out, but with a different outcome. Here, a clerical figure holds a sword behind his back while proffering an olive branch to 'Batavus'. Batavus, however, brandishes his own sword and protects himself with the shield

---

[17]   *Cort onderwijs eens liefhebbers des welstandts deser Nederlanden, waerinne allen christenen goede ghemeenten ende patriotten claerlijck bewesen wort: dat het wel gheoorloft is tegen te staen een coning* (Amsterdam, 1586). On the argument of *Vindiciae, Contra Tyrannos*, see for instance Van Gelderen, *Political Thought of the Dutch Revolt*, pp. 270–71, and Andrew Hadfield, *Shakespeare and Republicanism* (Cambridge, 2005), pp. 31–4.

[18]   Some of these tracts were translated into English and deeply offended King James; their use of biblical passages to support resistance theory caused the king to remark caustically that the Dutch might have made their point without 'wrest[ing] the Scriptures' (*CSP Scot.*, XII, 315).

Figure 5.1   Title page of Ellert de Veer's Tsamenspreeckinghe vant Recht der Coninghen (1598), a Dutch translation of Buchanan's *De Iure Regni*. Courtesy of the University Library, Vrije Universiteit, Amsterdam.

of 'diffidentia', realizing that the cleric's offer of peace is no more than a ruse.[19] The difference between Batavus and Arragonius is underscored by the fact that the former is wearing armour and stands on a steady pillar while the latter, unprotected in doublet and hose, balances precariously on a ball.[20] In case any further clarification was needed, behind the main figures on the title page we see a smaller image of Delilah cutting Samson's hair, illustrating – as De Veer points out in his introduction – that any peace offer made by the Spaniards is unlikely to be more sincere than Delilah's caresses, and that Samson's fate should alert the Dutch to the fatal consequences of misplaced trust. The caption reinforces all this once more by stating that

> Suspicion is the strongest weapon against the tyrant.
> By being too trusting, many a man has been deceived.

Thus Buchanan's book, already relevant in itself, was made more topical and used as evidence both for the justice of the Dutch cause and the need to continue the war against Spain. The fact that De Veer's *De Iure Regni* was reprinted, with its original title page illustration and introduction, in the first year of the Twelve Years Truce (1610) indicates its continuing relevance for the war party supporting Maurits of Orange against the more irenic efforts of the main architect of the Truce, Land's Advocate Johan van Oldenbarneveldt.

The political application of the second Dutch Buchanan translation, that of *Baptistes*, is less straightforward. Written in the early 1540s when Buchanan worked at the Collège de Guyenne in Bordeaux, *Baptistes* investigates the actions of the tyrannical King Herod, the influence of bad counsellors such as Queen Herodias and Rabbi Malchus, and the passive resistance of the persecuted John the Baptist. The nature of tyranny and the influence of counsellors were familiar subjects in political tracts and in the advice-to-princes tradition, and as such *Baptistes* is undeniably a political text. The precise nature of its message, however, beyond a general condemnation of tyranny and an admiration for stoicism in the face of persecution, has remained a source of endless speculation. Although the play is essentially non-specific where religion is concerned, many readers

---

[19]   The sword and the olive branch are used in a very particular way in these pamphlets. Usually, the combination of the two (especially when applied to kings) indicates a preference for peace but an equally strong resolution to fight in a just cause. In the Dutch pamphlets, however, the image has become one of duplicity: offering peace while secretly intending war. A clerical figure concealing a sword regularly appears in anti-Spanish pamphlets.

[20]   Arragonius' unstable position links him visually to Fortune, who is often depicted balancing on a sphere, while Batavus' secure pillar may allude to the Pillar of Faith. I am grateful to Arthur Williamson for bringing this to my attention.

have interpreted *Baptistes* in a context of religious reform. Among them were, apparently, the Lisbon Inquisitors against whose charges Buchanan had to defend himself in 1550. He did so by claiming that the tyrant in his play was not intended as a figure of the Catholic church but of Henry VIII: 'so far as the likeness of the material would permit' he had represented 'the death and accusation of Thomas More and set before the eyes an image of the tyranny of that time'.[21] This assertion may not have been much more than a convenient story to tell the Inquisition, but it is true that there are few (if any) concrete markers of Catholicism and Protestantism in the play and that its tyrannical characters could be taken to represent many kinds of oppression and corruption.[22] Nevertheless, *Baptistes* appears somehow to invite attempts at identifying allusions to historical figures and events: it has variously been interpreted in the context of Scottish, French and English politics either at the time of its composition (the 1540s) or its publication (the 1570s), and topical identifications of its characters have been suggested in later contexts as well.[23] In an English translation of the play that appeared in 1643 under the title *Tyrannicall-Government Anatomized*, for instance, it would not take a great stretch of the imagination to identify Herod as King Charles, Herodias as Henrietta Maria, and Malchus as Archbishop Laud. Of course, topical allusions in early modern texts are notoriously difficult to prove or disprove; if the various interpretations of *Baptistes* tell us anything about Buchanan's intentions it must be that the play was clearly meant to provoke political debate while leaving it up to the audience to fill in the details.

Considering the persistence with which Buchanan's readers across the centuries have linked the characters in his play to contemporary political figures, it is more than likely that his Dutch readership, too, responded to *Baptistes* in such a way. Unfortunately, the 1652 translation of the play – unlike De Veer's *De Iure Regni* – has no explicit paratext to indicate what the translator's interpretation of its political message may have been. The context in which it appeared, however, does provide some evidence as to his position in the renewed debate about tyranny and resistance that erupted after the execution of King Charles I.

---

[21]   From Buchanan's 'First Defence' before the Lisbon Inquisition, as quoted in James M. Aitken, *The Trial of George Buchanan before the Lisbon Inquisition* (Edinburgh, 1939), p. 25.

[22]   In general, Buchanan's ideas about resistance are not in themselves particularly 'Protestant'; it has been pointed out, for instance, that an argument similar to Buchanan's was put forward by the Spanish Jesuit Mariana in his *De Rege et Regis Institutione* (1599). See *Quatercentenary*, p. 282.

[23]   Various identifications of the characters, usually including Buchanan's adversary Cardinal Beaton in the role of the villainous Malchus, are discussed by the editors of Buchanan, *Tragedies*, pp. 10–13, and in Aitken, *Trial of George Buchanan*, pp. 128–35.

The Dutch translation of *Baptistes*, like the original, is a work of literature rather than a tract and offers few concrete clues as to the precise political intentions of its author. The translator, Jeremias de Decker (1609–66), was an Amsterdam merchant and a major poet who frequently and competently translated classical poetry and neo-Latin works by staunchly Protestant authors such as Buchanan, Beza and Scaliger. He tended to be attracted to biblical materials, producing, for instance, metrical versions of some of the Psalms of David and parts of the Lamentations of Jeremiah, as well as a long poem on the Passion of Christ. It is hardly surprising, then, that De Decker chose to translate Buchanan's *Baptistes*: both text and author were generally admired and fit neatly into the pattern of his literary interests.[24] In addition, there was a vogue in the Netherlands for art and literature based on biblical episodes, and the story of the Baptist was a particularly popular one. Some authors, including the most widely known Dutch poet and playwright of the seventeenth century, Joost van den Vondel, based the majority of their plays on biblical material. Vondel's work, for instance, includes a play about the episode that also formed the basis of Buchanan's *Jephthes*, and a long narrative poem (though not a play) about the Baptist: *Joannes de Boetgezant* (1662). Clearly Buchanan's *Baptistes* drew on popular subject matter. The dramatic appeal of the story is obvious, especially if – like many German medieval versions – one showed the dancing of Salomé and the decapitation of the Baptist on stage. What may have been an additional attraction in Protestant areas was the tradition of using the Baptist's tribulations to criticize Catholic authorities. In Heinrich Bullinger's *Tragedies of Tyrantes Exercised upon the Church of God* (1575), for example, John is treated as a proto-Calvinist martyr who was murdered for his exemplary faith.[25] De Decker may well have seen the story in this light. Although, as we shall see, the Dutch translation of *Baptistes* is not particularly propagandistic, the translator did share with his 'predecessor' Ellert de Veer a hatred of all things Spanish and Catholic; in De Decker's case, this has been attributed to the influence of his father, a refugee from Antwerp who had fought at the Siege of Ostend in 1604.[26]

De Decker's translation, however, does not reveal much about his religio-political beliefs. He did leave his mark on the text in the form of a number of deviations from the original, but on the whole these affect the literary aspects of the play more than its politics. It is especially in the final two acts that the translator significantly rearranged Buchanan's material,

---

[24]   The fact that the play was translated into French and German, too, is testament to its international popularity. See Berkowitz, *Baptistes*, pp. 269–70.

[25]   Henry Bullinger, *The Tragedies of Tyrantes. Excercised vpon the church of God* (London, 1575), fols 25r ff.

[26]   See e.g. J. Karsemeijer, *De dichter Jeremias de Decker* ([Haarlem], 1934), p. 48.

changing the order of speeches and even adding some scenes of his own.[27] These alterations mainly serve to clarify the development of the plot and to flesh out some of the characters, most notably Queen Herodias, who becomes much more directly involved in the tragedy. De Decker shows her plotting on stage with John's opponent, Rabbi Malchus, in an additional scene, and brings her back towards the end of the play to react with an almost cannibalistic enthusiasm to the sight of her daughter carrying the head of the Baptist on a platter – one of the more sensational elements of the traditional Baptist story that Buchanan had pointedly left off stage.[28] The deliberate evil of De Decker's manipulative Queen fits in well with the contemporary idea that tyrants were somehow 'feminized' in their lack of self-control and their tendency to 'shift shapes' while following their own selfish desires, and it has been suggested that the portrayal of Herodias' power over Herod in sixteenth-century drama was generally influenced by a dislike of female rule.[29] Mainly, though, the expansion of the role of Herodias adds to the dramatic plot.

There are, however, also certain political overtones to De Decker's version of the play. Of course, the original *Baptistes* deals with political issues already, and even in an entirely neutral translation certain passages would stand out naturally for their relevance to the Dutch Republic. The most obvious issue in this respect (and one of the main themes of the play) is the definition of good kingship as opposed to tyranny. Ironically, definitions of good kingship are offered throughout by Herod, who regularly lectures on the desired behaviour of kings and in the process keeps insisting on the legitimacy of his own rule – a prudent strategy, since his rise to power with the aid of Rome could easily be interpreted as usurpation. Even if his authority in itself is seen as legitimate, however, Herod is eventually persuaded by the *realpolitik* of Malchus, the Queen and her daughter into becoming a tyrant by oppression. He is all the more culpable for knowing what good kingship entails and then choosing to act otherwise; presumably this was the dire warning Buchanan had in mind for King James. Another character who frequently addresses the theme of tyranny and especially the limits of royal power is John the Baptist. His speeches are reminiscent at times of pamphlet defences of the Dutch Revolt; for example, when he asserts that his scorn is directed against

---

[27]   See ibid., pp. 114–17, for a scene-by-scene breakdown of the differences between original and translation.

[28]   It has been suggested that this 'taste for the sensational' in De Decker's play could be the result of 'the vivid portrayals' of the Baptist's head on a platter in seventeenth-century Dutch paintings (Berkowitz, *Baptistes*, pp. 272–3).

[29]   See Rebecca W. Bushnell, *Tragedies of Tyrants: Political Thought and Theater in the English Renaissance* (Ithaca, NY, 1990), pp. 9, 109–10, and Tricia McElroy's Chapter 2 above.

royal abuses rather than against kings in general, and when he remarks
that although Herod has

> ... the power to force others,
> God the King of all things
> Has that right over [Herod] and all kings.[30]

It is particularly in the telling differentiation between the king's *power* to
command others and God's *right* to do so that the text seems to echo a
point often made in Dutch defences of their 'rebellion' as an instrument of
divine retribution.

In addition to the political significances already there in Buchanan's
text, some of De Decker's changes to the original can also be seen as overtly
political. One example of this is the expansion of the role of Gamaliel, the
moderate rabbi who tries to defend the Baptist. Whereas in Buchanan's
version he disappears after the third act, in the Dutch translation Gamaliel
remains throughout as a voice of reason within the church. He overhears
the plotting between the Queen and Malchus and is given two additional
scenes in which he laments the wickedness of the times. In addition to
offering properly sober Calvinist comments on Herod's drinking and
Salomé's dancing – such wanton pastimes are, after all, bound to result
in tragedy – Gamaliel also emphasizes certain religio-political aspects of
the story. First of all, he is particularly preoccupied with ecclesiastical
corruption: De Decker makes him exclaim against 'the hunger of the
Church', which 'sucks from the teat' the profit for which others have to
sweat (p. 9). Furthermore, the rabbi warns against the dangers of mixing
religious authority with secular power, as the worst kind of tyranny ensues
when 'priestly envy' is coupled with 'courtly hate' (p. 40). Such remarks
could easily be taken as slurs on the Roman Catholic church, especially
considering the portrayal of Rabbi Malchus in the rest of the play. Malchus
and the corrupt religious authorities that he represents are more clearly
associated with Catholicism in the Dutch text than they are in the original.
For instance, when Malchus repeatedly refers to John as a 'heretic', who
by preaching against the 'yoke of foreign rule' is taunting 'Romish force
of arms' (p. 19), the accumulation of loaded terms suggests that it is not
merely *classical* Rome that is being referred to here.

In addition to such anti-Catholic tendencies, the Dutch text also refers
noticably more often than Buchanan does to concepts related to monarchy.
Buchanan's Chorus, for example, at one point describes heaven as a place

---

30   Jeremias de Decker, *Baptistes of Dooper, Treurspel*, in *J. de Deckers Gedichten*
(Amsterdam, 1656), p. 22. My translation.

of peace that has never been tainted by war or corruption. De Decker adds to this that in heaven,

No foolish king for the sake of a silly sceptre
Draws his sword, mad and drunk with desire for power;
Nor scatters peoples like worthless chaff
In order to strut around ridiculously with a crown;
Nor uses the sweat and the extorted blood
Of the poor kneeling before him
To feed splendour, idleness or wicked lusts;
Nor for the price of unknown souls
(O vanity!) buys famous titles,
Mere titles and shadows of thrones. (p. 54)

This description, of course, alludes to the traditional attributes of a tyrant, but it is provoked by the word 'king'; the passage could be taken to imply that monarchy in general is perilously close to tyranny and that there is something inherently 'silly' or 'ridiculous' about sceptres and crowns.[31] The theme of crowns then returns in the dying words of the Baptist, who is reported as saying that Herod may take his head, but one day God will make the king pay for this with his crown (p. 56). This brings us back to the notion of contract-based kingship: kings ignore God's will at their peril and may lose their power as a result. In short, in what seems almost a knee-jerk reaction, the rhetoric of the early Revolt still comes pouring out as late as 1652 at the mention of monarchs such as Herod who fail to recognize that there are limits to their authority. Such ideas were clearly deeply ingrained in De Decker's thinking.

It would be easy, therefore, to detect a republican – or at least somehow anti-monarchical – bias in the Dutch *Baptistes*, even if its author did not reveal his intentions as explicitly as Ellert de Veer had done half a century earlier. However, we should be careful when assigning specific political significances, let alone topical interpretations, to De Decker's translation. Had this text been written in England in the early 1650s, it could easily be identified as sympathetic to the parliamentarian cause, as was the English translation of the play published as *Tyrannicall-Government Anatomized* in 1642/3. We certainly cannot exclude the possibility that this is indeed how De Decker's play was received by some Dutch readers at the time – as we have seen, the republican sentiments in the text would justify such a

---

[31] The fact that the phrase 'to strut around ridiculously with a crown' ('Om met een' kroon belachelijck te proncken') could also support the translation 'to strut around with a ridiculous crown' adds to this subversiveness by locating the absurdity in the crown (and thus, by extension, in the institution of monarchy itself) rather than in the particular individual who wears it.

reading. However, external evidence suggests that it would be a mistake to consider De Decker hostile to monarchical rule on principle.

The example of De Decker illustrates the risk of over-simplification involved in guessing at seventeenth-century Dutch attitudes to resistance. Although the theme of tyrants and their victims runs through his work, the division of these roles is not as 'republican' as one might expect. In the following passage, for instance, De Decker compares two characters: one 'threatens, roars and raves', while the other

> ... stands firm and unmoved,
> Laments the state of his country, smiles at [the other's] rage,
> And approaches death quietly and courageously.
> He lifts up his eyes and prayers to heaven,
> As though he longed
> To step out of an earthly palace into a heavenly one.

This could easily be a confrontation between Malchus (or a proverbial roaring Herod) and John the Baptist. It is, however, a passage from a poem by De Decker, printed in the same collection as his *Baptistes* translation, and the patient saint it describes is King Charles I facing his executioners. The poet's attitude to the regicide here is one of unambigous condemnation:

> Did you have to dig your claws into that anointed one,
> And stain your mad [or blunt] axe with that holy blood?
> You hack down the great pillar of your state,
> And even dare to cover such dirty stains
> With the pretence of zeal in God's honour[.]

After a lengthy description of the English as barbarous patricides, De Decker concludes by warning the murderers they will not profit from their godless deed for long, because '[t]hose who raise their hand against Kings' never die quietly in their beds.[32]

These are not exactly the sentiments one might expect from the pen of a Dutch translator of Buchanan, especially when comparing them to De Veer's use of *De Iure Regni* in 1598. However, although their methods were different, De Decker and De Veer did essentially set out to do the same thing: they were both participating in propaganda campaigns on behalf of the House of Orange. De Veer, as we have seen, supported Maurits in continuing and intensifying the war effort after the Franco-Spanish peace of Vervins. When De Decker was writing, another

---

32   Jeremias de Decker, 'Klagte Over de dood des Konings van Groot Britaengien, Uytgestort tegens de Koningslachters', in *J. de Deckers Gedichten*, pp. 144–7. My translation.

propaganda campaign associated with the House of Orange was being mounted, and it demanded a rather different approach to the issue of resistance.

The execution of Charles I met with a mixed response in the Netherlands. Stadholder William II, who was married to Charles's daughter Mary, did his best to help his Stuart in-laws by orchestrating inflammatory condemnations of the regicide (to which De Decker's poem contributed), while on the other hand the States General were torn between their wish not to offend the new Calvinist government in England and their need to acknowledge the loyalty most Dutch people felt for the House of Orange.[33] In fact, the Stadholder's decision to support the Stuarts became inextricably entangled with Dutch domestic politics. The House of Orange had been trying for some time to formalize its *de facto* powers, an ambition perceived as worryingly 'monarchical' by the more republican-minded cities.[34] The States and the cities were naturally irritated by the stadholders' occasional high-handedness, but the underlying issue was presented as one of principle. In a political climate in which kingship and tyranny had come very close to meaning the same thing, any hint of royal aspirations in the House of Orange tended to provoke loud protests to the effect that the Netherlands had not rid themselves of one form of tyranny to replace it with another. Despite such attempts to associate the Princes with tyranny, however, public opinion tended to be firmly on the side of the House of Orange, particularly because it provided military leaders who promised a strong emphasis on national security.[35] After the official end of the war with Spain in 1648, when doubts were expressed as to the Dutch Republic's ability to survive as a unified whole in the absence of an external enemy, the stadholders tried to capitalize on people's fears by pointing out that only the House of Orange could provide a leader strong enough to

---

[33]   For a detailed discussion of such propagandistic texts in the early 1650s, see Paul R. Sellin, 'Royalist Propaganda and Dutch Poets on the Execution of Charles I: Notes Towards and Inquiry', *Dutch Crossing: A Journal of Low Countries Studies*, 24/2 (2000): pp. 241–64. See also Willem Frijhoff and Marijke Spies, *1650: Bevochten eendracht* (Den Haag, 1999), pp. 72–3. Frijhoff and Spies mention at least 214 Dutch pamphlets on the regicide appearing in 1649. For a detailed discussion of the relationship between the stadholders and the Stuarts, see Pieter Geyl, *Orange and Stuart: 1641–1672*, trans. Arnold Pomerans ([1939]; London, 2001).

[34]   See e.g. Frijhoff and Spies, *Bevochten eendracht*, pp. 98 ff.

[35]   When with the Act of Seclusion in 1654 the Oranges were banned from the stadholdership of Holland, the States reaped little profit from this victory over the stadholders; as the States had been pressured into the Act by Cromwell during the peace negotiations, public opinion considered it an example of spinelessly giving in to the enemy, and Orange became even more strongly associated with patriotism. See Geyl, *Orange and Stuart*, pp. 116ff.

maintain cohesion in a country racked by internal (religious) differences.[36] Supporting the Orange party was once again presented, as it so often had been in the past, as an act of patriotism: to be a patriot for De Veer in the 1590s meant using Buchanan's resistance theory to encourage Maurits's military campaign against the King of Spain, while for De Decker in the 1650s it meant demonizing the English regicides in order to support the Stadholder's Stuart relatives, even if their ideas about authority did not exactly sit well with what might be termed the spirit of the Dutch Republic.

Even without the efforts of Orange, however, by the 1650s there was little enthusiasm in the Netherlands for revolutionary republicanism, whatever the English parliamentarians may have hoped for. Apart from the fact that political upheaval was not good for trade, the Dutch did not feel any 'natural sympathy' for regicides. The United Provinces may have had a reputation for being averse to monarchical rule, but in reality the Revolt had been born out of practical circumstances rather than republican ideology. Furthermore, the Dutch had tried to legitimate their actions by emphasizing that their Revolt was conducted 'properly': although they had been forced into taking up arms in their own defence, they had never resorted to physical violence against the person of the king. Renouncing one's allegiance to one's feudal overlord was one thing; trying and executing one's anointed king was quite another. In addition, the Dutch population had had a vested interest in declaring Philip II a tyrant. They were far less eager to do the same for Charles, whose tyranny – if it was that – had not affected them directly. Removing any doubt as to a king's descent into tyranny was, of course, all-important; as Buchanan points out in De Iure Regni, the 'common people ... approve of the murder of tyrants but are concerned at the misfortunes of kings'.[37]

The lack of enthusiasm in the Netherlands for labelling Charles a tyrant was not only connected to the family bond between the Stuarts and the stadholders but also to the mounting tensions between England and the United Provinces that led to the outbreak of the first Anglo-Dutch war in 1652. It is in the context of this war that De Decker wrote his pro-Stuart verses. In the early 1650s, the foreign enemy against whom all Dutch patriots were called upon to unite was no longer Spain but England – Republican England, to be precise. As hostilities between the two countries escalated into open war, public support for the Orange war party – and, by extension, the Stuarts – grew, and once again De Decker made a poetic contribution to the debate.[38] In addition to the poem about

---

[36] See e.g. ibid., p. 78.
[37] Buchanan, De Iure Regni, p. 13.
[38] See e.g. Frijhoff and Spies, Bevochten eendracht, p. 131.

Charles quoted above, the volume in which the translation of *Baptistes* appeared also contains several patriotic works about the war, describing the English as tigers and wolves and effectively transposing onto them the accusations of exceptional cruelty that earlier pamphleteers had levelled against the Spanish. The regicide plays an important part in this process of demonization. In De Decker's poem *Encouragement by the Free Netherlands to their naval heroes*, for instance, the personified Netherlands argue that the English Civil War has produced a nation of monsters rather than a 'Free State and an Honourable Parliament':

> And, Sons, see how narrow a channel of water
> Divides your Mother from these furious Pests,
> These enemies of the human race,
> Who just recently robbed their lawful rulers
> The father and his lawful son,
> O horror! so cruelly,
> One of his head, the other of his crown.

Drunk with looting their own country, the poem continues, these pirates now turn their attention to their neighbours:

> Yea, with their mouths and never-satisfied claws
> Still dripping, still damp with patricide
> They greedily attack my rich ships,
> My hard-earned and honest profits;
> Although I have never interfered with what is theirs,
> But have always behaved as Britain's friend.

After some detailed gloating about various naval victories over the English, the speaker finally describes the Dutch as the rod in the hand of God, expressing the hope that one day they will 'wrest the oppressed Britannia from the hand of the cruel thief'.[39] In short, it is the parliamentarian regime that has now resorted to both types of tyranny by oppressing its own people and attempting to usurp its neighbours. The rhetoric is clearly similar to that employed by De Veer and the anti-Vervins pamphleteers in 1598, and so is De Decker's goal of supporting the House of Orange's military efforts while 'weaker' civil authorities would prefer to sue for peace. The only substantial difference is that De Veer used resistance theory to agitate against the King of Spain, whereas De Decker's interests required him to condemn regicide in the strongest

---

[39] 'Eer-spore Of moedigende Aenspraecke van 't Vrye Nederland aen sijne Zee-Helden', in *J. de Deckers Gedichten*, pp. 128–33. My translation.

possible terms, which inevitably meant downplaying the people's right
to resist. It would go too far to suggest that De Decker's translation of
Baptistes was a factor in the pro-Stuart propaganda campaign of the
early 1650s; the text does not provide us with sufficient evidence to
make any claims as to an intended topical interpretation. However, a
'parliamentarian' reading of the translation, although possible on the
basis of its contents, becomes problematic in view of the political climate
in which De Decker was working. After all, his translation was prepared
for the press at the same time as his poems in condemnation of regicide
in general and its recent occurrence in England in particular. It is highly
unlikely, therefore, that De Decker himself saw *Baptistes* as in any way
supportive of the English regicides, despite any 'republican' sentiments
in the text itself.

In conclusion, it is clear that Buchanan's writings were of great
interest to the Dutch, partly due to their author's reputation as a scholar,
poet and reformer, but mainly because of their applicability: Buchanan's
preoccupation with the subject of tyranny meant that his work was bound
to strike a chord in the Netherlands. Thus, *De Iure Regni* was used after
the Peace of Vervins in 1598 and again at the beginning of the Twelve
Years Truce to illustrate the argument that the Dutch Revolt was not
only justified but necessary, since trusting the King of Spain would spell
disaster for the commonwealth. *Baptistes* is a more general investigation
of stoicism in the face of persecution, and its translator provides little
guidance as to any particular interpretation of the story. Given the
reception history of *Baptistes*, however, there can be little doubt that
his readers drew their own conclusions. There are enough indications
of republicanism, or at the very least a wariness of kings, in the Dutch
translation of *Baptistes* to justify reading it as an expression of republican
feeling. This, however, was almost certainly not De Decker's intention,
considering the sympathy for Charles he expressed elsewhere and his
deliberate application of the label of tyranny to the English Parliament.
Whereas De Veer's interpretation of *De Iure Regni* belongs in many ways
to a simpler age in which it made sense to cast kings as natural tyrants
and their subjects as innocent victims, De Decker's *Baptistes* appeared at
a time when the United Provinces were forced to confront the confusing
and no doubt rather uncomfortable fact that it was now in the national
interest to discredit another republican regime. De Decker's translation
leaves its readers with several options. Herod could be considered a
typical example of a tyrannical king in the style of Philip II or, perhaps,
Charles I, oppressing his godly subjects as personified by John the Baptist.
On the other hand, Dutch readers may also have found that Charles I,
like John the Baptist, had been wrongfully beheaded, while those who
had executed him were, like Herod, adamant but not entirely persuasive

in their attempts to justify their actions. In the end, it is the fate of all texts to be interpreted, as the dramatist George Chapman put it, to 'the intendment of the Reader', and this is clearly true of Buchanan's political writings.[40] Tyranny, it appears, is in the eye of the beholder.

---

[40] George Chapman, *A Free and Offenceles Ivstification, of Andromeda Liberata* (London, 1614).

CHAPTER 6

Buchanan and the German Monarchomachs

Robert von Friedeburg

The term 'monarchomach' was coined by William Barclay in his *De Regno et Regali Potestate adversus Buchananum, Brutum, Boucherium et Reliquos Monarchomachos Libri Sex* (Paris, 1600). Given the deposition of Mary Queen of Scots (1567), the assassinations of William of Orange (1584), Henry III (1589) and Henry IV (1610), and the various plots against Elizabeth and James VI & I, it is perhaps not surprising that some contemporaries, including King James himself, genuinely believed in a conspiracy of king-killers. However, not only James, infamous for his alleged lack of courage, but also the English divine David Owen and the German neo-Aristotelian Henning Arnisaeus agreed with him in condemning monarchomach conspiracies.[1] And so too did other treatises as late as 1639.[2] A decade later, moreover, the execution of Charles I was followed by a wave of treatises condemning and defending the regicide, most prominent being the controversy between John Milton and the Dutch scholar, Claudius Salmasius. Those condemning the regicide also referred to a conspiracy of king-killers: for example, Peter Gartz (*Puritanischer Glaubens- und Regimentsspiegel*, 1650) and Caspar Ziegler (*Circa regicidum Anglorum*, 1652).

Most think primarily of Buchanan, 'Brutus', or the anonymous authors of the *Vindiciae contra Tyrannos*, Beza and Boucher, as monarchomachs.[3] But by 1614, Eberhard von Weyhe had added Guillaume Rossaeus

---

[1]   Henning Arnisaeus, *De autoritate principum in populum semper inviolabili* (Frankfurt, 1612).

[2]   Eberhard von Weyhe, *Verisimilia thelogica, iuridica ac politica: de regni subsidiis ac oneribus subditorum; Libro I. Samuelis cap. VIII traditis: per Philippum Melanthonem proposita: repetita & defensa discursim, contra Bartolum, Bodinum Rossaeum, Brutum, Zepperum et alios* (Frankfurt, 1606); Georg Lindenspirus, *De arcanis monarchici contra monarchomachos* (Ingolstadt, 1639).

[3]   These names became famous not least because they were mentioned in the titles of the polemical tracts directed against them, such as William Barclay's *De Regno et Regale Potestate*.

(perhaps William Reynolds[4]) and Juan Mariana to the list. By 1620 David Owen had included the German reformed theologian David Pareus, and already in 1612 Henning Arnisaeus had included Johannes Althusius. Indeed, Beza had published his *Droit des Magistrats* in 1574 disguised as a pamphlet from the German town of Magdeburg that had resisted the execution of the Imperial Interim in 1549–51, and that had been made famous by the historical works of Johannes Sleidan. The Magdeburg Confession argued that it was the duty of all magistrates, including inferior magistrates, to defend the true faith, even against their own superior authorities.[5]

With the exception of Johannes Althusius, neither the Magdeburg Ministers nor most of the German authors listed in 2001 by Horst Dreitzel as 'German Monarchomachs', ever gained as much fame in Europe as the above-named authors.[6] Dreitzel listed around a dozen German authors under this term, and one might add a few more.[7] Among them were Lutheran legal scholars such as Friedrich Pruckmann, Heinrich Bruning, Valentin Forster, Bartholomaeus Volcmar, and Jakob Multz; Lutheran theologians like Johann Gerhard and Jacob Fabricius; reformed theologians like David Pareus; Lutheran authors of *politica* – systematic analyses of the nature of society and government – like Reinhard Koenig and Christian Liebenthal, and reformed writers in the same genre like Hermann Kirchner and Althusius. The date of their publications ranges from Mathias Cuno's *De Pactis Liber* of 1590 to Reinhold Condit's *Repraesentatio Majestatis* of 1690. Liebenthal's *Politica* of 1619 was reprinted in 1652 in Amsterdam and again in 1677. However, the later 1590s and the first three decades of the seventeenth century was the major period for the publication of these tracts, as it was for *politica* more generally. Indeed, it was precisely in these decades that German public constitutional law became a genre of its own (*Reichspublizistik*). The reception of Bodin and the exceptional legal, political and religious strife of these years, led to a significant increase in the number of legal and political treatises about the nature of power relations

---

[4]   The identity of the author remains disputed: see Eckehard Quin, *Personenrechte und Widerstandsrecht in der katholischen Widerstandslehre Frankreichs und Spaniens um 1600* (Berlin, 1999), pp. 145–6.

[5]   Robert von Friedeburg, 'Confusion around the Magdeburg Confession and the Making of Revolutionary Early Modern Resistance Theory', *Archiv für Reformationsgeschichte*, 97 (2006): pp. 307–18.

[6]   Horst Dreitzel, 'Politische Philosophie', in *Grundriss der Geschichte der Philosophie. Die Philosophie des 17. Jahrhunderts. Vol. 4: Das Heilige Römische Reich deutscher Nation. Nord- und Ostmitteleuropa*, ed. Helmut Holzey and Wilhelm Schmidt Biggemann (Basel, 2001), pp. 609–866.

[7]   Jacob Fabricius, *Einundreissig Kriegsfragen* (Stettin, 1631), for example, on whom see Robert von Friedeburg, *Widerstandsrecht und Konfessionskonflikt. Notwehr und Gemeiner Mann im deutsch-britischen Vergleich 1530–1669* (Berlin, 1999), pp. 90–97.

in the empire, to the emancipation of German public law from Roman law, a process mainly completed by the 1660s, and to the emergence of the genre of the *politica* itself.

Several main lines of argument are distinguishable in the hundreds of major works published during this development. Dreitzel's recent overview gives *circa* 70 for the 'monarchomachs', 250 for the neo-Aristotelians, 100 treatises written by Lutheran, Reformed and Catholic clerics, and yet another 100 on reason of state and Tacitism.[8] My own inclusion of someone in the monarchomach group is based on two overlapping criteria. First, some of them were labelled monarchomachs by their opponents, such as Althusius by Arnisaeus and Pareus by Owen. Second, all of them, in one way or another, not only held that the polity was an independent body of its own, with specific laws and procedures, to which its supreme magistrate was bound, but they also identified certain groups, persons or officers in society entitled to correct, punish or even depose the supreme magistrate, or the governing prince, should he fail to govern according to these laws and procedures.

Beyond this feature, the variety among these writers is bewildering and Dreitzel's categorizations disputed.[9] Lawyers in this group argued their case on different grounds from theologians; reformed theologians on different grounds from Lutheran theologians; theologians used legal and political arguments; lawyers referred to Luther and Melanchthon and their defences of the Schmalkaldic League.[10] The situation is further complicated by Germany's two level process of state-building: the empire and its constituent territories. Some of the German monarchomachs explicitly included in their argument princes to be corrected by estates; others did not exclude this possibility, but cited citizens and inferior noblemen suing their prince, such as in Hesse in the 1650s. Only a few have received thorough investigation that allows firm conclusions to be drawn, these being the four internationally known writers Gerhard, Besold, Arnisaeus and Althusius.[11] What follows is largely restricted to these writers. First,

---

[8]   For a concise overview, see Robert von Friedeburg and Michael Seidler, 'Germany', in Howell Lloyd *et al.* (eds), *European Political Thought, 1450–1700: Religion, Law and Philosophy* (New Haven, CT, 2007), 102–75.

[9]   Dieter Wyduckel, 'Einleitung', in Frederick S. Carney, Heinz Schilling and Wyduckel (eds), *Jurisprudenz, Politische Theorie und Politische Theologie* (Berlin, 2004), pp. ix–xx.

[10]   See further below. As we shall see, Johann Gerhard for instance based his claims on the character of Germany as an electoral monarchy and on Horace, while Volcmar quoted some of Melanchthon's and Luther's statements from the 1540s.

[11]   On Althusius, see recent volumes such as Carney, Schilling and Wyduckel, *Jurisprudenz*, and Emilio Bonfatti, Giuseppe Duso and Merio Scattola (eds), *Politische Begriffe und historisches Umfeld in der Politica methodice digesta des Johannes Althusius* (Wiesbaden, 2002), that reflect the very heterogeneous state of research; on Arnisaeus, Horst Dreitzel, *Protestantischer Aristotelismus und absoluter Staat. Die 'Politica' des Henning*

in section I, I outline why the idea that the body politic was a political and legal entity in its own right, with laws to which any magistrate was bound and which were enforceable by inferior magistrates against a superior magistrate, was so deeply entrenched in Germany. In section II, I link Buchanan to the frontline of German debate where he was cited as a king-killer and condemned alongside others for his terrible deeds, as is the case in Arnisaeus' attack on the monarchomachs.[12] Alternatively, he figured as an example of a certain academic position on the possibility of the supreme magistrate being held to account by an Ephorate, often as one opinion among many. That was the approach of Christoph Besold, who was reluctant to take sides too clearly. Buchanan was also referred to in support of the view that such punishment was possible, advisable and practical, as was the case with Althusius. Johann Gerhard, another German monarchomach, however, referred to Buchanan in order to illustrate a point rather than to support his own argument, and he even opposed other monarchomachs. In illustrating these various uses of Buchanan, I shall not refer in any detail to Arnisaeus, who simply condemned him, but it is useful to see how Besold referred to him, because he shared some of the monarchomachs' legal arguments, if not their view of the actual feasibility of resistance. In section III, I examine the references to Buchanan in the writings of Gerhard and Althusius, while finally, in section IV, I reflect on what, if anything, such a review of the evidence tells us about either the German monarchomachs or George Buchanan.

I

The utterly heterogeneous character of the authors and books labelled 'monarchomach' and the varied circumstances in which they were

---

Arnisaeus (ca 1575–1636) (Wiesbaden, 1970); on Besold: Horst Dreitzel, *Absolutismus und ständische Verfassung in Deutschland: Ein Beitrag zur Kontinuität und Diskontinuität der politischen Theorie in der frühen Neuzeit* (Mainz, 1992), and Barbara Zeller-Lorenz, *Christoph Besold (1577–1638) und die Klosterfrage* (Tübingen, 1986). His conversion and the unusually complicated state of his publications have so far prevented any comprehensive treatment of him similar to that of Arnisaeus or Althusius. In the case of Johann Gerhard, his theological writings have been the subject of research, although less has been done on his arguments on the secular magistrate. However, see Johann Anselm Steiger, *Johann Gerhard (1582–1637). Studien zu Theologie und Frömmigkeit des Kirchenvaters der lutherischen Orthodoxie* (Stuttgart, 1997); Johann Anselm Steiger, *Doctrina et pietas: Zwischen Reformation und Aufklärung* (Stuttgart, 1997).

12   Henning Arnisaeus, *De Autoritate Principum in Populum semper inviolabili, commentario Politica Opposita seditiosis quorundam scriptis qui omnem Principum Majestatem sujiciunt censurae Ephorum et populi* (Frankfurt, 1612). I used the Strassburg edition of 1636.

written or which they addressed raises the question of whether such a group really exists. Buchanan's *De Iure Regni apud Scotos* (1579), the *Vindiciae, Contra Tyrannos* (1579), Jean Boucher's *De Iusta Henrici Tertii Abdicatione e Francorum Regno libri IV* (1589), Guillaume Rossaeus' *De Iusta Reipublicae Christianae in reges impios et haereticos authoritate: Justissimaque catholicorum ad Henricum Navareum et quemcumque haereticum a regno Gallicae repellendum confoederatione* (1592), and Juan Mariana's *De Rege et Regis Institutione* (1599) are obviously very different texts making very different points. Critics of the monarchomachs, however, pinpointed two common charges against them. First, monarchomachs shared a view of the body politic as an entity independent of the *imperium* or *dominium* of the supreme magistrate, possessing rights and customs of its own. Second, they insisted there were groups in the body politic capable of enforcing these laws and customs against the supreme magistrate. As noted already, Besold was clear about the former point, but did not say much about the latter. The German monarchomachs regularly referred to the first point, but also identified specific groups qualified on various specific grounds to coerce and punish the prince. This latter insistence was the basis of their inclusion among the monarchomachs. In 1612, Arnisaeus included Brutus, Rossaeus, Buchanan, Hotman, Boucher, Althusius, Hoenonius, Danaeus and also John of Salisbury in the group, but not Aquinas, who had differentiated between certain kinds of tyrants and the means of opposing them. In his *De Iure Maiestate Libri III*, Arnisaeus again attacked Buchanan, Althusius and Brutus for distinguishing between *imperium* as such and its exercise by the supreme magistrate holding it. He also rejected any idea of mixed monarchy and insisted that, in a monarchy, kingship is transferred by the *lex regia*, conquest, or succession to the person of the monarch alone and is subsequently held only by the supreme magistrate.[13] To him, the very functioning of a state depended on the *imperium* being exercised by a single clear-cut authority. That authority might be a large number of men, as in a polity (with a majority of heads of household actively participating in government) or an aristocracy, but *imperium* could not be shared with any group of persons beyond the group possessing it. Thus, in chapter III, he refers to Bodin's view that kingship and majesty cannot be separated. On that basis, the arguments of Althusius, Buchanan and Boucher (on the right of the popes to depose) are refuted on legal, historical and functional grounds.

Clearly, this argument is absurd: lumping someone like Buchanan together with Catholic monarchomachs who insisted on the power of the pope to depose kings must be so. Yet, at that moment in history, the

---

[13] Henning Arnisaeus, *De Iure Maiestate Libri Tres* (Strasbourg, 1635), c. III.

argument about the supreme magistrate being only an officer of the body politic was taking on a life of its own, and in the eyes of many French and English men, was being transformed from an entirely banal insight of late medieval law and political philosophy into a highly contested means of limiting absolute power. Not so in Germany where absolutism only thrived, if it thrived at all, after the 1660s. While theories of absolutism were developing in France (Bodin, Barclay) or Scotland and England (James VI & I) from the 1590s, the German debate took a very different turn. Barclay was not only arguing, as Bodin had done, that for functional reasons monarchy must be in principle free from the intervention or supervision of human agencies. He was also adamantly opposed to the idea that kingship was merely an office and that kings, like other magistrates, must exercise that office according to the laws, customs and procedures of the community they served, and that they could and must be corrected, punished or even deposed if they failed to fulfil their office. A whole tradition of late medieval and sixteenth-century thought was given a distinctly monarchomach twist as the French debate took this crucial turn.[14]

Late medieval Europe had seen a whole range of depositions. However, while in England, as Christine Carpenter has argued, they were seen as an embarrassment that could not be allowed to bear any systematic theoretical fruit,[15] in Germany, as Ernst Schubert has shown, depositions had never caused disastrous turmoil.[16] Indeed, the fact that the German emperor was elected following certain procedures and that his actions could and must be resisted if they did not follow the laws and procedures of the empire was a commonplace for German lawyers throughout the fifteenth and sixteenth centuries. As Eberhard Isenmann has shown in a seminal essay on German legal counsel in this period, the imperial *plenitudo potestatis* was regularly assumed to be exercised legally only within the framework of existing customs and procedures, not according to the will of the natural person of the emperor.[17] Recent work on the Swabian league, for example, shows how Maximilian had to submit to the procedures of the

---

[14]   One need only mention here that authorities from Figgis to Tierney have insisted on the importance of late medieval conciliar ideas of the representation of the community in relation to the supreme magistrate.

[15]   Christine Carpenter, 'Resisting and Deposing Kings in England in the 13th–15th century', in Robert von Friedeburg (ed.), *Murder and Monarchy: Regicide in Medieval and Early Modern Europe* (Houndmills, 2004), pp. 99–121, at pp. 9, 106–12.

[16]   Ernst Schubert, *Königsabsetzung im deutschen Mittelalter* (Göttingen, 2005).

[17]   Eberhard Isenmann, 'Der römisch-deutsche König und "imperator modernus" als "monarcha" und "princeps" in Traktaten und in deutschen Konsilien des 15./16. Jahrhunderts', in *'Panta Rei': Studi dedicati a Manlio Bellomo*, vol. III (Rome, 2004), pp. 15–79.

league as a member of that league, equal to its other members.[18] In other words, the fact that all imperial fiefs had to be transferred by the king and emperor neither translated into a *dominium regale* nor into the amount of social dignity, legal right or political authority that Scottish or English kings could count on. On these grounds the Schmalkaldic League had been founded to defend its members against illegal infringements of Catholic neighbours and the emperor, and on these grounds Catholic princes let go when the rebel Protestant Princes in 1552 nearly captured Charles V and then enforced the Passau compromise, the blueprint for the 1555 Augsburg Peace of Religion.[19]

English contemporaries recognized these differences between England and Scotland on the one hand and the empire on the other. Most used Sleidan as their source. Johannes Sleidan, the Lutheran historian, spread the message of the constitutional nature of the empire in Europe, and the English divine Thomas Bilson informed English readers in 1585 in his comments on the qualified nature of obedience due from princes in Germany, as also in the Netherlands, where the estates were free to defend their own possessions.[20]

Regarding the relationship of princes to their own vassals and subjects, different strands can be distinguished in contemporary German thought. For a variety of different reasons, some theorists stated that princes could and must rule their territories without any interference from their own subjects. In some cases, such as Arnisaeus, this rested on a functional analysis of monarchy. In other cases, it rested on the vision of the prince as a *pater familiae* and head of a territorial household comprising the tenant farmers of his own demesne land. Propaganda for Catholic dynasties such as the Wittelsbach in Bavaria or Habsburgs in Austria praised them as lineages of saints. Some of these theories amounted to alleging a *Lex Regia* in favour of the prince. But none amounted to a divine right of kings. There was plainly no act of anointing for either the emperor or the German princes. The empire as a whole was holy, not the elected emperor; and all the princes remained vassals. But all these very different strands of argument insisted on obedience from anyone who was subject to a prince. Arnisaeus was a major proponent of this strand, and as we have seen he condemned both Althusius and Buchanan in 1612. For him, *imperium* is held by virtue of conquest, *Lex Regia* or inheritance, and

---

[18]   Horst Carl, 'Landfriedenseinung und Ungehorsam', in Robert von Friedeburg (ed.), *Widerstandsrecht in der frühen Neuzeit. Erträge und Perspektiven der Forschung im deutsch-britischen Vergleich* (Berlin, 2001), pp. 85–112, at 102.

[19]   Robert von Friedeburg, *Self-defence and Religious Strife in Early Modern Europe: England and Germany, 1530–1680* (Aldershot, 2002), ch. 2: 'Torgau to Magdeburg'.

[20]   Thomas Bilson, *The True Difference between Christian Subjection and Unchristian Rebellion* (Oxford, 1585).

by one, few or many; it constitutes the body politic, the *res publica*, and cannot be challenged by men subjected to it. There are no grounds for such challenge legally or politically, and what is more, the body politic would collapse should the exercise of this right be hindered in any way, for only the undisturbed exercise of the right of majesty in itself constitutes the *res publica*. Writers like Buchanan or Althusius were thus wrong and not only endangered princes, but also society as a whole.[21]

However, Arnisaeus was a medical doctor by training, and his political and philosophical analysis did not engage in detail with the real nature of the German electoral monarchy and princely power. Lutheran and reformed lawyers such as Heinrich Rosenthal and Bartholomaeus Volcmar, *politica* writers from Johannes Althusius to Reinhard Koenig, and theologians from Johann Gerhard to Jacob Fabricius, all had to hand ample practical examples of the estates within princely jurisdictions possessing considerable room for manoeuvre in resisting the prince. Their common assumptions about the constraints on monarchy, not only that of the emperor, but also of the princes, were rooted in the importance of feudal law within the empire. By feudal law I do not mean any alleged early medieval Germanic roots such as were used to provide proof of certain constitutional arguments from the mid-seventeenth century onwards, in particular by Conring. Rather, the actual legal relations between the emperor, the princes and other noblemen, cities or the church were mainly regulated by enfeoffments and the complicated legal framework around them. Neither the imperial *plenitudo potestatis* nor the later princely *superioritas territorialis* ever managed completely to overcome the rights of and safeguards for vassals. During the later part of the sixteenth century, *superioritas territorialis* (*fürstliche Landshoheit*, that is, princely superiority over a given group of vassals and subjects) was modelled on the wide-ranging rights of the Roman *presides provinciarum*. By the early seventeenth century it was meant to be a single all-encompassing right to rule that had come to the princes during the middle ages. Most lawyers agreed that German princes had, one way or another, received many originally royal rights, such as coinage, blood, and other superior jurisdictions during the middle ages. Since the 1580s, however, evidence of such rights over a specific group or over a particular number of locations was increasingly understood to be just a token of a general right of superiority over all noblemen and cities in a certain geographical area. On a case-by-case basis, princes managed to avoid having to prove with specific evidence whether a specific village or noble family was or was not in a relation of inferiority to them. Rather, they could argue that physical settlement within this spatial district alone proved inferiority. But even then, feudal law provided for intervention by

---

21   Arnisaeus, *De Iure Maiestatis*; Arnisaeus, *De Autoritate Principum*.

the emperor or the right to resist by vassals if they were maltreated. Thus, Heinrich Rosenthal still insisted in 1610 that, while a vassal may never injure his lord and *dominus* ('laedere personam domini'), he could resist, and so could his own sub-vassals ('sed aliter ei vel eius subsidiaries resistat'), the illegal actions of the lord. The vassal could, as long as the body of the lord was not injured, confront his lord, in court and otherwise. In the case of an illegal interference of the lord with the enfeoffed goods, even injuring the lord in their defence remained legitimate.[22] This underlying understanding of relations among princes and their inferior nobilities, and sometimes even citizens, as essentially those of lords and enfeoffed vassals, was never entirely pushed to the margins by the political terminology of majesty, territorial superiority and subject-hood.

As Ernst Schubert has shown, these notions rested on the rise in the reputation of the *corpus iuris civilis* in the late medieval and Renaissance periods. Canon law had provided no substantial arguments to counter threats from kings or lords. But glosses to Roman law commented on the *vim vi repellere*. One argument bore particular fruit. It insisted that the illegal actions of superiors, including the emperor and princes, had to be understood as null and void; their implementation could thus be resisted. That had few practical consequences in medieval Germany, for the higher nobility did not need scholarly advice to act when they did. But the invention of the printing press, the Protestant Reformation and conflicts about the church and taxation, together with the notion of territorial superiority, led to an explosion of legal and political thought rooted in fifteenth- and sixteenth-century legal practice and counsel. At the height of the ascendance of legal humanism around the first half of the sixteenth century, Ulrich Zasius, generally acknowledged as its leading German legal exponent, pointed out that it was not the pope, but the electoral princes who could depose the emperor, no matter what Baldus had said on the issue.[23] More then that, he acted as counsel in real legal proceedings in the first two decades of the sixteenth century, helping a citizen of the empire, for example, to overrule the protection of a debtor by Maximilian – provided by Maximilian's imperial *plenitudo potestatis* – in order to collect the debts owed to his client.[24]

Lutheran ideas on resistance reiterated points long established and combined them, primarily in the writings of Melanchthon, Regius Selinus

---

[22]   Heinrich Rosenthal, *Tractatus et Synopsis totius Iuris Feudalis* (Cologne, 1610), c. 10, concl. 20, 58–60, concl. 33, 125–8. See in particular p. 59: 'Vasallo dominum pro defensione sui cum moderamine offendere licit; Magistratum contra ius vim in bonis inferentem, etiam in persona laedere licitum.'

[23]   Schubert, *Königsabsetzung im deutschen Mittelalter*, pp. 74–9.

[24]   See Steven Rowan, *Ulrich Zasius: A Jurist in the German Renaissance, 1461–1535* (Frankfurt, Ius Commune 31, 1987).

and the later Magdeburg Confession, with arguments on the legitimacy of the defence of the laws and constitutions of Germany and its *civitates*, its lands and cities, by a diverse range of inferior magistrates.[25] The late medieval glossators developed the *vim vi repellere* into the possibility to resist the actions of inferior judges and their servants. These ideas were applied during the 1530s to the emperor as elected superior judge and to the princes as true 'powers', according to Romans 13, in the empire. Should the emperor act in a case beyond his jurisdiction – e.g., faith and conscience – and contrary to legal procedure – e.g., without proper consideration of the issue in question at a general church council – he acted contrary to his oath and duties against his vassals, who could defend themselves and had to protect their subjects. Diethelm Böttcher admirably traced the development of this line of argument until 1530. He makes three crucial points. First, the fact of the electoral character of the imperial office did not play an important role here, for the majority of princes, ecclesiastical and secular, had gone along with the reinvigoration of the Edict of Worms in 1530. The empire as represented by some or all of the princes was at this point not prepared to support the new heresy. Thus, the older arguments on the possibility of the deposition of an emperor, for instance of Wenzel in 1400 or back to Lupold of Bebenburg and the election of Ludwig the Bavarian, were not pertinent to the problem in question.[26]

Second, he also showed that both Luther and Melanchthon knew their canon and Roman law better then the lawyers sent out to persuade them. They knew there was no direct application of the *vim vi repellere* argument to the issue in hand, because this argument had only pertained to inferior judges, not to a prince, let alone to an emperor.[27] The natural law right to self-defence had been restricted to magistrates as these were instituted among mankind in order to revenge evil on earth. Indeed, Imperial Statute Criminal Law, the *Carolina*, had transformed the vague natural law claim of self-defence into regular statute law, defining precisely under what conditions inferiors could shed blood. The main punch-line of the 1530 arguments in favour of resisting the emperor was to translate the unwritten privileges of the German higher nobility into their status as the 'powers' referred to in Romans 13 and thus not subject to the emperor in the ordinary sense of the word, but bound by specific regulations, including his election and their enfeoffment, allowing them to defend themselves and obliging them to defend their subjects in areas not properly enforced by the emperor. From here, challenging the legality of the Edict of Worms and

---

[25]   Friedeburg, *Self-defence and Religious Strife*, ch. 2.

[26]   Diethelm Böttcher, *Ungehorsam oder Widerstand? Zum Fortleben des mittelalterlichen Widerstandsrechts in der Reformationszeit* (Berlin, 1991), p. 80.

[27]   Ibid., pp. 59–96.

the 1530 reinvigoration of its enforcement led to a right to resist an illegal attack of the emperor in this matter.

In the early 1540s, Melanchthon added a further point. In pursuit of a generalized basis for ethics he expanded the realm of the law of nature. In Melanchthon's own writings magistrates were no longer seen to be a result of the Fall, but were part of the natural order created by God. In the 1530s, Melanchthon had insisted that the law of nature did not allow for self-defence, but that magistrates had the privilege of revenge. But in his reworking of his *loci communes* in 1543 he distinguished the revenge of magistrates from the self-defence of individuals by the law of nature.[28] In later pamphlets, specific historic incidents such as the capture of Düren by Spanish troops and the alleged atrocities during that capture served as examples where subjects had been allowed collectively to defend themselves by the law of nature, clearly going beyond the statutory provision of German Criminal law that allowed self-defence only for individuals within the household. In pamphlets of 1547 and 1548, Melanchthon and Basilius Monnerus argued that a whole *civitas*, a corporate body of people under a law, had also a right to defend itself, but remained cautious about collective action by subjects. Lutheran lawyers like Monnerus described the jurisdictions of princes as polities under the law with customs and procedures of their own, and princes as magistrates under the law. By that time – 1547 – the jurisdictions of princes were also described by legal scholars as spatial legal districts similar to the late Roman provinces. In sum, legal thought established the scattered rights of princes as rights over spatial territories, but by the same token, these territories were thought to have laws and customs of their own that were defendable even against the illegal actions of the territorial prince himself.[29]

The legacy of the tumultuous years between 1529 and 1555 was thus a reinvigoration of the mutual bonds and responsibilities of vassals to each other and to their lords and of the limited bonds of obedience between vassals and lords at all levels of government, including relations within the emerging territories. Three kinds of arguments were used to defend organized collective military violence against superiors. First, the princes and other imperial estates insisted on the defence of their privileges against each other and the emperor; second, violent action remained legitimate in defending one's own goods against any illegitimate attack from anyone

---

[28] Robert von Friedeburg, 'The Office of the Patriot: The Problems of Passions and of Love of Fatherland in Protestant Thought, Melanchthon to Althusius, 1520s to 1620's', *Studies in Medieval and Renaissance History*, 3rd series, 3 (2006): pp. 241–73.

[29] Robert von Friedeburg, 'In Defence of *Patria*: Resisting Magistrates and the Duties of Patriots in the Empire 1530s–1640s', *Sixteenth Century Journal*, 32/2 (2001): pp. 357–82. The context and implications of this development are more fully explored in the first part 'I: 1450–1555' of Friedeburg and Seidler, 'Germany'.

at all levels of society at the entry at one's own household, in particular
if the threat was *atrox* and *notorius*, that is, it could not be stopped by
referral to the appropriate courts and was clear cut in its nature (here the
statutory regulations of the Carolina applied); third, this latter argument
was applied, but now clearly beyond the bounds of the *Carolina*, to the
collective defence of a *patria* – a *civitas* such as a city or a territory – and
its right to defend itself against immediate and illegal attack.[30]

The increasing weight of the assumption of the imperial estates' *ius
superioritatis* over a more or less ill-defined group of subjects and vassals
helped shape this situation, but it did not change it radically. Some major
legal scholars, like Tobias Paurmeister, stressed the limits of the power of
the emperor vis-à-vis the princes, but insisted that everyone physically in a
territory must also be subject to the prince enfeoffed with the principality
of this geographical region.[31] But the leading authority Christoph Besold
distinguished between *in territorium* and *de territorio*.[32] Thus, even the
invention of the *ius territorialis* (the right over a territory as a spatial legal
district, including a varying number of privileges and rights of rule) did not
transform all vassals into simple subjects. Indeed, imperial enfeoffments
did not specify what precisely was or was not part of an enfeoffment,
who exactly the subjects of, say, the upper and lower principality of
Hesse really were. This left a good deal of room for interpretative conflict
between an imperial enfeoffment and the realization of power over a given
person in town and countryside, or over a specific holding, in particular
where members of the lower nobility and ecclesiastical corporations were
concerned. This in turn opened up the possibility of charging a prince with
alleged misdeeds against one's goods and person.

Once such a misdeed was identified, German monarchomachs suggested
that resistance and punishment of the prince was part of the regular
machinery of law and of political society in the empire. Such suggestions
were by no means the preserve of the 1570s and 1580s, but remained
embedded in German legal thought right into the 1630s and 1640s. For
example, in 1618, Bartholomaeus Volcmar published his *De Iure Principum
Aliorum Magistratum Synoptica Tractatio* in which chapter IX dealt with

---

[30]   For a more detailed elaboration of these three major lines of argument on resistance
in the empire, see Friedeburg, *Self-defence and Religious Strife*, pp. 56–90; and more
concise Friedeburg and Seidler, 'Germany', pp. 118–20. With regard to the arguments used
in the pamphlets issued in favour of Magdeburg in 1549–51, see Robert von Friedeburg,
'Magdeburger Argumentationen zum Recht auf Widerstand gegen die Durchsetzung des
Interims (1550–1551) und ihre Stellung in der Geschichte des Widerstandsrechts im Reich,
1523–1626', in Luise Schorn-Schütte (ed.), *Das Interim 1548–1550* (Gütersloh, 2005), pp.
389–437.

[31]   Tobias Paurmeister, *Iurisdictione Imperii Romani Libri II* (Hannover, 1608), c. VIII,
nn. 21, 31, 39, pp. 514–58.

[32]   Christoph Besold, *De Aerario Publico Discursus* (Tübingen, 1619), quaestio II, 89.

the problem of what kind of defence was appropriate against the prince. Like many others, he denounced the killing of a father and any illicit action taken by the subjects; he reminded readers that Luther had warned against any war in opposition to Charles V. It remained characteristic of these authors to approach the issue with caution, in particular with regard to individual subjects. However, Volcmar then reminded his readers with reference to Scripture (1 Kings 12), Bodin and Althusius, that the people had no obligation to a tyrant – whether a usurper void of title or a tyrant *ex exercitio*. Lord and vassals were obligated to the *patria*. In this context, it was typical to use this term for the territory in question.[33] The actions of a prince beyond the bounds of legality were seen as null and void ('proterea eius decreta nulla sunt'). Self-defence to secure life and limb was legitimate, the defence of religion even more so ('multo magis in causa religionis'). The task of correcting and defending rested with the Ephors, quoting a letter from Luther of 1547 edited by Melanchthon and Nehemiah 4. Volcmar also cited the three different kinds of resistance outlined above, that is, the defence of one's *patria*, based on allegiance to the *patria*, not the prince (p. 117); the licit defence of one's life (p. 118); and the specific privileges of groups in Germany to correct a superior magistrate (pp. 123–6), without any clear indication of who these persons were.

In Germany, these three kinds of resistance were justified by four different sets of arguments, overlapping with each other and used as a resource from one writer to the next in very different ways. The most important was the construction of the historic constitution of the Empire of the German Nation and of each *patria* or territory within it, culminating in the publications of Friedrich Hortleder in 1618 and of Hermann Conring in the 1640s. In 1643, Conring denied that Roman law had ever been used as the basic legal norm in Germany and based all law on the historic constitution of Germany since the early middle ages. The power of princes was now understood to be historically implemented during the middle ages *alongside the legal privileges of their subjects*.[34] Second, the Lutheran

---

[33]   See Bartholomaeus Volcmar, *De Iure Principum Aliorum Magistratum synoptica Tractatio* (Frankfurt, 1618), c. XI, p. 117. For other examples, see Robert von Friedeburg, 'The Making of Patriots: Love of Fatherland and Negotiating Monarchy in Seventeenth Century Germany', *Journal of Modern History*, 77 (2005): pp. 881–916.

[34]   Important among his publications in this regard were: Hermann Conring, *De Origine Iuris Germanici Commentarious Historicus* (Helmstedt, 1643); *Germanorum Imperio Romano* (Helmstedt, 1644); on his methodological approach, see his *Dissertatio de Optimo Republica*, in *Opera Bd. III* (Braunschweig, 1730); see on Conring, Dietmar Willoweit, 'Hermann Conring', in Michael Stolleis, *Staatsdenker in der frühen Neuzeit* (München, 1987), pp. 129–47; Michael Stolleis, *Geschichte des öffentlichen Rechts in Deutschland*, vol. I (München, 1988), pp. 231–3; Michael Stolleis (ed.), *Hermann Conring, 1606–1681: Beiträge zu Leben und Werk* (Berlin, 1983); Constantin Fasolt, *The Limits of History* (Chicago, IL, 2004).

'three estates doctrine' asked both magistrates and heads of households to defend true religion in the case of an emergency. However, this argument only pertained to religious infringements, not to infringements of the goods of vassals. Third, the humanist topoi of Ephors and the duties of 'patriots' was used at both the Imperial and territorial level. The conflict between princes and noblemen in Hesse from the 1620s to the 1650s is a case in point. The territorial nobility described itself as the *optimates*, the *ephors* and as the *patriots* described by Althusius for various levels of legitimate resistance against a superior magistrate.[35] Fourth, independent of political considerations, the law provided for resisting the actions of a magistrate who threatened not only life and limb, but also the goods of the vassal and subject.[36] In particular in Germany, where princely politics led whole areas into devastation during the Thirty Years War, the natural law defence of body and goods was used to justify the collective actions of peasants both against invaders and against soldiers of their own prince, as in Bavaria in the 1630s.[37] Against this background, let us look at two particularly prominent examples of references to Buchanan, by Christoph Besold, who was never charged with being a monarchomach, and by Althusius, the most prominent of them in Germany.

II

Christoph Besold was born in 1577 and matriculated in Tübingen University in 1591, becoming doctor *utriusque iuris* in 1599 and Professor of Law in 1610, dean from 1612, and seven times rector of the university from 1614 onwards. As Professor of Law and counsellor in legal cases across the empire, he was one of the major German authorities of the first three decades of the seventeenth century. His legal dictionary (*Thesaurus Practicus*) was reprinted until the 1740s, but his overwhelming legal authority translated also into the writing of *politica* on the nature of government and law in Germany in general. Two issues merit attention before we address his references to Buchanan. First, Besold argued that *imperium* rests with the body of the polity *itself* (the *universitas*) and that magistrates are entitled to act only in accordance with the laws and procedures of that polity. Obedience and order are necessary, for otherwise no harmony among men could be established. The commonwealth itself (*res publica*) is thus not only the holder of *imperium*, but the functional

---

[35]   Friedeburg, 'Making of Patriots'.

[36]   See Heinrich Rosenthal, quoted above, note 22.

[37]   Friedeburg, *Self-defence and Religious Strife*, chapter 'Peasants and Patriots'.

need for *imperium* is the reason for the existence of the commonwealth.[38] 'Majesty' as a right is thus, following the Marburg lawyer Kirchner, divided into real and personal majesty, the former due to those representing the *res publica*, the other due to the supreme magistrate.[39] Only in a democracy would they be identical. But in any case the prince had to keep the laws of the kingdom ('princeps enim tenetur legibus regni'). Second, Besold converted in 1630 to Catholicism, subsequently moving to Ingolstadt where he reworked some of his earlier publications to bring them more into line with the arguments of this Jesuit-dominated institution. However, the works examined here were written and published prior to his conversion.

Besold was never accused of being a monarchomach. Indeed, he cited Hotman, Althusius and Buchanan for erring in their belief that all monarchies were necessarily mixed in nature. Besold interpreted their arguments on resistance as claiming that those who had that right also had to have a share of sovereignty. To him, some monarchies were indeed mixed, but some were not. Absolutism existed; however, it was not a general principle of all true monarchies, but a specific historic and regional phenomenon, evident in some monarchies, like Spain, but not in others, like Germany. This principled constitutional relativism set Besold apart from Althusius or Buchanan.[40]

In pursuing this general line of argument, he not only quoted Althusius' *Politica* throughout his *Politicorum Libi Duo*,[41] but included a whole chapter on resistance, just as Althusius had done. Authors like Althusius, but also Philip Hoenonius (*Libri Duo Disputationum*, Herborn, 1608) and Danaeus, were particularly referred to in order to explain the nature of the magistrate, while Lipsius was attacked for his emphasis on the magistrate's personal dignity.[42] Chapter IX of the second book addressed how to 'cure' the commonwealth, reviewing the debate between Arnisaeus and Althusius over whether the prince can be corrected or punished by Ephors. He finally advises recourse to the imperial chamber court to sue the superior magistrate. Rather then directly advising resistance, Besold refers to authors such as Johann Gerhard and Keckermann (two of the German monarchomachs), but also to Mariana, the *Vindiciae, Contra Tyrannos* (the 'Calvinist Model'), and to Buchanan. But to him Buchanan is just one

---

[38]   See for instance his *Politicorum Libri Duo* (Frankfurt, 1620), Lib. I, c. I, 11–19, 26–38.

[39]   Ibid., c. II 'De Maiestate'.

[40]   Christoph Besold, *De Iure Maiestatis* (Tübingen, 1625), p. 227.

[41]   References to Althusius occur throughout the work, not least in key places, together with Aristotle; for instance on the origin of society, Lib. I, c. I, para. 2, p. 19. His emphasis on harmony among the members of society resembles Althusius' argument about harmony as a potential among human beings, to be brought to fruition by the labours of magistrates.

[42]   Ibid., Lib. I, c. II, p. 58.

of many authors, 'qui omnem principum majestatem Ephorum et populi censurae per omnia subjiciunt'. A less prominent reference to Buchanan occurs in his *De Aerario Publico* of 1619 on public finance. There, in his deliberations on question II on the nature of princely authority as *ius superioritatis*, Besold addressed the extent to which princes could muster their subjects for war and ask them for financial contributions to wage war. Referring to Buchanan's *Rerum Scoticarum Historia* (1582), lib. 29, Besold argues that, in Scotland, the most prestigious Scots (*proceres*), exhausted by various wars and faced with an empty treasure, levied taxes in proportion to what the most mighty among them could gather. Although I have failed to locate this reference in Buchanan's *Historia*, Besold not only referred to him as a monarchomach, but used him as a source of historical information to illustrate his argument.[43]

III

German monarchomachs used a wide range of arguments in support of their position. For example, the Lutheran divine Johann Gerhard drew on two different sources: Acts 5 (you must obey God rather than man) and positive constitutional law.[44] He did not invoke any general philosophical or political argument in favour of resistance. Indeed, in his German pamphlet of 1623 he agreed with Barclay and Arnisaeus that Brutus and Rossaeus had been wrong, insisting instead on an interpretation of Romans 13 and Peter 2.13 that *any* authority, including the tyrant, had been established by God and could not be resisted.[45] Thus, high taxes or other maltreatment did not in themselves constitute grounds for resistance, nor did such acts of cruelty for which Asian despots were famous. In his *Loci Theologici*, he quoted Buchanan's *De Iure Regni* as an example of a writer dwelling on these cruelties. He was not using Buchanan as a scapegoat like Brutus or Rossaeus, as an example of erring writers already refuted. But neither was he agreeing with him.

Rather, although all magistrates and tyrants were established by God, that did not mean that all their orders must be obeyed indiscriminately. In the *Loci Theologici* Gerhard insisted that men must not obey impious

---

[43]   Besold, *De Aerario Publico*, quaestio II, 89. The reference to Buchanan's 'lib. 29' must be an error as there are only 20 books in the *Historia*.

[44]   Johann Gerhard, 'Ob alle und jedwede Untertanen in einer jedweden Policey ihrer von Gott ihnen vorgesetzten Obrigkeit ohne Unterscheid also zum Gehorsam obligeret ...', in Dominicus Arumaeus, *Discursus Academicorum de Iure Publicum* (Jena, 1623), vol. 4, no 18, pp. 73–89; Johann Gerhard, *Loci Theologici*, 1610–1622, ed. F. Frank (Leipzig, 1885), vol. 4, 'De magistrato politico', pp. 547ff.

[45]   Gerhard, 'Ob alle ...', p. 74.

orders and can defend themselves and their families against physical coercion used in enforcing such impious orders. But taxes and other dues were still owed even to the heretical magistrate, as long as true religion was observed. Second, he maintained the Lutheran principle of *evangelium non tollit leges*. Thus, where princes were bound by written laws, as they were in the empire, estates could and should enforce these written pacts. Often, the persons making up the estates were not simple subjects (*meros subditos*), but a group of mixed subjects (*subditos mixtos*). They had certain rights to govern themselves. The right to defend the body and family of all subjects was generally acknowledged, but this defence was the office of the estates (*ordines*) in a given jurisdiction.[46] It is difficult not to see here a direct reflection of developments in Brandenburg, where Elector Sigismund had converted to Calvinism in order to inherit some reformed counties on the western fringes of the empire, and the estates and the church had enforced the establishment of Lutheran doctrine in Brandenburg against the will of the prince, while the prince was allowed to have his own service in his palaces in Berlin and elsewhere. To Gerhard, the positive laws of the empire, including the 1555 Peace of Augsburg, and the evolving 'constitution of Brandenburg', had effectively protected the Lutheran churches in this territory and provided the means to justify armed defence against emperor and princes and political coercion within each territory. Thus Gerhard rested his argument entirely on faith and positive constitutional law. All other arguments, in particular those of the *Vindiciae*, and of Rossaeus, that subjected the prince to some sort of *foedus* or to the power of the pope, were entirely rejected.[47] Also in his German pamphlet he was keen to distinguish his own argument in favour of the duties and rights of territorial estates from broader arguments on inferior magistrates in general.[48] Gerhard is concerned with magistrates destroying the state (*tyrannus ... ex reipublicae destructione*), not with violations of citizens or subjects. For the state is the institution protecting the legal order, and the legal order protects the church. The welfare of the fatherland (*patriae salus*), is thus more important then the prince, the prince is minor to the state embodied in the estates, and the prince, only an officer of the state (*Princeps est propter rempublicam minor*). This state is described as the *patria*, and the welfare of this *patria* is more important then the lust of any tyrant. It is to the state as *patria* that the prince is inferior, not to the citizens as a group.[49] To estates attempting to use this argument, service to the territory and to the family of the prince became the mould according to which the reality of resistance had to be shaped.

---

[46] Gerhard, *Loci*, pp. 558–9.
[47] Ibid., pp. 560–61.
[48] Gerhard, 'Ob alle ...', pp. 78–9.
[49] Gerhard, *Loci*, p. 561.

Althusius similarly insisted on the integrity of the *regnum* rather than the community of citizens. But he is much more forthcoming in his references to Buchanan. His *Politica* of 1614 contains five references to Buchanan, though the *Vindiciae*, Hoenonius and Danaeus are all cited more often. In particular chapter XVIII on the Ephors, where Buchanan is referred to, also contains references to Beza, Brutus, Hotman, Danaeus and Mariana, while chapter XIX on the office of the king as a commission on behalf of the community contains references to Brutus and Rossaeus. Thus, most Catholic and Protestant monarchomachs were referred to. The *Vindiciae, Contra Tyrannos* and Hotman served also as evidence for the ancient laws of France. However, throughout the *Politica*, legal authorities such as Bodin, Paurmeister, Pruckmann, Rosenthal, Tholosanus and Vasquez were virtually omnipresent. References to other monarchomachs are concentrated in places where issues such as the authority of the community and those groups entitled to enforce it are discussed.

The reference in chapter XVIII on the duties of the Ephors specifies their right to intervene should the *populus* by error or fraud be misled and place itself in servitude. In that case, their rights must be reinstituted, as Buchanan rightly asserted. Three further references occur in the next chapter in relation to kingship as a commission. That the law of the state (the *ius* of the *consociatio universalis*) and of the body politic (*corpus politicus*) pertains to that body itself is supported by references to Pruckman, Molina, Paurmeister, Vasquez and Buchanan. The fact that the people exercise their right via the Ephors, to whom they subject themselves, is supported by Hotman (*Francogallia*) and Buchanan. It is stressed that this does not give the people complete licence with regard to the magistrate. Finally, it is asserted that the Ephors must protect the true religion if the prince has a different one. Here, Althusius refers to Buchanan's *Historia*, book 6. A final reference is in chapter XX on the oath of submission or allegiance: while the supreme magistrate is obligated unconditionally by his oath, the people are only obligated under the condition that he rules with justice and piety. This time, Buchanan is referred to alongside Vasquez and Rossaeus.

Buchanan is not referred to in Althusius' famous chapter XXXVIII on the remedies against tyranny. Tholosanus, Augustinus and Aristotle are the major sources used to define tyranny, while Pareus is invoked to add specific cases of procedural mistakes and lack of adequate defences. To explain the right of the Ephors to intervene, Althusius mentions the nature of the mutual obligation, the limited nature of the jurisdiction of the magistrate, the implicit standards of piety and justice the magistrate has to adhere to, the power of the people exercised by the Ephors, the qualitative difference between the obligation between parents and children or master and servant and that between people and magistrates, the right to defend what is rightfully yours, and so on. He also stresses the duty of the *optimates* towards the fatherland and the protection of its laws and liberties. Althusius comes up with a few examples: the Helvetic federations, and the deposition of Mary Queen of Scots for tyranny and the murder of her husband, are mentioned among other cases, and the *ordines Scotiae regni* figure as the Ephors, though Buchanan himself is not referred to (n. 45). Hotman and Danaeus figure as sources.

IV

However, on the next page, apart from Ephors and *optimates*, the Ciceronian *cives patriae amantes* (taken from Cicero's letter to his friend Atticus) are mentioned. Cicero responded with this formula to the question, what to do now that Caesar had captured Rome. Cicero advised that all *cives patriae amantes* should roam the sea like pirates to fight the tyrant.[50] The formula suggested that love of the fatherland made breaches of the law permissible. Most German monarchomachs came up with some specific ethical or religious commitment that distinguished those fit to resist from ordinary subjects who had to obey in almost all circumstances. In most cases, they clearly identified the estates, the inferior nobility within the emerging territories, as the group of men possessing these attributes. This commitment was either described by reference to an office directly given by God, in particular by Lutherans referring to Luther's disputation of 1539, or it was described in terms of commitment to the *patria* in the shape of the territorial *res publica*, with reference to Horace and Cicero. Althusius referred to Cicero's formula, Gerhard to Horace.[51] Within this realm of commitment to the *patria*, German monarchomachs shared with Buchanan an emphasis on civic virtue, but strictly in the service of and subject to the state. They were understood accordingly: humble noblemen quoted Althusius when suing their prince.[52]

The notion of the priority of the body politic over the magistrate, commonly held by authorities like Besold and Althusius, together with

---

[50]   Marcus Tullius Cicero, *Epistolae ad Atticum*, 9, 19, 3: 'Nos quoniam superum mare obsidetur, infero navigabimus, et, si Puteolis erit difficile, Crotonem petemus aut Thurius et *boni cives amantes patriae mare infestum* habebimus'; Cicero, *Pro Milone*, ed. A.B. Poynton (Oxford, 1892); for the reception of this formula among German monarchomachs, see for instance Althusius, *Politica*: 'omnes et singuli *patriae amantes* optimates & privati resistere & possunt & debent' (c. XXXVIII n. 68); 'subditi resistentes & cives *patriae amantes*' (c. XXX n. 48); Reinhard König, *Disputationum Politicarum Methodice*, Disputatio XVI, 'De Principiis, conditionibus et causis bellorum gerendorum': 'subditi & cives patriae amentes, qui salvam Rempublicam volunt'.

[51]   Gerhard, *Loci*, p. 547: 'pro ea mortem obeundo, si alter fieri nequeat, de qua morte Horaz cenit: Dulce et decorum est, pro patria mori'.

[52]   Friedeburg, 'Making of Patriots', *passim*.

the emphasis on the state as a public order securing the compliance of men, explains the relatively large social and intellectual support for the idea of violent resistance to princes in Germany right into the 1650s. Arnisaeus never managed entirely to discredit this group. It was the new secular theories of natural law and the success of Pufendorf that led to their demise. By 1719, quite different authorities were being cited and other arguments were being developed to explain resistance to princes. But that is another story.[53] During the late sixteenth and the early seventeenth centuries, the idea of the *patria* provided German monarchomachs with an argument justifying resistance by virtuous citizens and patriots.

German monarchomachs remained primarily oriented towards positive law and the emerging constitution of the empire. But the difference between Althusius, Gerhard and other German monarchomachs and Buchanan was not so rooted in their reluctance to invest individual subjects as such with a right to resist – Buchanan was here also highly circumscribed.[54] Indeed, their argument that men of virtue were duty bound to defend the *patria*, even when that meant violating social and legal hierarchies, is an important similarity between them and the Scottish humanist. The main difference was that to German monarchomachs such as Althusius or Gerhard, no matter how different their argument in detail, the welfare of the civil order remained embedded in the legal order of the state, not the community of citizens. Nor did they consider for a moment that all subjects were endowed with sufficient rational capacities. Only those subjects sufficiently endowed with a love of their fatherland could also carry out the duties of a patriot. When it came to arguments over groups with problematic claims to a right in positive law to resist their own superiors, reference to the fatherland was thus crucial for the German monarchomachs.

53   Robert von Friedeburg, 'Natural Jurisprudence, Argument from History and Constitutional Struggle in the Early Enlightenment: The Case of Gottlieb Samuel Treuer's Polemic against Absolutism in 1719', in T.J. Hochstrasser and P. Schröder (eds), *Early Modern Natural Law Theories* (Dordrecht, 2003), pp. 141–68.

54   See Roger A. Mason, 'People Power? George Buchanan on Resistance and the Common Man', in Robert von Friedeburg (eds), *Widerstandsrecht in der frühen Neuzeit. Erträge und Perspektiven der Forschung im deutsch-britischen Vergleich* (Berlin, 2001), pp. 163–84, 175–7.

CHAPTER 7

The Reception of Buchanan in Northern Europe in the Seventeenth Century

Allan I. Macinnes

The historical writings and political thought of George Buchanan, as Scotland's foremost Renaissance humanist, carried an international resonance from the sixteenth to the eighteenth centuries. Buchanan's influence on state formation in the early modern period may not have been as pervasive as that of his French contemporary Jean Bodin, nor as that of the two foremost jurists of the seventeenth century, the Dutchman Hugo de Groot, alias Grotius, and the German, Samuel Pufendorf. Yet Buchanan, as a supporter of and propagandist for a Protestant Reformation carried out in defiance of the Scottish Crown, made a telling contribution to the relationship between monarchy and the commonwealth in terms of elective kingship, rights of resistance and their exercise in Northern Europe. In the course of the seventeenth century, this contribution had not just a recurring relevance for revolutions, civil wars and state formation within Britain. Through the brokerage of mainly Dutch publishing houses, Buchanan's writings served to check moves towards absolute monarchy in Denmark–Norway and to justify rebellion within the commonwealth of Poland–Lithuania.

Mapping Antiquarianism

After James VI of Scotland became James I of England in 1603, the new Britannic monarchy sought to claim *ius imperium*, an exclusive right of empire by land and sea, in and around the British Isles. This imperial construct was underwritten by an Anglocentric version of organic kingship propagated primarily by the antiquarian, William Camden, and the cartographer, John Speed. Buchanan's historical writings provided, from the perspective of civic humanism, a potent Scottish antidote to the authoritarian Britannic aspirations of James and his Stuart successors. It was this anti-imperial and anti-absolutist message that was to resonate throughout continental Europe, but particularly in the North Sea and Baltic States.[1]

William Camden was dismissive of the British origin myths about Brutus the Trojan that were fabricated on the Welsh marches in the twelfth century. Nevertheless, his humanistic conception of a territorially expansive Britain, which he depicted in his final version of *Britannia* (1607), underwrote English claims to be an exclusive empire. For the English comprised an elect Protestant nation with a Christian tradition under erastian episcopacy unbeholden to Rome. Conquest and invasion had refined their civilizing mission. Thus, London, the old Roman foundation, was now the metropolitan capital of a composite empire whose territories encompassed the Anglo-Saxon heptarchy as well as Wales and Cornwall. This composite empire could be deemed Britannic in laying claim not only to Ireland but also to that part of Scotland formerly held by the Picts. Though barbarians, they were not irredeemably so, like the Irish and Scots, whom Camden classified negatively as of Gothic stock. He was adamant that the Picts were actually Britons who had lived outwith the boundaries of Roman civilization; the classical if far from accurate demarcation that ensured such redeemable Gothic influences as the Saxons, Danes and Norsemen had enriched rather than destroyed Britain. These northern boundaries, which were settled at the Forth–Clyde division of Scotland, conformed to the division between the ancient Scottish kingdom of Alba and the Saxon kingdom of Northumbria. Following his accession to the English throne, the imperial vanity of James Stuart was certainly enhanced by the notion that he was the fabled heir to both the emperor Constantine the Great, who had spread Christianity from the British Isles to all territories under the sway of Rome, and King Arthur, who had expanded his British dominions into France. Repeated print runs of Camden's *Britannia* throughout the seventeenth century fuelled rather than dispelled English claims to superiority over Scotland and Ireland as well as Wales.[2]

The portraying of the three kingdoms as a composite empire was illustrated graphically by John Speed, whose *Theatre of the British Empire*, first published in 1612, remained the template for the subsequent

[1]   A.I. Macinnes, *The British Revolution, 1629–1660* (Basingstoke, 2005), pp. 8–24; see also on Scottish reactions to Camden and Speed, Roger Mason's Chapter 1 above.

[2]   D.R. Woolf, *The Idea of History in Early Stuart England: Erudition, Ideology, and 'The Light of Truth' from the Accession of James I to the Civil War* (Toronto, 1990), pp. 55–64, 115–27; William Camden, *Britain, or A Chronological description of the most flourishing kingdomes, England, Scotland and Ireland, and the islands adjoining, out of the depth of antiquity* (London, 1610 and 1637); William Camden, *The abridgement of Camden's Britannia* (London, 1626); William Camden, *Camden's Britannia newly translated into English with large additions and improvements* (London, 1695).

mapping of Great Britain and Ireland for much of the seventeenth century. In representing a male Britannia as barbarous but noble, then refined by Saxons, Danes and Normans in the guise of classical heroes, Speed was illustrating the importance of progressive civility to the Stuart dynasty's imperial agenda. Again following Camden, the composite empire was constructed from composite kingdoms. Thus England was a composite based on the Anglo-Saxon heptarchy: Scotland was a composite of the Scots, the Picts and the Isles; and Ireland of its four provinces of Munster, Leinster, Connacht and Ulster together with Meath. Even the principality of Wales had a tripartite division of North, South and Powys. Abridged versions of his maps issued from 1632, though purportedly depicting England and Wales, Scotland and Ireland as multiple kingdoms, still adhered to the basic structure of a composite empire.[3] This Britannic representation of Camden and Speed effectively appended Scotland, Ireland and the rest of the British Isles onto detailed topographical descriptions of the English and Welsh shires. This representation was duly accorded international recognition by the leading Dutch cartographer, Wilhelm Blaeu, whose map of *Britannia* was published posthumously in 1645.[4]

As a firm advocate of the belief that kingship was divinely interposed between God and civil society, James I of Great Britain viewed his composite empire as the first step towards perfect union under godly monarchy. Such a union opened up the prospect of British leadership in a Protestant Europe battling to resist Antichrist in the form of the papacy and the whole panoply of the Counter-Reformation. This imperial vision of godly monarchy was initially enunciated in *The True Lawe of Free Monarchies* (1598) and followed up in *Basilikon Doron* (1599), essentially a manifesto for his divine right to succeed to the English throne. On the one hand, James drew demonstrably on traditional English claims to be an empire free from papal control. On the other hand, he rebutted presbyterian claims to the autonomy of the Scottish kirk, whereby government through bishops, the erastian preference of imperial monarchy, faced replacement by an autonomous hierarchy of ecclesiastical courts.[5]

In his promotion of British Union, James had also brought into play Scottish origin myths, but not as interpreted by his former tutor, George

---

[3]   John Speed, *The Theatre of the Empire of Great Britain: presenting an exact geography of the kingdomes of England, Scotland, Ireland and the isle adjoyning* (London, 1616 and 1627); John Speed, *England, Wales, Scotland and Ireland described and abridged* (London, 1632).

[4]   C. Moreland and D. Bannister, *Antique Maps* (London, 2000), pp. 209, 213–16; J. Goss, *World Historical Atlas, 1662* (London, 1990), pp. 72–3.

[5]   J.H. Burns, *The True Law of Kingship: Concepts of Monarchy in Early Modern Scotland* (Oxford, 1996), pp. 222–54; J. Wormald, 'James VI and I, *Basilikon Doron* and *The Trew Law of Free Monarchies*: The Scottish Context and the English Translation', in L.L. Peck (ed.), *The Mental World of the Jacobean Court* (Cambridge, 1991), pp. 36–54.

Buchanan. These myths were largely the product of the Wars of Independence of the late thirteenth and fourteenth centuries and had borrowed heavily from Irish origin mythology. Notably embellished by Hector Boece in his *Scotorum Historia* (1527), these myths had underwritten not only Scottish pretensions to the longest unbroken line of kings in Europe but also the imperial aspirations of their Stewart monarchy since the fifteenth century. For Achaius, the sixty-fifth king of Scots was leagued in friendship, not clientage, with Charlemagne, the Holy Roman Emperor, around 790; a league that had laid the foundation of the 'auld alliance' between Scotland and France that was consolidated by the Wars of Independence. James, however, was particularly indebted to John Mair's vision of a composite British Empire that was to be achieved by dynastic union and was articulated in *Historia Maioris Britannia* (1521). But Mair's vision requires wider international contextualizing. When James commenced the Stuart dynasty's agenda for Britannic Empire in 1603, the Spanish monarchy had already established an Iberian World Empire for which Mair had been the principal apologist from the British Isles.[6]

However, the main opponents of World Empire within the three kingdoms were also Scots. All were staunch upholders of Protestant Reformation at home and abroad. Although they were anti-imperial, they were by no means antipathetic to British Union. Whereas the critique of John Knox was formulated from a biblical and apocalyptic perspective, George Buchanan was the foremost classical exponent of aristocratic republicanism. Both viewed post-Reformation Scotland as a virtuous commonwealth that should be open to wider federative arrangements to counter universal monarchy, especially as the political absolutism of the Habsburgs was now tied to the Counter-Reformation being promulgated by the papacy. Buchanan had firmed up Boece's fabricated line of kings in order to demonstrate the capacity of the Scottish commonwealth to remove tyrannical monarchs. By the Reformation, ungodly monarchy had become tyrannical monarchy. Buchanan, whose *Rerum Scoticarum Historia* (1582) was published four years before the first edition of Camden's *Britannia*, placed his political analysis within a descriptive framework of pertinent cultural, social and environmental themes. Camden, who acknowledged a shared scepticism about origin myths with Buchanan, followed a similar thematic structure that had become the accepted standard of Renaissance historiography. Camden's imperial perception of continuity and stability was assured through virtuous and hereditary monarchy. In marked contrast, Buchanan stressed that a virtuous monarchy was an elective

---

    [6]   P. McGinnis and A. Williamson, 'Britain, Race, and the Iberian World Empire', in A.I. Macinnes and J. Ohlmeyer (eds), *The Stuart Kingdoms in the Seventeenth Century: Awkward Neighbours* (Dublin, 2002), pp. 70–93.

monarchy that depended on the consent of the political community. This notion of popular sovereignty, basic to Buchanan's conception of civic humanism, had its roots in Cicero's classical questioning of the legitimacy of government. Buchanan's polemical advocacy of the right of resistance to monarchy, which upheld trusteeship over sovereignty, made his *De Iure Regni apud Scotos Dialogus* (1579) a ready target for proscription by successive Stuarts in the seventeenth century.[7]

The fundamental reconfiguration of Britain was also a prime concern of Andrew Melville, humanist, educational reformer and founder of Scottish presbyterianism. It was Melville who first suggested the merging of the two rival formulations of Britain. In a pastoral eulogy on the birth in 1594 of Prince Henry, eldest son of James VI, he anticipated that future regal union would join Scotland and England in a united commonwealth of the Scoto-Britannic people. This new commonwealth, however, was but the first step in a grand confederation of free Protestant states. David Hume of Godscroft, the leading Presbyterian intellectual in Jacobean Britain, was no less committed to full integration. In 1605, he promoted a complete political and religious union that would lead to the fusion of the British peoples. Nonetheless, the creation of a universal British commonwealth under the Stuart dynasty to challenge Spain and the papacy sat awkwardly with the aristocratic republic that he, like Buchanan, idealized. The Iberian menace pointed to new political directions that were not necessarily liberating. As a civic humanist vehemently opposed to withdrawal from public life yet reluctant to condone outright resistance to monarchy, Hume had no clear alternative to counteract the non-cooperation of the Stuart monarchy with his vision. Buchanan, on the other hand, had afforded an incisive and unequivocal critique of hereditary, absolute and imperial monarchy to which the Scottish Covenanters and later the British Whigs proved notably receptive when instigating revolts against the Stuarts.[8]

This Scottish perspective, like the Britannic to which it ran counter, attained international recognition. Dutch typographers and cartographers turned to Buchanan, supplemented by Boece, when seeking an alternative to the composite delineation of Great Britain by Camden and Speed. In 1627, Bonaventure and Abraham Elzevirus, as part of an occasional series of topographical discourses on European states, published *Respublica, sive Status Regni Scotiae et Hiberniae*. Although they used topographical

---

[7]   Burns, *True Law of Kingship*, pp. 283–95; Roger A. Mason, 'Imagining Scotland: Scottish Political Thought and the Problem of Britain, 1560–1650', in Mason (ed.), *Scots and Britons: Scottish Political Thought and the Union of 1603* (Cambridge, 1994), pp. 3–16.

[8]   *The British Union: A Critical Edition and Translation of David Hume of Godscroft's 'De Unione Insulae Britannicae'*, ed. P.J. McGinnis and A. Williamson (Aldershot, 2002), pp. 1–53; D. Allan, *Philosophy and Politics in Later Stuart Scotland* (East Linton, 2000), pp. 47–58, 116–21.

material drawn from Camden, Buchanan's historical polemic was accorded precedence. Accordingly, their selective representation, together with a summative history of the 'auld alliance' with France, underlined Scotland's status as a classical commonwealth independent of England. For Ireland, however, the evidence drawn predominantly from Camden and Speed was loaded in favour of its status as an English dependency. The Dutch publishers did not have access to the one work of Renaissance scholarship that served as a corrective to both the antiquarian pretensions of the Scots and the hegemonic claims of the anglocentric Britons. *Foras Feasa ar Éirinn* by Séathrún Céitinn (Geoffrey Keating) was a history purged of fable but written in Irish around 1634 and subsequently circulated in manuscript only. Nevertheless, this Dutch differentiation between an independent commonwealth and a dependent kingdom was sustained by the publication of Joan Blaeu's *Atlas Maior* in which Scotland was covered in volume XII of the Amsterdam edition of 1654. The accompanying topographical sections were prepared primarily by Sir Robert Gordon of Straloch, an Aberdeenshire laird firmly wedded to the Graeco-Egyptian origins of the Scots, to the antiquity of the Scottish kingdom as established by Boece and Buchanan, and to the emphatic rebuttal of Camden.[9]

Contested Dominions

The mapping of rival pretensions and perspectives was not just an antiquarian exercise. It had immediate relevance to issues of sovereignty, especially to that of contested dominion by land and sea. Thwarted in his endeavours to promote full union between Scotland and England, James VI & I had embarked upon foreign, frontier and colonial policies that promoted his British agenda internationally and, simultaneously, demonstrated the sovereign independence of his three kingdoms under imperial monarchy. The formal annexation of Orkney and Shetland to the Scottish Crown between 1611 and 1614 was partly an extension of frontier policy in that culturally distinctive Norse customs were eradicated in favour of the standardized administration of law throughout Scotland. There was undoubted imperial symmetry in the imposition of Scots law over the Northern Isles to complement the contemporaneous imposition of English common law throughout Ulster. No less pertinently, control over Orkney and Shetland also opened up the prospect of British collaboration

⁹   [Bonaventure and Abraham Elzevirus], *Respublica, sive Status Regni Scotia et Hiberniae* (Leiden, 1627); Joan Blaeu, *Scotiae Quae Est Europae, Liber XII* (Amsterdam, 1654 and 1662); B.Ó. Buachalla, *Foras Feasa ar Éirinn, History of Ireland: Foreword* (Dublin, 1987), pp. 1–8.

to compete effectively with Dutch dominance of the herring fishing in the North Sea.[10]

However, there was a wider imperial concern in annexing islands mortgaged to Scotland by the Danish–Norwegian crown in the mid-fifteenth century. The consolidation of the territorial waters around the British Isles into the Stuarts' imperial dominions served as a practical rebuttal to the claims for *mare liberum* articulated by Grotius in 1609. These Dutch claims for open access, though primarily directed against the Spanish in the East and West Indies, also had North Sea ramifications. Ten years earlier, John Dee, as naval adviser to Elizabeth Tudor, had advocated national security and imperial expansion based on exclusive maritime dominance, which not only termed all territorial waters as the 'British Seas' but also laid claims over the Atlantic waters from Florida to Greenland and into the Arctic. Rather than have recourse to unsound civil law compilations to justify closed seas, James VI & I preferred to rely on two Scottish jurists, William Wellwood and Thomas Craig of Riccarton, to sustain his intellectual case for *mare clausum* around his Britannic Empire.[11] James did reach an accommodation with his brother-in-law, Christian IV, not to resurrect Danish territorial claims on the Northern Isles. However, following the accession of Charles I in 1625, deteriorating personal relations between the new monarch and his Danish uncle, meant that this Stuart–Oldenburg accommodation came under increasing diplomatic strain. In the process, Christian IV's endeavours to establish the Oldenburg dynasty as a hereditary absolute monarchy faced an intellectual challenge that affirmed Buchanan's subversive influence internationally.

Christian IV had used his diplomatic accord with the Spanish and Austrian Habsburgs in 1629/30 as an opportunity to claim exclusive jurisdiction over fishing in the north-eastern Atlantic and to license access of English and Scottish whaling ventures to Greenland and Arctic waters. Ostensibly to control piracy by the Dunkirkers, Christian covertly agreed to provide Spain with a base in the Northern Isles from which they could pursue economic warfare at the expense of the Dutch herring fleet.[12] In order to uphold his *ius imperium* to the seas surrounding the British Isles, Charles I, unlike his father, preferred to rely on English lawyers, most notably Sir John Borough and John Selden. As defenders of Charles I, they

---

[10]   Macinnes, *British Revolution*, pp. 40–73.

[11]   W.H. Sherman, *John Dee: The Politics of Reading and Writing in the English Renaissance* (Amherst, 1995), pp. 148–200; D. Armitage, *The Ideological Origins of the British Empire* (Cambridge, 2000), pp. 208–13.

[12]   R[igsarkivet] C[openhagen], TKUA, Alm.Del I Indtil 1670, 'Latina' vol. 10, fols 33–5, 103–4, 240; *Danmark-Norges Traktater (1626–49)*, ed. L. Laursen (Copenhagen, 1917), pp. 87–93.

were less concerned with issues of jurisprudence grounded in civil law than with the precedents and processes of English common law reinforced by the case load of English parliamentary statutes. By 1637, Johannes Pontanus, a Dutch scholar with Danish roots in Elsinore on the Baltic Sound, had prepared an overt refutation of the Britannic case for *mare clausum* that was based on both historical precedents and jurisprudence. The 'British Seas' were not the internationally recognized waters around the British Isles, but merely the Channel between England and France, a view endorsed by Dutch cartographers and engravers.[13]

In undertaking his work of refutation, Pontanus was effectively seeking a measure of rehabilitation at the Danish court for his *Rerum Danicarum Historia* (1631), published in Amsterdam. As early as 1618, Pontanus had been commissioned as a royal historiographer by Christian IV. He was to provide a national history in Latin to ensure that Denmark–Norway in general and the Oldenburg dynasty in particular should be commemorated internationally. Pontanus had actually been twice admonished in 1622 and 1626 to expedite this work, which drew heavily on the thematic approach, the chronological narrative and the presentational style of Camden and Buchanan. Although he had a longstanding acquaintance with the former, Pontanus, as evident from the similarity of titles, was primarily influenced by the more intellectually rigorous Scottish humanist rather than the English antiquarian, Buchanan's *Rerum Scoticarum Historia* having recently been republished at Frankfurt am Main in 1624 for circulation in Northern Europe. But another historiographer royal, again a Dutch scholar, had also been appointed that year initially to supplement and then to supplant the work of Pontanus. This was Johannes Meursius, who, though less intellectually equipped than Pontanus, had produced *Historica Danica* at Copenhagen in 1630, which covered the reigns of the first three Oldenburg kings from 1448 to 1523. Meursius, indeed, was to prove a more pliable propagandist and apologist. Pontanus had not only borrowed Buchanan's historical methodology, but he had also endorsed the elective nature of monarchy. Accordingly, Pontanus terminated his work in 1448 with the accession of the Oldenburgs. In 1638, Meursius duly completed an extended version of his *Historica Danica* that went over the ground covered by Pontanus from the origin of the kingdom until 1448 but then endorsed the continuity brought by the first three Oldenburg kings. This revised work, published in Amsterdam, was notably more supportive of

13   Moreland and Bannister, *Antique Maps*, pp. 217–33; T.W. Fulton, *The Sovereignty of the Sea: An Historical Account of the Claims for Dominion of the British Seas* (Edinburgh, 1911), pp. 338–75. All maps accompanying the texts of Camden and Speed, as those by Blaeu and other Dutch cartographers, confined 'the British Seas' to the waters of the Channel. Contemporaneous English maps were Dutch engraved, with the result that Dutch ships were depicted sailing freely around the British Isles on open rather than closed seas!

the imperial aspirations of the Oldenburgs and their endeavours to resist Swedish territorial claims on the Danish provinces to the east of the Baltic Sound and on the dependent kingdom of Norway.[14]

Christian IV has been commemorated as a leading patron of the Renaissance in Northern Europe. But he never achieved his goal of hereditary absolute monarchy prior to his death in 1648. When he was predeceased by his son and designated heir, also named Christian, who was addressed as the Elected Prince in diplomatic protocols, the succession passed to his younger son Frederik. For twelve years, Frederik ruled through a central council and provincial commissions that were not so much the equivalent of Buchanan's aristocratic republic as a fractious oligarchy that embroiled Denmark–Norway in further disastrous wars against Sweden. Although Frederik III was acclaimed as hereditary absolute monarch in 1660, his kingdom had suffered extensive territorial losses to Sweden, most notably the three key provinces to the east of the Baltic Sound, Halland, Blekinge and Skåne. The claims of the Danish Crown to dominion by land and sea from the Baltic to the Arctic lay in tatters.[15]

Exporting Revolution

By 1660, the Buchanan-inspired Covenanting Movement in Scotland was also in tatters. The attempts of Charles I, from his accession in 1625, to impose administrative, social, economic and, above all, religious uniformity with England provoked a revolt by the political nation – the estates of the nobility, gentry, burgesses and clergy – that culminated in the issuing of the National Covenant in 1638. The ideological basis of Covenanting was rooted in the rights of resistance as interpreted at the Scottish Reformation of 1560–67 by John Knox and, more especially, George Buchanan. Knox had appealed to the lesser magistrates, that is, to the political nation as a whole, not just the nobility, to band together against the regency government of Mary of Guise. But Buchanan had gone on to claim that the perpetuation of ungodly monarchy against the wishes of the commonwealth justified tyrannicide.[16] Because the Reformation was

---

[14] K. Skovgaard-Petersen, *Historiography at the Court of Christian IV* (Copenhagen, 2002), pp. 23–40, 92–3, 152–7, 179–88, 369–74; K. Skovgaard-Petersen, 'Pontanus' og Meursius' Danmarkshistorier: Nogle Betragtninger over deres plads i Historiografiens Historie', *Historisk Tidsskrift*, 99/2 (1999), pp.387–405.

[15] BL, Trumbull Papers, Vol. CXCV, Add. MSS 72,436, fols 5–6; T. Munck, *Seventeenth Century Europe: State, Conflict and Social Order in Europe, 1598–1700* (Basingstoke, 1991), pp. 62–6, 228–30.

[16] Roger A. Mason, *Kingship and the Commonweal: Political Thought in Renaissance and Reformation Scotland* (East Linton, 1998), pp. 139–64; Burns, *True Law of Kingship*, pp. 185–221.

carried out in defiance of rather than in concert with the crown, upholders of the rights of resistance claimed by the Scottish commonwealth looked for intellectual reinforcement primarily from fellow Calvinists in Northern Europe rather than in England. In this context, the concepts of resistance articulated by French monarchomachs and Dutch republicans in the later sixteenth century further refined the revolutionary ideology of the Covenanting Movement in opposing Charles I on patriotic as well as godly grounds.

Notwithstanding the more substantive contribution of Huguenot and Dutch thought to the formulation of Covenanting rights of resistance, Buchanan was undoubtedly an acknowledged influence on Sir Archibald Johnson of Wariston and Alexander Henderson, who drew up the National Covenant of 1638 and subsequently the Solemn League and Covenant of 1643, which allied the Scottish Covenanters with the English Parliamentarians against the Royalist forces of Charles I. Thus, the Covenanters exported Scottish rights to resist the king and the supremacy of the commonwealth over the monarchy in the course of promoting confessional confederation with England. Buchanan's *Rerum Scoticarum Historia* was also republished in Edinburgh and Amsterdam to mark the occasion. In justifying recourse to defensive arms during the Bishops' Wars of 1639–40, Alexander Henderson had further endorsed the Covenanters' separation of the office of monarchy from the person of the king, a separation manifestly inspired by Buchanan. Another covenanting ideologue, Samuel Rutherford, who explicitly acknowledged his intellectual debt to Buchanan in *Lex Rex* (1644), formalized this right of resistance against the king's person as a coactive power exercised by the political nation to sustain godly monarchy. Charles I should be opposed but the Stuart monarchy retained.[17] However, more radical elements in the Covenanting Movement, led by Archibald Campbell, 8th Earl and subsequently Marquess of Argyll, had contemplated the Buchanan ideal of elected monarchy as early as 1640, when it became apparent that Charles I could not be trusted personally to reach any accommodation to limit his monarchical powers. Indeed, Buchanan's historical and polemical works were deemed in the Restoration era, particularly by those who recanted their engagement with the Covenanting Movement, as incendiary and the chief inspiration for revolution under the radical leadership of Argyll.[18]

James Graham, Marquess of Montrose, opposed to Argyll – initially as a conservative Covenanter, then as a Royalist leader – claimed that his bitter

---

[17]   Macinnes, *British Revolution*, pp. 111–51; Samuel Rutherford, *Lex Rex: The Law and the Prince* (Edinburgh, 1848), pp. 56, 143–8, 199.

[18]   Duke University Library, North Carolina, 'Buchanan Revised', in 'Tracts Criticall and Historicall compiled by Sir James Turner Knight', fols 1–2, 5–9, 11, 13, 15, 18–19, 134, 196–7.

rival was driven solely by personal ambition. However, the Covenanters had an identifiable, ready alternative that would not have required setting aside the Stuart dynasty. This was Louis Philippe, the expropriated Elector Palatine, whose mother, Elizabeth of Bohemia, 'the Winter Queen', was a sister of Charles I. The backbone of the Covenanting forces had been constructed from officers and troops returning from Swedish and Dutch service. As veterans of the Thirty Years' War, their engagement overseas had been marked by a strong loyalty to Elizabeth of Bohemia and a pronounced desire to see initially her husband and then her son restored to their patrimony in the Palatine from which they had been evicted in 1618 by the Holy Roman Emperor, Ferdinand II, head of the Austrian branch of the Habsburgs. When Louis Philippe had accompanied Charles I to Edinburgh in 1641, he had been warmly received by the Scottish Estates as they completed their constitutional limitations on monarchy in kirk and state. Charles I became increasingly frustrated that his status was being reduced to that of the relatively powerless Doge of Venice. He was left with little to do but play golf after his efforts to plot against the Covenanting leadership were exposed and discredited. At the same time, Argyll and the Covenanting leadership were expressing a strong desire to aid Louis Philippe recover his patrimony once the political situation within the British Isles was resolved. But rebellion in Ireland and civil war in England used up the military energies of the Covenanting Movement, which remained unable to release forces to aid recovery. The Palatinate was duly restored to Louis Philippe as part of the Peace of Westphalia that resolved the Thirty Years' War in 1648. Nevertheless, Louis Philippe remained in contact with the Covenanting leadership, particularly when they were invited onto the Committee of Both Kingdoms, which oversaw the parliamentary war effort in England and Ireland and became the main conduit for the allies' foreign intelligence between 1644 and 1646.[19]

The unilateral execution of Charles I by Oliver Cromwell and the regicides in 1649 promoted a patriotic accommodation of Covenanters and Royalists. Charles II was promptly proclaimed as heir to his father not just as King of Scots, but as King of Great Britain and Ireland. At his coronation on 1 January 1651, the new king was obliged to subscribe both the National Covenant and the Solemn League and Covenant. In the process, he publicly acknowledged the right of resistance vested in the Scottish commonwealth. Robert Douglas, who preached for two hours at the coronation at Scone in Perthshire, reminded Charles II that

---

[19]   BL, Trumbull Papers, Vol. CXCVI, Add. MSS 72,437, fols 20–29; S. Murdoch, 'The Scottish Parliament and European Diplomacy, 1641–1647: The Palatinate, The Dutch Republic and Sweden', in Murdoch (ed.), *Scotland and the Thirty Years' War, 1618–1648* (Leiden and Boston, 2001), pp. 77–106; S. Murdoch, *Britain, Denmark–Norway and the House of Stuart, 1603–1660* (East Linton, 2000), pp. 208–15.

his compulsory subscription of the Covenants was to deny absolutism, for 'total government is not upon a king'. The Covenanters' past use of force was bluntly justified with respect to Charles I, who had, 'in a hostile way, set himself to overthrow religion, parliaments, laws and liberties'. On a radical reading of Buchanan, the exercise of rights to resist was an expression of popular sovereignty. However, Covenanting ideologues from Wariston to Douglas were adamant that the people's rights to resist did not vindicate any attempt by a private citizen to assassinate Charles I as a tyrant. Charles I may have been ungodly, but he was also the legitimate monarch. The right of the people to resist a lawful king who had threatened to become tyrannical was to be exercised corporately by the political nation. The coactive power over monarchy was deemed to have been vested in 'the estates of a land': that is, initially in the Tables that had assumed control of the revolutionary movement at its outset and, subsequently, in the Scottish Estates meeting as a parliament from 1640 and, in the intervals between parliaments, in the Committee of Estates. But the exercise of legislative and executive powers by the Covenanting Movement conformed less to Buchanan's ideal of an aristocratic republic than to a centralized oligarchy that imposed unprecedented demands for ideological conformity, financial supply and military recruitment during the 1640s. In the process, the Movement became embroiled in civil war, then split and finally sundered as Scotland came under the sway of Oliver Cromwell, who enforced incorporation into the English Commonwealth then the English Protectorate during the 1650s.[20]

The constitutional settlements that followed on from the Restoration of Charles II in 1660 revived the Stuarts' *ius imperium* but ruled out any return to a confessional confederation united by allegiance to the Covenants. Internationally, the Stuart's Britannic perspective was highlighted by the Dutch academic, Rutgerius Hermannides, who nevertheless chronicled continuing English hegemony over Scotland as over Ireland. The alternative Scottish perspective as articulated by George Buchanan was seemingly laid to rest by the German jurist, Samuel Pufendorf, who came to view England as a composite monarchy with Scottish and Irish dependencies. Charles II was carrying on the mantle of Cromwell in maintaining English greatness through dominion over the seas and the promotion of commerce.[21] Notwithstanding the failure of the Covenanting Movement to limit monarchy through British confessional confederation, some distinctive

---

[20] J. Kerr (ed.), *The Covenants and the Covenanters* (Edinburgh, 1896), pp. 348–98; A.I. Macinnes, 'Covenanting Ideology in Seventeenth-century Scotland', in J.H. Ohlmeyer (ed.), *Political Thought in Seventeenth-century Ireland* (Cambridge, 2000), pp. 191–220.

[21] Rutgerius Hermannides, *Britannia Magna* (Amsterdam, 1661); Samuel [von] Puffendorf, *An Introduction to the History of the Principal Kingdoms and States of Europe* (London, 1699).

associations can be made with Polish rights of resistance as affirmed through a *rokosz*, first in 1606–1608 and more especially in 1662–66, events that once again brought Buchanan's ideas into play.

The Commonwealth of Two Nations

The *rokosz* as a tangible expression of rebellion in Poland–Lithuania in the seventeenth century was marked by oath-taking and by the greater and lesser nobility, who essentially constituted the political nation, confederating to assert rights of resistance that elevated their Commonwealth over the monarchy. These rights had both general and particular roots. The general derived from the conciliarism of the late medieval church, especially as rationalized by Marsiglio of Padua, and from the individual right of conscience to dissent as enshrined in canon law. The particular can be traced back to the later fourteenth century, when the Jagellonian dukes of Lithuania became elected kings of Poland. The elective nature of the Polish crown offered opportunities for bargaining to strengthen the privileges of the nobility, the provincial diets and – after the creation of the Commonwealth of Two Nations by the Union of Lublin in 1569 –the central diet or *sejm*. The legal right of resistance was first invoked by the nobility to justify the Commonwealth's revolt in 1606–1608 against Sigismund III, who was suspected of seeking to establish absolute monarchy in the Vasa line.

The next invocation of 1662–66, which occurred after the Commonwealth had been torn asunder by wars against Sweden and Russia, was directed against the endeavours of the last Vasa, John Casimir, to secure the succession during his own reign and thereby strengthen the central powers of the monarchy. A key element of this *rokosz* was the accompanying polemical controversy. The case for a strong centralizing if not absolute monarchy had been made by the eminent German political and legal theorist, Hermann Conring, a professor at Helmstedt who had been attached to the Swedish court as a doctor of medicine. Jan Sachs (Marinius Polonus) from Fraustadt in Wielkopolska, who later became secretary of the city of Thorn in Polish Prussia, mounted a spirited defence of the Commonwealth and its nobility. His *De Scopo Reipublicae Poloniae contra Conringium*, which was published in Breslau in 1665, appealed not only to theorists such as Bodin and Grotius to uphold rights of resistance within the Commonwealth. It also made use of Buchanan's *Rerum Scoticarum Historia* to affirm the elective nature of the Polish crown and the right of the nobility to uphold this by resistance if necessary, as had been the case in Scotland when James IV had been backed forcibly by the nobility to replace his father, James III, in 1488.[22]

Scottish history can be given a further Polish spin. The rights of the Scottish commonwealth to resist ungodly and tyrannical monarchy, as articulated in particular by Buchanan, can lead the Protestant Reformation of 1560–67 to be viewed as a Scottish *rokosz*, as can the fundamental limitations in kirk and state imposed on Charles I by the Covenanting Movement in 1640–41. Likewise the Claim of Right, which forfeited his second son James VII & II in 1689 and laid the basis for the Revolution settlement in Scotland, asserted similar rights to resist and replace an ungodly and unconstitutional monarch. Thus James VII was deposed in favour of his daughter Mary and his son-in-law William of Orange, whereas in England, as James II, he was merely deemed to have abdicated the throne.[23]

However, the Revolution Settlement of 1689–90 in Scotland differed in two important respects from the constitutional settlement achieved in 1640–41. Firstly, the political estates actually changed the monarchy by electing to offer the crown to Mary and William of Orange on condition that they accepted limitations on their prerogative powers and reintroduced presbyterianism in the kirk. Secondly, the removal of episcopal control over the kirk was effected for strictly erastian reasons – that it was contrary to the general inclinations of the people, not that it was a covenanting imperative or a requirement for a godly commonwealth. The lack of reference to covenanting reflected the movement's shift from a position of power to that of protest following the restoration of Charles II in 1660. In the process, control had largely passed from nobles, gentry and burgesses to farmers, artisans and itinerant preachers. Polemicists such as Sir James Stewart in his *Jus Populi Vindicatum* (1669) and Alexander Shields in his *A Hind Let Loose* (1687) had reinvigorated a radical interpretation of Buchanan's *De Iure Regni* in broadening the social basis of those entitled to resist ungodly and tyrannical monarchy beyond the accepted political nation as comprised by the Scottish Estates. Accordingly, the Scottish

---

[22]   I am greatly indebted to Professor Edward Opalinski, Institute of History, Polish Academy of Sciences, Warsaw, for his insights on *rokosz*, and to Dr Karin Friedrich, School of Divinity, History and Philosophy, University of Aberdeen, for her diligence in unearthing and contextualizing Buchanan's Polish connection. For further background on the Commonwealth, rebellion and resistance, see E. Opalinski, 'The Path towards the Commonwealth of the Two Nations', in Macinnes and Ohlmeyer (eds), *Stuart Kingdoms in the Seventeenth Century*, pp. 49–61, and R. Frost, *After the Deluge: Poland–Lithuania and the Second Northern War, 1655–1660* (Cambridge, 1993), pp. 1–25, 168–79.

[23]   E. Opalinski, 'Von der Krise der ständischen Monarchien bis zur Revolution (ca. 1600–1789)', in R.G. Asch (ed.), *Der europäische Adel im Ancien Regime* (Böhlau, 2001), pp. 77–104; A.I. Macinnes, *Union and Empire: The Making of the United Kingdom in 1707* (Cambridge, 2007), pp. 267–9.

Estates at the Revolution, no less than Sir George Mackenzie of Rosehaugh and other stalwarts of the outgoing Restoration regime, wished to distance themselves from all socially subversive challenges to established authority in kirk and state.[24]

Buchanan's historical and polemical writings were pressed into service in England more than in Scotland in the build-up to the Revolution, the first English translation of Buchanan's *De Iure Regni* having been published in 1680. At this juncture, the emergent Whig interest in England was attempting, through the Exclusion Crisis of 1678–81, to prevent James, Duke of York (the future James VII & II), a professed Roman Catholic, succeeding his brother Charles II. The Whigs, who subsequently became embroiled in assassination attempts such as the Rye House Plot of 1683, were also associated with two abortive rebellions in Scotland and England, led respectively in 1685 by Archibald Campbell, 9th Earl of Argyll, and James Scott, Duke of Monmouth, an illegitimate son of Charles II. Only a few Scottish nobles, gentry and burgesses had sided with the Whigs, but their leading British ideologue, Algernon Sydney, executed for his involvement in the Rye House Plot, professed admiration for Buchanan's political thought and affirmed that a virtuous commonwealth was enhanced by elective monarchy as exemplified by the Polish crown. For their rebellious activities and their seeming preference for elected over hereditary monarchy, the Whigs were castigated by their Tory opponents as the Polish faction. Their leader, Anthony Ashley-Cooper, Earl of Shaftesbury, was lampooned as the 'King of Poland'.[25]

The association of contested elections with rebellion, rights of resistance and elevation of the commonwealth over the monarchy gained added significance with the election of the Elector of Saxony as Augustus II in 1697 and subsequently the *rokosz* mounted against him in Poland–Lithuania in 1704. The French were intimately involved in these events, the first having taken place at the conclusion of the Nine Years' War, which had lined up Louis XIV against William of Orange, and the second occurring after the renewal of Anglo-French hostilities in the War of the Spanish Succession. No less significantly, the *rokosz* of 1704 occurred in

---

[24] *A Source Book of Scottish History, Volume III (1567–1707)*, ed. W.C. Dickinson and G. Donaldson (London and Edinburgh, 1961), pp. 198–217; T. Harris, 'Reluctant Revolutionaries? Scots and the Revolution of 1688–89', in H. Nenner (ed.), *Politics and the Political Imagination in Later Stuart Britain* (Rochester, 1997), pp. 97–117.

[25] *A Modest Vindication of the Earl of S[...]y: in a letter to a friend concerning his being elected King of Poland* (London, 1681); *The Last Will and Testament of Anthony King of Poland* (London, 1682); *The King of Poland's Last Speech to his Countrymen* (London, 1682); *The Case is Alter'd Now: or, The conversion of Anthony King of Poland, published for satisfaction of the sanctifyed brethren* (London, 1683); *A Congratulation of the Protestant-joyner to Anthony King of Poland, upon his arrival in the lower world* (London, 1683); Algernon Sidney, *Discourses Concerning Government* (London, 1704).

the midst of the political sparring between the Scottish Estates and the English Parliament that materially affected the attitude of Queen Anne and her English ministry to parliamentary incorporation.[26]

Union and Rebellion

The first negotiations for Anglo-Scottish union in the reign of Queen Anne took place just after her accession, primarily to avert the War of the Spanish Succession becoming the War of the British Succession. In 1701, the English Parliament had passed an Act of Settlement, which unilaterally prescribed the succession of the house of Hanover, as the nearest surviving Protestant heirs of the Stuarts through Elizabeth of Bohemia. Following the death of William's designated successor and sister-in-law, Queen Anne, then Princess of Denmark, the English throne would pass to Sophia, Electress of Hanover (or her son, the future George I). However, on the death of James VII & II that same year, Louis XIV had immediately proclaimed the exiled king's son as James VIII & III. Carrying out the dying wishes of William of Orange in 1702, Anne had authorized negotiations for political incorporation between commissioners from the Scottish Estates and the English Parliament. However, three months of negotiation proved fruitless by February 1703 as the Scots held out for substantive reparations for Darien, their colonial enterprise on the Panama Isthmus that had failed three years earlier after William had deemed it expendable.[27]

Notwithstanding the aborted negotiations, the prospect of political incorporation led to rival perspectives on comparative state formation, which set the scene for further polemical jousting on the issue of British Union. The Country Party, opponents of political incorporation as advocated by the Court Party, benefited from a revitalized Scottish perspective provided by George Ridpath, a committed Presbyterian given to extolling the historical insights of Buchanan. A former Whig polemicist based among the Scottish community in London, Ridpath did not rule out some form of federative union, but his preferred constitutional option was a return to the revolutionary arrangements of 1640–41 that had

---

[26]   NAS, Hamilton Papers, GD 406/1/4176, /6407, /6433–5, /6505; Papers of Lord Polwarth, GD 157/3310; Macpherson of Cluny Papers GD 80/854; Breadalbane Muniments, GD 112/39/175/7, /15; Bernard Connor, *The History of Poland in several letters to persons of quality* (London, 1698), pp. 1–32.

[27]   The National Archives, State Papers Scotland, series II, A Journal of the Proceedings upon the Union between the Kingdoms of England and Scotland, 1702–03, SP 54 /2/1; W. Speck, *The Birth of Britain: A New Nation, 1700–1710* (Oxford, 1994), pp. 44–5; D. Watt, 'The Management of Capital by the Company of Scotland 1696–1707', *Journal of Scottish Historical Studies*, 25 (2006): pp. 97–118.

secured limited monarchy and English recognition of Scottish sovereignty by the Treaty of London. Confederation would advance the Revolution Settlements in both countries.[28]

After a general election had significantly altered the party balance in the Scottish Estates, the Country Party took advantage of disunity over parliamentary priorities on the part of the Court Party to push through a radical agenda to redress the interference of English ministers in Scottish affairs, to promote the probity and accountability of Scottish officials and judges, and to defend the acclaimed rights and liberties of Scotland. This programme caught the English ministry off guard and initiated the legislative war of 1703–1705. The Scottish Estates duly passed two key acts that restricted the prerogative powers of the monarchy. The first was the Act anent Peace and War, which laid claim not so much to an independent foreign policy as to a binding commitment on Queen Anne's successor, if the common monarchy continued, to gain consent from the Scottish Estates before any war could be declared. Although the sovereign was to be free to take all requisite measures to suppress any insurrection or repel invasion from abroad, any treaties for peace, alliance or commerce also required ratification by the Estates. The curbing of unwarranted intrusion by the English ministry in Scottish affairs, which had become an incrementally marked feature since the Revolution, was also a feature of the second measure, the Act of Security. In this case, however, the presumption was made that the common monarchy would not continue unless prior to the death of Queen Anne 'there be condicions of government settled and enacted' that recognized the honour and sovereignty of the separate crown and kingdom; the freedom, frequency and power of parliaments; and that the religion, liberty and trade of the nation should not be subject to English or any foreign interference. The Scottish Estates were insistent on their sole right to elect a hereditary successor from the Stuart line provided he or she was Protestant on the twentieth day following Anne's death. The new sovereign was committed within thirty days if resident in Britain or within three months if resident overseas to accept the limitations prescribed in the coronation oath and any further limitations imposed by the Scottish Estates up to Anne's death and in the twenty days thereafter.[29]

James Douglas, Duke of Queensberry, empowered to validate legislation as the Queen's Commissioner, was prepared to accept the Act anent Peace and War. But, as he was also leader of the Court Party, he deferred giving consent to the Act of Security until he received fresh instructions from London. The English ministry were willing to pass

---

[28] [George Ridpath], *A Discourse upon the Union of England and Scotland* (Edinburgh, 1702).

[29] *A Source Book of Scottish History*, vol. 3, pp. 472–7.

both acts with a view to rescinding them in a later parliamentary session. Nevertheless, according to the Danish ambassador, Ivar Rosenkrantz, a close confidant of the Queen's consort, Prince George, Anne emphatically rejected what she deemed the exorbitant demands of the Scots. Once the Estates were notified that royal consent was withheld, they declined to vote supply for the Scottish forces in the standing army held in reserve at home pending service on the continent with the English against the French.[30] The Queen was now faced with a choice. She could reject the Act of Security and disband the forces on the Scottish establishment or accept limitations on the prerogative that could serve as a precedent for similar action in the English Parliament. The triumph of the Country Party, however, was far from complete. They had failed to press home their advantage to secure the election of commissioners to negotiate a treaty with their English counterparts, a manoeuvre that would either have restricted negotiations to a federative arrangement or forced their outright collapse. At the same time, the proroguing of parliament denied them the opportunity to carry the fundamental programme of limitations advocated by the radical constitutional reformer Andrew Fletcher of Saltoun, who had been implicated in the abortive Rye House Plot. More significantly in Anne's eyes, the Scottish Estates had strayed onto dangerous constitutional grounds in their discussions on limitations linked to state formation in contemporary Europe, especially when these discussions now included Poland–Lithuania.[31]

Among the Country Party, the elevation of the Commonwealth of Two Nations above its elective monarchy seemed to provide grounds for further limiting prerogative powers if Scotland was to have the same monarch as England after the death of Queen Anne. The fundamental constitutional checks on monarchy sought by Fletcher of Saltoun and his associates would have required a radical reform of the Revolution Settlement in Scotland; a situation anathema to Queen Anne and her authoritarian consort George, who, as a prince of Denmark–Norway, came from probably the

---

30   [George Ridpath], *Proceedings of the Parliament of Scotland begun at Edinburgh, 6th May 1703. With an Account of al the Material Debates which occur'd during that Session* (Edinburgh, 1704); BL, Sidney, 1st Earl of Godolphin: Official Correspondence. Home 1701–1710, Add. MSS 28,055, fols 7–8, 300–302; Hatton-Finch Papers: Letters to the Earl of Nottingham, Secretary of State, vol. II (1703–1725), Add. MSS 29,589, fols 97, 107–8; RC, TKUA England, Akter og Dokumenter nedr Sofart og Handel: Order med Bilag, 1703, A.III/ 207/45, /46, /50, /55–7, /59, /61–63, /65–7.

31   D[umfries] H[ouse, Ayrshire], Colonel Wm Dalrymple, Parliamentary Notebook, 1704–1705, A 817/1, pp. 2–49; RC, TKUA England, Akter og Dokumenter nedr Sofart og Handel: Order med Bilag, 1704, A.III/209/35, /44–5, /47–8, /49, /52–4; J. Robertson, 'Empire and Union: Two Concepts of the Early Modern European Political Order', in Robertson (ed.), *A Union for Empire: Political Though and the Union of 1707* (Cambridge, 1995), pp. 3–36.

least admired but most accomplished absolute regime in Europe.[32] Her firm resolve to defend her prerogative powers was bolstered by details of the latest *rokosz* against Augustus II carried in the newsletters and annual political commentaries for 1704. Simultaneously, Whigs ambitious for office in England were keen to distance themselves from their past characterizations as a Polish faction at the Exclusion Crisis.[33]

The Whig position was of critical importance in the aftermath of the Scottish parliamentary session of 1704. The Tories in the English Parliament mounted a sustained attack on Anne's foremost minister, Sidney Godolphin, Earl of Godolphin, for persuading the Queen to assent to the Act of Security. Godolphin, who as treasurer had financial oversight of English engagement in the War of the Spanish Succession, was only spared a motion of censure in late November by the Whig leadership, known as the Junto, coming to his rescue.[34] The Whig Junto was duly instrumental in promoting the Alien Act in December 1704, which eventually passed through both houses of the English Parliament by February 1705. This act, which was readily endorsed at Court, threatened to treat Scots as foreign nationals rather than as subjects of a common monarchy. They would be subject to discriminatory tariffs and commercial embargoes unless they agreed to treat for Union by Christmas 1705. As the English backlash against the Scottish offensive during the legislative war, this act marked a signal switch in public policy. The English ministry was no longer concentrating on securing the Hanoverian Succession but on giving priority to political incorporation both as a means of pre-empting the Scottish programme of limitations and bringing Scottish commerce at home and abroad under regulation from Westminster.[35]

By the outset of 1706, Union was on course as an English initiative. Through Union, England stood to gain much needed manpower for empire, manufacturing and war. At the same time, Union offered a meaningful prospect of terminating the disruptive impact of Scottish commercial

---

[32]   P.H. Scott, *Andrew Fletcher and the Treaty of Union* (Edinburgh, 1994), pp. 83–4, 227–8; RC, TKUA England, Akter og Dokumenter nedr Sofart og Handel: Order med Bilag, 1702–1705, A.III/207/56, /62–6 & /209/45, /48 & /210/38, /42–3, /45–6; Robert Molesworth, Viscount Molesworth, *An Account of Denmark as it was in the year 1692* (London, 1694), pp. 258–71.

[33]   Patrick Gordon, *Geography Anatomiz'd: or, the geographical grammar* (London, 1704), pp. 140–42; David Jones, *A Compleat History of Europe: or, a view of the affairs therein, civil and military for the year 1704* (London, 1705), pp. 85–7; John Toland, *Anglia Libera: or the limitations and succession of the crown of England explain'd and asserted* (London, 1701), pp. 108–9.

[34]   DH, Colonel Wm Dalrymple, Parliamentary Notebook, 1704–1705, A 817/1, pp. 49–55; RC, TKUA England, Akter og Dokumenter nedr Sofart og Handel: Order med Bilag, 1704–1705, A.III/209/60, /68–72, /75 & 210/1–2, /7.

[35]   *A Source Book of Scottish History*, vol. 3, pp. 477–8.

networks, particularly their carrying trade, on England's transatlantic commerce and woollen industry. By securing the Hanoverian Succession, Union seemingly lessened the prospect of a French invasion through Scotland in the guise of supporting Jacobitism (the followers of James VIII & III). Queen Anne was an enthusiastic advocate of a Union that would terminate the Scottish Estates, as was the Court Party in Scotland, intent on upholding the royal prerogative, conserving the Revolution Settlement in Kirk and State, and securing new places and profits in the British Empire.[36]

But there was to be one last flutter of Buchanan's reception in Northern Europe. As the third clause in the Treaty of Union was being debated in the Scottish Estates on 18 November 1706, an anonymous protest was raised – in all probability by Saltoun and his associates – that this clause for a common British Parliament did not respect the sovereignties and privileges of the two nations, unlike the union of Poland and Lithuania.[37] The accomplishment of political incorporation through the creation of the United Kingdom of Great Britain from 1 May 1707 duly marked the triumph of the English concept of a commonwealth in which sovereignty was exercised by the king or queen through parliament. The Buchanan-inspired, Scottish concept of a commonwealth challenging established monarchy and exercising rights of resistance was not entirely abandoned, however, as Scottish Jacobitism episodically took over the tradition of *rokosz*.[38]

---

[36]   Macinnes, *Union and Empire*, pp. 277–309; C.A. Whatley with D. Patrick, *The Scots and the Union* (Edinburgh, 2007), pp. 224–42.

[37]   DH, Colonel Dalrymple's Memorandums, particularly during 1706–1707 debates in the last Parliament of Scotland, A 817/2, pp. 53–4.

[38]   A.I. Macinnes, 'Jacobitism in Scotland, An Episodic Cause or National Movement?', *Scottish Historical Review*, 86 (2007): pp. 225–52.

PART THREE
Buchanan and Revolutionary Britain

CHAPTER 8

The Ciceronian Theory of Tyrannicide from Buchanan to Milton

Martin Dzelzainis

On Monday 16 July 1683, in the wake of the so-called Rye House Plot to assassinate King Charles II and his brother James Duke of York, the hebdomadal council of the University of Oxford instructed William Jane, Regius Professor of Divinity, together with the university's leading doctors of divinity to identify the subversive political principles that had inspired the outrage. Within six days, these pillars of the Anglican establishment had assembled a comprehensive list of twenty-seven propositions that were then read out in full by Jane to the University's convocation on Saturday. The convocation in turn unanimously passed its *Judgment and decree ... against certain pernicious books and damnable doctrines, destructive to the sacred persons of princes, their state and government, and of all humane society.*[1] Of these propositions, the one that is most relevant to the theme of this chapter is the twenty-third, according to which

> Wicked Kings and Tyrants ought to be put to death, and if the Judges and inferior Magistrates will not do their office, the power of the sword devolves to the People; if the major part of the People refuse to exercise this power, then the Ministers may excommunicate such a King, after which it is lawful for any of the Subjects to kill him, as the People did *Athaliah*, and *Jehu Jezebel*.[2]

---

[1] For these events, see R.A. Beddard, 'Tory Oxford', in Nicholas Tyacke (ed.), *The History of the University of Oxford, Volume 4: Seventeenth-century Oxford* (Oxford, 1997), pp. 891–8.

[2] *Oxford Decree*, p. 6. For the Latin version, see *Judicium & decretum Universitatis Oxoniensis latum in convocatione habita Jul. 21, an. 1683, contra quosdam perniciosos libros & propositiones impias quae capitibus sacratissimorum principum, eorum statui & regimini, & omni humanae societati exitium intentant* (Oxford, 1683), p. 6: 'Tyranni & impii Principes morte multandi sunt; quod si Judices & inferiores Magistratus officio suo desint, jus gladii redit ad populum, quo si major pars uti nolit, Pastores & Ministri Ecclesiastici debent Principes Satanæ tradere, & post sententiam Excommunicationis latani, quibuslibet subditis licebit eos occidere, eodem jure quo subditi *Athaliam*, & *Jehu Jezabelem*'.

Those who are said to have held this doctrine about who may put to death a tyrant include '*Buchanan, Knox, Goodman, Gilby, Jesuits*'. This represents a confessional melange of Calvinists, in the shape of Scotsmen (George Buchanan and John Knox) and Englishmen (Christopher Goodman and Anthony Gilby), and Jesuits (in this case, Robert Parsons and Robert Bellarmine).[3] Although the collection of names may strike us as eclectic, it had long been an Anglican belief that resistance theory was associated with the confessional extremes. Indeed, it can be argued that there was more than a grain of truth in what the Oxford convocation was alleging. As Quentin Skinner has observed in his account of the development of Calvinist political thought, since 'the arguments taken by the Calvinist from the Lutherans had originally been taken by the Lutherans from the civil and canon law, we may say with very little exaggeration that the main foundations of the Calvinist theory of revolution were in fact constructed entirely by their Catholic adversaries'.[4]

However, proposition 23 is manifestly a composite text, synthesizing a range of views on who was able to punish the ruler. No individual theorist ever advocated following the entire sequence of steps for legitimating tyrannicide that it sets out, according to which, if magistrates default, then it becomes the duty of the people and, if the people should default, then – once ministers have excommunicated the tyrant – any subject can kill him, as was warranted by Scripture. If we leave the Jesuits to one side, how well do the various Calvinists singled out by the Oxford divines measure up to this conspectus? While all of them refer to magistrates, none of them actually uses the phrase 'inferior magistrates' in apposition to private persons as was routinely done by Lutheran and Calvinist theorists. This may be a key distinction for proponents of resistance theory like Theodore Beza or the author(s) of the *Vindiciae, Contra Tyrannos* (1579), but it does not feature in the work of the British Calvinists. The latter were in

---

[3]   The 'Jesuits' in question were identified as Parsons and Bellarmine by Anthony Wood in his annotated copy of the convocation's decree; see Beddard, 'Tory Oxford', p. 893 n.209. The mistaken inclusion of the presbyterian clergyman Anthony Gilby (*c.*1510–85) gives a clue as to how Jane and the divines set about their task. In wrongly assuming that Gilby, rather than his fellow exile John Ponet (1514–56), was the author of *A Shorte Treatise of politike power, and of the true Obedience which subiectes owe to kynges and other ciuile Gouernours* ([Strasbourg], 1556), they were following the lead given in compilations of political unorthodoxy such as those by George Bancroft, *Davngerous Positions and Proceedings, published and preached within this Iland of Brytaine, under pretence of Reformation, and for the Presbiteriall Discipline* (London, 1593), pp. 34–9, 62, and Sir Thomas Aston, *A Remonstrance, Against Presbitery* (n.p., 1641), sig. G3r (and see G4r for a form of words close to that of proposition 23). For John Milton's reliance on Aston, see Milton, *Political Writings*, ed. Martin Dzelzainis (Cambridge, 1991), pp. 25, 41.

[4]   Quentin Skinner, *The Foundations of Modern Political Thought* (2 vols, Cambridge, 1978), vol. 2, p. 321.

fact much more open than their continental counterparts to the idea of popular revolution. In the 1550s, John Knox, Christopher Goodman and John Ponet all published works that appealed directly to the people as a whole to resist their rulers. It is significant, as Richard Tuck has pointed out, that their writings 'derived stylistically from the sermon rather than the legal treatise', for their basic concern was to instil a sense of the religious duty to resist idolatry and tyranny.[5] Thus Knox argued that, in the case of an idolatrous ruler, 'not only the Magistrate, to whome the sword is committet, but also the people are bound by that oath, which they haue made to God, to reuenge to the vttermost of their power the iniuirie done against his Maiestie'. And he was even willing to countenance individual action in the event of 'vniuersal defections' from true religion. For example, in the case of Catholic countries, since 'no ordinarie iustice can be executed', the punishment of idolatrous rulers 'must be reserued to God': he will appoint the 'meanes' to punish them just as he 'raised vpp Iehu' when the 'hole people' of Israel 'togethir conspired against God'.[6]

Goodman and Ponet (though not Knox) also differed from their Calvinist successors in placing much more emphasis on the private-law theory of resistance.[7] This theory was ultimately based on the civil and canon law premises that, according to the law of nature, it is lawful to repel force with force (*vim vi repellere licere*), and that a judge who is proceeding unjustly may be forcibly resisted. These doctrines had been taken up and transposed into the public sphere by the Lutheran jurists who, in 1530, advised John of Saxony that a judge who exceeds his lawful authority automatically reduces himself to the status of a private citizen and can be resisted accordingly. The theory was reformulated most influentially in the Confession of Magdeburg in 1550, where it was argued that a ruler who behaves tyrannically can no longer be regarded as one of the powers ordained of God and can therefore be resisted in the same way as anyone who employs unjust force.[8]

What this theory implied was that not only inferior magistrates but the people as a whole – and arguably even private citizens – could act against a tyrannical ruler. But while the Lutherans tended to minimize

---

[5]   Richard Tuck, *Natural Rights Theories* (Cambridge, 1979), p. 43.

[6]   John Knox, *The Appellation of Iohn Knoxe from the cruell and most iniust sentence pronounced against him by the false bishoppes and clergie of Scotland, with his supplication and exhortation to the nobilitie, estates, and communaltie of the same realme* (Geneva, 1558), 35a–b (contractions expanded).

[7]   For the development of the private-law theory, see Skinner, *Foundations*, vol. 2, pp. 124–6, 197–204, 221–2; for the much more limited use made of the theory by, for example, the Huguenots, see *Vindiciae, Contra Tyrannos*, ed. and trans. George Garnett (Cambridge, 1994), pp. 45, 49, 92, 105, 149.

[8]   For further discussion of the development of these ideas in Lutheran Germany, see Robert von Friedeburg's essay, above ch. 6.

this aspect of their version of the private-law argument, it was positively exploited by Ponet and, with even fewer reservations, by Goodman. Thus Ponet's defence of forcible resistance in his *Shorte Treatise* of 1556 (the work that was routinely misattributed to Gilby) is based squarely on the fact that 'the lawes of many christiane regiones doo permitte, that priuate men maie kil malefactours, yea though they were magistrates, in some cases'. Ponet then goes on to list some of the standard examples discussed in the *Digest*. At the same time, however, he is not altogether sure that this practice can 'be mentened by Goddes worde'. Although his syntax becomes rather strained at this point, he seems to have in mind those extreme cases 'wher execucion of iuste punishement upon tirannes, idolaters, and traitorous governours is either by the hole state utterly neglected, or the prince with the nobilitie and counsail conspire the subuersion or alteracion of their contrey and people'. Ponet is prepared to allow that 'any priuate man maie kill' in those circumstances, but only if he has either been 'commaunded or permitted by common autoritie' (a possibility that Ponet himself seems just to have excluded) or if he has 'som special inwarde commaundment of surely proued mocion of God' as happened in the case of Moses, Phineas and Ehud.[9]

The same ambivalence can be seen in Ponet's more extended discussion of Ehud and Eglon later in the same chapter. On the one hand, Ponet emphasizes the parallels between the experience of Israel under the Maobites and England under Mary Tudor and Philip of Spain. Eglon had, for example, brought with him 'a great power of Ammonites and Amalekites' whose 'pride and filthinesse of life' is compared to the 'common nature of Italianes and Spaniardes'. This would suggest that Ponet was advocating individual acts of violence against the Marian regime. However, when Ponet finally comes to pronounce whether Ehud's killing of Eglon was 'well done or euil', he proves most unwilling to endorse such an anarchic conclusion. He does allow that 'the dede is … commended in scripture', but he is at pains to emphasize that Ehud was not 'sent of the people to kill the king', and explains that he was forced to act in isolation because he would otherwise have certainly been betrayed by 'one Iudas or other' and been hung, drawn and quartered for his 'entreprise'. And Ponet concludes by stressing once again that 'the scripture saieth, that Ahud (being a private persone) was stered vp only by the spirite of God'.[10]

Substantially the same theory underpins *How Svperior Powers Oght to be Obeyd* (1558) by Buchanan's friend, Christopher Goodman. In Chapter X, for example, which deals with 'Obiections out of the olde Testament',

---

[9]   Ponet, *Shorte Treatise*, sigs G8r–v (contractions expanded).
[10]   Ponet, *Shorte Treatise*, sigs H5v–H6r (contractions expanded).

Goodman declares that, when 'kinges or Rulers are become altogether blasphemers of God, and oppressors and murtherers of their subiectes, then oght they to be accompted no more for kinges or lawfull Magistrats, but as priuate men: and to be examined, accused, condemned and punished by the Lawe of God, whereunto they are and oght to be subiect'. This conclusion is restated no less emphatically in Chapter XIII: rulers who use their 'publik auctoritie' unlawfully are 'no more publik persons' but 'are to be taken of all men, as priuate persones' and punished accordingly.[11]

But who exactly is to do the punishing in such cases? In the same chapter Goodman gives careful consideration to the problem of what the people should do if 'the Magistrates and other officiers contemne their duetie in defending Gods glorie and the Lawes committed to their charge'. The question this poses is whether it can ever be right that 'we that are subiectes take the sworde in our hands?' However, Goodman dismisses as 'vaine' any excuses that might be offered to justify the people's inaction in such a case. On the contrary, God has charged 'not onely the Magistrates and officers' with the duty 'to roote out evil' but also 'the whole multitude … to whom a portion of the sworde of iustice is committed' for that purpose. Goodman readily admits that one difficulty with this argument is that it may 'appeare at the firste sight a great disordre, that the people shulde take vnto them the punishment of transgression'. But his response is merely to reiterate that, when magistrates 'cease to do their duetie', and the people are as a result left 'without officers' and are even in a worse situation than 'if they had none at all', they can and must act by virtue of the fact that 'God geueth the sworde in to the peoples hande, and he him self is become immedialty [sic] their head'.[12]

Almost none of this holds true for Buchanan's De Iure Regni apud Scotos Dialogus, first published in print in 1579 though written some years earlier.[13] Indeed, strictly speaking, the only parts of proposition 23 to which his theory answers are the opening and closing clauses to the effect that tyrants should be put to death and that any subject may do it. When it comes to executing justice upon a tyrant, Buchanan does not assign a privileged role to the magistrate, inferior or otherwise. Nor is there any requirement to wait until ministers have excommunicated the tyrant. Nor

---

[11] Christopher Goodman, How Svperior Powers Oght to be Obeyd of their subiects: and Wherin they may lawfully by Gods Worde be disobeyed and resisted (Geneva, 1558), pp. 139–40, 187–8 (contractions expanded).

[12] Goodman, Svperior Powers, pp. 179–80, 185 (contractions expanded). It should be noted that Goodman's account of how the power of the sword (ius gladii) ends up in the hands of the people lacks the element of automaticity that characterizes the process of devolution outlined in proposition 23; that is to say, for Goodman, when magistrates default, power does not devolve to the people ipso facto but is in effect newly given to them by God.

[13] On the date of De Iure Regni, see McFarlane, Buchanan, pp. 392–6, and the 'Introduction' to Buchanan, De Iure Regni, pp. xxvii–xxxvii.

is there any need to appeal to scriptural precedents. It is true that Buchanan admits at one point that 'God frequently stirs up from the lowest ranks of the people (*de plebe*) humble and obscure men as avengers of the pride and violence of tyrants', but this is principally by way of countering the argument that God sets tyrants over people as a punishment. Buchanan's point is that divine commands cut both ways; if anyone tries to argue from St Paul that we are divinely enjoined to obey tyrants, he says, 'you will immediately have to face the objection that Ahab was also killed at God's command'.[14] More significantly still, although Buchanan is evidently familiar with the cases in the *Digest* upon which Goodman and Ponet based their arguments, he places no real weight on the private-law dictum that, as he phrases it, 'whatever is done by force can similarly be undone by force' ('quicquid per vim fiat simili vi solvi posse') when developing his own theory of tyrannicide.[15] This being so, however, it might well be asked upon what alternative theoretical grounds Buchanan is able to assert – as he does with great confidence – that private individuals can lawfully take up the sword of justice (*ius gladii*) by way of ridding themselves of tyranny. Or, to put it another way, what solution does he offer to the conundrum about the origins of the *ius gladii* that eventually led Thomas Hobbes to declare in Chapter 28 of *Leviathan* that there was still 'a question to be answered, of much importance; which is, by what door the Right, or Authority of Punishing in any case, came in'?[16]

Traditionally, there have been two answers to this puzzle. The first is that the punitive powers exercised by rulers are granted to them directly by God, who alone has the power of life and death. The second is that they acquire the right to punish from the community by which they are constituted as rulers. But this merely prompts the question of how the community came to possess the right that it then proceeds to transfer or delegate to the ruler. One school of thought held that the right to kill was a natural (and hence ultimately divine) power that only came into existence with the community itself. But another, and more radical, view was that communities possessed no rights other than those formerly enjoyed by individuals in the state of nature, including the right to use force not only for self-defence but also for punishment – what John Locke in the *Two Treatises of Government* later called the 'very strange Doctrine' that the

---

14   Buchanan, *De Iure Regni*, pp. 117, 125.

15   See ibid., pp. 96–7; and see p. 151.

16   Thomas Hobbes, *Leviathan*, ed. Richard Tuck (Cambridge, 1996), p. 214. For recent attempts to address this question in relation to Hobbes's own political theory, see Quentin Skinner and Yves Charles Zarka, *Hobbes: The Amsterdam Debate*, ed. Hans Blom (Hildesheim, 2001), pp. 71–87 ('Hobbes and the Right to Punish'), and Dieter Hüning, 'Hobbes on the Right to Punish', in Patricia Springborg (ed.), *The Cambridge Companion to Hobbes's 'Leviathan'* (Cambridge, 2007), pp. 217–40.

natural state of affairs is one in which 'every Man hath a Right to punish the Offender, and be the Executioner of the Law of Nature'.[17]

Where does Buchanan fit into this scheme of things? One view, proposed by Quentin Skinner in an influential essay in 1980, is that he belonged to the last and most radical of these schools.[18] What makes this suggestion appear plausible is the fact that Buchanan was extensively exposed to late medieval scholasticism during his formative years, and in particular to the thought of Jacques Almain (c.1480–1515) who was – like Buchanan – a pupil of John Mair (c.1467–1550). While it is undoubtedly true that Almain believed that the right of the sword is not conferred upon the ruler immediately by God but by the community as a whole, according to Skinner (in the first version of his essay), Almain further held that the community itself can only have acquired this right by virtue of the fact that each of its individual members had possessed it beforehand. And what this meant in turn was that when Buchanan came to address these issues more than half a century later all that he had to do in order to underpin his claim that it was open to private persons to kill tyrants was simply to recast this radical scholastic doctrine in a secular and humanist idiom. But Skinner's argument, as it relates to Almain, has been sharply contradicted by J.H. Burns. For, as Burns convincingly demonstrates, Almain never actually held the radically individualistic position attributed to him by Skinner. Indeed, as he points out, Almain explicitly rejected the 'suggestion that the derivation of political authority from the community is equivalent to deriving it from personae privatae'.[19] When Skinner revised his essay recently, he acknowledged that it is not the case for Almain 'that the community acquires this power from the fact that its individual members possess it', suggesting instead that the real 'reason why [Almain thought] the community must possess this power is that, by analogy with its individual members, any community must possess whatever rights are necessary for preserving itself' from threats to its existence.[20] The

---

[17]   John Locke, *Two Treatises of Government*, ed. Peter Laslett (Cambridge, 1988), p. 272 (II.2.8–9). It is sometimes suggested that Locke was following in the footsteps of Hugo Grotius, who also argued for the existence of a natural right to punish; see Tuck, *Natural Rights Theories*, pp. 62–3, 107–9, and Hugo Grotius, *The Rights of War and Peace*, ed. Richard Tuck (3 vols, Indianapolis, IN, 2005), vol. 1, pp. xx–xi, xxvii–xxviii. However, Locke may have also been indebted to his friend, James Tyrrell, or to John Milton; see John Locke, *Political Writings*, ed. David Wootton (Harmondsworth, 1993), pp. 80, 122 n.20.

[18]   See Quentin Skinner, 'The Origins of the Calvinist Theory of Revolution', in Barbara Malament (ed.), *After the Reformation: Essays in Honour of J.H. Hexter* (Manchester, 1980), pp. 309–30.

[19]   J.H. Burns, '*Jus Gladii* and *Jurisdictio*: Jacques Almain and John Locke', *Historical Journal*, 26/2 (1983): pp. 369–74 (at p. 374).

[20]   Quentin Skinner, 'Humanism, Scholasticism and Popular Sovereignty', in *Visions of Politics* (3 vols, Cambridge, 2002), vol. 2, pp. 245–63 (at p. 259 n.86); cf. Burns, '*Jus Gladii*',

connection that Skinner seeks to establish between Almain and Buchanan thus finally comes to rest on their supposed common adherence to the principle of *vim vi repellere licere*.[21] However, while it is true, as we saw earlier, that Buchanan alludes to this private-law dictum in passing, it would be incorrect to say that it occupies a significant place in his theory. Moreover, the principle could not in any case do the conceptual work that Skinner requires of it because the right of defending oneself from violence is analytically distinct from the right to punish, which involves exercising violence against those by whom one is not being directly and immediately threatened.[22] Despite Skinner's best efforts, therefore, the gap between Almain's insistence on the communitarian origins of the *ius gladii* on the one hand and Buchanan's individualistic account of it on the other appears to be unbridgeable.

An alternative line of argument – the one outlined in the remainder of this essay – is that when placing the sword in the hands of the single person Buchanan was actually deploying a straightforwardly Ciceronian theory of tyrannicide. Moreover, I shall argue, this same theory also informs two later but no less radical works of political theory, though the extent to which they may be directly indebted to Buchanan remains unclear. The first of these works was published anonymously in 1574; that is to say, after *De Iure Regni* had been written and was circulating in manuscript, but before it appeared in print.[23] This was the *Political Discourses* or, to give it its full title in French, *Discours politiques des diverses puissances establies de Dieu au monde, du gouernement legitime d'icelles, & du deuoir de ceux qui y sont assuiettis*. The tract appeared in the aftermath of the Massacre of St Bartholomew's Day in 1572 and, although it does not refer to those events (and may possibly have been written before them), was quite clearly published as a call to arms. Indeed, as Skinner says, it presents 'a more anarchic theory of resistance than any other work of Huguenot political thought'.[24] From 1578 onwards, it was able to reach a wider audience when Simon Goulart (Beza's colleague and eventual successor at Geneva) reprinted it in the third volume of the second edition of his *Memoirs of the State of France under Charles IX*. What is particularly striking is that, as the *Political Discourses* moves towards its concluding and climactic endorsement of tyrannicide, the author cites 'Hector Boetius chroniquer des Escossois' to illustrate the claim that when kings refuse to submit to

---

pp. 372–3. For Almain (loosely quoting Aquinas) on the analogy between the community and the individual, see *Conciliarism and Papalism*, ed. J.H. Burns and Thomas M. Izbicki (Cambridge, 1997), p. 136.

21   See Skinner, 'Humanism, Scholasticism and Popular Sovereignty', pp. 249, 259.
22   A point made by Burns, '*Jus Gladii*', pp. 371–2, and ignored by Skinner.
23   For evidence of its manuscript circulation, see Buchanan, *De Iure Regni*, p. xxvii.
24   Skinner, *Foundations*, vol. 2, p. 305.

justice in Scotland a single person ('vn particulier') could kill them without any penalty.[25] Given that there are times when the *Political Discourses*, although not formally a dialogue, almost reads like a paraphrase of *De Iure Regni*, the identity of this anarchic, Scottish-minded Huguenot writer would be well worth establishing.[26]

The other work, published 75 years after the *Political Discourses*, is John Milton's *Tenure of Kings and Magistrates*. As I have argued elsewhere, this tract pursues an anti-Scottish strategy, seeking to embarrass the presbyterians who opposed the trial and execution of King Charles I by reminding them that the Calvinist theory of revolution was a part of their intellectual heritage.[27] The claim he makes on the title page is that, despite this, the presbyterian-dominated Long Parliament had failed to bring the king to justice and that the Army had therefore been justified in intervening:

> That it is Lawfull, and hath been held so through all Ages, for any, who have the Power, to call to account a Tyrant, or wicked KING, and after due conviction, to depose, and put him to death; if the ordinary MAGISTRATE have neglected, or deny'd to doe it. And that they, who of late, so much blame Deposing, are the Men that did it themselves.[28]

This is reminiscent of proposition 23 to the extent that it is an argument about what happens when those who should act fail to do so. But what this default triggers immediately, without any intervening steps, is the radically populist situation in which the sword of justice is placed in the hands of 'any, who have the Power'. Like Buchanan, and like the anonymous author of the *Political Discourses*, Milton thus espoused a highly individualistic theory of the *ius gladii*.

---

[25]   Simon Goulart, *Memoires de l'estat de France sous Charles neufiesme: contenans les choses plus notables, faites & publiees tant par les Catholiques que par ceux de la religion, depuis le troisiesme edit de pacification fait au mois d'aoust 1570, iusques au regne de Henry troisiesme, & reduits en trois volumes, chascun desquels a vn indice des principales matieres y contenues. Seconde edition, reueue, corrigee & augmentee de plusieurs particuleritez & traitez notables* (Meidelbourg [Geneva], 1578), vol. 3, p. 294b. References hereafter supplied – page number only – parenthetically in the text.

[26]   The editor of the augmented edition of Boece's *Scotorum Historia* (Paris, 1574–75), Giovanni Ferrerio, can be ruled out on religious grounds. He knew Buchanan 'familiariter', but also supplied evidence against him to the Lisbon Inquisition: McFarlane, *Buchanan*, p. 78, and see pp. 26, 70, 133, 142, 417, 421; Nicola Royan, 'Ferrerio, Giovanni (1502–1579)', *ODNB*. For further discussion of the relationship between Buchanan's thought and that of the author of the *Discours politiques*, see Arthur Williamson's essay, above ch. 4.

[27]   See Martin Dzelzainis, 'Milton, Macbeth, and Buchanan', *The Seventeenth Century*, 4 (1989): pp. 53–66.

[28]   Milton, *Political Writings*, ed. Dzelzainis, p. 1. Further reference to this edition will be given parenthetically in the text.

It is worth recalling at this point that the *Tenure* is a surprisingly anachronistic work, deeply engaged with sixteenth-century Lutheran and Calvinist writings on resistance while showing little trace of Jacobean and Caroline or, for that matter, Civil War theorizing.[29] It is often therefore assumed that Milton must have read *De Iure Regni*, especially since it was frequently issued together with Buchanan's *History of Scotland* (*Rerum Scoticarum Historia*), a work Milton *does* cite in the *Tenure*. But there is no unequivocal textual evidence to that effect.[30] What is just as likely is that Milton had read the *Political Discourses*, with which the *Tenure* shares a number of arguments. Thus both of them dismiss the orthodox Lutheran and Calvinist distinction between private persons and inferior magistrates. The author of the *Discourses* does momentarily defer to orthodoxy by conceding that it would be 'well to say in general that the private person should not make an attempt against the person of the prince' ('Bien peut on dire en general que la personne privée ne dit attenter a la personne du prince': p. 294a). However, he refuses to rule out such an enterprise and (as we shall see) actually goes on to endorse it in the most resounding terms. Milton likewise rejects the presbyterian argument that the Army that had carried out the Purge were 'but private persons' and that whereas

---

[29]   Quentin Skinner sees Milton as to some extent merely restating the 'monarchomach' arguments popularized by Henry Parker, the most important parliamentary apologist of the early 1640s: see Skinner, 'John Milton and the Politics of Slavery', in his *Visions of Politics*, vol. 3, pp. 293–9. But a more indicative guide to the sources of his thought is found in the second edition of the *Tenure* that advertises on its title page the '*many Testimonies … added out of the best & learnedest among Protestant Divines asserting the position of this book*'; for these, see Milton, *Political Writings*, ed. Dzelzainis, pp. 37–43.

[30]   It should be noted that Milton's reading did not include many works now regarded as canonical. For example, while he mentions the *Vindiciae, Contra Tyrannos* by name in the *Defensio Secunda* (1652) – attributing it, however, to Beza – there is no other evidence for his having read it, and we can be reasonably certain that he did not know Ponet's *Shorte Treatise*; see *Complete Prose Works of John Milton*, ed. Don M. Wolfe *et al.* (8 vols, New Haven, CT, and London, 1983–82), vol. 4, p. 659; and above note 3. However, he was very familiar with Goodman's *Svperior Powers*, and had been interested in the private-law theory of resistance since at least 1641–43, to judge from a note in his Commonplace Book from de Thou's *Historiarum sui temporis*: 'At the time of the siege of Magdeburg there was written a book (later, in the year 1574, published in France with many additional arguments and instances) in which it is shown that it is lawful for subjects to repel by force any other force exerted against them illegally, even by Magistrates' ('erat et Magdeburgicae obsidionis tempore scriptus liber, et in Gallia denuo an. 1574 multis rationibus et exemplis amplificatus, in quo licere ostenditur subditis vim etiam a magistratibus extra leges illatam vi repellere'): *The Works of John Milton*, gen. ed. F.A. Patterson (18 vols, New York, 1931–38), vol. 18, p. 213; translation adapted. The original Latin is a conflation of two passages from De Thou's *Historiarum sui temporis* (5 vols, Geneva, 1626), vol. 1, p. 169 and vol. 2, p. 909, and not only the latter as Ruth Mohl assumes (Milton, *Complete Prose Works*, vol. 1, p. 501). The book referred to was not, as Mohl argues, François Hotman's *Francogallia* (1573), but almost certainly Beza's *Du droit des magistrats sur leurs subjets* (1574), which associated itself with the Magdeburg Confession on its title page.

'the Lawes of God, Nature, and Nations, together with the Dictates of Reason' has allowed the two Houses of Parliament 'to take up Armes for their owne Defence' they did 'not allow' the same to 'a multitude of Private Persons' even though 'they have strength in their hands to effect it'.[31]

However, neither Milton nor the author of the *Political Discourses* chooses to attack the distinction itself. Instead they focus their attack on a related scholastic distinction between tyrants without title and tyrants by practice; that is to say, the distinction between those who have seized power illegitimately and otherwise legitimate rulers who have degenerated into tyranny. The usual view was that, while it may be lawful for private men to resist a tyrant without title, only the inferior magistrate could resist the tyrant by practice. However, in the *Political Discourses* the two types of tyrant are consistently treated as virtually indistinguishable. In Israel, the author says, kings could be condemned by the people or their deputies whether they were a usurper or an evil ruler ('mauuais administrateur': p. 216b). Nor can he see any difference between a tyrant by usurpation ('tyran vsurpateur') like Eglon or a tyrant by practice ('tyran oppresseur': p. 293b) like Joram. In fact, of the two he considers those who usurp power against the laws to be less harmful than those 'who have been legitimately established and have violated them to reign more despotically' ('qui y estoient legitimement establis qui les ont violees pour regner plus seigneurialement': p. 228b). When Milton comes to the pivotal case of Ehud and Eglon he too concludes that in relation to a tyrant 'it imports not whether forren or native'. For insofar as a 'native' prince 'professes to hold by law' and then breaks the 'Covnants and Oaths that gave him title … what differs he from an outlandish King, or from an enemie?'

And Milton too thinks that the case against the tyrant by practice is stronger than that against the usurper, for if the king of Spain were to invade and so 'might lawfully be put to death in captivity, what hath a native king to plead, bound by so many Covnants, benefits and honours to the welfare of his people' (pp. 7–18)?

The hostility of both writers to the distinction between foreign and native tyrants is, however, merely the expression of a further and more basic commitment to stoic, and specifically Ciceronian values. Cicero is the most frequently cited author in the *Political Discourses*, especially *De Officiis* and the second Philippic. And what the author turns to Cicero for, above all, is the stoic notion of the brotherhood of man. Throughout the tract he stresses that individuals must see themselves as subordinate to a larger whole: 'we are not born for ourselves alone', he says, quoting Cicero verbatim, 'but for the city, the country, and our lineage' ('nous ne

---

[31]   *A Serious and Faithfull Representation of the Judgements of Ministers of the Gospell within the Province of London* (London, 1649), p. 6.

sommes pas nez pour nous-mesmes seulement, mais pour la cité, le pays,
& nostre lignage': p. 238b; Cicero, *De Officiis*, I.22). But while there are
'several societies between men', 'none is so gracious (says Cicero) nor so
dear as that which each must bear to the republic' ('Il a plusieurs societez
entre les hommes; mais ... il n'y en a nulle si gracieuse (dit Ciceron) ne
si chere que celle que chascun auoir à la chose publique': p. 239b; cf. *De
Officiis*, 1.53, 57). And, still quoting from *De Officiis*, he remarks that
since '(as the stoics say) the earth and all it contains is made for the use
of men; therefore men are made and engendered for other men' and their
'mutual utility' ('(comme disent les Stoiciens) la terre & tout son contenu
est faite pur l'vsage des hommes: donc les hommes sont faits & engendrez
pour cause des hommes, afin qu'ils se conferent mutuelle vtilité': p. 242a;
cf. *De Officiis*, 1.22). There is, in fact, a 'sovereign and universal society'
that 'has domination over all the others' ('soueraine & vniuerselle societé
a domination sur toutes les autres': p. 241a) such that 'one could say the
world is one city' ('on pourroit dire le monde estre vne cité': p. 240b; cf.
Cicero, *De Legibus*, 1.23).

From this point of view, it was absurd to distinguish between a citizen
and an enemy (or between two types of tyrant) simply on the grounds
of where they came from rather than on the basis of the disposition that
they bore towards you. As the author of the *Political Discourses* puts it,
'A citizen and an enemy are not distinguished by the place of their natural
habitation, but by disposition and by actions' ('Vn citoien & vn ennemi
pas à distinguer par lieux de leur naturelle habitation, mais par la volonté
& par les faits': p. 253b). Milton's thinking in the *Tenure* is along exactly
the same lines:

> Nor is it distance of place that makes enmitie, but enmity that makes distance.
> He therfore that keeps peace with me, neer or remote, of whatsoever Nation, is
> to mee as farr as all civil and human offices an Englishman and a neighbor: but
> if an Englishman forgetting all Laws, human, civil and religious, offend against
> life and liberty, to him offended and to the Law in his behalf, though born in
> the same womb, he is no better then a Turk, a Sarasin, a Heathen. (p. 18)

Christopher Hill has suggested that this passage and others like it are
expressive of the 'revolutionary Protestant internationalism' that Milton
shared with William Sedgwick, Hugh Peters and others.[32] But it is in truth
a straightforward articulation of the view in Book III of *De Officiis* that
those 'who say that account should be taken of other citizens, but deny it
in the case of foreigners; such men tear apart the common fellowship of

---

[32]   Christopher Hill, *Milton and the English Revolution* (London, 1977), p. 283.

the human race'.[33] Or, as Milton phrases the same idea, 'Who knows not that there is a mutual bond of amity and brother-hood between man and man over all the World, neither is it the English sea that can sever us from that duty and relation' (p. 18).

In both cases, the outcome of this commitment to stoic values was to sweep away the distinctions upon which the Lutheran and Calvinist theories of resistance were built. But even if they eliminated the reasons usually given for excluding the private person from political action, it would still remain to be shown by what right he (or she) could carry out so drastic an action as executing a tyrant. To borrow Milton's terms, even if 'any, who have the Power' could put a tyrant to death, where did this power come from?

Like Buchanan, both Milton and the author of the *Political Discourses* explicitly rule out the idea of divine authorization. The latter dismisses as 'a great scandal' ('vn grand scandale') the opinion of 'some self-styled theologians' ('à quelques vns que se disent theologiens') that it 'does not belong except to persons who have a particular revelation from God and a special command to touch the life of a prince' ('qu'il n'appartient qu'aux qui ont particuliere reuelation de Dieu & commandement special de toucher à la vie du prince'). And, considering the examples of Ehud and Jehu, he cannot believe that 'if they had not had a particular revelation, the thing would have been unjust on that account, which had otherwise been executed by the command of God and by that manifested as just and equitable' ('ie demande si n'y ayant eu particuliere reuelation la chose seroit pour cela iniuste, qui a esté autrefois executee par com[m]andement de Dieu, & par là manifestee pour iuste & equitable? Ie ne le croy pas' (pp. 293a–294a). Milton likewise will have nothing to do with the idea that Ehud 'had special warrant to kill Eglon'. And while he does admit that *'Jehu* had special command to slay *Jehoram* a successive and hereditary Tyrant', he insists that 'it seems not the less imitable for that; for where a thing grounded so much on natural reason hath the addition of a command from God, what does it but establish the lawfulness of such an act' (p. 19). In the case of Jehu, that is to say, the divine command had a purely declarative function, confirming beyond doubt that the action was lawful but not as such constituting the grounds of its lawfulness. What ultimately made the action lawful was simply its conformity to 'natural reason'. For Milton, as for the anonymous author of the *Political Discourses* (and, indeed, Buchanan as well), divine commands were beside the point when it came to either legitimating or de-legitimating political actions.

---

[33]   Cicero, *On Duties*, ed. M.T. Griffin and E.M. Atkins (Cambridge, 1991), p. 110 (III.28); 'Qui autem civium rationem habendam, externorum negant, ii dirimunt communem humani generis societatem': Cicero, *De Officiis*, trans. Walter Miller (Cambridge, MA, and London, 1975), p. 294.

It is hardly surprising therefore that both writers display a high degree of hostility towards the Huguenot pastors and presbyterian ministers who seek to erect scriptural obstacles to political action, and an equally militant determination to find a secular origin for the *ius gladii*. Again, they look no further than Cicero, and in particular the premise of universal brotherhood, the basic value of which is peace. The only way in which someone can be excluded – or, more strictly, exclude themselves – from this brotherhood is by displaying hostility. On this view, an enemy (or a tyrant) is simply someone who has segregated himself from human society and has thus rendered himself liable to punishment. As Cicero says, 'there can be no fellowship between us and tyrants – on the contrary there is complete estrangement', adding in anti-Caesarist vein that 'the whole pestilential and irreverent class ought to be expelled from the community of mankind'.[34] The author of the *Political Discourses* simply adopts this phraseology, it being 'necessary above all things to suppress these plagues and insatiable murderers' ('necessaire sur toutes choses pour supprimer telles pestes & meurtiers insatiables': p. 245b). And Milton follows suit. His view is that 'he that bids a man reigne over him above Law, may bid as well as savage Beast'. If a 'just King' is (another Ciceronian phrase) 'the public father of his Countrie', a tyrant is 'the common enemie', and the people may lawfully proceed against him 'as against a common pest, and destroyer of mankinde' (pp. 13, 17).

One of the most significant features of this argument is its sheer economy. The process by which someone identifies themselves as a tyrant – by manifesting a hostile disposition that means they are no longer living in peace with you but are at war – is at one and the same time what confers upon you the right to punish them. There is no need to seek further authorization by virtue of the fact that it is always lawful to kill those with whom one is at war. This is what Cicero had in mind when he described tyrants as wild and savage monsters in human form who should be removed from the body of humanity ('sic ista in figura hominis feritas et immanitas beluae a communi tamquam humanitatis corpore segregenda est').[35] That is to say, the tyrant was someone to be regarded exactly as brigands or pirates were – as 'the common foe of all' ('communis hostis omnium'), and thus subject to attack by any and all.[36]

---

[34]   Cicero, *On Duties*, ed. Griffin and Atkins, p. 111; 'Nulla est enim societas nobis cum tyrannis, et potius summa distractio est … atque hoc omne genus pestiferum atque impium ex hominum communitate exterminandum est': *De Officiis*, trans. Miller, p. 298; III.32.

[35]   Cicero, *De Officiis*, trans. Miller, p. 298 (III.32).

[36]   Ibid., pp. 384–5; III.107. Note, however, that Cicero does not actually use the phrase that came to define the pirate in Roman and, later, international law: 'hostis humani generis'. On this latter phrase, see now my 'Milton and the Regicide', in Paul Hammond and Blair Worden (eds), *John Milton: Life, Writing, Reputation* (Oxford, 2010), pp. 91–105.

This Ciceronian line of argument is the one that was in due course taken up and rehearsed by the figures of Buchanan and Maitland in the climactic passage from *De Iure Regni*. Buchanan begins by asking Maitland whether 'a war waged against an enemy of the whole human race, that is, against a tyrant' ('Quid in eo quod cum totius humani generis hoste, hoc est, tyranno, geritur?') would be just. When Maitland agrees that it would be, Buchanan immediately follows up by asking him the crucial question: in that event, is it 'the right not only of the people as a whole but also of individuals to kill the enemy?' ('ius est non modo universo populo sed singulis etiam hostem interimere?'). And when Maitland concedes that it is, Buchanan restates with even greater clarity what follows from their agreed characterization of the tyrant as a 'public enemy' ('hostem publicum'): which is, that his status as an enemy of humankind means that 'any individual from the whole mass of the human race [may] lawfully exact from him all the penalties of war' ('... singuli e tota generis humani multitudine iure omnes bellorum poenas ab eo expetere possunt').[37] And with that Buchanan effectively rests his case.

While it may prove impossible for us to determine whether Milton or the author of the *Political Discourses* actually read *De Iure Regni*, there can be little doubt that all three writers converged on an identical theory of the right to punish tyrants, and deployed it in turn against the houses of Valois and Stuart. Milton's summary of the argument in *Defensio Secunda* (1654) was both elegant and, as it proved, valedictory:

> In short, my opinion is, that (if a man has any use of his reason) he, against whom we make war, is considered by us as an enemy; that, to put an enemy to death has always been lawful, by the same right as we oppose him; and as a tyrant is not simply our enemy, but the general enemy as it were of the whole human race, that, by the same right as he may be attacked with arms, may he likewise be put to death.[38]

It really was that simple.

---

[37] Buchanan, *De Iure Regni*, pp. 152–5.

[38] 'Equidem in ea sum sententia, contra quem bellum gerimus, eum, siquis rationis aut judicii usus sit, hostem à nobis judicari; hostem autem tam interficere quàm oppugnare, eodem semper jure licuisse: Tyrannus igitur cùm non noster solùm, sed totius propè generis humani publicus hostis sit, eum quo armis oppugnari, eodem posse & interfici': *Works of John Milton*, ed. Patterson, vol. 8, pp. 196–7 (translation slightly adapted).

CHAPTER 9

George Buchanan and the Scottish Covenanters[1]

John Coffey

On 19 April 1664, the Scottish Privy Council issued a Proclamation against 'an old seditious Pamphlet'. It warned that, despite the blessing of the Restoration, 'some seditious and ill-affected persons endeavour to infuse the principles of rebellion in the minds of many good Subjects'. For that end, they had 'adventured to translate in the English Tongue, *De Iure Regni apud Scotos*, whereof Mr George Buchanan was the author', and had 'dispersed many Copies of the said Translation, which may corrupt the affections of the Subjects, and alienate their minds from their obedience to the Laws and his Majesties Royal Authority'. Noting that Buchanan's work had been condemned by an Act of Parliament in 1584, the Council ordered that all copies of 'the said Pamphlet or Book' be handed over to its Clerk, and it prohibited anyone from copying or dispersing the new translation. Those who contravened this order, would be considered 'seditious persons, and disaffected to Monarchical Government', and would be 'proceeded against' 'with all rigour'.[2]

Thus a century after its composition, *De Iure Regni* retained its reputation as an inspirational and dangerous text. For Scottish Covenanters, it was a work worthy of translation and circulation. Yet despite its continuing currency, historians have done little to explore the reception of Buchanan's political writings in Covenanter Scotland.[3] I want to make a start on this

---

[1]   I am grateful to the British Academy for a Small Research Grant that assisted my work on this chapter.

[2]   [Scottish Privy Council], *Edinburgh, The Nineteenth Day of April, One Thousand Six Hundred and Sixty Four* (Edinburgh, 1664).

[3]   There is, in fact, relatively little serious scholarship on Covenanter political thought, but see the following works published since 1980: I.M. Smart, 'The Political Ideas of the Scottish Covenanters, 1638–1688', *History of Political Thought*, 1 (1980): pp. 167–93; E.J. Cowan, 'The Making of the National Covenant', in J. Morrill (ed.), *The Scottish National Covenant in its British Context* (Edinburgh, 1990), pp. 68–89; E.J. Cowan, 'The Political Ideas of a Covenanting Leader: Archibald Campbell, Marquis of Argyll, 1607–1661', in Roger A. Mason (ed.), *Scots and Britons: Scottish Political Thought and the Union of 1603* (Cambridge, 1994), pp. 241–62; J.D. Ford, '*Lex, rex iusto posita*: Samuel Rutherford on the Origins of Government', in Mason (ed.), *Scots and Britons*, pp. 262–90; J.D. Ford, 'The

task, by discussing the uses to which Buchanan was put by Covenanters in the half century from 1638 to 1688. We shall see that Covenanters appealed to both *De Iure Regni* and the *Rerum Scoticarum Historia*. But I shall also suggest that, for all his usefulness, Buchanan was a less formative influence than one might expect.

Covenanter Use of *De Iure Regni*

The leading Covenanter theorists were well aware of Buchanan's famous defence of armed resistance against tyrants. In January 1639, as the early Covenanters faced the prospect of war with the king, we find Archibald Johnston of Wariston (that key architect of the movement) sitting down 'to draue up reasons of resistance *in thesi, in hypothesi*'. Unsure of how to accomplish his task, Wariston decided to mine classic Calvinist political texts: 'I set to work to exstract my remarques out of Knoxe and Buchanan for the hypothese, and to turne Althusius reasons and De Jure Majestatis to Inglisch'.[4] Subsequent Covenanters followed in Wariston's footsteps, claiming Buchanan as one of their own. For Samuel Rutherford, he fitted into a grand tradition of Protestant resistance, which included the French Huguenots, the Calvinists of the Dutch Revolt, the early Lutheran divines, 'Calvin, Beza, Pareus, the German divines, Buchanan, and an host...'.[5] In his preface to *A Hind Let Loose* (1687), the last major work of Covenanter resistance theory, Alexander Shields insisted that 'there is nothing here but what is confirmed by Authors of greatest note and repute in our Church, both ancient and modern, namely, *Buchanan, Knox, Calderwood, Acts of General Assemblies, Causes of Wrath, Lex Rex, Apologetical Relation, Naphtali, Jus Populi, History of the Indulgence, Banders Disbanded, Rectius Instruendum*, and some other Authors

---

Lawful Bonds of Scottish Society: The Five Articles of Perth, the Negative Confession and the National Covenant', *Historical Journal*, 37 (1994): pp. 45–64; John Coffey, *Politics, Religion and the British Revolutions: The Mind of Samuel Rutherford* (Cambridge, 1997), ch. 6; A.I. Macinnes, 'Covenanting Ideology in Seventeenth-century Scotland', in J.H. Ohlmeyer (ed.), *Political Thought in Seventeenth-century Ireland: Kingdom or Colony* (Cambridge, 2000), pp. 191–220; Robert von Friedeburg, 'From Collective Representation to the Right of Individual Defence: Sir James Stewart's *Jus Populi Vindicatum* and the use of Johannes Althusius's *Politica* in Restoration Scotland', *History of European Ideas*, 24 (1998): pp. 19–42.

   [4]   *Diary of Sir Archibald Johnston of Wariston, 1632–1639*, ed. G.M. Paul (Edinburgh, 1911), p. 408. For other references to Reformed resistance theorists, see ibid., pp. 310, 348, 410.

   [5]   [Samuel Rutherford], *Lex Rex, or the Law and the Prince* (London, 1644), p. 372. See also p. 418, where the 'host' of Lutheran and Reformed resistance theorists is named more fully, and includes 'Knox of blessed memory, Buchanan, Junius Brutus, Bouchier, Rossaeus, and Althusius'.

much respected'.[6] Buchanan and Knox, in other words, were identified as the fountainheads of a consistent Scottish tradition that was faithfully perpetuated by Calderwood, Rutherford, James Guthrie, John Brown, James Stewart, Robert McWard and Shields himself.

Scottish critics of the Covenanters largely concurred with this view. Indeed, it was often suggested (or implied) that Covenanter resistance theory was little more than a restatement of Buchanan. The royalist Sir James Turner claimed that Buchanan was invoked so often in 1638 that 'I imagined his ghost was returned to the earth to wander a little among the Covenanters'.[7] In 1639, William Drummond of Hawthornden satirized the dependence on Buchanan with a spoof recommendation to the Scottish Parliament: 'That Buchanan's Chronicle [i.e., his *History*] shall be translated into the vulgar Scottish, and read in the common schools; and, the Books of the Apocrypha being taken away from the Bible, his book *De Jure Regni* be in the place thereof insert'.[8] In his *History of Scots Affairs*, James Gordon maintained that Alexander Henderson and Samuel Rutherford 'saide no mor than Junius Brutus and Buchanan, in his ridiculouse tractate, *De Jure Regni*'.[9] The Aberdeen Doctors tried to neutralize the Calvinist monarchomachs by citing the Reformed theologian Andreas Rivet, whose *Jesuita Vapulans* (1635) had argued that Buchanan and Knox were not representative of mainstream Protestant opinion. 'The rashnesse of those writers', Rivet had suggested, was to be ascribed 'partly to the hard and perilous times of persecution, wherein they lived, and partly, *Scotorum praefervido ingenuo, & ad audendum prompto*'.[10] The episcopalian John Corbet remarked that if the Covenanters had really respected these great men they 'ought to have covered their nakedness' instead of displaying it once again to the world.[11]

Writing after the Restoration, George Hickes was still convinced that Buchanan was a chief authority for Presbyterian principles of rebellion. Like the Jesuits, he insisted, Buchanan had taught that kings can be excommunicated, and that subjects owe no obedience to excommunicated

---

[6] [Shields], *Hind Let Loose*, sig. A3r.

[7] Cited in E. Cowan, *Montrose* (London, 1977), p. 14; see also Clare Jackson's Chapter 10 below.

[8] Cited in D. Masson, *Drummond of Hawthorden: The Story of his Life and Writings* (London, 1873), p. 326.

[9] James Gordon of Rothiemay, *History of Scots Affairs from 1637 to 1641* (2 vols, Aberdeen, 1841), vol. 2, p. 203. For his comment on Rutherford and Buchanan see vol. 2, p. 170.

[10] John Forbes *et al.*, *Generall Demands concerning the Late Covenant; together with Answers to them, and Replies to those Answers* (1638), p. 8. See also John Forbes *et al.*, *Duplyes of the Ministers and Professors of Aberdene* (Aberdeen, 1638), p. 26.

[11] John Corbet, *The Ungirding of the Scottish Armour* (Dublin, 1639), p. 46. Corbet noted that Buchanan's *De Iure Regni* had been 'expressly condemned by Act of Parliament'.

kings; that if the king fails to perform his part of the reciprocal agreement with his people, they ought not to perform theirs; that supreme power is originally lodged in the people, who may reclaim it from a prince if he abuses it; that the primitive Christians did not take up arms against the persecuting Emperors simply for lack of opportunity.[12] In 1684, George Mackenzie complained, 'Amongst the other wicked Instruments in these Rebellions, I must confess that our Countrey-men *Buchannan* (one of the chief Ornaments, and Reproaches of his native Country) the Authors of *Lex Rex*, *Naphtali*, and *Jus Populi Vindicatum*, have been Ring-leaders, who have endeavoured extreamly to poison this Nation' with their seditious doctrines. For Mackenzie, these writers were united by their anti-monarchical principles and by their blatant disregard for 'the positive Law of *Scotland*'.[13]

In its famous 1683 *Judgement and Decree ... against Certain Pernicious Books and Damnable Doctrines*, the University of Oxford also set *De Iure Regni* alongside *Lex Rex* in a group of works by Calvinist (and Catholic) resistance theorists. Once again, Buchanan and Rutherford were heard singing in the same key, part of a monarchomach choir that included the French Huguenots, the Catholic Bellarmine, the regicidal Independents, Milton and Goodwin, and the odd man out, Richard Baxter, who must have been angry about being placed in this company. All of these non-Anglicans were alleged to have taught the same three doctrines: '(1) That all civil authority is derived originally from the people ... (2) That there is a mutual compact, tacit or express, between a king and his subjects, and that if he perform not his duty, they are discharged from theirs ... (3) That if lawful governors become tyrants, or govern otherwise than by the laws of God and man they ought to do, they forfeit the right they had unto their government'.[14]

Yet Buchanan had not merely argued that tyrants forfeit their right to government; he had also advanced a remarkably populist theory of tyrannicide. As the University noted in its twenty-third proposition, Buchanan, Knox, Goodman, Gilby and the Jesuits had taught that '[w]icked kings and tyrants ought to be put to death; and if the judges and inferior magistrates will not do their office, the power of the sword devolves to the people. If the major part of the people refuse to exercise this power, then the ministers may excommunicate such a king; after which it

---

12   George Hickes, *The Spirit of Popery Speaking out of the Mouths of Phanatical-Protestants* (London, 1680), p. 13 n. 10.

13   Mackenzie, *Jus Regium*, pp. 4–5.

14   'The Judgement and Decree of the University of Oxford, Passed in their Convocation, July 31 1683', in David Wootton (ed.), *Divine Right and Democracy: An Anthology of Political Writing in Stuart England* (London, 1986), p. 121.

is lawful for any of the subjects to kill him'.[15] The same doctrine had been highlighted years earlier by John Corbet. Writing under the pseudonym Lysimachus Nicanor, a Jesuit admirer of the Covenanters' rebellious principles, he reminds them that, if they have learned properly from Knox and Buchanan, they will not baulk at killing the king himself: 'Let that golden sentence of Buchanan never be forgotten. Whiles he saies, *It were good that rewards were appointed by the people, for such as should kill tryants, as commonly there is for those, that have killed either Wolves or Beares, or taken their whelps'.*[16]

The early Covenanters, however, had little use for Buchanan's populist theory of king-killing. They looked to aristocratic support, not plebeian uprising; to victorious generals, not lone assassins. It was the later Covenanters who would reach for the most radical arguments of *De Iure Regni*, especially after the defeat of the Pentland Rising in 1666. George Hickes blamed Buchanan for promoting the 'damnable doctrine of Heroical Impulse [which] hath poisoned the whole Sect', and 'instigated many Inhumane Butcheries and Rebellions', before they imbrued their hands in the 'sacred Blood' of Scotland's Primate, Archbishop James Sharp of St Andrews. To prove the point, Hickes also cited Buchanan's notorious statement: 'That it is lawful and meritorious to kill Tyrants, as Wolves and Bears ... if he will not come to be Judged, they may kill him like a Night-Thief any way'.[17]

Hickes probably exaggerated Buchanan's influence. *Naphtali*, branded as the incendiary pocket-book of assassins and revolutionaries, did not cite Buchanan at all. This was largely due to the fact that it was a popular and accessible text unencumbered by scholarly apparatus. But *Naphtali* did cite *Lex Rex*, and it seems probable that lay Covenanters were familiar with recent works of Covenanter political theory but had little direct knowledge of earlier works by Buchanan (or even Knox). George Hickes alleged that *Naphtali* and *Jus Populi* were 'the pocket-books of the Field-Conventiclers', but he made no similar claims about the popularity of *De Iure Regni*.[18] Sharp's would-be assassin, James Mitchell, cited Knox at second hand from *A Cloud of Witnesses*, and his papers did not refer to Buchanan at all. Instead he declared his fidelity to the canon of recent Covenanter texts, *Lex Rex*, *The Causes of Gods Wrath*, the *Apologetical*

---

[15] Ibid., p. 123.

[16] [John Corbet], *The Epistle Congratulatorie of Lysimachus Nicanor* (1640), p. 44. Lysimachus Nicanor also cites Buchanan approvingly on pp. 45, 58–9. Corbet's authorship is asserted in a later edition: *The Epistle Congratulatory of Lysimachus Nicanor* (Oxford, 1684), pp. 4–7.

[17] [Hickes], *The Spirit of Popery*, pp. 69, 29.

[18] Ibid., p. 67.

Relation, *Naphtali* and *Jus Populi*.[19] These were the books most readily available to field-preachers and conventiclers.

Yet *De Iure Regni* did have some keen readers. In 1681, one of Sharp's assassins, James Russell, affixed a libel to the door of the parish church of Kettle, in Fife, in which he declared that Charles II had 'forfeited his right of the Crown and Kingdom of Scotland, and is no more a King, but is become a Tyrant'. Russell supported his declaration with two quotations from Buchanan: 'When the King breaks the Contract and Covenant that was betwixt Him and the People, and doth contrair to that He covenanted to do, whatever Right or Privilege did belong to him by that Agreement or Covenant is then lost'. Likewise he saith: 'When the King does those things which are directly for the dissolution of society, for the continuance whereof he was created, He is a Tyrant'. 'If we will believe Buchanan and other sound Writers', Russell went on, '[a] Tyrant has no just authority over a People' and has become their enemy so that there is 'a just and lawful War' between them. Moreover, Buchanan had taught that, in such a just war, 'it is lawful not only for the whole People to kill that Enemy, but for every one of them'.[20] One wonders if Russell had read Buchanan some time before that fateful Saturday in May 1679, when he and his accomplices ambushed Sharp on Magus Moor and slaughtered him in front of his daughter. Perhaps not. Russell's own account of the assassination says nothing about his reading habits – beyond predictable references to finding inspiration in biblical texts – and none of the killers had enjoyed a university education.[21] Buchanan's *De Iure Regni* was only finally published in English translation in 1680.[22] Prior to that, most lay Covenanters would only have known of his arguments at second hand. The likelihood is that Russell acquired the English translation *after* the assassination, and found in its pages a reassuring vindication of his earlier actions.

When Alexander Shields set out to defend tyrannicide in 1687, he too turned to Buchanan's notorious pamphlet. In the 200-page discussion of tyrants in *A Hind Let Loose*, 'our Renowned Country man Buchanan'

---

[19]   See 'The Papers left by Mr James Mitchel', published in the third edition of *Naphtali, or the Wrestlings of the Church of Scotland* (1693), pp. 397–433, citations on pp. 408, 412. Mitchell's papers had previously been printed in [George Hickes], *Ravillac Redivivus, Being a Narrative of the Late Tryal of Mr James Mitchel* (London, 1678), pp. 17–31.

[20]   *A True and Exact Copy of a Prodigious and Traiterous Libel, Affixt upon the Church-door of Kettle, in Fife, the third of this instant, being Easter-day, written and subscribed by James Russel, one of those bloody and Sacrilegious Murtherers of the late Lord Primate of Scotland, his Grace* (Edinburgh, 1681), pp. 4–5.

[21]   See 'Russell's account of the murder of Archbishop Sharp', appended to James Kirkton, *The Secret and True History of the Church of Scotland from the Restoration to the Year 1678*, ed. C.K. Sharpe (Edinburgh, 1817), pp. 399–482.

[22]   *De Jure Regni apud Scotos, or, A Dialogue ... translated out of the original Latin into English by Philalethes* (1680).

emerges as the most important authority.[23] In a subsequent section, vindicating 'the extraordinary execution of judgement by private men', the great sixteenth-century scholar was again to the fore: 'As Buchanan says of a tyrant, de jure regni, A Lawful war being once undertaken with such an enemy as a Tyrant is, every one out of the whole multitude of mankind may assault with all the calamities of war a Tyrant, who is a publick Enemy'. Shields added a series of Buchanan's examples from classical history, and concluded with six arguments in favour of killing tyrants, 'here and there scattered in his book de jure regni'.[24] As Colin Kidd explains elsewhere in this volume (Chapter 13), Buchanan's famous tract was one important source for the Covenanters' assassination principles.

Covenanter Use of Buchanan's *History*

If Covenanters found *De Iure Regni* useful, Buchanan's *Rerum Scoticarum Historia* (1582) was if anything more important. Buchanan the historian provided the Covenanters with a usable past. Firstly, he had presented Scotland as a nation with an ancient church free of government by bishops. As Roger Mason has observed, he 'effectively reworked the chronicle of Hector Boece in such a way as to demonstrate, not only that the Scots had always really been Protestant, but that they had always really been Presbyterian'. It was his 'signal achievement to supply the new reformed kirk with the historical legitimacy it required but which Knox had failed to provide'.[25]

His account of primitive Scottish Christianity was eagerly transmitted by the Covenanters. In his preface to the 1644 edition of Knox's *History of the Reformation*, David Buchanan turned to his namesake to supplement Knox and fill in the pre-history of the presbyterian kirk.[26] In his *Apologetical Relation* (1665), John Brown of Wamphray again recycled Buchanan's version of history. John's disciples had evangelized Scotland, and its first Christians were proto-presbyterians.[27] Alexander Shields divided Scottish church history into six periods, beginning with the Culdees, for whom his source was inevitably Buchanan. Using Knox for the Lollards and the Reformation, and Calderwood for the fourth period from 1570–1638, one could construct a powerful narrative in which the pristine purity of

---

[23] [Shields], *Hind Let Loose*, Pt III, Head ii (pp. 268–468), quotation at p. 343.

[24] Ibid., Pt III, Head vi (pp. 633–93), quotations at pp. 654 and 660.

[25] Roger A. Mason, *Kingship and the Commonweal: Political Thought in Renaissance and Reformation Scotland* (East Linton, 1998), p. 181.

[26] [John Knox], *The Historie of the Reformation of the Church of Scotland* (London, 1644). See Mason, *Kingship and the Commonweal*, pp. 181–5.

[27] [John Brown], *An Apologetical Relation* (1665), pp. 5, 7.

Scottish Christianity was continually threatened by popish and prelatical pollution. Presbyterians, on this account, were the heirs of the Culdees, the Lollards and the Reformers.[28]

Having such a story really mattered, especially after the Restoration, for the Covenanters' critics accused them of representing Christianity's deviant extremes – of being the Scottish equivalents of the ancient Donatists and Gnostics, the continental Anabaptists and the English Sectaries. Episcopalians and Presbyterians fought to claim the centre ground, and Buchanan was part of the argument. The Tory George Hickes poured scorn on the presbyterian version of church history – as he explained to his English readers:

> Unless you are vers'd in our Historian Buchanan, you will wonder why [it is asserted] that the Government of our Church was Presbyterian from the first Plantation of the Gospel in 205 or rather 203 till the arrival of Palladius in the middle of the Fifth Century. You must know therefore that all the Authority our Presbyterians have for this assertion is from Buchanan, that furious Enemy of Bishops, who in the Fifth Book of his History, writes that the Church in the aforesaid time was not governed by Bishops but by the Monks or Culdees.

Thankfully, noted Hickes, this 'groundless assertion' had been confuted by Archbishop Spottiswoode.[29] Covenanters were untroubled by Spottiswoode; in their eyes, the authority of Buchanan was quite sufficient to establish the true history of Scotland's ancient church. As Sir John Lauder noted, the Covenanters sought to make Spottiswoode's *History* look 'ridiculous' by 'using to refute him the auctority of Buchanan, an auctor more suspected then himselfe'.[30]

Alongside his ecclesiastical history, Buchanan had constructed an equally palatable version of Scottish political history. Covenanters turned again and again to Buchanan's work on the Scottish monarchy. Robert Baillie took it for granted in his reply to John Corbet, even if he did not cite Buchanan directly.[31] In the penultimate chapter of *Lex Rex*, Rutherford rehearsed Buchanan's long list of Scottish kings created, censured, imprisoned and even deposed by parliament.[32] Later Covenanters followed suit. John Brown of Wamphray praised Buchanan as 'the renowned Historian', 'a man well acquainted with the lawes and

[28] [Shields], *Hind Let Loose*, pp. 8–9 (Buchanan on the Lollards).
[29] [Hickes], *Ravillac Redivivus*, p. 17.
[30] See *Journals of Sir John Lauder, Lord Fountainhall, 1665–1676* (Edinburgh, 1900), p. 139.
[31] Robert Baillie, *Ladensium Autokatakrisis, The Canterburians Self-Conviction* (1640), 'A Postscript for the Personate Jesuite Lysimachus Nicanor', pp. 8, 12.
[32] [Rutherford], *Lex Rex*, ch. 43.

constitutions of Scotland'. Buchanan had demonstrated that the kings of Scotland had no power to make war without parliament's consent, and that 'it was the common practice of the Parliaments of Scotland ... to rise in armes against their Kings, when they turned tyrants'.[33] Critics of the Covenanters challenged Buchanan's history, but they could also use it for their own purposes. Andrew Honyman noted that even Buchanan could not 'produce any one instance of our lawful Parliaments or Peoples taking on them, in a judicial way, in cold blood, and under forms of process, to punish or destroy their Kings, howsoever evil'. Kings had admittedly 'perished' in insurrections, but not once had the Scots sat 'as Judges on their Soveraigns in cold blood', as the English had done in 1649.[34] Honyman's use of Buchanan was unusual, but it confirmed the importance of his historical narrative in Scottish political debate.

Indeed, it may well be the case that the Covenanters valued Buchanan more as a historian than as a political theorist. In *Jus Populi Vindicatum*, James Stewart appeals to Buchanan only when discussing Scotland's tradition of calling kings to account; he never once draws on the theoretical arguments of *De Iure Regni*.[35] Of the seventy-eight authors referred to by Stewart, the prime authorities are Althusius (who is cited over thirty times) and Rutherford (whose 'unanswerable book' *Lex Rex* is cited on fifty pages).[36] For Stewart, Buchanan the historian was irreplaceable; but as a political theorist he had been superseded by later (more elaborate) writers.

Covenanter Divergence from Buchanan

As this suggests, the relationship between Buchanan and the Covenanters was not as straightforward as they and their critics maintained. While Covenanters did refer to Buchanan with some regularity, he hardly dominates. Wariston turned to him, but also to Knox, Pareus, Althusius and the famous Huguenot tract, *Vindiciae, Contra Tyrannos*. Buchanan is cited on no more than a dozen of *Lex Rex*'s 466 pages; the same can be said of Brown's *Apologeticall Relation*; *Naphtali* (as we have noted) never mentions him once; *Jus Populi* cites authorities far more frequently,

---

[33] [Brown], *Apologetical Relation*, pp. 142–3. See also pp. 120–25.

[34] [Honyman], *A Survey of the Insolent and Infamous Libel, entituled, Naphtali* (1668), p. 78. For a further refutation of Buchanan's argument concerning Scottish kings see [Honyman], *A Survey of Naphtali* (1669), pp. 90–91.

[35] See the following passages referring or alluding to Buchanan's historical arguments: [Sir James Stewart], *Jus Populi Vindicatum, or the Peoples Right to Defend Themselves and Their Covenanted Religion Vindicated* (n.p., 1669), pp. 91–4, 124–7, 135–7, 392–4.

[36] E.C. Beisner, 'His Majesty's Advocate: Sir James Stewart of Goodtrees (1635–1713) and Covenanter Resistance Theory' (unpublished PhD thesis, University of St Andrews, 2003), Appendix B: 'Index of authors cited directly in *Jus Populi*'.

but in its 500 pages, Buchanan is directly cited just a handful of times; in Shields' *A Hind Let Loose*, Buchanan appears on around twenty pages out of 600. This still makes him one of the Covenanters leading authorities, but for large stretches of their writing he is out of sight (and presumably out of mind). And there is little evidence that Covenanters read or used his political poetry – his *Baptistes* was translated and published in London in 1643 by order of the Westminster Parliament under the title *Tyrannicall-Government Anatomized, or a Discourse concerning Evil-Counsellors*, but whether the Scots had any involvement in this publication is unknown.

Moreover, the Covenanter works of resistance theory differ from Buchanan's *De Iure Regni* in significant respects. Henry Guthry tells us that, at the General Assembly of the Kirk in 1645, every member 'had in hand that Book lately published by Mr Samuel Rutherford ... [which was] so idolised that whereas Buchanan's treatise *De Iure Regni apud Scotos*, was looked upon as an oracle, this coming forth, it was slighted (as not anti-monarchical enough) and Rutherford's *Lex Rex* only thought authentic'.[37] Guthry is probably not the most reliable authority, and it is hard to see how one could complain that Buchanan was 'not anti-monarchical enough', particularly since Rutherford is markedly more reluctant to sanction tyrannicide by private persons. However, the suggestion that Covenanter clergy found *Lex Rex* more conducive than *De Iure Regni* is not implausible. Rutherford's book was a work of the moment, and it must have made Buchanan seem outdated – Mary Stuart was ancient history now, whereas Rutherford's bitter invectives against Charles I and his popish Queen could not have been more contemporary. Moreover, for all the similarity in their political doctrines, it is hard to imagine two books more different. Buchanan's Latin work was written for (and reached) a European readership (both Protestant and Catholic); Rutherford's English work was clearly intended for a British Protestant audience. Buchanan composed an elegant humanist dialogue of just 25,000 words; Rutherford wrote an elaborate scholastic treatise approximately five times greater in length. Buchanan's tone was generally urbane; Rutherford was often vitriolic. Buchanan cited predominantly classical authorities; Rutherford drew on a far wider range of sources, including a host of modern jurists and theologians. Buchanan's treatment of the Bible was relatively limited, involving a striking contextualization and neutralization of Paul's teaching in Romans 13; Rutherford's biblical exegesis was exhaustive, marked by intensive engagement with numerous biblical texts.

The differences between *De Iure Regni* and *Lex Rex* reflect significant developments in the intellectual culture of Reformed Protestantism

---

[37] *Memoirs of Henry Guthrie, Late Bishop of Dunkel in Scotland* (London, 1702), p. 139.

between 1570 and 1640. Calvinists had participated in a massive revival of scholastic learning in the late sixteenth and early seventeenth centuries, partly prompted by the need for increasingly sophisticated polemic and increasingly precise formulations of doctrine.[38] At the same time, they had endeavoured to construct a systematic biblical politics based on meticulous scriptural exegesis. *Vindiciae, Contra Tyrannos* (published in the same year as *De Iure Regni*, 1579, though probably written some time after Buchanan's work was originally composed in 1567) led the way – its biblical references outnumbered all other citations by five to one.[39] In Calvinist nations that saw themselves as New Israels, the Old Testament came to be seen as the primary political textbook, worthy of intensive study beyond that afforded to classical histories.[40] Althusius's *Politica*, published in 1603, was packed with biblical citation, a point easily missed by readers of Carney's English translation, which unhelpfully cut most of this out. In the preface to the third edition, Althusius commented: 'I more frequently use examples from sacred scripture because it has God or pious men as its author, and because I consider that no polity from the beginning of the world has been more wisely and perfectly constructed than the polity of the Jews'.[41]

In the Scottish Reformed tradition, of course, intensive mining of the Old Testament went back to Knox himself. The Covenanters inherited his conviction that the Bible – specifically the Old Testament – was the definitive sourcebook for Protestant politics. It is here that the contrast with Buchanan is sharpest. Buchanan, who had spent only a small portion of his life in Calvinist circles, who was steeped in the classics, who was addressing an audience both Protestant and Catholic, devoted relatively little space to Scripture, and placed significantly less weight on it than other Calvinist writers. He showed no interest in amassing biblical examples to back up his argument, and concentrated on neutralizing biblical texts quoted against resistance (I Samuel 8 and Romans 13). He did so by 'employing a radically historicist approach', one that relativized the text and denied its contemporary political relevance. As Roger Mason has emphasized, the author of *De Iure Regni* is clearly a historically minded humanist rather than a biblical literalist. In advising his interlocutor 'to leave Scripture

---

[38]   See R.A. Muller, *Post-Reformation Reformed Dogmatics: The Rise and Development of Reformed Orthodoxy, ca. 1520 to ca. 1725* (4 vols, Grand Rapids, MI, 2003).

[39]   See A. McLaren, 'Rethinking Republicanism: *Vindiciae Contra Tyrannos* in Context', *Historical Journal*, 49 (2006): p. 32.

[40]   See L.C. Boralevi, 'Classical Foundation Myths of European Republicanism: The Jewish Commonwealth', in Martin van Gelderen and Quentin Skinner (eds), *Republicanism: A Shared European Heritage* (2 vols, Cambridge, 2002), vol. 1, ch. 12.

[41]   *The Politics of Johannes Althusius*, translated and abridged by F.S. Carney (London, 1964), p. 10.

aside ... and go back to school to learn from the philosophers', he displays 'extreme distrust of scriptural "case law"', and reveals 'an attitude worlds apart from that normally associated with Calvinist resistance theorists'.[42]

Of course, Buchanan was no Spinoza, and his Protestant contemporaries did not detect dangerous heterodoxy in his use of biblical texts. Rutherford, in fact, endorses one aspect of his predecessor's exegesis of Romans 13: 'We affirm with Buchanan, that Paul here speaketh of the office and duty of good magistrates, and that the text speaketh nothing of an absolute king, nothing of a tyrant'.[43] But his own treatment of Romans 13 differs markedly from Buchanan's,[44] and he places enormous weight on biblical precedent. Unlike *De Iure Regni*, Covenanter works were drenched in biblical citation. Stewart's *Jus Populi*, for example, contained 450 citations from the Bible, 90 per cent from the Hebrew Scriptures.[45] The Covenanters' obsession with the most obscure of Old Testament personages would later be lampooned in Sir Walter Scott's *Old Mortality*, where characters like Habbakuk Mucklewrath, Ezekiel Kettledrumme and Ephraim Macbriar displayed a virtuoso command of the books of Kings and Chronicles.

Few biblical figures loom as large in Covenanter discourse as Phineas, the prototype of the godly lone assassin. As the University of Oxford noted in the twenty-fifth proposition of its *Judgement and Decree*, *Naphtali* had maintained that 'the example of Phineas is to us instead of a command, for what God has commanded or approved in one age must needs oblige all'. The Oxfordians observed that the same claim had been advanced by a sixteenth-century Scottish writer – not Buchanan, but Knox.[46] In his defence of *Naphtali – Jus Populi Vindicatum* – James Stewart devotes an entire chapter to Phineas, and appeals to Knox against those who claim that such actions were 'extraordinary' and 'not to be imitated'. Indeed, Stewart loved to quote at length from 'our worthy and Noble Reformer famous Mr Knox' – several of his quotations in *Jus Populi* are three or four pages long. Buchanan, by contrast, is cited very little, and not at all in the chapter on Phineas, for he had nothing to say about this obvious biblical precedent for tyrannicide.[47] When Alexander Shields addressed the 'Extraordinary executing of Judgement upon Notorious Incendiaries ...

---

[42] See Mason, *Kingship and the Commonweal*, pp. 222–4; see also 'Introduction' to Buchanan, *De Iure Regni*, pp. xlvii–xlviii. For Buchanan's discussion of Romans 13, see pp. 110–23.

[43] [Rutherford], *Lex Rex*, p. 265.

[44] See [Rutherford], *Lex Rex*, Question 33 (pp. 350–55).

[45] See Beisner, 'His Majesty's Advocate', Appendix A: 'Scripture References in *Jus Populi*'.

[46] 'The Judgement and Decree', in Wootton (ed.), *Divine Right and Democracy*, p. 125.

[47] See [Stewart], *Jus Populi*, ch. 20, esp. pp. 418–19. See also Beisner, 'His Majesty's Advocate', Appendix B.

by private Persons', he did cite Buchanan's defence of tyrannicide, and employed a number of his classical examples, but the bulk of his sixty-page discussion was given over to biblical precedents, including the godly assassins Phineas and Ehud. His references to Buchanan are buried in a text that bristles with biblical citations, and it is no surprise to find that Shields too appeals to the authority of John Knox.[48]

The gap between Buchanan's classical humanism and the Covenanters Hebraic biblicism may account for a strange misquotation in Hickes's *Spirit of Popery*. Hickes is referring to the 'damnable Doctrine of *Heroical Impulse*', which motivated vigilante killings. In the margin, he demonstrates his point with a citation from Buchanan, *De Regni*: 'The only remedy against Tyrants is Ehuds Dagger, to which as the Supreme Court of Justice, Moses brought the Egyptian, Phineas Zimri and Cosbi, Ehud Eglon, Samson the Philistines, Saul Agag, and Jehojadah Athalia'.[49] As those familiar with *De Iure Regni* will recognize, this quotation is nowhere to be found in Buchanan's tract – he never cites the famous example of Phineas, which was so dear to Covenanter militants, or any other Old Testament assassinations. The source of Hickes' quotation is in fact Edward Sexby's anti-Cromwell tract, *Killing noe Murder* (1657), a work that supports tyrannicide with a wealth of biblical evidence.[50] It is telling, I think, that, in trying to trace Covenanter assassination principles to their supposed source, Hickes has to put words into Buchanan's mouth. For while Buchanan does endorse the execution of justice by private persons, the assassins he names are all Greek and Roman rather than biblical figures. *De Iure Regni* differs from Covenanter tracts in its humanist form, its urbane tone and its overwhelmingly classical citations.

Moreover, Buchanan's work has little or nothing to say about idolatry or the defence of true religion. It is, of course, a stridently anti-papal tract, but the focus is on the *tyranny* of the papacy and not on its *idolatry*. Carlos Eire has written, 'If there is one single word or concept that stands out as some sort of red blinking light in all the Calvinist theories from Calvin to Buchanan, it is precisely the issue of idolatry'.[51] He is surely right that this is a central characteristic of Calvinist resistance theory, but he would have been better to say 'Calvinist theories from Calvin to Knox', for in Buchanan's famous tract the concept of idolatry is conspicuously absent. In Knox, however, it is a theme of cardinal importance. Richard Kyle has argued that the crusade against idolatry was 'the great motivation of

---

48   See [Shields], *Hind Let Loose*, pp. 633–95.
49   [Hickes], *The Spirit of Popery*, p. 69.
50   See William Allen [i.e. Edward Sexby], *Killing Noe Murder* (1657), in Wootton (ed.), *Divine Right and Democracy*, p. 377.
51   C. Eire, *War against the Idols: The Reformation of Worship from Erasmus to Calvin* (Cambridge, 1986), p. 308.

Knox's career' and 'the primary motivation for Knox's notions of resistance to idolatrous men'.[52] In this respect, as in his preference for classical over biblical precedents, Buchanan's political theory looks far less Calvinist than that of Knox. For their part, Covenanter writings about politics bear a greater resemblance to Knox than to Buchanan. In Rutherford's *Lex Rex*, for example, one finds ferocious attacks on popish idolatry (which is pronounced 'as abominable as the worshipping of Dagon or the Sidonian gods').[53] The theme of idolatry recurs in later Covenanter works, especially *A Hind Let Loose*. For the Covenanters, as for Knox, the struggle between true and false religion is at the very heart of their theories of resistance. The same cannot be said of *De Iure Regni*.

This is not to imply that Buchanan would have disapproved of Covenanter writing, any more than he would have taken exception to the pamphlets of John Knox. His fulsome poetic tributes to Calvin and Beza demonstrate his passion for the Reformed faith, and his anti-clerical poems reveal a man who fully shared the Scottish Reformer's iconoclastic zeal.[54] As a defender of tyrannicide and an enemy of bishops it is hard to imagine him shedding tears over Archbishop Sharp. The elements of *De Iure Regni* that set it apart from quintessentially Calvinist works are less to do with any principled ideological disagreement with the Reformed tradition, and more to do with Buchanan's own intellectual formation and his cosmopolitan audience. But the difference remains, and it helps to explain why Covenanters found Buchanan less useful than one might expect.[55]

Conclusion

This essay has confirmed what we all suspected – that Buchanan was a significant source for the Scottish Covenanters. They plundered both his *De Iure Regni* and his *History*. But we have also suggested that Buchanan and the Covenanters were not always singing from the same psalm sheet. The most radical element of Buchanan's political theory – his defence of tyrannicide – was taken up by the later Covenanters in the years following their defeat at Pentland in 1666, but it was far less useful to the earlier Covenanters, and may have been something of an

---

[52]   R. Kyle, 'John Knox and the Purification of Religion: The Intellectual Aspects of his Crusade against Idolatry', *Archiv für Reformationsgeschichte*, 77 (1986): pp. 265–80.

[53]   See [Rutherford], *Lex Rex*, p. 369. On Rutherford's vehement iconophobia, see Coffey, *Politics, Religion and the British Revolution*, esp. pp. 182–3.

[54]   Buchanan, *Political Poetry*, pp. 112–17, 246–9; see also Arthur Williamson's discussion of Buchanan's spirituality, above ch. 4.

[55]   The divergence between Buchanan and the Covenanters is also emphasized in Ford, 'Lex, rex iusto posita: Rutherford on the Origins of Government', esp. pp. 263, 272–3.

embarrassment. Moreover, while the Covenanters rehearsed Buchanan's ancient constitutionalism, and shared his Aristotelian natural law theory, they showed relatively little interest in the third major strand of his political thought – his Stoic civic humanism.[56] Finally, two characteristic features of Calvinist politics are stamped all over Covenanter writings, but relatively marginal to *De Iure Regni* – intensive reliance upon scriptural rather than classical precedent, and a consuming passion for the destruction of false religion. Although Covenanters owed much to George Buchanan, they had more in common with John Knox.

---

[56] These three strands are discussed in Mason's 'Introduction', Buchanan, *De Iure Regni*, pp. l–lxxi.

CHAPTER 10

Buchanan in Hell: Sir James Turner's Civil War Royalism*

Clare Jackson

Imprisoned in Hull in 1649, Colonel James Turner was depressed. Disillusioned by his experiences in active service for the Covenanters, he had initially welcomed the formation of the Engagement as an opportunity to promote anew Charles I's cause, but strategic confusion, combined with poor troop discipline, had obliged Turner and the men under his command to surrender to English parliamentarian forces at Uttoxeter, in Staffordshire, in July 1648. As he later recalled in his *Memoirs of His Own Life and Times*, published posthumously in 1829, the subsequent regicide of January 1649 only confirmed that what 'was intended for the Kings reliefe and restoration, posted him to his grave'.[1] Moreover, the ensuing abolition of both the Stuart monarchy and the English House of Lords prompted Turner to feel 'more out of love with Buchanan, whom I looked on as one of these, who had plentifully sown the seed of that Rebellion, which had procured all these dolorous Mischiefs'.[2] Indeed, Turner recalled how, on returning from mercenary employment on the continent to join the Covenanting forces in Scotland during the 1640s, he had discovered that not only could every army minister cite the works of George Buchanan 'as readilie as a Bible', but also that the majority of army officers 'carried Buchanan about with them likewise, and so universally was he cry'd up by all, that I imagin'd his ghost was return'd to earth to wander a little among the Covenanters'.[3] Fortunately for Turner's vivid imagination, the parliamentarian governor at Hull, Colonel Robert Overton, indulged his request to 'furnish me with any books I called for',

---

* I would like to thank Margaret Storrie for first bringing the existence of Turner's manuscript account of 'Buchanan in Hell' to my attention. I would also like to thank Amy Blakeway, Patricia Glennie, Mark Goldie, Colin Kidd, Steve Murdoch, David Stevenson and Jenny Wormald for reading and commenting on an earlier draft of this chapter.

[1] Sir James Turner, *Memoirs of His Own Life and Times M.DC.XXXII–M.DC.LXX*, ed. Thomas Thomson (Edinburgh, 1829), p. 77.

[2] NLS, Advocates MSS. 31.1.15, 'Buchanan Revis'd by Sr James Turner. Annotations or Animadversions on Buchanan's Historie and his Dialogue, De Jure Regni', fol. 1r.

[3] Ibid., fol. 4r.

together with paper, pen and ink, during his enforced confinement, and the result was a manuscript entitled 'A novell against Buchanan, giveing a faithfull and true account of his descent and reception into Hell, and his entertainment there'.[4] Later, Turner described this satirical novel as being 'bot Raillerie': a literary fancy that was in no way intended to detract from the much more extensive set of 'annotations and animadversions' on both Buchanan's *Rerum Scoticarum Historia* and his *De Iure Regni apud Scotos*, which Turner had started several years previously, and which he had also found time to complete, while imprisoned at Hull between September 1648 and November 1649.

In bringing Turner's 'novell against Buchanan' to historical notice, this chapter comprises four sections. The first provides a biographical conspectus of Turner's life, while the second examines both the genre and contents of Turner's picaresque account of Buchanan's descent into Hell. The third reflects on Turner's fictional account in the light of the critique of Buchanan's political philosophy that he presented in a longer manuscript entitled 'Buchanan revis'd'. The fourth contextualizes Turner's account of 'Buchanan in Hell' by considering another fictional account, later penned by Turner, describing Oliver Cromwell's arrival in Hell and his subsequent underworld experiences.

More broadly, this chapter advances three related arguments in its analysis of Turner's writings. The first illustrates the extent to which the experiences of fighting in the British civil wars of the 1640s evidently provoked a profound interest, on Turner's part, in the political ideas over which the wars were being fought. As a foreign mercenary, he had previously defended an ostensible right to eschew political partisanship, but following his imprisonment in 1648 Turner developed a detailed royalist theory of non-resistance that thereafter underpinned his staunch support for Charles I and his descendants. Secondly, this chapter excavates the reasons behind Turner's insistence on the critical and pervasive influence of Buchanan's political ideas on Covenanting opposition to Charles I. For, interestingly, Turner's avowal of the importance of Buchananite ideology in the civil wars effectively gainsays the historiographical assessments of other contributors to this volume that tend to accord only a limited role to Buchanan in the formation of Covenanting ideology. Paradoxically, Buchanan could thus be held to have occupied a more prominent place in the arguments of his mid-seventeenth-century royalist critics than among those who might have been regarded as his natural ideological heirs.

---

[4]   Duke University Library [DUL], North Carolina, 'A Novell ag^t Buchanan giveing a faithfull and true Account of his Descent and Resception [*sic*] into Hell and his Intertainment there', in 'Tracts Criticall and Historicall compiled by Sir James Turner Knight', fols 197–229. A later copy of this 'novell' is appended to the Advocates' MSS. copy of 'Buchanan Revis'd', cited above at fols 92v–105v.

Finally, this chapter draws attention to the characteristically cosmopolitan nature of much mid-seventeenth-century Scottish royalism by considering the intellectual and personal parallels Turner subsequently perceived between Buchanan's iniquitous influence and that of the mid-century Lord Protector, Oliver Cromwell.[5]

I

Born around 1615, James Turner was the eldest son of Patrick Turner, minister of Borthwick, near Edinburgh, and his second wife, Margaret Law, daughter of James Law, Archbishop of Glasgow between 1615 and 1633.[6] After graduating MA from Glasgow in 1631, Turner took time to immerse himself in reading published controversies between Protestants and Roman Catholics, 'so I might not, in traversing the world, be carried away with everie wind of doctrine', as he later claimed.[7] Resisting family pressure to seek ordination, in 1632 Turner instead enlisted as an ensign in a Scots levy raised to fight in Germany under the renowned Protestant defender, Gustavus Adolphus of Sweden. Thereafter, Turner spent most of the 1630s fighting under Swedish command and, by his own account, achieved successive promotion from ensign to lieutenant, captain-lieutenant and captain. His *Memoirs* provide a personalized and vivid account of the death and destruction unleashed in central Europe by the Thirty Years' War. Describing the desperation of the local peasantry in the plundered Werra region of Germany in 1638, for example, Turner deemed events a rueful 'object of pitie to any tender hearted Christian, and did show us with what dreadfull countenance that bloodie monster of warre can appear in the world'.[8] At the same time, however, Turner later recalled that foreign mercenary service ensured he 'had swallowed without chewing ... a very dangerous maxime', namely, 'that so we serve our

---

[5]   Lamenting the extent to which scholars have long been 'enchanted, besotted and beguiled by Parliamentarians, Puritans and so-called "radicals" of every hue', Jason McElligott and David Smith have described Interregnum royalist thought as 'significantly under-studied' ('Introduction: Rethinking Royalists and Royalism during the Interregnum', in McElligott and Smith (eds), *Royalists and Royalism during the Interregnum* (Manchester, 2010), pp. 2, 1.

[6]   For more biographical detail concerning Turner, see not only Turner's own *Memoirs*, but also David Stevenson, 'Turner, Sir James (*b. c.* 1615, *d.* in or after 1689)', *ODNB*, and, by the same author, 'The Literary Mercenary: Sir James Turner', in his *King or Covenant? Voices from the Civil War* (East Linton, 1996), pp. 79–94.

[7]   Turner, *Memoirs*, p. 3.

[8]   Ibid., p. 10; for more on this subject, see John Theibault, 'The Rhetoric of Death and Destruction in the Thirty Years' War', *Journal of Social History*, 27 (1993–94): pp. 271–90, and Geoff Mortimer, *Eyewitness Accounts of the Thirty Years' War* (Basingstoke, 2002).

master honnestlie, it is no matter which master we serve'.[9] Accordingly,
when a quarrel with his colonel provoked his resignation from active
service in 1639, and the outbreak of the civil wars in Britain presented new
opportunities for military employment, Turner subsequently claimed to
have been indifferent as to whether he served Charles I or the Covenanters,
resolving only 'to goe with that ship I first rencounterd' at Gothenburg,
'without examination of the justice of the quarrell, or regard of my dutie
to either prince or countrey'.[10] When the first ship available proved to be
a Danish one being sent to supply the Covenanting armies, Turner was
duly given a commission in a Covenanting regiment, and served first in
Scotland and England, before participating in the attempted suppression
of Catholic rebels in Ulster between 1642 and 1644.

It was thus amid particularly brutal atrocities and prolonged siege
warfare in Ulster that Turner started compiling a treatise entitled 'Buchanan
Revis'd', suggesting that he too had started to revise his original belief that
'it was no matter which master' a soldier served. Having also met a Catholic
woman, Mary White, who would later become his wife after her conversion
to Protestantism, Turner returned to Scotland and served the Covenanting
cause until the end of the first civil war. Turner was, however, increasingly
a 'conservative' Covenanter who supported the stance adopted by James
Hamilton, Marquis of Hamilton, and therefore effectively changed sides
from armed opposition to Charles I's regime to qualified support. Serving
under Hamilton's command, Turner obtained commissions to suppress
opposition to the pro-royalist Engagement in Glasgow, Ayrshire and
northern England before, as indicated above, a chaotic disintegration of
discipline obliged his surrender to English parliamentarian forces in 1648
and his subsequent imprisonment. In Hull, Turner was not only visited
by his wife but also finished his treatise 'Buchanan Revis'd', wrote his
novel 'Buchanan in Hell' and penned a number of shorter essays on an
eclectic range of subjects, including the duties of sovereigns and subjects,
the nature of sovereignty, monarchy, aristocracy and democracy, as well

---

[9]   Turner, *Memoirs*, p. 14. A degree of disingenuity has, however, been alleged with
respect to this oft-quoted assertion. Steve Murdoch, for instance, has contended that, since
Turner wrote his *Memoirs* after the Restoration, when Charles II's administration was
engaged in brutal suppression of presbyterian Covenanters, he was evidently 'trying to
place as much distance between himself and the Covenanters as possible' (Steve Murdoch,
'The House of Stuart and the Scottish Professional Soldier: A Conflict of Nationality and
Identities', in Bertrand Taithe and Tim Thornton (eds), *War: Identities in Conflict 1300–
2000* (Stroud, 1998), p. 44). Similarly, William S. Brockington has insisted that Turner's own
claim should not be 'swallowed without chewing' and '[n]or should his assertion be applied
indiscriminately to all who served foreign masters for pay' ('Robert Monro: Professional
Soldier, Military Historian and Scotsman', in Steve Murdoch (ed.), *Scotland and the Thirty
Years War, 1618–1648* (Leiden, 2001), p. 218).
[10]   Turner, *Memoirs*, p. 14.

as reflections on oratory, magic, Judaism, friendship, imprisonment, anger, revenge, dueling and cruelty.[11] In his *Memoirs*, Turner later described the parliamentarian governor at Hull, Colonel Robert Overton, as 'a great Independent ... [and] a schollar, bot a little pedantick' who 'promisd to befriend me as much as he could, without his oune prejudice'.[12] To this end, not only did Overton disregard instructions received directly from Oliver Cromwell that Turner be kept in chained confinement, but he also allowed him both 'the reading of all the Gazets and Diurnalls' and to write 'with so much confidence and freedome, as if I had beene at my full libertie' and 'to cary all my papers with me untouchd and unseene by himselfe or any other'.[13]

Their profound political differences notwithstanding, Overton's friendship evidently also led to Turner's release from prison. Initially, he went to the continent, but returned to serve the royalist cause, as colonel of a regiment, at Worcester in 1651, before suffering recapture by the Parliamentarians, from which he staged a dramatic escape and fled, once more, to the continent, where he spent most of the 1650s engaged in various employments, including service in the armies of Denmark–Norway. Residing in Bremen, and later The Hague, in the late 1650s, Turner was also obliged to rewrite the whole of his treatise 'Buchanan Revis'd', as well as a number of other political writings, after his manuscripts had been destroyed in September 1651, when Cromwellian forces had sacked the town of Dundee, whence Turner had sent his papers to his wife for safe keeping.[14] At some point, he also composed another fanciful fiction, set in

---

[11]   See BL, Add. MSS. 12,067, 'Miscellaneous Essays and Poems by Sir James Turner'.

[12]   Turner, *Memoirs*, pp. 78–9.

[13]   Ibid., pp. 83, 88. Ironically, similar courtesies were not accorded to Overton himself when, in 1655, he was imprisoned by the Cromwellian authorities, following the discovery, in Overton's possession and in his own handwriting, of a copy of a satirical verse entitled 'The Character of a Protector'. Overton remained in prison until after Cromwell's death, and was never subjected to a formal trial. For more information, see Andrew Shifflett, '"A Most Humane Foe": Colonel Robert Overton's War with the Muses', in Claude J. Summers and Ted-Larry Pebworth (eds), *The English Civil Wars in the Literary Imagination* (Columbia, MI, 1999), pp. 159–73.

[14]   A similar fate afflicted the works of another royalist contemporary, Sir Thomas Urquhart of Cromarty, whose imprisonment after the fateful defeat at Worcester in 1651 coincided with the loss of his literary manuscripts. From the 'six score and eight quires and a half' composed by Urquhart, only one 'together with two other loose sheets' were recovered, representing the loss of manuscripts 'treating of metaphysical, mathematicall, moral, mythological, epigrammaticall, dialectical, [and] archaeological matters in a way never hitherto trod upon by any' (*The Works of Sir Thomas Urquhart of Cromarty Kt.* [ed. J. Maitland] (Edinburgh, 1834), pp. 189–90).

1659, concerning the descent into Hell and underworld experiences of the former Lord Protector, Oliver Cromwell.[15]

Following the restoration of the Stuarts, Turner returned to London, where he obtained a knighthood and appointment as major of Charles II's footguards in Scotland, followed by promotion as lieutenant-colonel in July 1666, in which capacity he earned enduring obloquy for his role in the Restoration government's persecution of presbyterian nonconformists. Most notoriously, when sent to suppress resistance in Dumfries in November 1666, Turner was ignominiously seized by a group of Covenanting rebels 'in his night-gown, night-cap, drawers and socks', as the Covenanter, John Blackadder, later recounted.[16] Thereafter, he was unceremoniously marched around Lowland Scotland by his captors for a fortnight, before staging another dramatic escape during the Covenanters' military defeat at Rullion Green. Unfortunately, however, Turner duly became the scapegoat for government failures and, after an inquiry, was censured and stripped of his commission. He then devoted the following decades to writing his lively and entertaining memoirs, partly in retrospective vindication of his conduct. Following the publication in 1683 of his twin folio collection of military essays, entitled *Pallas Armata: Military Essayes of the Ancient Grecian, Roman and Modern Art of War*, dedicated to the Duke of York, Turner enjoyed a brief rehabilitation and was given a new military command, before retiring in 1685 and dying, in relative obscurity, at some point in or after 1689.[17] A decade before their eventual publication, however, Turner's memoirs provided Sir Walter Scott with irresistible inspiration to create one of his finest comic characters, Dugald Dalgetty of Drumthwacket, in *A Legend of Montrose* (1819). Admired by William Thackeray and John Buchan, Dalgetty comprises such 'a strange mixture of shrewdness and idealism, of practicality and pedantry, of aggression and caution, of cosmopolitan experience and simple Scottish prejudice, that he provokes our disgust, excites our amusement, and finally earns our respect'.[18]

---

[15]   BL, Add. MSS. 12,067, 'A Letter from Dom Francisco of Quevedo to Philander of Sitwald, who wrote the continuation of Quevedos Visions, concerning some discourses which passed in the infernall court, between the late usurper, Oliver Cromwell, the late Chancellor Sweden, Axell Oxenstierne, and the Lord Lilienstrome, sent by the post of hell, in the year 1659. English'd out of hie Dutch', in 'Miscellaneous Essays and Poems', fols 133v–151r.

[16]   *The Life and Diaries of Lieut. Col. John Blackadder*, ed. Andrew Crichton (Edinburgh, 1823), p. 139. Since Blackadder himself was, however, only a young child at the time of this incident, he was presumably recounting anecdotes that he was told much later.

[17]   The title of Turner's military essays was, presumably, inspired by the earlier appearance of Sir Thomas Kellie's *Pallas Armata, or Militarie Instruction for the Learned &c.* (Edinburgh, 1627).

[18]   J.D. Mackie, 'Dugald Dalgetty and Scottish Soldiers of Fortune', *Scottish Historical Review*, 12 (1915): p. 221; see also John Robert Moore, 'Defoe and Scott', *Proceedings of*

II

While Turner's satirical vision of George Buchanan's arrival in Hell may have provided an outlet for personal frustration during his imprisonment in 1649, Turner's manuscript account also embraced an ancient literary genre in supplying an account of life in the infernal world.[19] In Book XI of Homer's *Odyssey*, for example, Odysseus travels to the Greek underworld, Hades, to consult the blind seer, Tiresias, while in Turner's time, John Boys published an English translation in 1660 of Book VI of Virgil's *Aeneid*, entitled *Æneas, His Descent into Hell*.[20] Similarly, while Virgil himself guided the pilgrim, Dante, through the three worlds of the 'beyond' in Dante's *Divine Comedy*, both Erasmus and Sir Thomas More had produced English translations of Lucian of Samosata's satirically mordant *True History, Charon and Dialogues of the Dead*. As parliamentarian opposition to Charles I gathered pace, however, a flurry of anonymous new titles appeared in 1641, including *A Dreame, or Newes from Hell, A Description of the Passage of Thomas, Late Earl of Strafford, over the River Styx, Newes from Hell, Rome and the Inns of Court* and *The Hellish Parliament being a Counter-Parliament to this in England*.[21]

For his part, Turner self-consciously modelled his manuscript account of Buchanan's descent into Hell on the inventive 'sueño del infierno', from the *Sueños y Discursos*, or 'Dreams and Discourses', that had been written by the Spanish poet and prose writer Francisco Quevedo y Villegas between 1605 and 1621, and which had circulated widely in manuscript, before being translated into a variety of languages throughout Europe.[22] An unattributed English translation was first published by Richard Croshawe in 1640, entitled *Visions, or Hels Kingdome, and the World's Follies and Abuses*, while another unacknowledged translation by Edward Messervy,

---

the *Modern Language Association*, 56 (1941): pp. 718–19.

[19] See, e.g., Benjamin Boyce, 'News from Hell: Satiric Communication with the Nether World in English Writing of the Seventeenth and Eighteenth Centuries', *Proceedings of the Modern Language Association*, 58 (1943): pp. 402–37.

[20] John Boys, *Æneas, His Descent into Hell &c.* (London, 1660).

[21] Other similar titles published during the 1640s included *An Epistle Written from Lucifer* (1642), *A Disputation betwixt the Devil and the Pope* (1642), John Taylor's *Mercurialis Infernalis; or Orderless Orders, Votes, Ordinances and Commands from Hell* (1644), Sir Francis Wortley's *Mercurius Britanicus, His Welcome to Hell* (1647), James Howell's *A Trance, or Newes from Hell* and the anonymous *A Declaration of the Great Lucifer, Prince of Ayre, and of the Divells, and of all the Damned Crew in Hell* (1648).

[22] For a modern edition, see Francisco de Quevedo, *Dreams and Discourses*, ed. and trans. R.K. Britton (Warminster, 1989). For more information about Quevedo's infernal vision, see Sofie Kluge, 'The Dialectics of Redemption, Autonomous Language, Heresy and Divine Truth in Francisco de Quevedo's Dream of Hell', *Orbis Litterarum*, 59 (2004): pp. 416–38, and William H. Clamurro, 'The Sueños and the Ideology of Agudeza', in his *Language and Ideology in the Prose of Quevedo* (Newark, DE, 1991), pp. 88–119.

entitled *Hell Reformed, or a Glasse for Favourits* appeared the following year.[23] It was not until the Restoration, however, that Quevedo's *Sueños* became widely popular, following the lively and didactic translation produced by Roger L'Estrange, entitled *English Visions*, which went through eleven editions by 1715.[24]

Both Turner's manuscript account of 'Buchanan in Hell' and his later narrative of Cromwell's infernal experiences were presented in the form of a series of letters dispatched from the underworld. The first, claiming to supply 'the storie of the prodigious conception of George Buchanan', was ostensibly sent by Quevedo on 1 March 1506 (a month after the real date of Buchanan's birth) to a Spanish friend and Calatravian knight, Don Juan Acuña. It begins by admonishing sceptical readers not to question how such an additional account could predate those of Quevedo's other visions, explaining that Quevedo himself had actually died around 1490, but that before his death, Quevedo had promised to write to his friend 'from the Infernal World, such Occurrences, as he thought worthy his knowledge'.[25] Since such occurrences had been recounted in private letters between friends, they had evidently not been thought suitable for inclusion in the original collections of Quevedo's *Sueños*, allegedly printed by Quevedo's great-grandchild. The second letter, describing Buchanan's arrival in Hell, was dated 29 September 1582 (a day after the real date of Buchanan's death) and was not written by Quevedo, but by 'Philander of Sitwald' to a German friend, Caspar, Baron of Isenstein. In this instance, Turner's inspiration appears to have been the satirical writings of the German Lutheran, Johann Michael Moscherosch, who wrote under the pseudonym 'Philander von Sitwald' and whose most famous work was published in two volumes between 1641 and 1643 entitled *Wunderliche und Wahrhafftige Gesichte Philanders von Sitwald*, or the 'Peculiar and true visions of Philander von Sitwald'.[26] Modelled on Quevedo's *Sueños*, Moscherosch's satires lampooned the culture and *mores* of mid-seventeenth-century Germany from the perspective of a Lutheran patriot. Similarly, Turner's later account of Cromwell's descent into Hell was

---

[23]   [Francisco de Quevedo], *Visions, or Hels Kingdome, and the Worlds Follies Strangely Displaied by R. C. of the Inner Temple Gent. Being the first fruits of a reformed life* (London, 1640), and [Francisco de Quevedo], *Hell Reformed, or A Glasse for Favorits, their falls and complaints, also the complaints of princes against their favourites, with the dangerous mischiefs of state politicks, flatterers, suborders, secret accusers, false witnesses &c.* (London, 1641).

[24]   R[oger] L['Estrange], *The Visions of Dom Francisco de Quevedo Villegas, Knight of the order of St James* (London, 1667).

[25]   DUL, 'A Novell ag.[t] Buchanan', fol. 198.

[26]   For a modern edition, see Johann Michael Moscherosch, *Visiones de Don Quevedo: Wunderl. u. Wahrhafftige Gesichte Philanders von Sittewald*, ed. J.P. Mulben (2 vols, Hildesheim, 1973).

presented in the form of a letter sent by Quevedo to Philander of Sitwald, evidently following the latter's successes in disseminating 'the continuation of my Visions'.[27]

Turner's first fictional letter thus set out to provide an explanation of Buchanan's birth. According to Quevedo's dispatch from Hell, it was around the year 1505 that the ghost of King Macbeth of Scotland had first detected a general disquiet pervading the underworld, evidently occasioned by its head, King Pluto, suffering from a 'squeasie Stomach', which was deemed curious, on account of the immorality customarily accorded to devils.[28] Diagnosed to be suffering from 'a Superabundance of Pride and Rebellion', Pluto was directed to take an emetic and immediately 'vomite up some of his Rebellious humours' that, preferably, would be discarded in a cold and inhospitable climate in the terrestrial world, to prevent sickness of pride from festering.[29] Moreover, Macbeth's ghost was informed that Pluto had selected Scotland as the most suitable location in which to dispose of his excess pride and rebellion, since he harboured a historic grudge against Scotland, for the country's speedy embrace of Christianity and its concomitant rejection of paganism. Indeed, Pluto had prognosticated a pleasing potential to create future strife in Scotland, given the forthcoming onset of the Protestant Reformation. According to Quevedo's account, a year then elapsed before Macbeth's ghost learned that Pluto had insisted that any of the pride and rebellion he had disgorged had been carefully preserved in a pair of unicorns' horns. An incubus and a succubus had been dispatched with the contents of the unicorns' horns to imbue Pluto's diabolical rebelliousness into a peasant man and his wife, who were thereafter to spawn a child who would not only 'equally partake of the humane and diabolicall natures' but would also 'prove, the greatest firebrand of Rebellion that ever poor Scotland saw'.[30] Accordingly, nine months later, in early 1506, a baby boy had evidently been born, 'begot with the help of four individuals, a man, a woman, a hee divell and a shee divell, so that in outwards shape, he may prove and appear a Man, but inwardly, he will be a divell'.[31] The baby boy's name was, unsurprisingly, George Buchanan.

Turner's tale continues with a second letter dispatched from the underworld, dated 29 September 1582, recounting how, the previous day, a ghost had arrived at the River Styx, imperiously demanding transport across the river. Having identified itself as being the ghost of George

---

27   BL Add. MSS. 12,067, 'A Letter from Dom Francisco', in 'Miscellaneous Essays and Poems by Sir James Turner', fol. 133r.
28   DUL, 'A Novell ag^t Buchanan', fol. 199.
29   Ibid., fol. 202.
30   Ibid., fol. 206.
31   Ibid., fol. 207.

Buchanan, a diabolical herald had informed Hell's inhabitants that, since Buchanan had achieved unparalleled renown in seeking 'to reduce Rebellion to ane Art, and Method, and [had] publickly taught Lessons of it', all of Hell's inhabitants were to 'come out of their caves and cells, and congratulate the Arrivall of this great Doctor of Impietie, Wickedness, Confusion and Rebellion'.[32] Making its stately progress through the underworld, Buchanan's ghost was duly accosted by a number of Hell's inhabitants, including the spectre of Photius, the ninth-century emperor of Constantinople, who wished that he had 'had Thee, or one like thee, near Me, when I usurped the Impyre of Greece', before lamenting the barbaric manner in which he had subsequently been put to death by his subjects. Buchanan's ghost remained unmoved at Photius's regrets, insisting that Photius should have beheaded his predecessors with more 'shew of Justice' to his subjects than he had displayed, to ensure thereby that 'both desire and power of Revenge is taken from them'.[33] Thereafter, Buchanan's ghost had been detained by another apparition, 'whose head was very untowardly sew'd to his neck', revealing itself to be an equally disgruntled ghost: that of King Macbeth. For its part, Macbeth's ghost bluntly denied that any reader should take the time to read Buchanan's writings, since he himself had pursued precisely the same precepts for which Buchanan later assumed credit, not only in confirming the ancient, elective character of the Scots monarchy, but also in an act of 'Singular Good Service to Scotland', by removing King Duncan, under whose rule Scotland had risked being surrendered to the Danes.[34] Moreover, Macbeth's ghost claimed thereafter to have reigned justly, at least for the first decade, despite later being calumniated as 'a Cruel Tyrant' and 'Perfidious Villain' in Buchanan's *Rerum Scoticarum Historia*. In response, Buchanan's ghost remained unaffected, replying to Macbeth's ghost that, whereas he had indeed heartily endorsed the more recent deposition of Mary Queen of Scots, 'you lived in an other age, and therefore, I beseeche you, learne to distinguish the times'.[35]

---

[32]   Ibid., fol. 213.

[33]   Ibid., fol. 215.

[34]   Ibid., fol. 216. In studying William Shakespeare's subsequent adoption of a 'Buchananesque mode in a tragedy on a Scottish theme', David Norbrook has drawn attention to the fact that, since the historical King Macbeth was 'a regicide who was condemned equally by Buchanan and by conservatives, and yet had half-buried associations with constitutionalist traditions', he was always likely to 'evoke ambivalent responses' from humanists interested in drawing Senecan contrasts between harmonious good government and chaotic misrule ('*Macbeth* and the Politics of Historiography', in Kevin Sharpe and Steven Zwicker (eds), *Politics of Discourse: The Literature and History of Seventeenth-century England* (Berkeley, CA, 1987), pp. 113, 116).

[35]   DUL, 'A Novell ag.[t] Buchanan', fol. 216. In envisaging this exchange, Turner may, however, have allowed his own rhetorical polemic to eclipse his insistence on quoting

Subsequently, however, Buchanan's ghost was impressed to encounter the ghost of the Roman emperor, Julius Caesar, whom he reverentially addressed in perfect classical Latin and confirmed his regret at the violent manner in which Caesar had met his death, before magnanimously insisting that, had he been alive at the time, he could have written so powerfully in his defence, that Caesar would certainly have escaped death. Notwithstanding, Caesar's ghost retorted by denouncing Buchanan's ghost as a 'Presumptuous Pedant', devoid of insight into practical politics. Indeed, Caesar's ghost proceeded to inform Buchanan's ghost, 'let it be known to thee, base wretch, that I would have choosed to have been murther'd ten thousand times over and over againe ... before I would have had my life spared by such a vile Harlot, as thou art knowen to be'.[36] Another altercation then ensued between the ghost of Buchanan and that of the assassinated Regent Moray, whose ghost had appeared 'all bloody, occasion'd by a wound he had gott in his bellie', and who seemed to be constantly trying, in vain, to snatch hold of an elusive royal crown.[37] When blamed by Moray's ghost for having failed to secure him the Scottish throne, Buchanan's ghost responded by attributing Moray's assassination instead to his cowardice in failing to remove Mary Queen of Scots permanently, simply deposing her as queen rather than killing her, together with his arrogant conduct thereafter as royal regent.

The culmination of Turner's fictional tale then occurs when Buchanan's ghost was finally presented to the head of the underworld, King Pluto. After Buchanan's ghost offered a deeper bow to Pluto 'then ever he did it, either to Queen Mary or King James', Pluto had fulsomely paid tribute to the gloriously diabolic effects on earth of Buchanan's actions and writings.[38] As Pluto confirmed, '[t]he whole Senate of the Hierarchie of Hell acknowledges that since Adam by my instigation, sinn'd against his Maker, there hath not been such an Architector of Rebellion as your selfe'.[39] Notwithstanding, Pluto then informed Buchanan's ghost that it was hereafter to be held in solitary confinement, lest the infectious character of both his rebellious nature and his political teachings conspired to undermine Pluto's own governance of the underworld. As Pluto had subsequently confirmed to his diabolical colleagues, 'this Abominable Pestilential fellow, who was so declared an Enemie to Absolute Monarchie on Earth, can never be a

---

Buchanan faithfully. For, in his *Historia*, Buchanan had indeed conceded that, of Macbeth's seventeen-year reign, 'in the first Ten, he performed the Duty of a very good King; in the last Seven, he equalled the Cruelty of the worst of Tyrants' (George Buchanan, *The History of Scotland*, trans. J. Fraser (London, 1690), p. 214).

[36]   DUL, 'A Novell ag.' Buchanan', fol. 217.
[37]   Ibid., fol. 218.
[38]   Ibid., fol. 220.
[39]   Ibid., fol. 221.

friend to the purely Monarchical Government of Hell'.[40] In similar vein, one of the devils later explained to Buchanan's ghost that Pluto may love Buchanan's treasonable ideas, but not the traitor himself. En route to his solitary confinement, Buchanan's ghost had a final, unfortunate, encounter with the ghost of the fifteenth-century Burgundian writer and statesman Philip de Commines, who treated Buchanan's admiring salutations with the same contempt as Julius Caesar's ghost, denouncing him as an 'Ignorant Blockhead' whose political thought was confused and whose historical analysis was erroneous.[41] In response, Buchanan's ghost had been obliged to console itself with a maxim from Commines's own *Mémoires*, to the effect that those who perform the greatest services are often unjustly rewarded with the greatest ingratitude. Deeply dejected, Buchanan's ghost was informed by one of Pluto's mirthful devils that, were he to publish a record of his recent conversations and encounters in Hell, it would be read 'with more pleasure ... [and] sure with more profitt than that damned pamphlet of yours, De Jure Regni apud Scotos'.[42]

III

Turner himself deemed the two fictional letters that comprised 'Buchanan in Hell' as being 'bot Railleries': a literary fancy that should not detract from his more extensive set of manuscript 'annotations and animadversions' on Buchanan's *Historia* and the *De Iure Regni*. Entitled 'Buchanan Revis'd', Turner's commentary extended to around 65,000 words and, according to its preface, was intended to demonstrate Buchanan's 'Inadvertencies, Inconsistencies, false citations, Inexcusable Ignorance in the Histories of our neighbour Nations, Blasphemies, Insolencies, arrogant contempt of Superiour powers ... frequent speaking ill of dignities, his Lessons and Dictates of Rebellion, his misregard of Holy Scripture, his malicious untruth, Downright Lies and most dishonourable Language of those in lawfull Authority'.[43] In this context, the vituperative tone of Turner's attack echoed earlier denunciations of Buchanan's political precepts by English and Scots royalists alike. In 1639, for example, the Anglican divine, Henry Valentine, published a sermon he had just preached at St Paul's in London, entitled *God Save the King*, which denounced Buchanan's doctrine of resistance as 'the *imprimis* in the blacke Catalogue of the Doctrine of the Devils, it is the Doctrine of Beelzebub the Prince of devils, it is the bane of mens soules, the blemish of Christian religion, and the breach of all

---

40   Ibid., fol. 228.
41   Ibid., fol. 223.
42   Ibid., fol. 225.
43   NLS, Adv. MS. 31.1.15, 'Buchanan Revis'd', fol. 1r.

common tranquillity'.[44] For his part, Turner embarked on a page-by-page dissection of both of Buchanan's major works, 'well knowing', as he put it, that 'I shall have the whole swarme of the Buchananists about my ears, who will perhaps charge me with little less than pettie blasphemie'.[45] From the outset, however, Turner was evidently insistent that he did not intend 'to make my observations publick', despite the care he had taken to rewrite his critique, following its original destruction in 1651.[46]

In terms of its content, while Turner devoted the greater part of 'Buchanan Revis'd' to enumerating numerous chronological and genealogical inaccuracies identified in Buchanan's historical account of the Scots monarchy, a broader ideological critique also emerges. Most notably, Turner attributed the radical aspects of Buchanan's political precepts to his personal impiety and to his failure to adhere to a single religious conviction throughout his life. Claiming that Buchanan had 'fitted his religion according to the mode of the place where his Destinie cast him', Turner also drew attention to allegations concerning Buchanan's involvement in Judaism, previously advanced by the Scots Catholic writer, David Chalmers, in his *De Pietate, Fortitudine et Doctrina Scotorum* (Paris, 1631).[47] Irrespective of the accuracy of such charges, Turner emphasized Buchanan's disregard for scriptural authority in denying the legality of resistance, articulated for example, in the books of Samuel, Kings and Chronicles, claiming that Buchanan had seemingly 'looked on them as tales of Robin Hood'.[48] Furthermore, he attacked Buchanan for effectively denying the universal validity of biblical teachings, as evidenced by his deeming St Paul's famous injunction regarding obedience to superior powers (Romans 13: 1–2) to be 'bot a temporarie command to these men and women who compos'd the Roman Church at that tyme, when the Apostle wrote the Letter, and not a generall law or order to all Christians to the end of the world'.[49] As Turner concluded, if such reasoning was valid, the moral and political teachings of

[44] Henry Valentine, *God Save the King. A Sermon Preached in St Paul's Church, the 27th March 1639, being the Day of Maiesties Happy Inauguration, and of his Northern Expedition* (London, 1639), pp. 26–7. Valentine's sermon was licensed for the press on 28 March, the day after it was preached, and entered into the Stationer's Register on 29 March (Jonquil Bevan, 'Henry Valentine, John Donne and Izaak Walton', *Review of English Studies*, 40 (1989): p. 198).

[45] NLS, Adv. MS. 31.1.15, 'Buchanan Revis'd', fol. 4v.

[46] Ibid. Indeed, Turner confessed his 'wish that Buchanan had keep'd his book from the presse, as well as I shall keep these papers, and that he had been as readie to burne his Historie … as I shall be at the desyre of any honest man to throw these papers of mine into the fire' (ibid.). Notwithstanding, Turner also insisted that, 'if any man will read these animadversions', he needed to have copies of both Buchanan's *Historia* and the *De Iure Regni* to hand, 'that he may see I quote him faithfully both book and page' (ibid., fol. 1r).

[47] Ibid., fol. 42r.

[48] Ibid., fols 9v–10r.

[49] Ibid., fols 44r.

St Paul, together with those of the other apostles, might be cast 'in a fire, as such we owe no reverence to'.[50]

Moreover, while Turner's own political proclivities emerge largely by inference in 'Buchanan Revis'd', he elsewhere articulated more fully his adherence to Jacobean divine-right theories of absolute kingship. In an essay on the duties of sovereigns and subjects, for example, he held that 'all the armes, subjects may use against their soveraignes, are prayers and teares' and insisted that Scripture remains 'our guide, the rule, whereby we s[h]ould square all our actions ... a full and perfite pedagogue to teach us our Duties to God, to the king, to all our superiours, to our equals, and inferiors'.[51] In particular, Turner held the misappropriation of Scripture, for nefarious political ends, to be the most heinous political sin, bitterly attacking those who 'can counterfeit pietie so well, as they are esteem'd not only relligieous [sic], bot the very Patrons of Religion'.[52] Deeming the miserable mischiefs unleashed by civil war to be tenfold worse that any inconveniences suffered 'under the tirranous misgovernment of the most Monstrous Nero', Turner insisted that it was always 'better to endure the greatest oppressions that can be excogitated by the greatest of tyrants'.[53] Hence he bitterly denounced those malcontents who 'inveigh against abuses of state ... talke of the oppression of the subjects, the enslaveing a free borne people, the tirranizing over consciences of good Men', and thereby 'make their Zeale to the publicke good, and libertie of the nation, the pretext and specious cloake of all their hellish plots'.[54]

In an accompanying essay on monarchy, Turner proceeded to draw parallels between the political power exercised by a father over the microcosm of a family, and a monarch's role in the macrocosm as 'the sunne in the firmament ... the Moone, and all the starres, borroweing their light from him'.[55] Having subdivided monarchical government into three types (arbitrary, royal and tyrannical), Turner identified the Scots monarchy as being 'royal' in its adherence to divine, natural and civil law, while insisting that 'successive Monarchie, by many impartiall politicians

---

50   Ibid., fol. 78r.

51   BL Add. MS. 12,067, 'Of the Dueties of Soveraignes and Subjects', in 'Miscellaneous Essays and Poems by Sir James Turner', fols 38v, 45r.

52   Ibid., fol. 42v. Bitterly attacking his former Covenanting colleagues, Turner proceeded to contend that, while the majority of 'Covenanters either in Scotland or England' would readily denounce the French Catholic League as having been treasonous, rebellious and unlawful, '[c]hange bot the name of the Catholike religion, in true protestant religion, the holy league is directlie your oune Solemne League and Covenant' (ibid., fol. 43r).

53   Ibid., fol. 46r.

54   Ibid., fol. 42v.

55   BL Add. MS. 12,067, 'Of Monarchie', in 'Miscellaneous Essays and Poems by Sir James Turner', fol. 57v.

is reputed to be the best'.[56] In 'Buchanan Revis'd', however, Turner remained relatively pragmatic as to the qualitative character of magistracy, conceding that 'no government under the Sunn can be perfect', since 'the best modell'd Government that the heart of man can devise will be found defective, and have its imperfections'.[57] Moreover, Turner conceded that he would have been prepared to accept Buchanan's claims in the *De Iure Regni* if they had been presented as 'the pattern of such a Commonwealth as best pleas'd his own fancie', similar to the ideal society outlined in Sir Thomas More's *Utopia* (1516), but he denounced Buchanan's iniquity in claiming that his account reflected 'the antient government of the Kingdome of Scotland'.[58] Moreover, with reference to the Scots monarchy, Turner also denied Buchanan's identification of an inherent contractarianism. For Turner, indefeasible hereditary succession, including succession by a minor, was not only enjoined in Scripture, but also constituted 'our old fundamentall law' in Scotland.[59] Accordingly, the coronation of a Scots monarch was 'bot a Ceremonie', the witnessing whereof 'makes not the King, nor adds any thing to his authoritie'.[60] As Turner pointed out, Charles I had been 'reallie and truely longer king of Scotland before his Coronation there, then he was after', having wielded strong and effective power between his accession to the throne in 1625 and his coronation at Holyrood in 1633, but thereafter being obliged to reign 'bot precario', following the rise of Covenanting control from 1638 onwards.[61] Finally, in addition to having propounded theories of popular sovereignty and rights of resistance, Buchanan was also charged by Turner with prejudiced partiality and a lack of patriotism, particularly in his treatment of recent Scottish history and the circumstances surrounding the deposition of Mary Queen of Scots. Denouncing Buchanan for having disregarded 'the rules of Historie, one whereof is to write nothing bot Truth',[62] Turner claimed that, throughout Buchanan's writings, 'things which are ordinare with other princes, must be extraordinare crimes in Queen Mary, and hiely

---

[56] Ibid., fol. 56r.

[57] NLS, Adv. MS. 31.1.15, 'Buchanan Revis'd', fol. 9r.

[58] Ibid., fol. 89v.

[59] Ibid., fol. 14v. In identifying hereditary succession to be a fundamental law of Scotland, Turner was advancing the same argument as that subsequently asserted by Sir George Mackenzie of Rosehaugh in a tract also directed against the political theories of, *inter alia*, Buchanan entitled *That the Lawfull Successor Cannot be Debarr'd from Succession to the Crown: Maintained against Dolman [Robert Parsons], Buchannan [sic] and Others* (Edinburgh, 1684).

[60] NLS, Adv. MS. 31.1.15, 'Buchanan Revis'd', fol. 74r.

[61] Ibid., fol. 89v.

[62] Ibid., fol. 67r.

aggravated too, by magisteriall Buchanan'.[63] Indeed, Turner averred that Buchanan 'characters Queen Mary no otherwayes, than if she had been some wild Beare or Tiger',[64] thereby ensuring that no 'stranger can read two passages of his booke, besides many more, and not say, the Scots were a rude, savage, and a barbarous people.'[65] Regarding Buchanan's reservations about gynæcocracy, Turner insisted that not only did Scripture furnish examples of lawful and successful female rulers, such as Deborah, but also, '[t]here is no law in Scotland that excludes women from government'.[66] In a separate essay, Turner also insisted that 'all unbyass'd men ... look'd upon Mary of Scotland everie way equall to Elisabeth of England for wisdome, vertue, and those qualities which adorne the mind, farre superior to her in the Beautie of Bodie, tho[u]gh Inferior to her in the happie and fortunate event of all her actions.'[67] Moreover, Turner's concomitant attack on Elizabeth I's unforgivable jealousy of her cousin presumably explains why, in 'Buchanan Revis'd', he selected continental examples to demonstrate the achievements of female monarchs. As he contended, for example, Margaret, Queen of Sweden, Denmark and Norway, had successfully ruled all three territories with 'as much equitie, justice, courage, and magnanimitie, as ever they were govern'd before, or since that time', while Isabella of Castile had likewise 'govern'd with much equitie, prudence, and courage', both before and after her marriage to Ferdinand.[68] Accordingly, Turner charged Buchanan with unjustified misogyny for having eschewed a reasoned argument against female rule, but instead 'in a Pedantick furie', having sought to 'whip them all from their thrones, and chase them to their Gynocæa, and womenhouses, there to spin and card'.[69]

Interestingly, however, Turner's 'Buchanan Revis'd' simultaneously revealed Buchanan's success in obliging his intellectual enemies to focus

---

[63]   Ibid., fol. 42r. As Roger Mason argues, Buchanan depicts Mary 'as a tyrant, a latter-day Nero or Caligula, a victim of lust, greed and ambition, increasingly portrayed as a manipulative dissimulator', acknowledging that aspects of '[t]his farrago may bear little relation to the known facts of history, but it is rhetorically highly effective'. Roger A. Mason, 'George Buchanan and Mary Queen of Scots', *Records of the Scottish Church History Society*, 30 (2000): pp. 23, 25; see also 'Introduction', Buchanan, *De Iure Regni*, pp. lxvii–lxx.

[64]   NLS, Adv. MS. 31.1.15, 'Buchanan Revis'd', fol. 66v.

[65]   Ibid., fol. 50r.

[66]   Ibid., fol. 24r.

[67]   BL Add. MS. 12,067, 'Mary Steuart, Queene of Scots', in 'Miscellaneous Essays and Poems by Sir James Turner', fol. 275v.

[68]   NLS, Adv. MS. 31.1.15, 'Buchanan Revis'd', fol. 27r. For an account of how Buchanan's partisan interpretation of Scottish history could be appropriated by English commentators on female monarchy, see Amanda Shephard, *Gender and Authority in Sixteenth-century England: The Knox Debate* (Keele, 1994), pp. 155–8.

[69]   NLS, Adv. MS. 31.1.15, 'Buchanan Revis'd', fol. 27v.

on those moments in Scottish history that proved uncomfortable for defenders of divinely ordained, hereditary monarchy. As Roger Mason has shown, the murder in 1566 of Queen Mary's Savoyard servant, David Riccio, by Protestant noble conspirators, led by Patrick, Lord Ruthven, represents 'the climax of the entire *History*'.[70] For Turner, however, 'it were to be wish'd, that, that assassination had been buried in oblivion', rather than presented in Buchanan's *Historia* as 'a most heroick act',[71] whereas, rightly, Ruthven's actions should have been denounced as 'more savage and inhumane then the most barbarous Scithian, or American, that any historie ever mentioned.'[72] Instead, Turner drew parallels between Riccio and Buchanan, contending that, 'in their Lives, they differ'd but little': both were of low birth, both had 'travell'd over severall countreys in poverty and penurie',[73] both were artists in that Riccio had been a musician and Buchanan a poet, and both had ultimately benefited from royal patronage. Indeed, Turner accepted Riccio's intimate proximity to Mary on the grounds that '[o]ur Kings and Queens in these dayes, keep'd not that state they now doe'.[74]

In contrast to the gruesome events recounted in Buchanan's narrative, however, in 'Buchanan Revis'd', Turner envisaged an alternative scenario that might have occurred at some point during the political ascendancy of James Stewart, Regent Moray, who has subsequently been identified as the 'real hero' of Buchanan's *Historia* and 'the embodiment of civic virtue'.[75] In Turner's version, noble leaders loyal to Mary might just as readily have decided to eliminate Buchanan's pernicious and destabilizing influence, by seizing him forcibly from Moray's presence, whereupon Turner imagined 'twenty daggers are stabb'd in Buchanan's breast' or, alternatively, Buchanan being taken to Edinburgh's Mercat Cross to have both his 'seditious tongue' and his right hand removed, 'which hath writ all his invectives'.[76] Such fanciful speculations prompted Turner to ponder further parallels between Buchanan and the Roman author, Virgil, since both were poets with 'more of Atheism than Religion in them', who had obliged Mary Queen of Scots, and Dido Queen of Carthage, to share the misfortune of having their lives 'falsly and wickedly written by two matchelesse poets'.[77] Turner pursued this analogy, drawing attention to further similarities between the Regent Moray and Æneas, as the respective

---

[70] 'Introduction', Buchanan, *De Iure Regni*, p. lxix.
[71] NLS, Adv. MS. 31.1.15, 'Buchanan Revis'd', fol. 41r.
[72] Ibid., fol. 50v.
[73] Ibid., fol. 42r.
[74] Ibid., fol. 41v.
[75] 'Introduction', Buchanan, *De Iure Regni*, p. lxviii.
[76] NLS, Adv. MS. 31.1.15, 'Buchanan Revis'd', fol. 45r.
[77] Ibid., fol. 67v.

heroes of Buchanan and Virgil: both Moray and Æneas were bastards, both became traitors to their country and both ultimately betrayed the trust of sovereign queens.

IV

By the time of Charles II's restoration, Turner's interests in the potential parallels between Virgil's portrayal of Æneas, and Buchanan's account of Regent Moray may have been reawakened by John Boys's publication of an English translation of Virgil's *Æneas, His Descent into Hell* in 1660. Also published that year was an anonymous pamphlet entitled *A Parly Between the Ghosts of the Late Protector, and the King of Sweden, at their Meeting in Hell*.[78] In subject matter, this anonymous pamphlet was similar to Turner's second fictional vision, which was evidently composed more than a decade after 'Buchanan in Hell', since it presented 'some Discourses which passed in the Infernall Court' between Oliver Cromwell, the former Chancellor of Sweden, Axel Oxenstierna, and Oxenstierna's secretary, John Ahusen, later Lord Lillieström.

In this context, Turner's targets for fictional dispatch to the underworld were carefully selected. For, in blaming Buchanan for the bloodshed and rebellion that had engulfed Scotland during the 1640s, Turner was only anticipating Cromwell's own unsuccessful attempts to persuade the Scots to acquiesce in Charles I's regicide by resorting to 'a long discourse of the nature of royal power according to the principles of [Juan de] Mariana and Buchanan' in 1651.[79] On a personal level, Turner was also aware that not only had Cromwell specifically directed that he should be kept a chained prisoner in Hull in 1648, but it had only been 'so soone as Cromwell went out of England' for Ireland the following November, that Robert Overton had felt able to 'propose some way for my libertie'.[80] With regard to the content of his second 'novell', Turner also later recalled having 'made my particular application to the renoued Chancellor Oxenstern', while in Stockholm in 1640,[81] before becoming disillusioned by Oxenstierna's subsequent perfidy in effectively jettisoning the longstanding unofficial alliance that had subsisted between Scotland and Sweden in favour of forming an official Swedish alliance with the English Cromwellian republic in the mid-1650s.

---

[78]   Anon., *A Parly Between the Ghosts of the Late Protector, and the King of Sweden, at their Meeting in Hell* (London, 1660).

[79]   *Writings and Speeches of Oliver Cromwell*, ed. W.C. Abbott (4 vols, Cambridge, MA, 1937–47), vol. 1, p. 746.

[80]   Turner, *Memoirs*, p. 85.

[81]   Ibid., p. 13.

Taken together, Turner's two fanciful accounts of the misfortunes of Buchanan, Cromwell and Oxenstierna in the underworld can be read as didactic morality tales that, above all, attacked hypocrisy as the fatal progenitor of widespread civil war and destruction. Accordingly, just as Francisco de Quevedo's original *Sueños* had sought to unmask fictions and to expose hypocrisy in contemporary Spanish society, so Turner attacked Buchanan for 'hypocritically professing to be that which you never were, a Christian', and Scots Covenanting preachers for being 'arrogant, presumptuous and pertinacious hypocrites', in their readiness to invoke Scripture in order to legitimize civil dissension.[82] In similar vein, Turner deemed Cromwell to be the 'Worst of men, and Prince of Hipocrites',[83] and also inveighed against 'Suedish hipocriticall fetches and cheats'.[84] More broadly, Turner's second fictional tale also reveals the increasing prominence of Tacitean reason of state theory that simultaneously provided seductive legitimation of the pragmatic pursuit of statecraft alongside private withdrawal and self-protection in the face of irreconcilable differences and the deceptiveness of appearances. As Noel Malcolm has shown, the Thirty Years' War had rendered continental Europe 'a huge public laboratory in which the theories of reason of state – where high politics, diplomacy and the use of armed force were concerned – could be tested and demonstrated'.[85] Moreover, Turner's interest in this emergent form of theorizing also echoed ideas earlier shared in correspondence between Quevedo and the Flemish reason of state theorist, Justus Lipsius.[86]

As indicated previously, Turner's second tale was presented in the form of a letter, in two parts, sent by Francisco de Quevedo to Philander of Sitwald, ostensibly 'English'd out of hie Dutch' by Turner himself.[87] As in 'Buchanan in Hell', the first part of Turner's fictional account opens with the arrival of Cromwell's ghost in Hell, where it had evidently been concerned that it might be obliged 'to converse with meane people who knew nothing of the modern Reason of State', as opposed to being 'in the societie of those politicians who could discourse accuratlie of

---

[82] BL Add. MS. 12,067, 'Of Orators and Preachers', in 'Miscellaneous Essays and Poems by Sir James Turner', fol. 84r.

[83] BL Add. MSS. 12,067, 'A Letter from Dom Francisco', fol. 147r.

[84] Ibid., fol. 145r.

[85] Noel Malcolm, *Reason of State Propaganda and the Thirty Years War: An Unknown Translation by Thomas Hobbes* (Oxford, 2007), p. 31.

[86] In 1630, Quevedo was described as the 'Lipsio de España en prosa'; Henry Ettinghausen, *Francisco de Quevedo and the Neostoic Movement* (Oxford, 1972), p. 15.

[87] BL Add. MSS. 12,067, 'A Letter from Dom Francisco', in 'Miscellaneous Essays and Poems by Sir James Turner', fol. 133r. In his *Memoirs*, Turner confirmed his fluency in 'Hie Dutch' (i.e., German), claiming to have been taught the language by a 'very handsome, wittie and discreet' young widow in Oldendorpe in 1639 (Turner, *Memoirs*, p. 6).

state affaires'.[88] Accordingly, King Pluto had obligingly responded by permitting Cromwell's ghost to reside initially with the ghost of the former Regent and Chancellor of Sweden, Axel Oxenstierna, and the ghost of Oxenstierna's erstwhile Secretary, Lillieström. But whereas Cromwell's spirit expected to find Oxenstierna's ghost in possession of 'a faire librarie, adorn'd with the choycest bookes of law', it was dismayed to find the former Swedish Chancellor engaged in mending torn cloaks and repairing broken spectacles.[89] In presenting Oxenstierna in this way, Turner was conceivably drawing on the portrayal of the Roman emperor, Alexander, engaged in patching clothes in Hell, in Book II of Francois Rabelais's *Pantagruel* (1532), an English translation of which had been published by Turner's royalist colleague, Sir Thomas Urquhart of Cromarty in 1653.[90]

In response, however, Oxenstierna's ghost explained that the cloaks and spectacles were former tools of Swedish statecraft, the cloaks being made from sheepskin, but internally lined with the skins of foxes and wolves. Indeed, they were the 'cloaks of religion' that Swedish diplomats had successfully appropriated to pursue their territorial ambitions in, for example, Silesia, Livonia, Pomerania, Prussia and Brandenburg. Claiming to have become a 'Master of the moderne Ragione di Stato', Oxenstierna's ghost ascribed the success of such 'Lutheran perfidy' to the Swedes' successful exploitation of religion as the most effective means by which to persuade subjects to rebel against their lawful sovereigns.[91] With this, Cromwell's ghost concurred, acknowledging with rueful envy that he too had tried to avail himself 'of the pretext of Religion', in his opposition to the King of England, Charles I, and 'had a damned trick of my own to intrude myself in the secret councils of the Almighty' in order to 'tell, whom the great God had rejected, and whom he had ordained to rule on earth'.[92] Yet even with the assistance of John Milton's writings in his defence, Cromwell's ghost conceded that he had ultimately failed to convince Charles I's former subjects of the rectitude of the regicide. As for the broken spectacles, Oxenstierna's ghost informed Cromwell's spirit that these were likewise no ordinary glasses, but 'Swedish spectacles of state', formerly issued to plenipotentiaries on important occasions, such as the peace negotiations at Osnabruck in 1648, at the end of the Thirty Years' War, when they had served to prevent Sweden's enemies from seeing 'these

---

[88]   BL Add. MSS. 12,067, 'A Letter from Dom Francisco', fol. 133v.

[89]   Ibid.

[90]   S[ir] T[homas] U[rquhart of] C[romarty], *The Second Book of the Works of Mr. Francis Rabelais, Doctor in Physick, treating of the heroick deeds and sayings of the good Pantagruel ... now faithfully translated into England* (London, 1653).

[91]   BL Add. MSS. 12,067, 'A Letter from Dom Francisco', fol. 136r.

[92]   Ibid., fol. 135v.

fine tounes and cities, which we desir'd to be given us'.[93] Accordingly, when invited to try on a pair of the Swedish state spectacles to view a map of Pomerania, Cromwell's ghost was duly impressed that they indeed rendered entirely invisible the port city of Stettin, acquired by the Swedes at the Peace of Westphalia.

Shortly thereafter, Cromwell's ghost also learns that, since arriving in Hell, Oxenstierna's ghost had established a school, closely modelled on Oxenstierna's alma mater, the Saxon university of Wittenberg, except that, due to the intense heat of the underworld, Oxenstierna's school lacked the 'fine coole cellar, for beere, as that of Wittemberg hath'.[94] In the infernal school, however, Oxenstierna's ghost was 'senator, master and pedagogue', lecturing daily to groups of 'nubile Mephistopheles' on reason of state theory, as drawn from the political precepts of suitable authors, such as Tacitus, Grotius and Machiavelli.[95] In this context, the attention of Cromwell's spectre was drawn to the sole copy of a hitherto unknown work, entitled 'De Arcanis Belgii', ostensibly composed by the Dutch writer, Marcus Zuerius van Boxhorn, which Oxenstierna's ghost claimed to have secured 'with much difficultie' after Boxhorn had retracted all copies from circulation, following censure by the Dutch States General.[96] At this point, however, the first part of Turner's fictional tale concludes, as the authorities in Hell convened to decide whether Cromwell's ghost should be permanently accommodated 'with kings' or if 'a neu quarter s[h]ould be built for Protectors'.[97] In this context, another recurrent theme in Turner's underworld tales confirmed the fate that befell those individuals, such as Cromwell, who were originally of mean birth, who might cheat and trick their way to earthly power, but were subsequently disappointed to find Hell arranged in strict hierarchical order.

The second part of Turner's tale relates events that ostensibly occurred while this conference was being held, when Cromwell's spirit encountered

---

[93] Ibid., fol. 137r. The idea of 'spectacles of state' was a common trope in early modern reason of state literature. In an English translation of Traiano Boccalini's *Advertisements from Parnassus*, published in 1656, for example, reference is made to 'the purest Politick Spectacles ... lately made in Tacitus his forge', which enabled a wearer 'to see the truth of passions, which lay deeply hid in the breasts of modern men, who were so mysterious in all their proceedings, as their inward meanings appeared least outwardly' (Traiano Boccalini, *Advertisements from Parnassus; in Two Centuries, with the Politick Touch-stone ... put into English by the Right Honourable, Henry, Earl of Monmouth* (London, 1656), p. 377).

[94] BL Add. MSS. 12,067, 'A Letter from Dom Francisco', fol. 138r.

[95] Ibid., fol. 139r.

[96] Ibid. A prominent Dutch scholar of Tacitus, Boxhorn's publications included *Caii Cornelii Taciti quae exstant M.Z.Boxhornius recensuit et animadversionibus nonnullis illustravit* (Amsterdam, 1643), and *Dissertationes Politicae de Romanorum Imperio* (Amsterdam, 1651).

[97] BL Add. MSS. 12,067, 'A Letter from Dom Francisco', fol. 141r.

a group of ghosts of English soldiers who had recently drowned in the icy waters of the North Sea. Recognizing one spectre as that of a commander who had formerly served under him, Cromwell's ghost was thereupon alarmed to learn that, following his own death in 1658, not only were 'the craftie wayes he had used to aspire to the soveraigne power of the three nations' widely known, but also that the succession of his elder son, Richard, had been primarily supported by English royalists who had calculated that Richard's incompetence would, in the medium term, offer the surest route to secure a Stuart restoration.[98] Rejoined once more by the ghosts of Oxenstierna and Lillieström, Cromwell's ghost further learned that his son was currently considering offering military support to the Swedes against Denmark and Holland. Incensed by this news, Cromwell's ghost then subjected its listeners to a lengthy lecture on contemporary European history that emphasized the folly of those foreign powers that supplied military and financial assistance to Sweden and expected some form of mutual recompense. Drawing on his own experiences of fighting both under Swedish command in Germany during the 1630s, and subsequently for Denmark–Norway against Sweden during the 1650s, Turner's tale thereafter becomes a litany of the hard usage suffered by various former allies of Sweden, including the Landgrave of Hesse, the Duke of Mecklenburg and the Elector of Brandenburg.

Somewhat ironically, Cromwell's ghost was even moved to plead the righteous grievance of Charles I who had given around £43,000 sterling and sent up to 12,000 Scots and English soldiers, under the command of James, first Duke of Hamilton, to fight for the Swedes in Pomerania and Saxony in 1631–32. As Cromwell's ghost alleged, although this expedition had cost 'more money, then Sueden disbursed for the whole armie, with which the great Gustavus Adolphus invaded the Roman Empire', it had failed to yield 'one sixpence in returne', apart from further eroding Charles I's support domestically.[99] In similar vein, Cromwell's ghost also drew attention to the case of the Scotsman Hugh Mowatt, whose attempts to negotiate a triangular Anglo-Scottish–Swedish confederacy between 1644 and 1648 had been vitiated when the Swedes changed their position and thereby foreswore 'all your agents transactions ... threat[e]ned that poor man with hanging, for no fault of his ... and made him dy a starke Beggar'.[100] In response, Oxenstierna acknowledged the validity of such allegations, but insisted that, irrespective of prior obligation, 'the ultimate end, and mark of all the Suedish consultations, is no other then to bring

---

[98]   Ibid., fol. 143v.

[99]   Ibid., fol. 146v.

[100]   Ibid., fol. 147r. For more information concerning relations between Scotland and Sweden, see Alexia Grosjean, *An Unofficial Alliance: Scotland and Sweden, 1569–1654* (Leiden, 2003).

perfas, et nefas, as much of the European World, under their power, as possiblie they can'.[101] At this point, Turner's tale comes to an abrupt end, when a messenger from the diabolical council announced that – like Buchanan's ghost in 'Buchanan in Hell' – Cromwell's ghost was henceforth to be accommodated in solitary confinement, since none of the ghosts of former monarchs 'thought him worthie of their conversation'.[102]

To conclude, Turner's lively tales were, after all, evidently composed for private entertainment, rather than publication and analytical scrutiny. In this sense, they confirm their author's vivid imagination, which was doubtless also stimulated by notorious excesses while drunk. Gilbert Burnet later described Turner as a man who was 'naturally fierce, but was mad when he was drunk, and that was very often',[103] and Turner himself rued many an adverse 'effect of drinking, whiche I confesse, beside the sinne against God, hath brought me in many inconveniences'.[104] More seriously, however, as well as illustrating a wider royalist inclination to displace the horrors of civil warfare into humorous satire, Turner's attempts to interpret life from the viewpoint of death offer intriguing insight into the eclectic mental world of mid-seventeenth-century Scottish royalism. Whether actively fighting, or enduring exile or imprisonment, Turner's interest in the complex psychology of human motivation provided a rationalization of extraordinary events that could endure *sub specie æternitatis* in a fast-changing, dangerous world of civil and international warfare.

---

[101] BL Add. MSS. 12,067, 'A Letter from Dom Francisco', fol. 149v.

[102] Ibid., fol. 151r.

[103] *Bishop Burnet's History of His Own Time: With the Suppressed Passages of the First Volume &c.*, ed. Martin Routh (6 vols, Oxford, 1823), vol. 1, pp. 364–5.

[104] Turner, *Memoirs*, p. 43.

CHAPTER 11

George Buchanan, English Whigs and Royalists, and the Canon of Political Theory

Caroline Erskine

John Locke and Algernon Sidney have long been recognized as totemic figures in the birth of English Whiggism during the Exclusion Crisis of the late 1670s and early 1680s. Both wrote tracts to demonstrate the legitimacy of resistance against a tyrant, both fearful of the direction the Restoration monarchy might take should a Catholic, James Duke of York, succeed his brother Charles II to the throne of England. Locke's contribution, *Two Treatises of Government*, published in 1689, has made him one of the most securely canonical of early modern English political theorists. The career of Algernon Sidney, author of *Discourses Concerning Government*, first published in 1698, took him on a rather different route to political celebrity. The manuscript of the text was used as a witness against Sidney in the trial for treason in 1683 that resulted in his judicial murder, and this was a development that ensured the lasting fame of the man and his writing.

Like Locke and Sidney, George Buchanan was a radical theorist of resistance, but his posthumous reputation has followed an uneven trajectory, and he has not achieved the particular notoriety or canonical status enjoyed by the English Whigs. However, Buchanan's work has recently received a good deal of attention from historians of political thought,[1] and his most important tract *De Iure Regni apud Scotos* appeared in an authoritative translation with critical apparatus in 2004, and in an accessible paperback edition in 2006.[2]

---

[1] General studies of the history of political thought give full coverage of Buchanan's career, and he is now recognized as a political theorist of European significance: see, for example, Quentin Skinner, *The Foundations of Modern Political Thought* (2 vols, Cambridge, 1978), vol. 2; J.H. Burns and Mark Goldie, *The Cambridge History of Political Thought 1450–1700* (Cambridge, 1991).

[2] Buchanan, *De Iure Regni* (2004); George Buchanan, *A Dialogue on the Law of Kingship among the Scots*, ed. and trans. Roger A. Mason and Martin S. Smith (Edinburgh, The Saltire Society, 2006). Subsequent references to the *De Iure Regni* are to the 2004 edition.

What follows is neither an attack on the notion of a canon of classic political theories, nor a plea for the consolidation of George Buchanan's place in such a canon. Rather, it is an attempt to explore the historical idiosyncrasies of inclusion and exclusion that the development of the Anglophone canon of political theory has spawned. With a view to examining why Locke and Sidney enjoyed such high reputations in comparison to Buchanan, the varying resistance theories produced by these men in the late sixteenth and late seventeenth centuries will first be examined. Next, the process of the formation of the canon will be considered. While it is often assumed that the canon of political theory is a corpus of great ideas, great texts written, for the most part, by great men, and consisting of universal observations about human behaviour, the Whig canon of political theory was born out of violent conflict and resistance theory and only later became a reverenced institution of wisdom enshrined in classic texts. It is argued that membership of the canon is based not only on the intrinsic qualities of the texts or their authors, but also on contingent factors. Indeed, although Harold Bloom as a literary commentator is primarily concerned with the aesthetic qualities that make the Western canon of literature, his notion of the canon as a 'survivor's list' is a telling one.[3] The contexts of the Restoration period and the aftermath of the Revolution of 1688 will be considered to illustrate the receptions of Buchanan, Locke and Sidney in England.

The resistance theories of Buchanan, Locke and Sidney share similar characteristics. J.H.M. Salmon has traced the development of different strands of resistance theory from the late medieval conciliarists to the Revolution of 1688 and argues that there were two ideological routes: one that limited the agency of the people and confined the right of resistance to the nobility, or inferior magistrates; and a more radical strand that pointed towards popular sovereignty and permitted any individual to act against a tyrant. The French Huguenots are most closely associated with the first, more moderate route, whereas the more radical Buchanan, Locke and Sidney took the latter.[4]

Buchanan's *De Iure Regni apud Scotos*, written in 1567 against the background of the deposition of Mary Queen of Scots and published in

---

[3]   Harold Bloom, *The Western Canon: The Books and School of the Ages* (London, 1996), p. 38.

[4]   J.H.M. Salmon, 'An Alternative Theory of Popular Resistance', in his *Renaissance and Revolt: Essays in the Intellectual and Social History of Early Modern France* (Cambridge, 1987), p. 136. The classic statements of Huguenot resistance theory, all three of which stipulated that inferior magistrates should carry out resistance, are François Hotman's *Francogallia*, published in 1573; Theodore Beza's *Du Droit des Magistrats*, published in 1574; and the *Vindiciae, Contra Tyrannos*, usually ascribed to Phillipe Du Plessis Mornay, published in 1579. See *Constitutionalism and Resistance in the Sixteenth Century: Three Treatises by Hotman, Beza and Mornay*, ed. and trans. J.H. Franklin (New York, NY, 1969).

1579, endorsed popular resistance by arguing that the tyrant's misrule placed him (or her) in a state of war with the people:

> Now when a war has been undertaken against an enemy for a just cause, it is the right not only of the people as a whole but also of individuals to kill the enemy? [...] Cannot any individual from the whole mass of the human race lawfully exact from him all the penalties of war?[5]

John Locke's *Two Treatises of Government*, written during the Exclusion Crisis but published in the aftermath of the Revolution of 1688, treated rights of resistance as an escape hatch for people who were not bound to tolerate tyranny. The people could choose to overthrow a tyrant, dissolve their government and constitute a new one as they saw fit. He expressed his theory in terms not dissimilar to Buchanan: 'When a King has Dethron'd himself, and put himself in a state of War with his People, what shall hinder them from prosecuting him who is no King, as they would any other Man, who has put himself into a state of War with them'.[6] And Algernon Sidney's *Discourses Concerning Government* put forward the case for popular rights of resistance with the seemingly uncomplicated argument that 'Every man has a right of resisting some way or other that which ought not to be done to him'.[7] His concern was not merely to justify the overthrow of monarchical rule, but to outline a republican system that might replace it.

Of course, complicating factors militate against any straightforward interpretation of these resistance theories as populist and radical. In the case of Buchanan, it may be objected that only once in the text of the *De Iure Regni* did he explicitly state that the people themselves, or individuals, could resist tyranny.[8] Secondly, the bold rhetoric of the *De Iure Regni* was

---

[5]   Buchanan, *De Iure Regni*, pp. 152–3.

[6]   John Locke, *Two Treatises of Government*, ed. Peter Laslett (Cambridge, 1988), pp. 424–5.

[7]   Algernon Sidney, *Discourses Concerning Government*, ed. Thomas G. West (Indianapolis, IN, 1990), p. 339.

[8]   While Edward J. Cowan suggests that the single appearance of this argument constitutes an internal inconsistency within the *De Iure Regni*, and that Buchanan 'fumbled' the question of popular resistance, other commentators have attached greater significance to this statement. Roger Mason regards the *De Iure Regni* as giving an 'unequivocal endorsement of single-handed tyrannicide', tyrannicide that was permissible 'with no institutional checks on individual initiative', and Quentin Skinner holds Buchanan to be 'By far the most radical of all the Calvinist revolutionaries'. Edward J. Cowan, *'For Freedom Alone': The Declaration of Arbroath, 1320* (East Linton, 2003), p. 92; R.A. Mason, *'Rex Stoicus*: George Buchanan, James VI and the Scottish Polity', in John Dwyer, Roger A. Mason and Alexander Murdoch (eds), *New Perspectives on the Politics and Culture of Early Modern Scotland* (Edinburgh, 1982), p. 22; Roger A. Mason, 'People Power? George Buchanan on Resistance and the Common Man', in Robert von Friedeburg (ed.), *Widerstandsrecht in der frühen Neuzeit:*

counterbalanced by the more moderate narrative of Buchanan's *Rerum Scoticarum Historia*, published in 1582. In this text the nobility emerged as the main agents of resistance against tyrannical monarchs, such as in the recent instances of the deposition and murder of James III in 1488 and the deposition of Mary Queen of Scots in 1567.[9]

The interpretation of Locke's resistance theory entails similar problems. Firstly, he developed his radical ideas relatively late in his career. Between 1660 and 1662 he wrote the *Two Tracts*, to argue for a strong sovereign power and to assert that the civil magistrate could impose religious forms on the English national church.[10] Twenty years later, with the writing of the *Two Treatises of Government*, Locke displayed a wholly different attitude to the civil magistrate. Partly as a consequence of this shift in his thought, some commentators regard Locke as more conservative than a reading of his resistance theory alone might suggest. He insisted that the people were unlikely to resist a ruler without good cause. It is debatable whether Locke actually *encouraged* resistance, or merely *admitted* it as a last resort.[11]

In the case of Sidney, while the interpretation of the text of the *Discourses Concerning Government* leaves little doubt about the radicalism of his theory, and his implication in the Rye House Plot against the Stuart monarchy suggests a willingness to carry this through into action, it cannot be stated with certainty that the text was intended for publication. At his trial, naturally, Sidney insisted that his writing was mere private speculation.[12] And as Blair Worden observes, the long and convoluted nature of the text may suggest that it was unrevised and unintended for

---

Ertrage und Perspektiven der Forschung im deutsch-britischen Vergleich (Berlin, 2001), p. 179; Skinner, *Foundations*, vol. 2, p. 343 fn.

[9]   Mason resolves the dichotomy between the apparent radicalism of the *De Iure Regni* and the aristocratic moderation of the *Historia* by arguing that the difference between the two texts lies in their intention. The *Historia* was necessarily backward looking, while the *De Iure Regni* was bolder and 'looked to a brave new world of participatory popular politics': 'People Power?', p. 181.

[10]   Mark Goldie, 'Introduction', in John Locke, *Political Essays*, ed. Mark Goldie (Cambridge, 1997), p. 9.

[11]   Richard Ashcraft argues that Locke's resistance theory was truly radical, and must be seen in the context of the failure of Exclusion by parliamentary means: with the failure of institutions, only private action could spare the nation from the tyranny that was expected of a Catholic monarch. In contrast John Marshall contends that Locke, having demanded non-resistance in the *Two Tracts*, did not perform a complete U-turn in the *Two Treatises*. Resistance was admitted as a means to preserve limited government by giving it good reason to remain within its proper bounds. The theory of resistance was intended to deter the practice of it, and Locke was 'in some ways close to being as conservative a revolutionary as a revolutionary could be'. Richard Ashcraft, *Revolutionary Politics and Locke's 'Two Treatises of Government'* (Princeton, NJ, 1986), ch. 7, esp. pp. 304–10; John Marshall, *John Locke: Resistance, Religion and Responsibility* (Cambridge, 1994), pp. 217, 283.

[12]   Samuel March Phillips, *State Trials: or, A Collection of the Most Interesting Trials, Prior to the Revolution of 1688* (2 vols, London, 1826), vol. 2, p. 102.

publication in the condition in which it was found by the agents of the Stuart regime.[13] Sidney might be credited as the most radical Whig of the seventeenth century – Jonathan Scott regards him as 'the only theorist of this period to actually *justify rebellion*' – but it must be remembered that his writings were thrust involuntarily into the public sphere.[14]

It might also be questioned whether Buchanan's sixteenth-century resistance theory should be considered as an influence on the ideas conceived by Locke and Sidney almost a century later. Certainly it is known that both had some knowledge of Buchanan's texts. Sidney's *Discourses* cited Buchanan on numerous occasions, apparently regarding him as a prime example of a Protestant political theorist. For the most part, however, Sidney mined Buchanan's writings for historical examples to support his own ideas on resistance, rather than making use of the theory contained in the *De Iure Regni*. He paid particular attention to Buchanan's account of the embassy of the Earl of Morton to Elizabeth to justify the deposition of Mary Queen of Scots.[15]

Sidney was considerably more willing than Locke to name his sources. Indeed, Locke did not cite Buchanan at all in the *Two Treatises*, and Buchanan's name appears in the text only in the lengthy Latin citations that Locke took from William Barclay.[16] The possibility of Buchanan's influence on Locke is further complicated by the fact that, while it is known that Locke read the *De Iure Regni*, he did so in the 1660s at a time when he opposed its arguments on resistance.[17] These observations serve to illustrate the problems inherent in a corpus of ideas, where theorists of different persuasions and contexts could be appropriated, twisted or subverted to meet contingent polemical needs, and where many possible lines of transmission could be suggested. Counting citations and seeking to construct chains of influence linking political theorists across disparate contexts is an unsatisfactory approach to the transmission and reception of political thought. It can be surmised that Buchanan was available as a resource to seventeenth-century theorists, but the extent to which they digested his ideas is unquantifiable.

---

[13]   Blair Worden, *Roundhead Reputations: The English Civil Wars and the Passions of Posterity* (London, 2001), pp. 132–3.

[14]   Jonathan Scott, *Algernon Sidney and the Restoration Crisis, 1677–1683* (Cambridge, 1991), p. 262.

[15]   Sidney, *Discourses Concerning Government*, pp. 9, 11, 292, 398. For the account of Morton's embassy, see p. 546.

[16]   Locke, *Two Treatises*, pp. 420–21. For a discussion of William Barclay's theory of absolutism, which was written in response to Buchanan, see J.H. Burns, 'George Buchanan and the Anti-monarchomachs', in N. Phillipson and Quentin Skinner (eds), *Political Discourse in Early Modern Britain* (Cambridge, 1993), pp. 19–20.

[17]   Marshall, *John Locke*, p. 236.

The methodological problems of tracing transmission and reception are mitigated somewhat by the consideration that the men and the myths are as important in the attainment of canonical status as are the texts themselves. Conal Condren has sought to establish a methodology by which scholars can classify texts of political theory as 'classic' or 'great'.[18] His work follows on from Quentin Skinner's methodological warnings on the risk of creating 'mythologies' in the analysis of political texts, and classic political texts in particular. Skinner is particularly insistent that to attempt to chart the influence of one theorist upon another, or the extent to which an earlier theorist 'anticipated' later ideas, is effectively to debase the history of ideas to a 'search for approximations to the ideal type'.[19] Instead, Condren suggests, commentators should take up a vocabulary of 'usage', looking to describe how one political theorist 'used' another, rather than how one political theorist 'was influenced by' another. Users, then, can be acknowledged for their creative appropriations from older texts, and not merely treated as passive receivers.[20]

Condren discusses the expectations and criteria by which a text can be judged:

> We expect theses to be *original*, essays to make *contributions*, arguments to be *coherent*, concepts to be *unambiguous*. And what we deem 'the great books' of the past are commonly held, ideally, to be paradigmatic confirmations of these expectations.[21]

He goes on, however, to demolish the importance of these categories, for reasons that might be illustrated by the interpretative questions raised above of Buchanan, Locke and Sidney. None was entirely original in his ideas, although perhaps there was originality in their expression of them. None was entirely coherent and unambiguous. And their contributions, to one another and to political discourse in general, cannot be isolated or quantified with any confidence.

Condren argues instead that the development of the canon of political theory has been an ongoing dialogue between ambiguous texts and

---

18   Conal Condren, *The Status and Appraisal of Classic Texts* (Princeton, NJ, 1985).

19   Quentin Skinner, 'Meaning and Understanding in the History of Ideas', in his *Visions of Politics: Regarding Method* (Cambridge, 2002), p. 63.

20   Condren, *Classic Texts*, p. 136. Oakley has endorsed Condren's suggestion that the concept of 'usage' is preferable to 'influence', but he nonetheless argues that it is an inescapable fact that thinkers have influenced one another. 'The influence concept', he declares, has 'an important and probably indispensable role to play in the history of ideas. It should be permitted to play it.' See Francis Oakley, '"Anxieties of Influence": Skinner, Figgis, Conciliarism and Early Modern Constitutionalism', *Past and Present*, 151 (1996): pp. 60–100, at p. 110.

21   Condren, *Classic Texts*, p. 3.

exploitative users. 'What then gives texts classic status? At its simplest, the intellectual communities that need them: they are fashioned as man's gods and ancestors have been in his image and likeness.'[22] Beyond the appraisal of the text, the canonical status of a political theory can also be related to the celebrity of its author. The greatness of a political theory is more than just a definition of how much the text itself deserves our attention. Indeed, certain political theorists have enjoyed a celebrity beyond their texts, and Algernon Sidney is a definitive example whose life, death and rhetoric contributed more to his posthumous reputation than did his ideas themselves. As Blair Worden notes, many eighteenth-century readers came to know Sidney through quotations rather than through the full text of the *Discourses*: 'Ever less about his life (as distinct from his death) was mentioned. He had become, for many who cited his example, more a symbol than a person.'[23]

Recent research has done much to explore the agency behind the making of reputations and canonical texts – Condren's 'intellectual communities' – in historical contexts. The adoption of political theorists as figureheads, sometimes as unlikely figureheads, for later causes, contributed much to the shaping of their posthumous reputations and the reception of their political texts. This adoption could involve varying degrees of commitment. A user might wish to cite an earlier political theory that he admired. Or a user might wish to go further, to edit, package and sell a new edition of an older text to make it speak for a new cause. The period of the Restoration and the aftermath of the Revolution of 1688 are fruitful contexts for the consideration of Locke and Sidney as contemporaries, and Buchanan as an earlier resource.

The Revolution of 1688 gave way to a boom in publishing, as the Licensing Act that ran from 1685 to 1695 was interrupted, and Roger L'Estrange removed from his all-knowing position as government censor. In this window of opportunity, a raft of new publications appeared to justify the alteration in the royal succession, ranging from cautious endorsements of change wrought by providence to radical explanations of the Revolution as an act of resistance.[24] In addition numerous texts of resistance theory from the sixteenth and seventeenth centuries were reprinted, reread and reconsidered. The first English translation of Buchanan's *De Iure*

---

[22] Ibid., p. 284.

[23] Worden, *Roundhead Reputations*, pp. 133, 176. On Sidney's posthumous reputation, see also Alan Craig Houston, *Algernon Sidney and the Republican Heritage in England and America* (Princeton, NJ, 1991); Jonathan Scott, *Algernon Sidney and the English Republic, 1623–1677* (Cambridge, 1988).

[24] For a seminal study of contemporary justifications of the revolution, see Mark Goldie, 'The Revolution of 1689 and the Structure of Political Argument', *Bulletin of Research in the Humanities*, 83 (1980), pp. 473–564.

Regni had been produced in 1680 by an unknown translator under the pseudonym Philalethes, and was to become the standard translation for the remainder of the seventeenth- and into the eighteenth century. This translation was reissued in London in 1689, and was followed in 1690 by a translation of Buchanan's *History of Scotland*.[25] Other reprints included the Huguenot text *Vindiciae, Contra Tyrannos*, first published in 1579 and in English translation in 1648; Philip Hunton's *Treatise of Monarchy*, first published in the earliest phase of parliamentarian resistance against Charles I in 1643; John Milton's *The Tenure of Kings and Magistrates*, first published in 1649 to justify the regicide, and reprinted twice by 1691; and numerous texts from the Exclusion Crisis by Whig authors such as Robert Ferguson and Samuel Johnson.[26] By 1698, Locke's *Two Treatises* and Sidney's *Discourses* had also been published. The Whig canon had begun to coalesce, and Buchanan appeared to be an important and accepted member.

Blair Worden's extensive research into England's republican heritage has led him to argue that Whig editors and biographers, principally the Deist controversialist John Toland and his printer John Darby, were instrumental in the making of Whig reputations, and in the creation of the English canon of republican theory. From Darby's presses came Sidney's *Discourses Concerning Government*, a collected edition of Milton's *Prose Works*, and a new edition of Neville's *Plato Redivivus*, all in 1698; Toland's *Life of John Milton* in 1699; and the collected works of James Harrington in 1700. While each of these texts was polished by Toland to suit the literary tastes of the late 1690s, none was altered more than the *Memoirs* of the regicide Edmund Ludlow, whose republicanism was softened and his Puritanism almost entirely eradicated.[27] Through 'skilful editing and marketing', Worden observes, radical tracts could be made respectable.[28]

Was the reputation of George Buchanan affected by unfaithful editing? Not to a great extent – certainly Buchanan was not a victim of this process in anything like the way Ludlow was. While the publication of Buchanan's *Opera Omnia* by the Episcopalian Jacobites Thomas Ruddiman and Robert Freebairn in 1715 provoked howls of protest from Whigs, the Latin texts themselves are virtually unimpeachable, and the editors reserved

[25]   George Buchanan, *De Jure Regni Apud Scotos* (1680); George Buchanan, *De Jure Regni Apud Scotos* (London, 1689); George Buchanan, *The History of Scotland* (London, 1690). 'Philalethes', or 'lover of truth', was an enormously popular pseudonym in the early modern period; however, the *Dictionary of Anonymous and Pseudonymous English Literature* fails to yield any clues as to the identity of the translator of the *De Iure Regni*. S. Halkett and J. Laing, *Dictionary of Anonymous and Pseudonymous English Literature*, new edn ed. J. Kennedy, W.A. Smith and A.F. Johnson (9 vols, Edinburgh, 1926–34).

[26]   Goldie, 'Revolution of 1689', pp. 522–3.

[27]   Worden, *Roundhead Reputations*, pp. 39–121.

[28]   Ibid., p. 11.

their criticism of Buchanan for the preface and notes.[29] The controversy over the *Opera Omnia* acts as a reminder of the flexibility inherent in Buchanan's corpus of writing. Whig users could choose to emphasize his resistance theory, whereas royalist users could celebrate his Latin and his historical focus on the antiquity of the Stuart pedigree.[30]

Users, in other words, although they did not try to restyle his texts in their entirety, did try to remake Buchanan in their own image. Buchanan was not a victim of mistranslation of his texts, but arguably he was a victim of a form of mistranslation across contexts. And while the reputation makers of Ludlow, Sidney and Milton secularized their ideas, the opposite process had been at work with Buchanan in the seventeenth century. In the hands of the Scottish Covenanters, Buchanan, whose writings had a strongly secular cast, was given an extra injection of Calvinism.

As John Coffey makes clear elsewhere in this volume (Chapter 9), from the 1640s to the 1680s Covenanting political theorists such as Samuel Rutherford, James Stewart of Goodtrees and Alexander Shields borrowed extensively from Buchanan in their political and polemical writings, making increasing use of his resistance theory, while also plundering the *Rerum Scoticarum Historia* for examples of deposed and murdered monarchs. However, the secular rhetoric of the humanist Buchanan could be made to fit the Covenanters' needs only with a degree of distortion. This obstacle was surmountable, however, through the introduction of subtle, and indeed, often silent alterations to their citations from Buchanan's political theory and history. They sought to boost his Calvinist credentials, injecting a vocabulary of covenants, of providence, and of apocalyptic speculation that was almost wholly absent from Buchanan's own writing.[31] In Scotland, then, in the seventeenth century, association with the Covenanters and their canon of resistance theory dominated Buchanan's reputation. This was a canon that was parochial rather than international, and a route to obscurity rather than canonical celebrity.

Yet in a quirk of the transmission of ideas, Buchanan's resistance theory found a committed readership among theorists of divine right monarchy in both Scotland and England in the late seventeenth century. Arguably the creation of the canon owed as much to the period immediately before

---

[29]   George Buchanan, *Opera Omnia*, ed. Thomas Ruddiman (2 vols, Edinburgh, 1715); Douglas Duncan, *Thomas Ruddiman: A Study in Scottish Scholarship of the early Eighteenth Century* (Edinburgh, 1965), p. 62.

[30]   Colin Kidd, 'The Ideological Significance of Scottish Jacobite Latinity', in Jeremy Black and Jeremy Gregory (eds), *Culture, Politics and Society in Britain 1660–1800* (Manchester, 1991), pp. 110–30.

[31]   Caroline Erskine, 'Humanism and Calvinism in George Buchanan's *Rerum Scoticarum Historia*', *Records of the Scottish Church History Society*, 35 (2005): pp. 90–118, at p. 116.

the Revolution of 1688 as it did to the period immediately afterwards. Supporters of the Restoration monarchy, the opponents of resistance, did much to interpret resistance theories correctly, and to assemble the group of names and texts that would eventually comprise the Whig canon.

Royalists tended to read Buchanan accurately as they sought to bring radical ideas into the open in order to attack them, whereas those whose aim was to legitimize resistance in cautious terms had a predisposition to ignore or gloss over the radicalism of the resources they used. As David Wootton notes, the Laudian Scottish bishop John Maxwell, in *Sacro-Sancta Regum Majestas* (1644), was one of the first to understand the full logic of Protestant and Catholic resistance theories: that even if the authors of these theories denied it, their arguments pointed to the sovereignty of the people. Maxwell sought both to reach a subtle understanding of these resistance theories, and to attack each by association with the others. He attacked the English parliamentarians for their pretensions to moderation and confirmed the contemporary view of Buchanan as one of the most radical resistance theorists, arguing that he was the only one who had admitted the full radical import of his ideas.[32] Similarly, Robert Filmer's *Patriarcha*, composed in the late 1630s or early 1640s and first published in 1680, sought to associate the Jesuits with the 'Geneva discipline', and Parsons with Buchanan.[33] For much of the seventeenth century, before the emergence of Whiggism in England, the negative associations of Buchanan's name were second only to those of the Jesuit resistance theorists, such as Robert Bellarmine and Francisco Suarez, who were held in Protestant circles to advocate that immoral actions were justifiable in serving the ends of the Counter-Reformation.

In Restoration Scotland, Buchanan's name had become a touchstone for identifying opponents of the Stuart dynasty. Sir James Turner's lampooning of Buchanan, as described in the previous chapter by Clare Jackson, was perhaps hardly typical. Nonetheless, the *De Iure Regni* was the object of official censure by the Privy Council, as a proclamation of April 1664 stipulated that any who were found in possession of a copy would be

---

[32]   David Wootton, 'Introduction', *Divine Right and Democracy: An Anthology of Political Writing in Stuart England* (London, 1986), p. 47. Maxwell placed less emphasis on Buchanan's resistance theory and more on the emasculation of monarchs with his assertion that laws should be subject to the approval of the community before being passed. John Maxwell, *Sacro-Sancta Regum Majestas, or, The Sacred and Royal Prerogative of Christian Kings* (London, 1689), pp. 159, 203–4; Buchanan, *De Iure Regni*, p. 55.

[33]   Robert Filmer, *Patriarcha*, in J.P. Sommerville (ed.), *Patriarcha and Other Writings* (Cambridge, 1991), p. 3. The English Jesuit Robert Parsons wrote under the pseudonym Doleman, and his *Conference about the Next Succession to the Crowne* (Antwerp, 1595) had promoted hopes of a Catholic successor to Elizabeth I. His antimonarchical reputation derived from his view that hereditary claims alone were not sufficient to determine a successor, and that the needs of the English commonwealth must also be taken into account.

'proceidit against as seditious persons and disaffected to monarchicall government'. Interestingly, the proclamation alluded to the *De Iure Regni* as translated into English, although no such translation is known to have been published until 1680.[34]

In England, annual anniversary sermons in Anglican circles after 1660 commemorated the restoration of the monarchy and the martyred Charles I, and although they only rarely named theorists and actors behind the king's execution, a number of attacks on Buchanan suggest that there too he was a favourite bogeyman in royalist minds.[35] Polemicists also engaged with what they regarded as Buchanan's malevolent influence on English politics and were particularly concerned with situating him in a succession of proto-Whiggish resistance theorists and compiling lists of their most obnoxious principles. John Dryden's *Epistle to the Whigs*, which prefaced his attack on the Earl of Shaftesbury in *The Medall* of 1682, traced the intellectual origins of Whiggism to John Calvin, Theodore Beza and George Buchanan. Indeed, Dryden charged that John Milton's first *Defence of the People of England*, published in 1651, borrowed heavily from Buchanan's *De Iure Regni*. He thereby regarded Buchanan as a key figure in the development of Whig ideas, ideas he characterized as setting 'the People above the Magistrate'.[36]

Perhaps one of the most famous texts of Restoration royalism, and certainly one of the most comprehensive lists of offensive names and opinions to emerge in this period, is the *Judgement and Decree of the University of Oxford* of 1683, an attack on 'certain pernicious books and damnable doctrines', that harmed the political and social fabric of England. The *Decree* condemned twenty-seven political propositions such as that 'All Civil Authority is derived originally from the People'; that relations between monarchs and subjects were governed by contracts; and that wicked kings and tyrants could be resisted and killed.[37] In doing so, the *Decree* named authors responsible for disseminating such ideas

---

[34] *Register of the Privy Council of Scotland*, ed. P. Hume Brown, 3rd series, vol. 1 (Edinburgh, 1908), p. 527; Alastair Mann, *The Scottish Book Trade 1500–1720: Print Commerce and Print Control in Early Modern Scotland* (East Linton, 2000), p. 180.

[35] See the accusatory citations of Buchanan in John Spencer, *The Righteous Ruler. A Sermon Preached at St Maries in Cambridge June 28 1660* (Cambridge, 1660), p. 17; Robert South, 'A Sermon Preached before King Charles II at his Chapel in Whitehall, on the Thirtieth Day of January 1662/3', in Irene Simon (ed.), *Three Restoration Divines: Barrow, South, Tillotson* (2 vols, Paris, 1976), vol. 2, part 1, pp. 304, 307–8; Thomas Wilson, *A Sermon on the Martyrdom of King Charles I. Preached January 30 1681* (London, 1682), p. 16.

[36] John Dryden, *The Medall. A Satyre against Sedition*, in *The Works of John Dryden*, ed. H.T. Swedenberg Jr (20 vols, Berkeley, CA, 1972), vol. 2, p. 40.

[37] For further discussion of the *Oxford Decree*, see the chapters by John Coffey and Martin Dzelzainis above.

and ordered that their texts be burnt, including George Buchanan, as well as the reformers John Knox and Christopher Goodman, moderate parliamentarians of the 1640s such as Philip Hunton, the presbyterian divine Richard Baxter, Scottish Covenanters such as Samuel Rutherford, and Jesuit theorists of resistance such as Robert Bellarmine. Thomas Hobbes was condemned alongside the resistance theorists he despised.

Interestingly, the *Decree* reveals two royalist strategies at work: parallel desires to separate and to conflate theories of resistance. Each proposition tackled specific strands of resistance theory, whether biblical, classical or pertaining to the English constitution, and thereby identified a spectrum of radicalism and religious enthusiasm. Yet in tandem with these quite careful distinctions between resistance theories, the *Decree*, by ordering that all be burnt, still merged them and lumped the less radical with the more radical.

One year later in 1684 the Scottish Lord Advocate George Mackenzie of Rosehaugh published *Ius Regium: Or, the Just and Solid Foundations of Monarchy*, which he dedicated to the University of Oxford in support of its stance against political heresy.[38] Mackenzie noted the recent publication of Buchanan's *De Iure Regni* in English translation and argued that royalist theorists had not done enough to combat such ideas. He also provided a list of obnoxious principles that elevated the status of the people:

> That our Monarchs derive their Rights out of them.
> That therefore since they derive their Right from the People, they are accountable to them for their administration, and consequently they may be suspended or deposed by them.
> That the People may Reform without them, and may rise in Arms against them, if the Monarch hinder them to Reform.
> That the People or their Representatives may seclude the Lineal Successor, and raise to the Throne any of the Royal Family who doth best deserve the Royal Dignity.[39]

The subtitle of *Ius Regium* proclaimed its opposition to an apparently cohesive group of resistance theorists: *Buchanan, Naphtali, Dolman, Milton &c.* The names of George Buchanan and John Milton were coupled with a Covenanter and a Jesuit, and the 'etcetera' implied that

---

[38]   Clare Jackson, *Restoration Scotland, 1660–1690: Royalist Politics, Religion and Ideas* (Woodbridge, 2003), p. 216.

[39]   George MacKenzie, *Ius Regium: or The Just and Solid Foundations of Monarchy in General, and more especially of the Monarchy of Scotland, maintain'd against Naphtali, Dolman, Milton, &c.* (Edinburgh, 1684).

the readers themselves would be capable of making further associations.[40] Yet, however much Mackenzie sought to attack Buchanan's resistance theory, he could not help but express grudging admiration for Buchanan's *Historia* that emphasized the pedigree of the Stuart dynasty by dating the foundation of the Scottish monarchy to the year 330 BCE.[41]

Mackenzie's ideas and terms of reference were digested in English royalist discourse through John Northleigh's *The Triumph of our Monarchy* (1685). He also railed against Buchanan, Naphtali, Dolman and Milton, 'those Epidemick and most damnable Quacks of the Kingdom', and noted Mackenzie's recent attack on them.[42] The tone of Northleigh's tract was, as the title suggests, exultant, because the Stuart monarchy had survived the Exclusion Crisis of the early 1680s, the Catholic Duke of York had succeeded to the throne as James VII & II in 1685, and Monmouth's rebellion had been recently defeated. Nevertheless, Northleigh clearly felt that there were ideological battles still to be fought, and while the principal objects of his ire were tracts produced against the background of the Exclusion debates, he returned to sixteenth-century theorists of resistance to reel off a list of hated names both Catholic and Calvinist: Bellarmine and Buchanan, Parsons and Knox, Suarez and Calvin.[43]

After the Revolution of 1688 and the flurry of Whig publishing that accompanied it, the well-established conventions of royalist or Tory polemic against theories and theorists of resistance remained potent. The publication of Locke's *Two Treatises* and Sidney's *Discourses Concerning Government* in 1689 and 1698 respectively provided the Tories with two more bogeymen to attack, but they were slow to take up these opportunities, preferring instead to concentrate their energies on their traditional targets.

As Mark Goldie has emphasized, the rise to prominence of Locke's *Two Treatises* was slower than is often assumed, tempered by Locke's preference for anonymity within his own lifetime, by the radicalism of the text that even many Whigs regarded as excessive, and by the ongoing confidence of Tory polemic.[44] In what Goldie has characterized as 'the first sustained critique of Locke's *Two Treatises*',[45] published in the weekly paper *The Rehearsal* in 1705, the Irish Episcopalian and crypto-Jacobite Charles Leslie associated the Whigs with the anarchic notions of Calvinist

---

[40]   *Naphthali* was a Covenanting text of 1667 authored by James Stirling and James Steuart.

[41]   On the flexible and multifaceted nature of Mackenzie's engagement with Buchanan, see Jackson, *Restoration Scotland*, esp. ch. 3.

[42]   John Northleigh, *The Triumph of our Monarchy, over the Plots and Principles of our Rebels and Republicans, being Remarks on their most eminent Libels* (London, 1685), p. 9.

[43]   Northleigh, *Triumph of our Monarchy*, pp. 355–6, 552.

[44]   Mark Goldie, 'Introduction', in Goldie (ed.) *The Reception of Locke's Politics* (6 vols, London, 1999), vol. 1, pp. xxii–xxv.

[45]   Mark Goldie, 'Introduction to *The Rehearsal*', in ibid., vol. 2, p. 2.

and Catholic resistance theorists, in which Locke and Sidney were simply two more names added to a now familiar list:

> Let all the Whiggs and Common-wealth-Men in England know, That Neither Doleman alias Parsons the Jesuit, who led the Dance here, nor Buchanan, Knox, or Rutherford in Scotland; nor Harrington, Hobbs, Milton, Locke, or Sidney in England, or any other Orators for the Original Power of the People, either Antient or Modern, cou'd make any Other or Better Sense of it.[46]

Whiggish 'Revolution Principles' experienced a long and painful genesis in the years before 1714 as able critics such as Jonathan Swift assaulted resistance theory and popular activism. In an act of uncharacteristic assertiveness the Whigs found the courage to have the *Judgement and Decree of the University of Oxford* burned in 1710, but not before they had endured embarrassing scrutiny of their ideological underpinnings, accompanied by the barest judicial victory, in the furore over the High Churchman Dr Sacheverell's attack on Protestant Dissenters.

Supporters of Sacheverell were quick to revisit older arguments that saw Protestant Dissent and indeed Whiggism itself as products of Genevan and Scottish radicalism, and Buchanan as a figurehead. Indeed, so rooted were Tory arguments in pre-Exclusion Crisis terms of reference that they rarely bothered to add the names of Locke and Sidney to their list of enemies. Many pro-Sacheverell polemics relied to a considerable extent on Abednego Seller's *History of Passive Obedience* of 1689 and its *Continuation* of 1690, texts that summarized earlier royalist writings and presented them in an easily digestible form.[47]

This tendency to gloss and abridge earlier political theories and polemics inevitably stripped them of any subtlety. While royalists of the earlier 1680s had been careful in their attempts to define, differentiate and categorize proto-Whiggish arguments – while seeking to attack the entire corpus – the post-Revolution attempts to blacken Whiggism relied more broadly on damning by association and conflation. Seller merged the principles of George Buchanan and John Knox thus:

---

46   Charles Leslie, *The Rehearsal*, no. 49, in ibid., vol. 2, pp. 19–20. Similarly, 30 January anniversary sermons by the High Church Anglican Luke Milbourne grafted the names of Locke and Sidney to the list of earlier theorists, tracing the origins of the regicide to Jesuit political theorists, and arguing that their ideas were 'transferr'd into the Writings of our Knoxs, Buchanan's, Milton's, Baxter's, Sidney's, Lock's, and the like Agents of Darkness.' Luke Milbourne, *The Utter Extirpation of Tyrants and their Families* (London, 1708), p. 19.

47   See for example the following publications that draw to a considerable extent on the style, structure and content of Seller's texts: *A Defence of Dr Sacheverell. Or, Passive Obedience Prov'd to be the Doctrine of the Church of England* (London, 1710); *The Loyal Catechism: Wherein Every English Subject may be truly Instructed in their Duty to their Prince* (London, 1710); *Collections of Passages Referr'd to by Dr Henry Sacheverell* (1710).

That Princes for just causes may be deposed. That it is not Birthright only, nor Propinquity of Blood, that makes a King lawfully reign above a People professing Jesus Christ. If Princes be Tyrants against God and his Truth, their Subjects are freed from their Oaths of Obedience. The People are better than the King, and of greater Authority, &c.[48]

Such a summary overstated the religious imperative behind Buchanan's secular and humanist resistance theory, while exaggerating Knox's commitment to popular rather than aristocratic resistance against tyranny.[49]

The tactic of treating George Buchanan as a prophet of anarchy and associating him with Calvinist brethren, and often with Jesuit theorists of resistance as well, was a mainstay of royalist polemic before 1714. Only after this point did Whig mythology secure its position in the cultural mainstream in England, allowing the elevation of its own heroes, with John Locke and Algernon Sidney foremost among them.[50] Mark Goldie argues that, as the eighteenth century progressed, Locke came to be regarded less as a radical theorist of resistance and was promoted with increasing success as a modern, Protestant, enlightened icon. This was deliberate: 'a contrived act of forgetting, by which Locke's less salubrious intellectual predecessors could be dispensed with'.[51] These predecessors were the regicides, republicans and religious fanatics of the seventeenth century, but also the humanist polymath of the sixteenth century, George Buchanan. As a resource for Whigs and a target for Tories, Buchanan had served his purpose in England. The future of his posthumous reputation lay thereafter in Scotland, where he might also achieve the status of national icon, albeit in a smaller nation.[52]

To conclude, while George Buchanan did not come to attain the stature of John Locke or Algernon Sidney in seventeenth- and early eighteenth-

---

[48]   [Abednego Seller], *A Continuation of the History of Passive Obedience since the Reformation* (Amsterdam, 1690), p. 54.

[49]   In another example, William Oldisworth, High Church Sacheverellite and eventual active Jacobite merged Buchanan with Knox, Theodore Beza and the Huguenot theories of Hotman and the *Vindiciae, Contra Tyrannos*, producing an exaggerated summary of their principles: 'that all Power is in the People, deriv'd from them to the Magistrate, who may be depos'd, censur'd, judg'd, executed, and the Government revok'd or alter'd at Pleasure.' Such a generalized view assumed that one size of resistance theory fitted all sixteenth-century Calvinists, and was a particularly stretched interpretation of the moderate Huguenots. [William Oldisworth], *A Dialogue between Timothy and Philatheus* (3 vols, London, 1710), vol. 2, p. 211.

[50]   On the rise of the cult of patriotism in Hanoverian Britain, see Linda Colley, *Britons: Forging the Nation 1707–1837* (London, 1992); Christine Gerrard, *The Patriot Opposition to Walpole: Politics, Poetry, and National Myth, 1725–1742* (Oxford, 1994).

[51]   Goldie, 'Introduction', *Reception of Locke's Politics*, vol. 1, p. xxvi.

[52]   See Chapter 14, Caroline Erskine, 'George Buchanan and Revolution Principles, 1688–1788'.

century England, it is clear that he was a contested presence. To claim that Buchanan was a significant influence on theories and actions of resistance during the English Revolutions of the seventeenth century would be an overstatement; rather, his significance lay in the positive and negative associations that accompanied his name. Beyond the reception of political texts and the theories contained within them, the politics of association played an important part in shaping Buchanan's posthumous reputation, and the reputations even of securely canonical authors such as John Locke and Algernon Sidney. While Locke and Sidney deserve their canonical celebrity on the grounds of their scholarship, it should be acknowledged that additional factors, such as Locke's broad-ranging reputation as a philosopher and Sidney's heroic martyrdom, contributed to their fame. If George Buchanan has not achieved canonical celebrity, the explanation lies as much in the needs of later contexts in which he was used or ignored, as in the content of his own writings.

It might also be observed that Buchanan's Latin has not been a significant issue in his relative lack of celebrity as a political theorist. The above examples illustrate the extent to which Buchanan's posthumous reputation – unlike his own writing – addressed its readers in the English language. Political theorists and polemicists from the Covenanter Samuel Rutherford and the regicide John Milton to royalists such as John Maxwell and George Mackenzie tended to read Buchanan in Latin, but to quote or paraphrase his ideas in English. In so doing, and in glossing, summarizing or highlighting Buchanan's most significant ideas, these users potentially brought them to a wider audience.

The question of whether timing and other such contingent factors can affect the reputations of political theorists is one that has been considered by Michael Levin. Although he is ungenerous in suggesting that John Locke's 'originality was limited and his intellect unexceptional', Levin's contention that Locke was writing in the right place at the right time, in circumstances where his ideas were most likely to be favourably digested, has considerable merit.[53] While Locke must be regarded as deserving of his reputation on the grounds of the scholarship of the *Two Treatises*, and of his broader achievements as a philosopher, an element of 'good fortune' ought to be acknowledged in the making of his celebrity.[54]

If entry into the canon of political theory does not depend purely on the intrinsic merit of texts, but on contingent factors as well, then Buchanan was certainly not in the right place at the right time. The Scottish Covenanters believed themselves to be Buchanan's intellectual heirs, but

---

[53]   M. Levin, 'What makes a Classic in Political Theory?', *Political Science Quarterly*, 88 (1973): pp, 462–76, at p. 465.

[54]   Ibid., p. 466.

they were among his most unfaithful and inconsistent readers. Buchanan's absorption into the parochial and narrow-minded Covenanting tradition in the seventeenth century, and his continuing association with it into the eighteenth century, was detrimental to his reputation as a political theorist, and retarded his acceptance into the Whig canon of political theory at the moment of its birth from the 1680s.

Consideration of the posthumous reputation of George Buchanan in Restoration and post-Revolution England sheds light on the logic by which the users of political theory sifted through available resources and selected heroes and villains. While post-Revolution Whig biographers, editors and printers are rightly regarded as instrumental in the making of the canon of political theory, royalist polemicists had earlier made an important contribution in compiling what they regarded as an unholy canon of hated theorists, texts and ideas. Although Conal Condren argues that historians have been too willing to accept interpretations of resistance theory that originated with its royalist enemies, it is argued here that these enemies were at times subtle and accurate readers, notwithstanding their tactic of seeking to tar all resistance theorists, Calvinist and Catholic, with the same brush.[55]

Through reading and interpreting George Buchanan, royalists were able to create a demonic icon of considerable ideological value, and although the Stuart cause faltered in 1688, the negative caricature of Buchanan remained useful to Jacobite and 'Church and King' loyalist causes throughout the eighteenth century. As late as 1795 the English barrister John Reeves, chief organizer of the Association for the Protection of Liberty and Property against Republicans and Levellers, recalled the spirit of the *Oxford Decree* in seeking to neutralize the anarchic threat of French-inspired radicalism in Britain. He identified Calvin as an earlier insidious French influence upon the British Isles, complaining that Calvinism encouraged the people to believe that they themselves were 'the origin of all Civil Authority'. The malevolent disciples of Calvin he named as Theodore Beza, John Knox and George Buchanan.[56]

---

[55]   Conal Condren, *The Language of Politics in Seventeenth-century England* (Basingstoke, 1994), p. 134.

[56]   [John Reeves], 'Thoughts on the English Government. Addressed to the Quiet Good Sense of the People of England', in Gregory Claeys (ed.), *Political Writings of the 1790s* (8 vols, London, 1995), vol. 8, p. 232.

PART FOUR
Buchanan and the Enlightenment

CHAPTER 12

Scotland's Fabulous Past: Charles Mackie and George Buchanan

Esther Mijers

In the late 1710s, a group of Edinburgh scholars came to the defence of George Buchanan, 'that incomparably learned and pious author', who had recently suffered a vicious attack at the hands of Jacobites. According to these men, known as the Associated Critics, not only was Buchanan's reputation at stake but also 'their own Principles were so warmly attacked & vigerous attempts made to subvert the constitution upon which the libertie of the subject & the Protestant religion in Britain so much depends'.[1] This group was not alone in their concern with Buchanan. The relationship between George Buchanan and Scotland's Enlightenment historians is generally defined in terms of interpretations of Scottish Whiggism.[2] Charles Mackie (1688–1770), the first professor of the new discipline of Universal History at the University of Edinburgh, who taught some of these men, is usually included in this category. Indeed, Mackie was one of the key members of Buchanan's early eighteenth-century vindicators. Nevertheless, as a historian, Mackie has received very little attention while his Whig credentials have never been properly scrutinized.[3]

Mackie is not well known outside specialist circles and tends to be mentioned only in passing, usually in relation to his pupils. He never published anything of substance and ostensibly his main achievement was to have taught William Robertson, the most famous of the Enlightenment historians. Yet Mackie had a long and distinguished career, in which he kept up with the most recent (usually continental) publications, and incorporated them into his teaching and research. Both his methodology and his research interests reveal this, and Mackie was arguably a more sophisticated and modern scholar than is generally acknowledged.

---

[1] NLS, Advocates MSS 31.6.2/6, 'Proposals of the Associated Critics'.

[2] See Colin Kidd, *Subverting Scotland's Past: Scottish Whig Historians and the Creation of an Anglo-British Identity, 1689–c.1830* (Cambridge, 1993).

[3] L.W. Sharp, 'Charles Mackie: The First Professor of History at Edinburgh University', *Scottish Historical Review*, 91 (1961): pp. 23–45; Jeffrey R. Smitten, 'Mackie, Charles (1688–1770)', in ODNB. See also my *'News from the Republick of Letters'. Scottish Students, Charles Mackie and the United Provinces, 1650–1750* (Leiden, 2012).

Educated as a continental 'polyhistor', he was an active member of the early eighteenth-century Republic of Letters, and not only followed its historical debates closely but also promoted its ideals in Scotland. The traditional view that he was a rather dull antiquarian with Buchananite Whig leanings does not do him justice. As we shall see, Mackie certainly earned his Whig credentials, defending Buchanan against the Jacobite editors of his *Opera Omnia* and cooperating with the Dutch publisher, Johannes Langerak, and the Leiden Professor of History, Pieter Burman, in their attempt to publish a new, international edition of the same work.[4]

Nevertheless, although the Reformation was the key event in his Universal History course, Mackie's perspective was a continental rather than a specifically Scottish one, and he was not above questioning the value of Buchanan's *Rerum Scoticarum Historia* (1582) as a historical source on certain points. As a historian, Mackie was in the first place interested in correcting errors and exposing fables. He engaged with the two great debates over history as a discipline that exercised the contemporary Republic of Letters – chronology and historical criticism – while paradoxically showing a patriotic concern with Scotland's long history of independence as exemplified by the tradition of Scottish historical writing in which Buchanan loomed so large. This chapter will try to make sense of how Mackie saw the work of presbyterian Scotland's most revered historian in the context of his two key projects: the gathering and testing of accurate historical data and the fixing of them in their correct chronological order.

I

So who exactly was Charles Mackie? Born in the revolutionary year 1688, he was raised by his aunt Margaret Carstares, the sister of William Carstares, William III's chaplain and chief advisor on ecclesiastical affairs, and, after William's death, principal of the University of Edinburgh. Carstares apparently took an interest in his nephew's education from a young age.[5] As a student, Mackie attended the University of Edinburgh and, like thousands of other Scots in the late seventeenth and early eighteenth centuries, and possibly encouraged by his uncle, he rounded off his education in the Netherlands. But unlike most of his countrymen he did not attend the universities of Leiden or Utrecht; instead, he chose Groningen, in the far north of the Dutch Republic, famous for its tradition of 'philosophical freedom' and its Huguenot French professors, most

---

⁴   Kidd, *Subverting Scotland's Past*, pp. 92–4.
⁵   Sharp, 'Charles Mackie', pp. 23–45, at p. 23.

notably the law professor Jean Barbeyrac.[6] Mackie spent the year of the Union (1707–1708) in Groningen, studying law and history. He met some of his future Huguenot contacts there, and developed a lifelong interest in contemporary French scholarship. Seven years later, in 1715, Mackie returned to the Netherlands, this time as tutor to Alexander Leslie, the son of the 3rd Earl of Leven. They matriculated at the University of Leiden and stayed for four years, studying law and history. In 1719, Mackie returned to Scotland for good and was appointed professor of Universal History – a new discipline – at the University of Edinburgh. Mackie seems to have returned to the Netherlands only once thereafter, in 1720, shortly after his appointment, apparently to buy books.[7] For most of the rest of his long career, he kept in contact with a number of Dutch-based scholars and, especially, with the publications coming out of the Dutch printing houses and bookshops, which fuelled many of the contemporary scholarly debates.

Mackie's academic interests stretched well beyond his own immediate field and he became a keen collector of books and learned journals on a wide range of subjects. He was at the centre of an extensive personal network, which included students and former students at home and abroad, colleagues in Scotland, England and the Netherlands, and, most importantly, booksellers and printers in London, Leiden and Utrecht. He was, in short, an active member of the early eighteenth-century international community of gentlemen scholars and their learned exchanges, known as the Republic of Letters.[8] An avid reader, he ordered most of his books directly from the Netherlands, at least until 1735, when his close friend Thomas Johnson, an enigmatic Rotterdam-based bookseller and publisher of Scottish descent, with distinct early Enlightenment interests, died. Mackie's library shows an interesting mixture of the classical, the modern and the radical, and included

---

[6]   Esther Mijers, 'Scotland and the United Provinces: A Study in Educational and Intellectual Relations, 1680–1730' (unpublished PhD thesis, University of St Andrews, 2002), Ch. 5.

[7]   EUL, Mackie Papers, La.II.95/7, 8, John Mitchell to Charles Mackie.

[8]   This Republic of Letters had been in existence since Erasmus' time. Its members' main aim was the search for knowledge and truth, independent of the church. It has been the subject of extensive debate by historians, in particular the Republic of the late seventeenth and early eighteenth centuries and its relationship with the Enlightenment – many American historians, led by John Pocock and Anne Goldgar, see the two as opposites, whereas continental historians, most notably Daniel Roche, tend to consider them as (virtually) interchangeable. For a good overview of this debate, see John Robertson, *The Case for the Enlightenment: Scotland and Naples 1680–1760* (Cambridge, 2005), pp. 38–41. This chapter adheres to the view there was a close connection between the two. Cf. L.W.B. Brockliss, *Calvet's Web: Enlightenment and the Republic of Letters in Eighteenth-century France* (Oxford, 2002), pp. 1–19. For Mackie's engagement, see his extensive correspondence: EUL, Mackie Papers, La.II.90, Letters (357) to/from various correspondents, 1694–1765; La.II.91, Correspondence.

many contemporary works by Scottish, English and French authors.[9] These formed the basis of his teaching and research.

Mackie taught two courses at Edinburgh University, one on Universal History 'in which, beginning from the earliest account of time, he explains the great revolutions that have happened in the world', and one on Roman History, aimed specifically at law students.[10] Significantly, both courses were more or less imported from the Netherlands: they were adaptations of the courses Mackie and his pupil Alexander Leslie had taken at Leiden, with the Professor of History, Pieter Burman. Burman was not a very original scholar, advocating a rather staid humanism, in which the classics, the unity of all knowledge and a universal erudition were key elements.[11] As a self-proclaimed opponent of French learning, he preferred the traditional, classical approach to history, in which rhetoric and poetry served as the tools for understanding history, to the more modern, critical examination of historical texts and sources, and edited numerous Latin texts.[12] As was customary at the Dutch universities, he taught both Dutch and Universal History as well as giving occasional lectures on topical subjects. In addition, Burman also taught ancient history. Like Mackie's, his course on Roman antiquities was especially designed for law students. Burman wrote his own textbook for this class entitled *Antiquitatum Romanarum Brevis Descriptio*, which originally appeared anonymously in 1702 in Utrecht.[13] He also taught classes on separate authors as well as a 'Historicall College on Authors', presumably a course on historiography.[14]

---

[9]   EUL, Mackie Papers, Dc.8.51, Library Catalogue Charles Mackie, 'Libri historici, antiquarii, literatores, poetae etc'.

[10]   *Scots Magazine* (1741).

[11]   J. Roelevink, '*Lux Veritatis, Magistra Vitae*: The Teaching of History at the University of Utrecht in the Eighteenth and Early Nineteenth Centuries', *History of Universities*, 7 (1988): pp. 149–74, at p. 157. Cf. Anthony Grafton, 'The World of the Polyhistors: Humanism and Encyclopedism', *Central European History*, 18 (1985): pp. 31–48, at p. 34.

[12]   Anthony Grafton, *What was History? The Art of History in Early Modern Europe* (Cambridge, 2007), p. 11.

[13]   *Antiquitatum Romanarum Brevis Descriptio* (Ultrajecti, 1702). E.O.G. Haitsma-Mulier and G.A.C. van der Lem (eds), *Repertorium van Geschiedschrijvers in Nederland 1500–1800* (Den Haag, 1990), p. 81. The first edition under Burman's name appeared in 1711: *Antiquitatum Romanarum Brevis Descriptio* (Ultrajecti, ap. G. vande Water typ., 1711). For the Scottish editions, see John W. Cairns, 'Three Unnoticed Scottish Editions of Pieter Burman's *Antiquitatum Romanarum brevis descriptio*', *The Bibliotheck*, 22 (1997): pp. 20–33. Cairns discusses why these editions appeared anonymously, but the most plausible reason seems to be that the Scottish publishers followed the Dutch original.

[14]   NAS, GD247/177/6/16, 'Accounts of Wauchope of Niddry's expenses'. Apart from these he taught many more classes and lectures. For instance in 1720, he taught a course on Horace. *Bronnen der Leidsche Universiteit, IV (1682–1725)*, ed. P.C. Molhuysen (Den Haag, n.d.), 'Resoluties der Curatoren', p. 161.

Burman's teaching, but not his methods, had a significant influence on Mackie. Like his friend he taught contemporary and Roman history, using the work of a sixteenth-century Italian Jesuit, Orazio Torsellino (Tursellinus) entitled *Epitome Historiae Universalis* – the traditional universal history text at the Dutch universities since the late 1670s, singled out, despite its Catholic partiality, for its elegant style and strict chronology – and Burman's own *Antiquitatum Romanarum Brevis Descriptio*. Mackie quite literally imported Burman's course for lawyers, and the first Scottish edition of the latter's textbook was printed, without Burman's name on the title page, in 1721, the same year Mackie began teaching his course on Roman antiquities.[15] He also gave a number of topical lectures. Several of these survive, including one from 1734 on the recent treaty between Louis XV of France, Philip V of Spain and Charles Emmanuel of Sardinia, and one from 1741, following the death of the Holy Roman Emperor Charles VI, on the election of the German Emperors.[16]

In a famous description of the Edinburgh curriculum in the *Scots Magazine* of 1741, the sources for Mackie's universal history course were identified as Tursellinus' *Epitome Historiarum*, the *Grand Corps Diplomatique*, Rymer's *Foedera*, and other (unidentified) 'authentick vouchers, particularly the ancient treaties and alliances between Sovereigns, the foundations of several claims of Princes to particular territories etc.'[17] Rather than concentrating exclusively on the history of Scotland or even Britain, Mackie chose a broad European approach, in which Scottish historical events served as examples rather than as the central theme. Mackie started his lectures with an introduction in which he set out his methodology and chronology and commented on and recommended reading. He then followed Tursellinus' ten books closely, concentrating mainly on the political events 'from the beginning of the world to the year of Christ 1516'.[18] This was a fairly traditional history course, although he

---

[15]   Two editions followed, in 1733, by Thomas Ruddiman, who also printed the 1721 edition, and in 1759 by Hamilton, Balfour and Neill. The latter was possibly a reprint of the second Dutch edition printed in Leiden that same year. Cf. Cairns, 'Three Unnoticed Scottish Editions'; Haitsma-Mulier and Van der Lem, *Repertorium van Geschiedschrijvers in Nederland*, p. 81. As Cairns has pointed out, over the years 1744–47, Mackie's account with the Edinburgh bookseller John Paton was credited for the sale of sixty copies of a book entitled *Antiquitatum Descriptio*, which must have been Burman's text. EUL, Mackie Papers, La.II.90/6/1.

[16]   EUL, Mackie Papers, La.II.37/3–10, 'Lecture on Election of German Emperors (1741)'; Sharp, 'Charles Mackie', p. 33.

[17]   *Scots Magazine* (1741).

[18]   EUL, Mackie Papers, La. II.37/87–90, 'Prolegomena Historiae Universalis'; La. II.37/301–44, Lecture notes; La.III.237, 'Lectures on universal history based on O. Tursellino's *Historiarum … epitomae libri decem*, taken down by a student. 23 Dec. 1747 to 6 May 1748'. Cf. Sharp, 'Charles Mackie', p. 32.

used some very modern authors to supplement and correct Tursellinus. The publication of Thomas Rymer's multi-volume *Foedera* was only completed in 1735.[19] The first edition of the *Corps Universel Diplomatique du Droit des Gens* had appeared in 1726, but Pufendorf's supplement was not published until 1739.[20] Like his teacher Burman, Mackie was very keen to stress to his students the need to understand both the old and the new authors for the proper understanding and appreciation of universal history and, especially, to rectify Tursellinus' partiality and errors.[21]

The course began with two sections on chronology (*De Varia Ratione Computandi Temporis*) and periodization (*De Divisione Historicae*), a detailed discussion of the Persians, the Egyptians and the Jews, before continuing on to the Greeks and Romans and finally the medieval and early modern history of Europe until the Reformation. There are two surviving sets of manuscripts of these lectures. The first, in Mackie's own hand dating from around 1741, shows two columns with the narrative on one side and notes on sources and authors on the other. The second was taken down by a student and is dated 1747.[22] Mackie's periodization scheme was relatively modern, more or less secular and was based on the causes of religious, political and social and economic change. In contrast to his predecessors and colleagues in Church History, he apparently denied, or at least left out, the role of providence in (political) history.[23] An anonymous quote from one of his notebooks, on the Civil Wars under King Charles I, is revealing:

> Civil Discords are in ye political system somewhat like tempests in ye natural world, that cause indeed great commotion & disorder, & tear up al yt come in

---

[19]   Thomas Rymer, *Foedera, Conventiones, Literae, et Cujuscunque Generis Acta Publica, Inter Reges Angliae, et Alios Quosuis Imperatores, Reges ... Ab Anno 1101, Ad Nostra Usque Tempora, Habita Aut Tractata ... In Lucem Missa de Mandato Reginae* (Londini, per A. & J. Churchill, 1704–1735) (and other editions).

[20]   Jean du Mont, *Corps Universel Diplomatique du Droit des Gens, Contenant l'Histoire des Anciens Traitez ... Depuis les Tems le Plus Reculez Jusque à l'Empereur de Charlemagne* (2 vols, Amsterdam, P. Brunel, La Haye, P. Husson, 1726); Jean de Barbeyrac, *Supplement au Corps Universel Diplomatique du Droit des Gens, Contenant l'Histoire des Anciens Traitez ... Depuis les Tems le Plus Reculez Jusque à l'Empereur de Charlemagne* (8 vols, Amsterdam, les Janssons à Waesberge ..., La Haye, P. de Hondt, 1739). Mackie's lecture notes on German history, as part of his course on universal history, have survived and were indeed based on Pufendorf, alongside Burman. EUL, Mackie Papers, La.II.37/301–44.

[21]   NLS, Adv, MS 5/1/4, 'Petri Burmanni Dictata in Horatij Tursellini Historiam Epitomen'; EUL, Mackie Papers, La.II.37/87–90, 301–44; La.III.237. Cf. La.II.90/8, and Sharp, 'Charles Mackie', p. 36.

[22]   EUL, Mackie Papers, La. II.37/87–90, 301–44; La.III.237. More than likely these were part of the same lecture series.

[23]   Cf. David Allan, *Virtue, Learning and the Scottish Enlightenment: Ideas of Scholarship in Early Modern History* (Edinburgh, 1993), pp. 53–4.

their way, but at ye same time purge away noxious qualitys in ye atmosphere, & prevent stagnation wc wd be fatal. For ye most part, these ferments in a Nation throw off what is most aggressive & settle in ye end into a more eligible state. And tho' this can't be said to have been much ye case in our disorders under K. Cha: I or yt much was gain'd by them, yet 't is well known, very few of ye privileges we enjoy have not been gain'd by popular discontents & presev'd by popular opposition. It is certainly better to be visited once in some centurys with a brush of these hurricanes of civil discord & suffer its disorders for a few years, than to exchange them for ye fatal stagnation & deadly calm of quiet slavery for ever.[24]

Mackie divided history into Ancient History (biblical and Greco-Roman), the dark ages up to the reign of Charlemagne, the Middle Ages and the Modern period, which encompassed the Renaissance and, especially, the Reformation.[25] The latter was the crucial event in this course and was clearly as much a political and cultural watershed as a religious one. Despite Mackie's resolve to stick to the facts, this is where he showed himself at his most partial and Protestant. The dark ages had become really dark with the rise of popery and 'monkery' in the sixth century – it had brought 'ignorance and barbarity' and papal demands had encroached upon the rights of free men everywhere.[26] Interestingly enough, Mackie said little about the importance of the Reformation in liberating man from papal thraldom in general.

In the 1741 lectures, his discussion of the Reformation paid considerable attention to the United Provinces. The Dutch Revolt against Spain, the creation of the Republic, the Synod of Dordt and the conflict between the Stadholder Maurice and his Grand Pensionary Van Oldenbarnevelt all received detailed attention. The text of his lectures is annotated throughout, referring to Burman's lectures.[27] Yet Mackie certainly did not follow Burman and Tursellinus exclusively. His sources were an eclectic mix and included, aside from the ones highlighted by the *Scots Magazine* and the standard classical titles on history, philosophy and belles letters, many of the most recent works on both ancient and modern history, including Pierre Bayle's *Dictionnaire*, Ralph Cudworth's *The True Intellectual System of the Universe*, Rapin's *History of England*, Thomas Salmon's *Modern History*, old and modern texts on chronology

---

[24]   EUL, Mackie Papers, Dc.5.24¹, 'Common place book of Scottish History etc'. Martin Dzelzainis has suggested that Mackie was quoting Machiavelli, but I have not been able to verify this.

[25]   In the 1747 manuscript, he also included the discovery of America. EUL, Mackie Papers, La.237/563–5.

[26]   Ibid., La.III.237/371, 373, 405.

[27]   Frequently, Mackie wrote in the margins: 'Burman eas narravit 1717', 'Burman ita metulit hanc hist.', and 'Anno 1717 Burman ita habuit.' Ibid., La.II.37/301–44.

by Calvisius, Ussher, Nicolas Lenglet du Fresnoy and Isaac Newton, and complete runs of the French and English learned journals. He also owned works on the Persians, Greeks, Egyptians and Muslims, including several on the life of Muhammed, and on the history of the European countries. As far as Scotland was concerned, his main sources were Patrick Abercrombie, James Anderson, Bede, James Dalrymple, Bishop Elphinstone, Fordun, Thomas Innes, George Mackenzie, Henry Maul, Robert Sibbald, John Spottiswood, Robert Wodrow, and such mainstays of patriotic whig (and increasingly presbyterian) history as John Major, Hector Boece, David Calderwood, and of course Buchanan himself.[28]

The 1747 lecture series displays a much greater concern with Scotland and her history. Here, Mackie appears to follow the traditional line on Scotland's earliest history, as described in Buchanan's *Historia*, including the latter's description of the Scots' wars with the Romans, Picts and Britons, their preference for exile over conquest and occupation and their triumphant return under Fergus II, the story of their independent conversion to Christianity and the separate development of the Scottish Church and its unique class of priests, the famously learned Culdees, often interpreted (following Buchanan) as proto-presbyterian.[29] In the tradition of Scottish historical writing exemplified by Buchanan, Mackie was keen to highlight Scotland's independence from both the pagan Roman Empire and the Pope's Catholic one. He interpreted the history of the Scottish Church, both its independent origins and the Reformation itself, in cultural terms. Thus Scotland's thriving arts and letters, which were based on her proto-presbyterianism, had been suppressed by Rome but were liberated as a result of the Reformation, 'when the church was freed from popish tyranny'.[30] Throughout these lectures, Mackie stressed the importance of those alleged Scottish virtues, freedom and independence, as well as the flourishing of the arts. Roman walls and other archaeological artefacts were presented as proof. Quoting approvingly from Sir John Clerk of Penicuick's manuscript 'An Account of Some Roman Antiquities at Bulness (Bo'ness) in Cumberland', Mackie noted that Roman servitude had not extended into Scotland. 'Caledonians were resolved at all hazards to preserve the liberty of their country'. This spirit had continued until this day, and 'indeed in all ages & reigns ye Scots never fail'd of being amongst ye first in ye cause of British liberty'.[31]

---

[28]   Ibid., La.II.37; La.II.237; Dc.5.24; Dc.8.50, Mackie's notes, Dc.8.51.
[29]   Ibid., La.III.237/314–15, 329.
[30]   Ibid., La.III.23 /564–6.
[31]   Ibid., Dc.5.24^1/5–6. Clerk had sent his manuscript to Mackie for consultation on 19 October 1739. Cf. NAS 9D18/5050, 'Mackie to Sir John Clerk on Roman ramparts, walls and ditches, 1 Dec 1739'. See also EUL, Mackie Papers, Dc.5.24^1, section XIII.

In presenting Scotland's history to his students, Mackie showed the same concern to base his interpretations on facts, Roman artefacts and the latest historians, as he did in his many commonplace and notebooks, which give an insight into his research projects. At the same time, he was careful to set his history of Scotland in both a British and European context. As regards England, for example, the introduction of popery well before this happened in Scotland contrasted with the unparalleled development of her parliament and liberties, ensuring a neighbour with mixed comparative virtues. When talking about Europe's early history, Mackie paid particular attention to the Romans, the Danish (Viking) invasions and the Reformation. In his numerous note and commonplace books, in which he gathered miscellaneous information, Mackie presented Scotland in this larger European framework.[32]

Mackie's research agenda can then be gleaned from his substantial archive, which contains many notes and lists. Although he never published anything to speak of, he deserves more credit than might appear at first glance. He can be easily dismissed as a dull antiquarian, who, like his teacher Burman, worked in the continental polyhistoric tradition, striving for encyclopaedic erudition without doing much with it. However, as Anthony Grafton has shown, the work of the best of the polyhistors deserves credit for its breadth of knowledge and interests. Although some, like Burman, resisted the introduction of the new (French) learning, which transformed a 'Latin-speaking *Respublica litterarum* into a French-speaking *République des lettres*', others, Charles Mackie included, embraced the 'New History', which renounced rhetoric and put the emphasis on reason and a critical attitude towards sources and previous (particularly ancient) historians, that accompanied this process.[33] He was a committed member of this Republic of Letters, as both his contacts and his book-buying activities testify. The fact that he actively engaged in its debates proves that Mackie was more than just a spectator. His two main concerns were with the gathering of historical knowledge to rid history of fable and error and, more tangibly, to arrange this accumulated factual information to come to an accurate chronology of history.[34] It is true that Mackie's papers read like a virtual 'private universal library', and are filled with lists and tables, drawn from the histories, dictionaries and journals

---

[32]   Sharp, 'Charles Mackie', p. 32.

[33]   Grafton, 'The World of the Polyhistors', pp. 34, 42; Grafton, *What was History?*, pp. 12–13. In analogy with Descartes' New Philosophy, Jean Leclerc in his *Ars Critica* had called for a New History to replace the classical ideal of the humanist tradition and the authority of its historians.

[34]   Mackie set out their importance with regard to the study of history but unfortunately never acted upon his own advice. EUL, Mackie Papers, La.II.90/8, and Sharp, 'Charles Mackie', p. 36.

that he largely obtained from the Netherlands.[35] Yet these do not merely suggest a polyhistoric appetite for knowledge and information; they also show a concern with systematizing, rationalizing and periodizing history, and as such must be viewed as a contribution to the international debate on chronology and historical criticism. At the same time, Mackie's papers evince a genuine interest in the contested issue of the Scottish nation's earliest history and the challenge posed to the Buchananite view of the Scottish past by its main critic, Father Thomas Innes.

II

Chronology, both of biblical and ancient history, was a scholarly pursuit of great importance in the first half of the eighteenth century among Europe's antiquarians and classicists. As a discipline it had been around for a long time, but it was given particular credit in the late sixteenth century when Joseph Scaliger produced his famous *Opus Novum de Emendatione Temporum* (Paris, 1583). Scaliger's work inspired both awe and controversy; throughout the seventeenth century, scholars in Britain and on the Continent occupied themselves with the problem of establishing the correct dates of historical events and civilizations, and, very often, their theological implications for sacred time, the beginning and end of human history.[36] Chronology was at the centre of the historical discipline, and Jean Leclerc in his *Ars Critica* (1697) famously declared it, alongside geography, one of the eternal touchstones of the critical study of history.[37] In the early eighteenth century, new life was given to the discussion by the involvement of Sir Isaac Newton. The publication in 1720 of his manuscript entitled 'An Abstract of Chronology' caused great upheaval throughout antiquarian Europe.[38] Hitherto, for many of those concerned with chronological works, the motivations were religious. Now freethinkers and deists also entered the debate and began to challenge the

---

[35]   Jonathan Israel describes the scholarly ideal of building up a universal library, which encompassed all knowledge, in which the best modern as well as ancient authors, and the best editions, were represented. They were of course essential to any 'modern' scholar. Jonathan Israel, *Radical Enlightenment: Philosophy and the Making of Modernity, 1650–1750* (Oxford, 2001), p. 120.

[36]   In the British Isles the system of Bishop James Ussher (1581–1656), dating the foundation of the world to 23 October 4004 BCE, was commonly accepted. Alan Ford, *James Ussher: Theology, History, and Politics in Early-modern Ireland and England* (Oxford, 2007).

[37]   Grafton, *What was History?*, p. 7.

[38]   Frank E. Manuel, *Isaac Newton: Historian* (Cambridge, 1963), pp. 1–2. Much of this had been known in manuscript form since the 1690s. It was published without Newton's consent.

traditional belief that the world was only a few thousand years old, further emphasizing the religious implications of the study of chronology.[39]

At the same time, however, there were cultural and patriotic motivations: a carefully worked-out history of the ancient peoples could shed light on how these were mutually related and allowed a deeper insight into the cultural interactions of the remote past, which in turn had implications for the present. Mackie followed these discussions closely: he owned several copies of Newton's chronological writings in manuscript form, collected references to the ongoing discussion in the learned journals, and had his correspondents report on the debate on the continent.[40] Although he clearly appreciated the religious implications of the issue, he was mostly interested in its cultural and national dimensions. It may be argued that he was keen to fix the dates of British events, and particularly Scottish ones, because these bore upon questions of national honour and Scottish independence as well as the accurate reconstruction of the past. In other words, Mackie tried to find a place for Scotland and her past within the new world of post-Union Britain.

Mackie was fascinated with the origins of nations, and not just of the Scots. His numerous chronological tables as well as his lecture notes on classical and biblical civilizations bear witness to this.[41] Although he often referred to Scotland and the Scots in a wider context, whether Roman (there are lengthy notes on Roman artefacts and Scotland's history in Roman times) or European, he was keen to stress their history of independence, once again drawing on a tradition of Scottish historical writing exemplified by Buchanan. In particular, he noted the physical borders between Caledonia and the Roman Empire in the form of Roman walls.[42] At the same time, he also pointed out in one of his lectures that, while Scotland too had suffered invasions, noting the presence of Danes in Fife, nevertheless, unlike England, she had never succumbed

---

[39] For instance, two years after the discovery of Newton's original manuscript, the Huguenot Spinozist Simon Tyssot de Patot published a 35-page treatise on biblical chronology in Thomas Johnson's *Journal Littéraire*.

[40] For instance, in his Commonplace book, he wrote: 'see what has been argued for and ag^t [Newton's chronology], in ye Present State of ye Repub. of Letters, vol. 3 Art 11, 15, 28, 29, 41. vol 4 art 4, & 12. vol. 8. Art 14, 22.' EUL, Mackie Papers, Dc.5.24^2/118. In Autumn 1728, one of his main correspondents, John Mitchell, wrote, apparently in answer to Mackie's request, of the apparent lack of interest in Newton's chronology among the scholars at Leiden and Utrecht as a result of their poor or non-existent English. La II.90/23, John Mitchell to Mackie. Mitchell had recently arrived in London from the Netherlands. Around the same time, Alexander Boswell reported from Leiden that Burman had not yet given his opinion on the subject. La.II.91/61, Boswell to Mackie.

[41] Ibid., La.II.37/17v–33, Notes on chronology; La.III.237.

[42] Ibid., Dc.5.24^1/5–6; XIII. Roman Affairs in Britain; La.III.253, Mackie's Notes.

to the conqueror.[43] Moreover, Mackie noted that, like France, Spain and England, 'ye present inhabitants of Scotland be descended originally of different people cemented into one'.[44] At the same time though, Scotland was clearly an independent nation, if no longer politically then at least still in spirit. Scotland's honour lay in her character, her independent past and her distinction from England. It was especially Scotland's contributions to learning and Christianity that set her apart from her neighbour(s). Here Mackie kept to Buchanan, on the Culdees, the Picts and the Fergusian line of kings, as well as James Anderson's royal genealogy.[45] Disappointingly enough, he merely followed Buchanan, without offering any new insights of his own. Moreover, he did not discuss any of Buchanan's republican ideas, nor his understanding of an ancient Scottish constitution that featured elective monarchy, rights of resistance, and, arguably, popular sovereignty. It would seem that Mackie's use of Buchanan was one of mere patriotic convention.

He was, however, not uncritical of Buchanan. He corrected him in his papers as well as in his lectures, on the nature of the English defeat at Bannockburn, for example, but especially on the facts of Roman history, such as the place of Severus' wall.[46] Mackie was careful, however, simply to amend rather than demolish Buchanan's *Historia*, presenting his evidence within the wider context of the chronology debate. Interestingly enough, he began his lectures with a comparison between Ussher and Scaliger, favouring the former's dating scheme over the latter's.[47] The irony that it was Scaliger who had inadvertently reinforced the thesis on which the Fergusian line of kings was built, when he 'push[ed] back into the first century CE the evidence that the Romans knew the Scots – and accordingly, that the Scots already had some sort of national identity', and that Buchanan had used this thesis, must have escaped Mackie.[48]

This is where Mackie's engagement with the chronology debate merged with the great contemporary historical discussion in Scotland, that of

---

[43]   Ibid., La.237/395.

[44]   He does not say which peoples. Ibid., La.537/73, Commonplace book.

[45]   For an overview of the Fergusian myth in Scottish history, see H.R. Trevor-Roper, *The Invention of Scotland: Myth and History* (New Haven, CT, 2008). Part I, and Roger A. Mason, 'Civil Society and the Celts: Hector Boece, George Buchanan and the Ancient Scottish Past', in Edward J. Cowan and Richard J. Finlay (eds), *Scottish History: The Power of the Past* (Edinburgh, 2002), pp. 95–119.

[46]   EUL, Mackie Papers, La.III.237/521; Dc.5. 24¹/4. Cf. EUL, La.II.37/92–104, 'A Dissertation on the Sources of Vulgar Errors in History and How to Detect & Rectify them'. Read to the Philosophical Society, 4 March 1741, in which Mackie criticized Buchanan for his lack of originality.

[47]   Ibid., La.III.237/112.

[48]   Anthony Grafton, *Joseph Scaliger: A Study on the History of Classical Scholarship. II Historical Chronology* (Oxford, 1993), p. 80.

the debunking of the myth of the Scottish kingdom's first foundation by Fergus I in 330 BCE and the fabulous line of forty kings who allegedly succeeded him. Sparked by the publication of the Jacobite antiquarian Father Thomas Innes's *Critical Essay on the Ancient Inhabitants of the Northern Parts of Britain, or Scotland* in 1729, historians of all persuasions entered the debate over the nation's history, as well as over Innes's chosen methodology. Mackie too played his part, keen to disprove the myths of Scottish history, without replacing them with a new set, as he believed Innes had done.[49] Mackie's contribution to the debate was presented in a paper to the Philosophical Society in 1741, entitled 'A Dissertation on the Sources of Vulgar Errors in History and How to Detect & Rectify them'. In this he set out his, admittedly not strikingly original, methodology. The arguments he used had been around since Roman times.[50] 'Truth', Mackie declared, 'is the very soul of history',

> Yet in all ages it has been so much corrupted & mixed with Fables by many Writers on ye subject, that I imagine it may not be an improper enquiry to search into ye grounds & reasons of ye many vulgar errors which have crept into history, & to illustrate ym with a few obvious examples. Then I propose to give some rules, which if attended to, may assist us in ascertaining the truth of history & distinguishing between what is true & what is not; to paint out some Criteria by means of which we may lay a proper Foundation for a rational belief of historical Facts, & prevent on ye one hand, our being impos'd upon by Forgerys; & on ye other; ye hazard of running into ye contrary extreme of imagining all History to be spurious.[51]

Mackie identified 'a passion for illustrious origins' as one of the biggest problems in historical writing. Following Varro, he divided the past into three periods: '[the] obscure or unknown, [the] Fabulous and [the] Historical.' Applying this method to Scotland's own past, Mackie noticed that a large part of it came under the first two categories. He warned against

[49]   EUL, Mackie Papers, La.III.537/22–46, 'Notes on Innes' Critical Essay'. For the earlier history of this debate over the foundation of the kingdom, see Roger Mason's Chapter 1 above.

[50]   Mackie also appears to have been influenced by Leclerc's *Ars Critica* (1697), which was the topic of a polemical debate on the nature of historical criticism with Jacobus Perizonius, Burman's predecessor at Leiden, and champion of the humanist method, which Leclerc vehemently opposed in his work. Grafton, *What was History?*, pp. 1–20. After Perizonius' death Burman continued his battle with Leclerc and the influence of French scholarship. Although so far no evidence has been found that Mackie had read *Ars Critica*, he had read other works by Leclerc and followed the French learned journals closely. Cf. EUL, Mackie Papers, Dc5.24², Commonplace book. In 1726, John Mitchell mentioned the controversy between Burman and Leclerc, La.II.90/19, Mitchell to Mackie.

[51]   Ibid., La.II.37/92–104.

tradition as a guide for the history of these times. 'The most that can be expected from it, is to fix the certainty and dates of a few very remarkable and extraordinary occurrences [...] such as the Succession of Kings, or some bloody battles, But it can never fournish us with an uninterrupted series of events.' Mackie used the fourteenth-century chronicler, John of Fordun, as an example of an author who made the mistake of relying on tradition and hearsay: '[Fordun] wrote near 100 years after the time that it is said, the monuments and records of our History were destroyed or carryd off by King Edward I of England.' In fact, Mackie said, Scotland's history was 'somewhat singular' as many of the sources were lost due to the conflict between Robert Bruce and John Balliol. While this was a real problem, 'I would not be understood as if I meant to determine all that part of our history to be entirely spurious and fabulous'. He then went on to make a point of 'need[ing] say nothing of the subsequent writers of our History, the Chief of which are Jo. Major, Hector Boece, Jo Leslie Bishop of Ross, and Buchanan, who in the main copy after one another'. Mackie was careful not to pass judgement on these giants of Scottish patriotic historiography, although he denounced Boece for his use of fictional authors and criticized Buchanan for his lack of critical rigour.

The final and most critical Scottish historian to come under attack in his paper was Thomas Innes. Mackie acknowledged that Innes's *Critical Essay* contained 'some very ingenious things', yet he accused Innes of doing the same thing he accused others of doing: he replaced one tradition – of the Scottish line of kings from Fergus I to Fergus II – with another, 'a favourite scheme of high Pictish Antiquitys'. While criticizing 'our Historians' for their use of unreliable source material, Innes used merely a different set of equally unreliable documents to fit his agenda. What was worse, Innes readily acknowledged the unreliability of some Irish authors but was happy to bend his own rules, when it suited him. As a result, he had not actually debunked the Fergusian myth at all, and, Mackie added, 'the storry of our first 40 or 45 Kings, may still be true.'[52] In other words, Innes did not actually disprove the Fergusian line so much as set it aside and put a different line of kings in its place.

Mackie's paper then continued to argue that, aside from tradition, history also suffered as a result of forgeries, the marvellous, the stories of travellers, national and religious zeal, ignorance, credulity and superstition. The dangers of 'religious affairs' worried Mackie in particular. In ancient times, religious and political authority had been one and people 'had no separate interest of their own to advance, [...] but the case became greatly altered

---

[52]   In his lectures, Mackie's judgement of Innes was much harsher, dismissing his work as 'fabulous' and false. Ibid., La.III.237/387.

when under the specious pretence of advancing and promoting the best religion [...], a Spiritual hierarchy was set up'. 'Now', Mackie concluded,

> Mankind being divided in their opinion with regard to things of such high importance and with so much bitterness; it is easy to be conceived that the causes and sources of all these disorders and mischiefs, as well as the facts themselves must be differently represented by the several historians as they were addicted to this or t'other religious sect or party.[53]

Lastly, there were certain types of history of which Mackie strongly disapproved. Narrative (the 'itch of storytelling'), poetry, family annals and funeral orations all led to a distortion of the truth or even mythology. Mackie had little patience with the 'Monkish writers of Chronicles', who embodied everything that was bad about historical writing. Authentic sources, reason and logic ought to be the historians' sole tools. 'Besides', Mackie went on, 'men in low life [such as monks] have little access to be rightly informed of the truth of transactions.'

In this respect the ancient compilers of History have a great advantage over those of the middle ages and most of the moderns. Herodot, Thucydides, Xenophon, Polybius, Sallust, Livy, Tacitus, Plutarch, Dio Cassius, were most of them men of high birth, all men of eminency and distinguished rank, and many of them were deeply concerned in the direction of the public affairs of their times. So if any of them have failed upon some occasions to represent things fairly, it was not for want of knowledge and capacity.

Mackie's paper has traditionally been read as a plain Whig attack on Thomas Innes's 'Picto-Jacobitism', and more specifically on his Roman Catholicism and priestly background.[54] Yet Mackie seemed more concerned with his methods and the application of right reason to the historical craft, than with the political and religious implications of Innes' work. His 'Dissertation' was as much an engagement with the contemporary European discussion on chronology and the critical study of historical sources that accompanied it. Following his fellow Buchananite Whig, James Anderson, Mackie wrote in his Commonplace book of Scottish History that,

> An historian ought not to lay any stress upon authoritys yt are at in ye least liable to inspection, & when that wc he relates tends especially, to ye prejudice

---

53   Ibid., La.II.37/92–104.
54   Kidd, *Subverting Scotland's Past*, pp. 101–7, 117.

of any one's reputation, if he must speak out, he ought to say nothing [without] good proof wc demands a strict examination of both sides.[55]

Instead, he ought to 'preserve certainty, order and perspicuity' and to gather the best available sources.[56] Only 'principal occurrences' such as battles and the foundation and subversion of kingdoms could be known with certainty, and even then different authors could have different opinions. Mackie's 'Dissertation' was followed by what looks like a draft in which he tried to work out the Fergusian line, in response to Innes. He wrote, 'Chronology fix'd dates & other outward appearances of Hist no incontested proof of y[e] truth of it'.[57] So while he profoundly disagreed with Innes, he still saw room for debate. As a scholar, Mackie's main objective was always the critical study of history.

The practical side to Mackie's historical criticism was his own chronological project. Mackie not only gathered information but also compiled his own tables. Following the 'rules' he had set out, he tried to work out a new set of dates for both ancient and modern history by collecting and comparing as many data as possible. The result was a comparative table, comprising the full chronological spectrum from the traditional chronology of Calvisius, via Ussher and Petrie, to the contemporary tables of Newton and du Fresnoy.[58] Starting with biblical times, the table covered the history of the ancient world, Asia Minor, the countries of the Middle East and India, and most of Europe. Scotland had its own table of kings from Fergus I to Fergus II, based on Calvisius, Buchanan and the Leiden edition of Ruddiman's Buchanan.[59] So in the end Mackie chose to adhere to Buchanan's *Historia*, having concluded that Innes's alternative did not stand up to his rules of historical criticism. As a result, he preferred to correct what he saw as errors in the traditional account of Scotland's past rather than to dismiss it as altogether fabulous.

---

[55]   EUL, Mackie Papers, Dc.5.24²/118, 'Royal Genealogys by Ja. Anderson in 2 parts'. Cf. Dc.5.24¹/261. William Ferguson has called Anderson's critical appraisal of original sources and use of palaeography and diplomatic documents 'a completely new approach to the study of Scottish history'. Instead, it could be argued that Anderson, like Mackie, was part of the same European tradition as Jean Leclerc. W. Ferguson, 'Introduction', in J. Anderson, *An Historical Essay Shewing that the Crown and Kingdom of Scotland is Imperial and Independent*, Stair Society 39 (Edinburgh, 1991), pp. 1–130, at p. 9. Cf. Allan, *Virtue, Learning and the Scottish Enlightenment*, pp. 62–3; Grafton, *What was History?*

[56]   EUL, Mackie Papers, La.II.37/92–104.

[57]   Ibid., La.II.37/107v.

[58]   He seriously considered publishing it as a supplement to Lenglet du Fresnoy's work, in London, with a preface by John Ward, the Professor of Rhetoric at Gresham College, but he abandoned the project in 1740. In 1765, he drafted a manuscript, entitled 'A general table of chronology for the assistance of the memory', which was never published either. Sharp, 'Charles Mackie', p. 37. Cf. EUL, Mackie Papers, La.III.253.

[59]   Ibid., La.II.37/17v–33.

III

There was finally one further dimension of Mackie's engagement with Buchanan that needs to be taken into consideration. As Colin Kidd has shown, much was invested in the Fergusian legend as the basis for an acceptable presbyterian historiography.[60] This helps to explain Mackie's active participation in that most significant of pro-Buchanan activities, the defence of his reputation in the light of Jacobite attacks. In the early 1720s, Mackie acted as the spokesman for the 'Society of the Scholars of Edinburgh, to vindicate that incomparably learned and pious author [Buchanan] from the calum[n]y of Mr Thomas Ruddiman', also known as the Associated Critics, a group of Whig literati, who came to Buchanan's defence after the Jacobite and episcopalian Thomas Ruddiman (1674–1757) produced an edition of his *Opera Omnia* in 1715 that was particularly critical of Buchanan's personality, politics and presbyterianism.[61] The Associated Critics aimed to vindicate Buchanan's character and, by extension, his authority as a historian. They felt, moreover, that the entire Reformation was being attacked by 'Popish and pretended Protestant writers'.[62] Although the Associated Critics promised to produce an entirely new edition of Buchanan works, the project died a premature death and, as a result, their projected vindication of the Reformation came to nothing.

In 1723, however, the project was given a new lease of life when Mackie's old Professor at Leiden, Pieter Burman, wrote to him, informing him of the plans of a Leiden bookseller to reprint Ruddiman's Buchanan and asking Mackie for his advice.[63] The Associated Critics apparently tried to prevent this, asking Mackie to contact Burman about the possibility of publishing their edition instead.[64] The following year, the bookseller himself, Johannes Langerak, wrote to Mackie about the latter's correspondence with Burman concerning the Dutch edition:

> Je prens la liberté de vous prier par celle ci Monsieur, de vouloir convénir par un Contrac avec moy, pour envoyer a Mr le Proffr Burman oú a Mr Conningham Mackenzie oú a moi oú a quelque autre de vos amis, toute les annotat, Refutation, Correction et autres piece faîtes ou composeés par vous même oú par quelque autre savant, par les ajouter dans nostre Edition ....[65]

---

60 Kidd, *Subverting Scotland's Past*, p. 79.
61 Buchanan, *Opera Omnia*.
62 Robert Wodrow, *Analecta*, III (Edinburgh, 1843), p. 142. Cf. Cairns, 'Three Unnoticed Scottish Editions', pp. 24–5.
63 EUL, Mackie Papers, La.II.91/39, Petrus Burman to Charles Mackie.
64 Wodrow, *Analecta*, p. 142.
65 'I take the liberty to appeal to you, Sir, to enter into a contract with me, to send to Professor Burman, or to Mr Cunningham Mackenzie or to me or to one of your other friends, all annotations, refutations, corrections and other pieces written by yourself or any

Langerak promised to include the names of any contributors alongside Burman's. In return Mackie would receive as many copies of the new Buchanan as he wanted. Moreover, Langerak expressed the view that it would be better to have one complete edition, to avoid the need for a new Scottish one. Mackie's friend at Groningen, Robert Duncan, also knew about his involvement and discussed the Scotto-Dutch plans with the Huguenot professors, Jean Barbeyrac and Marc Rossal, who both expressed their approval.[66] Mackie thus appears to have been personally involved in the 'proposals from Holland for reprinting of Buchanan's work in 2 quartos, with a preface by Burman, at Leyden'.[67] Yet, again, the Associated Critics failed to deliver, and as a result Langerak decided to go ahead with reprinting Ruddiman's edition, essentially unaltered, but with an introduction by Burman. The Critics decided to try to prevent its publication, and we know that Mackie wrote to Burman to that effect but to no avail.[68] A year later, the Burman–Langerak edition appeared, with a list of international subscribers, including some Scots but none of the Associated Critics.[69]

Mackie's role in this episode seems somewhat murky and his commitment must be questioned. The original Associated Critics formed in 1717, when Mackie was still in the Netherlands with Charles Leslie. By the time he joined, or was invited to join, the original project had already failed. He apparently was not averse to cooperating with Langerak and Burman, and he certainly used Ruddiman's edition in his comparative chronological table. As a historian he must have appreciated Ruddiman's critical skills, being more concerned with the scholarship than with the Critics' wider aims. He certainly did not lack the contacts to bring the scheme to fruition – in 1722 he was involved with the bookseller Thomas Johnson in a joint project to print the *Complete Works* of Pierre Bayle for the Scottish market.[70] Mackie looked after the subscription list on Johnson's behalf and was involved in the shipping and distribution. This project, steeped in the ideals of the Republic of Letters, was clearly closer to his heart than the domestic Scottish affair that was Buchanan's reputation.

---

other scholar, to add to our Edition'. EUL, Mackie Papers, La.91/42, Johannes Langerak to Mackie.

66   Ibid., La.91/43, Robert Duncan to Charles Mackie. He expressed the concern that 'people are afraid here that it will run into a party business'.

67   Wodrow, *Analecta*, p. 142.

68   EUL, Mackie Papers, La.II.90/3/3, 5, Charles Mackie to Petrus Burman.

69   George Buchanan, *Opera Omnia … in Unum jam Collecta … Curante Thoma Ruddimanno … cum Indicibus … et Praefatione Petri Burmanni* (Lugduni Batavorum, apud Johannem Arnoldum Langerak, 1725). Neither Charles Mackie nor the scholars he approached feature on this list.

70   EUL, Mackie Papers, La.II.91/34, The Hague, May 1722, Thomas Johnson to Mackie. Johnson describes their cooperation as 'our Project for printing Bayle's works'.

Intellectually and politically, Mackie seems to have been essentially a 'chamber Whig'. Although he was a member of the Edinburgh Revolution Club and aided the Whig cause during the '45 by spreading anti-Jacobite rumours, he lacked the zeal of party.[71]

It would be easy to read too much into Mackie's work and Buchanan's place within it. His respect for the classics, his preoccupation with the history of the Dutch Revolt, his comments on the Civil War and providentialism, and of course his support for Buchanan's vision of early Scottish history, could all point towards a republicanism of sorts. At a stretch, this could then be seen as having been put into practice by his practical defence of Buchanan and the Reformation, and his membership of the Revolution Club. The Reformation certainly was the central event in his understanding of history – and his views of the papacy and 'monkery' are damning to say the least. Furthermore, he upheld the Fergusian line of Scottish kings and the development of a distinctive Scottish presbyterian kirk. He certainly made the right noise at the right time, to be seen, on the surface at least, as a Buchananite Whig. However, he also subjected the whole of Scotland's past to his rules of historical criticism, admitting that its earliest history lacked hard evidence and, though not necessarily fabulous, was likely to be so. He questioned several of its historians, including Buchanan, and he relied more on modern continental and English historians than on Scottish presbyterian writers. Innes' attack ought to have posed a problem for the historian Mackie, but the apparent holes in his argument and flawed treatment of the alternative evidence offered a way out, if one lacking in elegance, and allowed Mackie to use his critical method in defence of Buchanan rather than against him. Yet he never took a political stance in his work – his primary concern was always proper scholarship. Not only did Mackie make a contribution towards introducing a new critical method and applying it to the Scottish past, he also tried to recast the nation's independent history in a wider, European framework. At the end of the day Mackie belonged to the world of the Republic of Letters in which polite conversation and the exchange of ideas took precedence over the strife and polemics of partisan politics. In that world, the key historical debate concerned the universal problems of chronology and historical criticism. As a result, Buchanan was probably only of minor interest to Mackie. While he respected him because it was the proper thing to do, the debate over Scotland's early kings was both too obscure and too parochial to be of much concern in the cosmopolitan intellectual world to which Mackie belonged.

---

[71] Sharp, 'Charles Mackie', p. 45.

CHAPTER 13

Assassination Principles in Scottish Political Culture: Buchanan to Hogg[*]

Colin Kidd

Political leaders tend to consider assassination one of the remoter risks that attend what is otherwise a highly precarious and unstable way of life. However, in western Europe between the middle of the sixteenth century and the 1630s the threat of assassination came to loom very large indeed; though successful attempts at assassination were not so frequent that they lost their shock value. In the hierarchical world of the early modern era, when the lot of most ordinary people was undistinguished obscurity, the practice of political assassination was a guaranteed route to a kind of celebrity martyrdom (among the champions of one's cause) and, more generally, notoriety – not only in the camp of one's victim, but internationally in the new medium of print. Assassins were household names in early modern Europe. Most notorious of all, perhaps, was François Ravaillac, a Roman Catholic schoolmaster, who seized the opportunity to murder Henri IV of France in May 1610, stabbing him to death when the latter's coach became stuck in heavy Parisian traffic. When, in the late 1670s, the Anglican apologist, scholar and chaplain to the Duke of Lauderdale, George Hickes, was commissioned by his patron to write a pamphlet on the murderous ambitions of the Scots Covenanter, James Mitchell, it was published under the title of *Ravillac Redivivus* (1678; 2nd edn, 1682). Clearly, Hickes's readers in Britain might safely be assumed to know the identity of the original French assassin. The canonical rogues' gallery of early modern assassins also included the Dominican monk, Jacques Clément, who killed Henri III of France in August 1589, another stabbing; Balthasar Gérard, who shot William the Silent of the United Provinces in 1584 with a handgun; and John Felton, a disappointed former naval lieutenant, who killed the early Stuart court favourite George Villiers, Duke of Buckingham, with a cheap dagger in 1628.

In late sixteenth-century France many political careers – Catholic and Huguenot alike – ended in assassination. In 1563 the Duc de Guise was shot by a Protestant noble, Poltrot de Méré, and then in 1572 on St

---

[*] I should like to thank Clare Jackson, Gerry Carruthers, Karin Bowie and Thomas Munck for comments on an earlier draft of this piece.

Batholomew's Day the Huguenot leader, Coligny, was wounded by a shot
from a harquebus before being stabbed to death by a swordsman; and
in December 1588 the tables were once again reversed as three leading
Catholic politicians – Henri of Lorraine, the Duc de Guise and the Cardinal
of Lorraine – were stabbed on the orders of Henri III, who – as we have
seen – got his comeuppance the following year. Later, in 1617, Carlo
Concini, a Florentine noble who had become a leading royal adviser to
the Queen Mother, Marie de Medici, was stabbed to death by an assassin
on the orders of Louis XIII. Alongside the practice of assassination there
developed a very rich literature of controversy surrounding the politics of
assassination. It played a prominent part in Jesuit political theory, ranging
from Juan de Mariana's *De Rege* (1599), an outspoken legitimation of
assassination, to the extremely cautious endorsement of tyrannicide found
in the work of his fellow Spaniard Francisco Suarez,[1] while the subject also
featured in imaginative literature, most notably in Shakespeare's *Julius
Caesar* and *Hamlet*.[2]

The age of assassinations was, however, relatively short lived. As
the late Franklin L. Ford has argued in his wide-ranging history of
assassination, *Political Murder* (1985), there was an 'abrupt decline in
political assassination' from the mid-seventeenth century. Already in
1610, noted Ford, less than two months after the murder of Henri IV, the
General of the Jesuit order, Father Claudio Aquaviva, had issued a decree
on tyrannicide that set out the unlawfulness of killing princes. Protestant
authorities were similarly squeamish when it came to resisting monarchs.
The late seventeenth century witnessed a marked cooling of temperatures
in the early modern Wars of Religion: confessional differences still played
a pronounced part in domestic politics and international relations, but
politique statecraft was in the ascendant. Assassination attempts still
occurred from time to time, such as the unsuccessful stabbing of Louis
XV at Versailles by Robert-François Damiens in 1757 or the murder of
Gustavus III of Sweden in 1792, dying a fortnight after being shot in the
Stockholm opera house; but these became more infrequent and tended to
be less successful, in part no doubt because assassination had ceased to be
an accepted instrument of policy, as it had undoubtedly been – however
discreetly encouraged – at the height of the Wars of Religion.[3] Indeed,
it became a matter of policy rather to fan the flames of paranoia as a
justification for authoritarian reaction when assassination conspiracies
were foiled – however remote the plotters from realizing their goals – as

[1]   H. Höpfl, *Jesuit Political Thought: The Society of Jesus and the State, c.1540–1630* (Cambridge, 2004), ch. 13.

[2]   A. Hadfield, *Shakespeare and Republicanism* (Cambridge, 2005).

[3]   F.L. Ford, *Political Murder: From Tyrannicide to Terrorism* (Cambridge, MA, 1985), esp. pp. 180–83.

after the suppression of the Rye House Plot to murder Charles II and his brother James on their way back to London from the races at Newmarket in 1683 or after the plot to assassinate William III in 1696. In both cases the life of the monarch was never in serious danger, but it served the interests of the state to magnify the dangers of assassination.

The case of Scotland provides an interesting variation on the pattern detected by Ford. This is because assassination remained a central issue in Scottish history over a more prolonged period, running from the mid-sixteenth century through to the 1720s, and then enjoying a vigorous afterlife in the 1820s when the topic was revived as a central theme in the literature of the period. The sixteenth century in Scotland witnessed a series of dramatic murders of political and religious figures. Cardinal Beaton, the Archbishop of St Andrews, was murdered in May 1546 by a group of Fife lairds, and the scandalous reign of Mary Queen of Scots witnessed the murder of her Italian secretary David Rizzio in March 1566 and the curious killing in February 1567 of the Queen's second husband Henry Darnley whose house at Kirk o' Fields was blown up but whose body was found strangled nearby. Moreover, various passages in the works of John Knox as well as George Buchanan's *De Iure Regni apud Scotos* (1579) appeared to provide justification for the assassination of evildoers and tyrants. Nevertheless, the focal point of the Scottish debate on assassinations came a full century later, for what is, arguably, the most controversial assassination in Scottish history took place in 1679 – the murder of Archbishop James Sharp. Unlike previous assassinations, this was the cold-blooded killing of a Protestant cleric – the episcopalian primate no less – by fellow Protestants (albeit Covenanting presbyterians); and the deed provided bloody matter for a burgeoning intra-Protestant debate between Scots episcopalians and presbyterians over which was the legitimate Protestant Church of Scotland and, more pertinently, whether the violent associations of the Scots presbyterian tradition were accidental or indicative of an essentially un-Christian barbarity.

Yet although the Scottish debate over assassination principles – and the related issues that it threw up – was at its most lively in the decades between the murder of Sharp in 1679 and the appearance of the Reverend Robert Wodrow's monumental defence of the Covenanters, his two-volume *History of the Sufferings of the Church of Scotland* in 1721–22, the issue achieved its highest profile in Scottish culture during the early 1820s when a series of novels published in the wake of Walter Scott's *Old Mortality* (1816) revived some of the great themes of Calvinist theology and presbyterian political theory, including the issue of godly assassination, which featured prominently in John Galt's *Ringan Gilhaize* (1823) and in James Hogg's psychological exploration of the dark recesses of the Calvinist mindset, *The Private Memoirs and Confessions of a Justified Sinner* (1824).

I

It is not the aim of this chapter to trace the direct influence that Buchanan's justification of assassination had on Scottish political thought, but to explore a wider hinterland of political argument where deliberately treacherous ambiguities of quasi-appropriation, quasi-repudiation and subtle evasion make it very hard for the historian to parse influence with any certainty. Assassination principles, it transpires, occupied a central place in Scottish political culture, but often as a spectral presence within a culture of denial: for the most part an apparently wholehearted rejection of assassination principles was qualified by some slender and exceptional caveats. Of course, Buchanan's justification of assassination did have its open adherents on the radical extreme of the late seventeenth-century Covenanting movement. However, within the mainstream of Scots presbyterian culture, Buchanan left a more elusive legacy. Far from defining Scots presbyterian assassination principles, Buchanan's theory of tyrannicide gave rise rather to a body of presbyterian casuistry, in which anxious and embarrassed presbyterians sought simultaneously to exculpate their confession as a whole from the principles and practice of assassination, yet also to justify particular assassinations of the unrighteous as the workings of providence, an argument that was not derived from the robust secularism of Buchanan's own case for tyrannicide. Nevertheless, it is possible to discern the ghostly lineaments of Buchanan's theory of assassinations lurking behind these contorted triangulations. Buchanan, alongside Knox, had made the case for tyrannicide, a case that stuck; and although later generations asserted that all true presbyterians recoiled from the abomination of assassination, the fact that these condemnations were always accompanied by slippery extenuations suggests that nobody quite believed they meant it – neither their episcopalian opponents, nor themselves.

However explosive its implications, Buchanan's dialogue *De Iure Regni* was a somewhat stilted discussion between Thomas Maitland and a fictional George Buchanan. By way of the laboured exchange between these characters, Buchanan construed tyranny as a breach of the mutual pact between the ruler and the ruled. This situation created a state of war between the tyrant, who was by definition an enemy of the people, and his former subjects. The question then arose, whether within such a war it was the right not only of the people as a whole, but also of an individual to kill the enemy: 'ius est non modo universo populo sed singulis etiam hostem interimere?' Buchanan, through Maitland, offered an argument from the consensus of nations, that individuals were able to wage war on tyrants. Almost every nation had held the view that this practice was legitimate, according to Buchanan's mouthpiece, Maitland, who then went on to list numerous examples of the killing of tyrants or the supporters of tyrants from classical antiquity that had been lauded in the societies where they had occurred – the praise of Thebe for murdering her husband, Timoleon for killing his brother, Cassius for killing his son, Fulvius for killing a son who was about to join Catiline, and Brutus for killing his sons and kinsmen when he discovered they were about to restore a tyrant. The uncontradicted testimony of the world – meaning the world of the ancients – vindicated the assassination of tyrants. Curiously, however, Buchanan did not resort to biblical examples, except briefly to discuss the killing of Ahab; nor did he invoke any divine right by which the righteous might inflict bloody judgement on the ungodly. Most of the arguments and examples in the *De Iure Regni* were conspicuously profane.[4]

John Knox, on the other hand, had employed biblical exemplars to justify the slaying of idolaters. In *A Faithful Admonition to the Professors of God's Truth*, Knox prayed that God might 'stir up some Phineas, Elisha, or Jehu, that the blood of the abominable idolaters may pacify God's wrath'.[5] The name of Phineas was to resound at the radical extremes of Scots presbyterian political argument throughout the early modern era as an exemplar of righteous assassination. In the Old Testament, Numbers 25 told how Phineas had slain Zimri, an Israelite officer, as he lay in bed with a Midianite idolatress. Elisha and Jehu – who were also to be cited as noble examples of godly killers – had participated in the killing of the evil Queen Jezebel.

In *Leviathan* (1651), the English political philosopher Thomas Hobbes blamed the imitation of the classics – 'the reading of the books of policy, and histories of the ancient Greeks, and Romans' – for the dangerous rash of assassinations in the early modern era:

> From the reading, I say, of such books, men have undertaken to kill their kings, because the Greek and Latin writers, in their books, and discourses of policy, make it lawful, and laudable, for any man so to do; provided before he do it, he call him tyrant. For they say not regicide, that is, killing of a king, but tyrannicide, that is, killing of a tyrant is lawful.[6]

It is unclear how far Hobbes's analysis applies to assassination principles in early modern Scotland. Certainly, the authorities feared the arguments set out in Buchanan's *De Iure Regni*, and this work was banned by the Scottish authorities in 1584, 1664 and August 1688, and possibly also

---

[4]   Buchanan, *De Iure Regni*, pp. 116–17, 152–7.
[5]   John Knox, *Works*, ed. D. Laing (6 vols, Edinburgh, 1846–64), vol. 3, p. 309.
[6]   Thomas Hobbes, *Leviathan*, ed. C.B. Macpherson (Harmondsworth, 1968), Pt. II, ch. 29, p. 369.

in 1671.[7] Nevertheless, it was Phineas rather than Brutus who was the cynosure of presbyterian assassination principles.

Although Buchanan and Knox provided the initial justifications for righteous killing and tyrannicide in Scottish political culture, these foundational texts were supplemented in the second half of the seventeenth century by a group of Covenanting writings justifying violent resistance to malignant uncovenanted rulers, including *Naphtali* (1667), co-authored by Sir James Stewart and James Stirling, and Alexander Shields's *A Hind Let Loose* (1687). To the conservative Anglican and episcopalian opponents of Scots presbyterianism, this series of works from Knox and Buchanan to Shields appeared to constitute a coherent and consistent canon of Scots presbyterian political theory – 'all of them sing the same note' – and a body of pernicious ideas whose dangerous and obnoxious radicalism needed to be confronted directly in order to maintain the health of the body politic. As noted elsewhere in this volume, *The Judgement and Decree of the University of Oxford* in 1683 against 'pernicious books' and 'damnable doctrines' singled out the canon of Scots presbyterian political thought for explicit condemnation: Knox, Buchanan, David Calderwood, Samuel Rutherford, the Solemn League and Covenant, *Naphtali*. The twenty-third proposition to be condemned, ascribed to Buchanan and Knox, as well as to the Jesuits, was that 'wicked kings and tyrants ought to be put to death, and if the judges and inferior magistrates will not do their office, the power of the sword devolves to the people; if the major part of the people refuse to exercise this power, then the ministers may excommunicate such a king, after which it is lawful for any of the subjects to kill him, as the people did Athaliah, and Jehu Jezebel.' Similarly, Knox and the Covenanting pamphlet *Naphtali* were identified as proponents of the twenty-fifth proposition to be condemned in the Decrees, namely that 'the example of Phineas is to us instead of a command; for what God has commanded or approved in one age, must needs oblige in all.'[8] Indeed, Hickes attributed presbyterian assassinations to what he termed 'this damnable doctrine of heroical impulse' – most obviously, of course, the example of Phineas – that had 'poisoned the whole sect, and instigated them to many other inhuman butcheries and lesser rebellions, before they imbrued their hands in the primate's sacred blood'.[9]

Naphtali heartily praised the holy zeal of Phineas (as did Stewart's other notorious resistance tract, *Ius Populi Vindicatum*), and argued that his example of private and righteous killing was even more applicable to

---

7   A.J. Mann, *The Scottish Book Trade, 1500–1720: Print Commerce and Print Control in Early Modern Scotland* (East Linton, 2000), p. 180.
8   *Oxford Decree*, p. 6.
9   [George Hickes], *The Spirit of Popery speaking out of the mouths of Phanatical Protestants* (London, 1680), p. 69.

Restoration Scotland than to Old Testament Israel. Whereas God had approved Phineas's personal vigilantism, notwithstanding the existence of a godly magistracy among the Israelites, taking the law into one's own hands seemed even more worthy of emulation – and divine favour – in a society such as Scotland's where 'the supreme civil magistrate, the primores regni and other inferior rulers, [were] not only unwilling to do their duty, but so far corrupted and perverted', that they themselves were complicit in the very ungodly 'abominations' that required correction:

> as for the particular instance of Phineas, if the Lord did not only raise him up to that particular act of justice, but also warrant and accept him therein, and reward him therefore, upon the accompt of his zeal, when there was a godly and zealous magistrate able ... but also willing to execute justice; how much more may it be pleaded, that the Lord ... will not only pour out of that same spirit upon others, but also when he gives it, both allow them though they be but private persons, and also call them being otherwise in a physical and probable capacity, to do these things in an extremely necessitous, and otherwise irrecoverable state of the church, to which in a more entire condition thereof, he doth not call them.[10]

In response the episcopalian propagandist Andrew Honyman, Bishop of Orkney, claimed that the example of Phineas did not justify the assumption of the sword by private persons, for Phineas, Honyman claimed, had belonged to the priesthood and been a prince in his tribe. Such reservations did not deter presbyterian resistance theorists.[11] Alexander Shields's *A Hind Let Loose* (1687) cited the example of Phineas in his glorification of godly assassination. Shields also acknowledged the authority of Buchanan's *De Iure Regni*, but not as a neo-classical justification of tyrannicide; rather, he pressed Buchanan's arguments into serving the case for the private execution of blasphemers, idolaters and tyrants who suppressed religion. More appositely, perhaps, Shields also invoked Knox and *Naphtali*, for his argument was primarily religious. In particular, the scriptural prohibition on murder in the sixth commandment, Shields insisted, 'doth not prohibit all killing'. When 'enemies to God' were bent on furthering the cause of 'impiety', and when the lawful magistrates connived in such wickedness, then the 'extraordinary executing of judgment, upon notorious incendiaries and murdering public enemies, by private persons ... cannot be reduced to any case that can infer the guilt of murder'. In the 'pinch of extremity' it was no 'usurpation upon the magistrate, where there is none', even for

---

[10]   [James Stewart and James Stirling], *Naphtali* (n.p., 1667), pp. 23–4. See also [James Stewart], *Ius Populi Vindicatum* (n.p., 1669), pp. 409–26.

[11]   [Andrew Honyman], *A Survey of the Insolent and Infamous Libel, entituled Naphtali* (n.p., 1668), pp. 104–20.

the humbler sort to carry out killings in God's name. When God inspired ordinary people to execute His justice upon his adversaries, 'we should rather ascribe glory and praise to Him' who 'many times chooseth the weak and foolish things of the world to confound the mighty', than 'condemn His instruments for doing such things'.[12]

Assassination principles were clearly not alien to the presbyterian political tradition, albeit espoused most fiercely on its radical wing. However, the actual practice of assassination, in particular the murder of Archbishop Sharp of St Andrews on 3 May 1679, was too delicate an affair, at least so far as the presbyterian mainstream was concerned, for the direct application of theories of tyrannicide and godly assassination. The assassination of a Protestant man of God gave episcopalian pamphleteers and their fellow Anglican co-religionists a marvellous opportunity to demonize presbyterians as fanatical traducers of the gospel message. Atrocity literature rolled off the presses, including *A Narrative of the Horrid Murther committed on the body of the late Rt. Rev. James, Lord Arch-bishop of St Andrews* (1679), *A True Account of the Horrid Murther committed upon his Grace, the late Lord Archbishop of St Andrews* (1679) and *The Manner of the Barbarous Murder of James, Lord Arch-Bishop of St Andrews* (1679). Actually, the flood of condemnation had begun before Sharp's murder, in the context of the trial of James Mitchell who had made an earlier attempt on Sharp's life in 1668. It was the prosecution of Mitchell that had led to the publication of Hickes's pamphlet *Ravillac Redivivus* (1678), a forthright denunciation of presbyterian assassination principles. A further edition of *Ravillac Redivivus* appeared in 1682, and parts were later repackaged as *A Caveat against Fanaticks under all Denominations* (3rd edn, 1717). In the meantime, Hickes had produced a further work, *The Spirit of Popery speaking out of the mouths of Phanatical-Protestants ... With Animadversions, and the History of the Archbishop of St Andrews his murder, extracted out of the Registers of the Privy-Council* (1680), which described the killing of Sharp as a vivid demonstration of the ways in which presbyterians borrowed their murderous principles from the Jesuits – an influential anti-presbyterian smear and one that continued to inform episcopalian rhetoric into the 1720s. The presbyterians rallied to justify the killing of Sharp by way of a pamphlet that blackened Sharp's reputation, *A true Relation of what is Discovered concerning the Murder of the Archbishop of St Andrews* (1680).

The Revolution of 1689 transformed the significance of the presbyterians' murderous reputation, for the Jacobite commitments of the Scottish episcopate forced a reluctant William of Orange to replace an episcopalian establishment in 1690 with a presbyterian kirk. Disappointed episcopalians

---

12   [Shields], *Hind Let Loose*, pp. 648, 651–2.

and their co-religionist allies in the established churches of England and Ireland campaigned to destabilize the new kirk by questioning the probity of the violent and disloyal sect of presbyterians who now manned the Scots establishment.[13] Could any monarchs – even the beneficiaries of a Whig Revolution – entrust power in the church to a body of radicals committed to levelling principles of democracy in church and possibly state, who had risen in rebellion against duly constituted authority, who were guilty of regicide, having delivered up Charles I to his enemies, and who subscribed to, and practised, obnoxious assassination principles? Lacking the necessary discipline that an episcopal system of hierarchy brought to a church, had presbyterianism not degenerated into a form of reckless enthusiasm, a cult in thrall to a religion of violence? Indeed, had not Shields, the most vociferous exponent of assassination principles, rejoined the ministry of the kirk in 1690? According to the Reverend Robert Calder, the Scots presbyterians had shown themselves to be the 'gun-disciples of Christ', armed militants who perverted the gospel message. After all, Jesus had not 'advanced his kingdom with balls of cannon, nor bullets of guns', nor had he trained up his true disciples 'to fight his cause with pistols or muskets'.[14] The Union of 1707 further dented the confidence of kirkmen, for it effectively left the Scots presbyterian establishment at the mercy of a sovereign Anglican legislature. In precarious possession of the privileges of establishment after decades of persecution, presbyterian kirkmen attempted to answer Anglican and episcopalian slurs, perhaps even to disown some of the bloodier moments in their troubled past, though without jettisoning the distinctive principles of the presbyterian tradition or betraying the sacrifices of those martyrs for the presbyterian cause who had perished during the tyrannous reigns of Charles II and James VII. In such a milieu, assassination theories in general, and the assassination of Sharp in particular, were acutely sensitive issues.

A further round of debate on the specific question of assassination was inaugurated in 1719 with the publication of a presbyterian interpretation of Sharp's life and fate, *The Life of Mr James Sharp, From his Birth to his Instalment in the Archbishoprick of St Andrews written in the time of his life … With an Appendix containing an Account of Some of Mr Sharp's Actions, during the Time of his Being Archbishop: And the Manner and Circumstances of his Death, by one of the Persons concern'd in it*, which provoked an outraged episcopalian response in 1723, attributed to David Symson, *A True and Impartial Account of the Life of the Most Reverend Father in God, Dr James Sharp, Archbishop of St Andrews*. However,

---

13   C. Kidd, 'Constructing a Civil Religion: Scots Presbyterians and the Eighteenth-century British State', in J. Kirk (ed.), *The Scottish Churches and Parliament, 1707–1999* (Scottish Church History Society supplement, 2001).

14   *Mr. Robert Calder's Vindication of his Sermon Preach'd January 30, 1703* (Edinburgh, 1703), pp. 4–6.

this pamphlet also constituted a response to Robert Wodrow's magnum opus *History of the Sufferings* (1721–22), which contained an evasive whitewash of Sharp's death. Wodrow's *History* also elicited a powerful episcopalian critique from Alexander Bruce, in *The Scottish Behemoth Dissected* (1722).

Wodrow took on the mammoth task of squaring the events of the Restoration era in Scotland with the demands of civility and anti-presbyterian suspicions prevalent in post-1688 British political culture. Central to Wodrow's project was his attempt to equate presbyterian resistance to established authority during the tyrannies of the Restoration era with the eventual success of the Revolution in 1688–89.[15] If Covenanting principles were to all intents and purposes Revolution Principles, the episcopalian critics of Scots presbyterianism could be more easily identified as what Wodrow believed them to be – that is, Jacobite enemies of the Whig constitution. While it was plausible to rehabilitate the popular Covenanting risings of 1666 and 1679 as unsuccessful Revolutions *avant la lettre*, it was not possible to use the same broad brush to depict the assassination of Sharp as an act that foreshadowed the Revolution. After all, the principal glory of the Revolution of 1688–89 was its conservatism. The Revolution had been relatively unbloody, at least in England; had not threatened the social hierarchy; and had not led to the demise of the monarchy. Its achievement lay in preserving rather than overturning the existing constitution and social order. Contemporaries were all too acutely aware of the differences between the great rebellion of the 1640s – which culminated in what Anglican pamphleteers continued to refer to as the 'murder' of Charles I and whose proto-whiggish associations were therefore the cause of some embarrassment – and the non-regicidal Revolution of 1688–89. On the other hand, critics of the Revolution, not least among episcopalian critics of the Scots presbyterian tradition, were only too keen to yoke together regicide and assassination as the vivid manifestation of a naked presbyterianism, its hypocrisies unmasked. In defence, Wodrow needed to resort to a very precise and particular presbyterian casuistry in accounting for the killing of Sharp. Neither a straightforward statement of principle nor a direct narration of events would suffice in this very special instance.

In relating the demise of Sharp, Wodrow resorted with euphemistic delicacy to the passive voice – but to a providentially assured passive: 'this bloody and perfidious man was cut off, and came to this fatal exit, by no premeditated and formed design; but circumstances offering an occasion, it was very suddenly given into.' The opportunity to strike at Sharp was a gift of Providence. So too Wodrow planted the suggestion, while

---

[15]   C. Kidd, *Subverting Scotland's Past* (Cambridge, 1993), pp. 67–8.

appearing to retract it, that Providence might have enabled the *actual* perpetrators to escape scot free the forces of the regime. The cunning of Providence seemed to have drawn the authorities to misidentify and punish the lukewarm bystanders rather than the zealous men of blood, at least in Wodrow's disconcerting and circuitous account. Indeed, whereas Wodrow's *History of the Sufferings* was, for the most part, the work of a robust and judgemental narrator, who normally wasted little time in winnowing ungodly persecuting cavaliers from heroic presbyterian victims, the discussion of Sharp's death was hedged with apparent equivocation: 'by far the greater, and the most knowing part of Presbyterians, yea, of sufferers, did disapprove of the action, and yet humbly adored the righteousness of the Lord's way with this ill man.' Yet Wodrow's nods and winks to the role of Providence in the affair suggest that his even-handedness was little more than superficial:

> Upon the whole, though the most part of good people in Scotland could not but observe and adore the holy and righteous providence of God, in the removal of this violent persecutor and spring of the most part of the former severities, at such a juncture when just upon new and violent projects, yet they could not approve of the manner of taking him off, nor would they justify the actors.

Nevertheless, Wodrow's discomfort at the assassination was real enough.[16]

On the other hand, his episcopalian critics sensed Wodrow's embarrassment. Symson argued that Wodrow studiously declined to call the death of Sharp a 'murder', but termed it 'only a violent death, a violent taking away etc'. While Wodrow declared it an injustice to charge the death of Sharp upon the presbyterians as a whole, Symson contended that, almost 'with the same breath', he discovered Wodrow 'shuffling in such extenuating circumstances (all of them by the by false in fact) to palliate and excuse the wickedness, that one would be almost tempted to believe, that if he was not one of the conspirators himself, he does at least approve of the deed, by his intitling it to the providence of God'. What most appalled Symson was the blasphemous equation of Providence and de-factoism, that the presbyterians made 'God the author of their foulest actings', that in the absence of *a priori* arguments, they brought in 'this piece of Turkish divinity as an argument a posteriori, viz. the success of the action to justify their villainies'.[17] On another note, Bruce highlighted similarities between the assassination principles of the presbyterians and

---

[16]   Robert Wodrow, *History of the Sufferings of the Church of Scotland* (2 vols, Edinburgh, 1721–22), vol. 2, pp. 28, 33.

[17]   [David Symson], *A True and Impartial Account of the Life of the Rev Father in God, Dr. James Sharp, Arch-bishop of St Andrews* (n.p., 1723), 'Preface', pp. xxv, xxvii–xxviii, xxx.

the Jesuits,[18] a further group associated in the Protestant worldview with a treacherous casuistry.[19]

The dominant ideological trend in the eighteenth-century kirk led away from the militant presbyterianism of the Covenanting movement towards an uncombative style of religious moderation. In part, this was because many of the kirk's leaders shared the aspirations of the Scottish Enlightenment to create a polite and commercial society at a conscious remove from the bitter sectarian conflicts that had disfigured Scottish life during the sixteenth and seventeenth centuries; some pragmatic kirkmen also acknowledged that the Church of Scotland was the minority establishment of a diminished North British province within the British state, and needed to trim its pretensions accordingly.[20] Nevertheless, the militancy of the older Covenanting tradition persisted, first within the tiny, but vociferous Covenanting minority – the Cameronians – that remained outside the kirk establishment after 1690, and then among the Seceders, who had broken from the kirk during the 1730s in disgust at its growing moderation.[21] Assassination principles continued to circulate within this culture of radical estrangement from the kirk. *Naphtali* was reprinted in 1721 and 1761, and *A Hind Let Loose* in 1744, 1770 and 1797. Nevertheless, even within the Secession, one of its leading intellects, John Brown of Haddington (1722–87), Professor of Divinity in the Associate Synod, resorted to careful triangulation on the subject of Sharp's demise.[22]

Within the presbyterian mainstream, Wodrow's equivocations were upheld, restated and popularized by the Reverend William Crookshank, Minister of the Scots Congregation at Swallow Street in London, in his *History of the State and Sufferings of the Church of Scotland from the Restoration to the Revolution* (1749), which was in effect an abridgement of Wodrow's massive tomes. Crookshank complained that Sharp's death had been 'most unjustly charged on the whole body of the Presbyterians' when the very 'actors themselves' had not intended to make an attempt on Sharp's life until he happened to come their way. It was crucial

---

[18]   [Alexander Bruce], *The Scottish Behemoth dissected* (Edinburgh, 1722), pp. 5–6, 8–9.

[19]   M. Sampson, 'Laxity and Liberty in Seventeenth-century English Political Thought', and J.P. Sommerville, 'The New Art of Lying: Equivocation, Mental Reservation and Casuistry', both in E. Leites (ed.), *Conscience and Casuistry in Early Modern Europe* (Cambridge, 1988), pp. 72–118 and pp. 159–84.

[20]   I.D.L. Clark, 'From Protest to Reaction: the Moderate Regime in the Church of Scotland, 1752–1805', in N.T. Phillipson and R. Mitchison (eds), *Scotland in the Age of Improvement* (Edinburgh, 1970), pp. 200–224.

[21]   C. Kidd, 'Conditional Britons: The Scots Covenanting Tradition and the Eighteenth-century British State', *English Historical Review*, 117 (2002): pp. 1149–76.

[22]   John Brown, *A Compendious History of the British Churches* (new edn, 2 vols, Edinburgh, 1820), vol. 2, p. 336.

to make this final point about the role of contingency in the killing of Sharp, for the very lack of a plan allowed Crookshank to answer the slur that the assassination was 'one of the dismal effects' of presbyterian 'field-meetings, these rendezvous of rebellion, as they were called'. If the killing had only been decided upon at the very last minute, in the light of an unexpected opportunity, then it removed a direct link between conventicling and assassination. This 'violent death' – to use the standard euphemism – had been effected 'by a few private persons' and, moreover, in the absence of 'any premeditated design'. The event and its aftermath were, moreover, providential: 'whether the actors were right or wrong, [Sharp] met with the just reward of his deeds, and God was righteous in his providence.' Indeed, Crookshank noted, by Sharp's death, 'new designs of cruelty were prevented'. Nonetheless Crookshank engaged respectfully with the criticism heaped upon presbyterians after Sharp's murder 'that, let the bishop have been ever so bad, yet the actors had no right to pursue him to death; for none of them had the power of the sword, nor were in any public judicative capacity'. There was, however, a powerful counter-argument, for he perceived that it had been virtually impossible for the presbyterians persecuted by Sharp 'to have recourse to the magistrate for justice, the constitution of government being overturned' and that as a consequence the suffering presbyterians fairly 'looked upon themselves as in a state of war, and consequently as having a right to cut off their great enemy, by whom they and others were persecuted to death'.[23]

Godly assassination scarcely featured *per se* within the discourse of the Scottish Enlightenment, though various casuistical stratagems were deployed within William Robertson's *History of Scotland* (1759), which prudently omitted the horrors of the seventeenth century, including the problem of how one explained away the murder of Sharp, and focused almost exclusively on the sixteenth-century Reformation. Robertson apologized for the violence of the Scottish Reformation by ascribing it to the mores of an unenlightened age. The assassination of Cardinal Beaton he attributed to 'private revenge, inflamed and sanctified by a false zeal for religion', noting that it was 'not the temper of the man [Norman Lesley, son of the Earl of Rothes], or the spirit of the times, quietly to digest an affront.'[24] Critical raillery, rather than apology, was the dominant note in David Hume's assessment of presbyterian violence. Hume alluded somewhat indirectly to godly assassination in his essay 'Of Superstition and Enthusiasm', which described the two main types of 'false religion', where he included the Scots Covenanters among his list of historical examples of

---

[23]   William Crookshank, *History of the State and Sufferings of the Church of Scotland from the Restoration to the Revolution* (2 vols, London, 1749), vol. 1, pp. 432–3.
[24]   William Robertson, *History of Scotland*, in *Works* (London, 1831), p. 81.

religious enthusiasm and described the psychological processes by which the religious enthusiast – under the supposition of divine illumination – came to reject reason and morality as 'fallacious guides' and might commit extreme acts of cruelty. Unsurprisingly, in his *History of Great Britain* (1754) Hume attributed the murder of Sharp to the fanaticism of the Covenanters, a species of religious enthusiasm reinforced and informed by Old Testament precedents of militant action in the cause of righteousness. The possible influence of Buchanan's classical exemplars went unmentioned. Rather, it seemed to Hume, it was the 'blind zeal' of the Covenanters that 'had often led them, in their books and sermons, to praise and recommend the assassination of their enemies, whom they considered as the enemies of all true piety and godliness. The stories of Jael and Sisera, of Ehud and Eglon, resounded from every pulpit.' Nevertheless, Hume appeared to be sanguine that enlightened Scotland had seen the worst of what was generally a short-lived phenomenon, for enthusiasm's 'fury is like that of thunder and tempest, which exhaust themselves in a little time, and leave the air more calm and serene than before'.[25]

II

Assassination principles became a central feature of Scottish political culture once more in the early 1820s, in the wake of the controversy provoked by Walter Scott's novel *Old Mortality* (1816), which presbyterians read as an indictment of the late seventeenth-century Covenanting movement.[26] The bitter sectarian conflicts of the Covenanting era were resurrected in Scottish literature, including the topic of assassination. Indeed, the theme of godly killing provided some of the most compelling matter for a distinctive body of Scottish romanticism, where the romantic fascination with primal forces, the individual will, the powers of the imagination, and dreams and illusions took a Calvinist turn. The issue of righteous assassination occupied a central place in Scots presbyterian romanticism alongside quintessential Calvinist preoccupations with predestination, election, damnation, and the treacherous proximity of Calvinism to the doctrine of antinomianism, the heretical belief that salvation is compatible with a reckless disregard for the moral law. In the Scots presbyterian novel, the hesitations and the recoil from decisive judgement that marked the

---

[25]   David Hume, 'Of Superstition and Enthusiasm', in *Essays*, ed. E.F. Miller (Indianapolis, IN, 1987), pp. 74, 76–7; idem, *History of England* (6 vols, Indianapolis, IN, 1983), vol. 6, p. 372.

[26]   D. Mack, 'The Rage of Fanaticism in Former Days', in I. Campbell (ed.), *Nineteenth-century Scottish Fiction* (Manchester, 1979), pp. 37–50.

casuistical approach to assassination were now reflected in fictional form, in narrative instability and uncertainty.

Old Mortality was arguably more balanced and latitudinarian in its sympathies than Scott's critics perceived. Indeed, the novel contains a very accurate mapping of presbyterian assassination principles. At one point Scott reviews

> the various opinions maintained among the insurgents concerning the murder of Archbishop Sharp. The more violent among them did, indeed, approve of this act as a deed of justice, executed upon a persecutor of God's church through the immediate inspiration of the Deity; but the greater part of the presbyterians disowned the deed as a crime highly culpable, although they admitted, that the Archbishop's punishment had by no means exceeded his deserts.[27]

Nevertheless, Scott's uninhibited parodies of a variety of fanatical and ludicrous presbyterian preaching styles, put in the mouths of a series of preposterous clerical characters, most notoriously Ephraim MacBriar and Habbakuk Mucklewrath, obscured for his critics his measured bipartisan interpretation of the Scottish past. Nuance was lost on Scott's foremost antagonist, the Reverend Thomas McCrie of the Auld Licht Antiburghers, a branch of the Secession, who reviewed the novel at enormous length in the Edinburgh Christian Instructor.[28] Sectarian passions were further inflamed with the publication of Charles Kirkpatrick Sharpe's edition of The Secret and True History of the Church of Scotland from the Restoration to the year 1678, the work of the presbyterian historian James Kirkton (1628–99), to which Sharpe appended An Account of the Murder of Archbishop Sharp, by James Russell, an actor therein. An episcopalian and a friend of Scott, Sharpe argued that late seventeenth-century presbyterians had formed as close an attachment to the assassination principles of the Covenanting canon – Naphtali, Ius Populi Vindicatum and A Hind Let Loose – as to the Bible itself, and also reprimanded Wodrow for his account of Sharp's murder, which seemed to express 'the most fraternal sympathy and apologetic tenderness, like a genuine disciple of John Knox'.[29] Nevertheless, the responses of Scotland's leading presbyterian

---

[27]   Walter Scott, Old Mortality (Harmondsworth, 1975), p. 262.

[28]   Thomas McCrie's three articles from the Christian Instructor for Jan., Feb. and March 1817 are reprinted in McCrie, Works (7 parts, Edinburgh and London, 1855–56), vol. 7, pp. 5–128.

[29]   James Kirkton, The Secret and True History of the Church of Scotland from the Restoration to the year 1678, to which is appended an Account of the murder of Archbishop Sharp, by James Russell, an actor therein, ed. C.K. Sharpe (Edinburgh, 1817), pp. 407 fn, 450 fn.

novelists, John Galt and James Hogg, injected a new strain of ambivalence into the debate, at least where it touched upon godly assassination.

Despite his rejection of Scott's unsympathetic portrayal of the Covenanters – at least to Galt's eyes – Galt himself responded with an otherwise partisan novel, *Ringan Gilhaize* (1823), which, nevertheless ends, surprisingly, on an uncertain note. Throughout the novel, Galt is unsparing in his celebration of the heroism of the presbyterian tradition, but as the novel concludes, also seems to hint at the dark psychology underlying the godly assassination to which some Covenanters were ultimately driven. Some of Galt's most brilliant fictions took the form of compelling life stories told by winning yet unreliable narrators, such as the Reverend Micah Balwhidder in *The Annals of the Parish* (1821) or Provost Pawkie in *The Provost* (1822), both of whom engage the reader's sympathy yet prove to be deluded, whether by self-importance or by a failure to discern the true causes of events. It is not entirely clear whether this pattern is repeated in *Ringan Gilhaize*, for here Galt covers his tracks in ambiguity. The novel, as a whole, is a heroic Scots presbyterian family saga, which depicts the struggles of three generations of the Gilhaize family on the side of the Scots Reformation, the Covenants and the presbyterian cause, between the mid-sixteenth century and the Revolution of 1689. The novel climaxes with the killing of John Graham of Claverhouse, Viscount Dundee, the persecutor of the Covenanters, by the novel's eponymous hero, Ringan Gilhaize. From his vantage point on a hill overlooking the pass of Killiecrankie, Gilhaize picks out Claverhouse and tries three times to shoot him with his carabine, the third time successfully after kneeling devoutly in prayer with the gun in his hand. Read straight, the conclusion affirms and magnifies the heroism recounted throughout this desperate saga of holy suffering: the long era of persecution is brought to an end at last by the indomitable Gilhaize, who, under the inspiration of the Holy Spirit, carries out the work of God's reformation by slaying its foremost enemy in Scotland. Yet, read ironically, as one is compelled to do to make sense of the other deluded personae in Galt's oeuvre, this novel seems to show the progressive disorientation of its hero, whose family having been killed by persecuting Cavaliers, eventually becomes so detached from reality that he believes himself God's chosen instrument of vengeance, the divinely appointed killer of Claverhouse.

Gilhaize starts out as a reliable narrator, albeit with strong commitments to the Covenanting cause. At one stage he is questioned by the authorities about the assassination of Sharp, and answers robustly, though in a level-headed and reasoned fashion, that Sharp deserved to be killed, and that there was no other way in the circumstances for those he had oppressed to punish his crimes. However, the narrative voice becomes increasingly fanatical. On finding his wife and daughters killed in a Cavalier atrocity,

Gilhaize prays in his anguish that God might 'make me an instrument to work out the purposes of thy dreadful justice, which in time will come to be'. But is Gilhaize what he thinks he is – an instrument of Providence – or a man unhinged by ideology and by the horror of his circumstances? The immediate context of Claverhouse's demise is itself a site of ambiguity. The slaying of Claverhouse occurs not in the heat of battle, but in the confused aftermath of the battle of Killiecrankie, which blurs the distinction between killing in open conflict and assassination. When Gilhaize shoots Claverhouse, he does so in full awareness that 'Claverhouse had won', with only some 'scattered firing, which was continued by a few'. Gilhaize then hears 'the voice of an oracle crying in the ears of my soul, "The victory of this day is given unto thy hands!" and strange wonder and awe fell upon me, and a mighty spirit entered into mine, and I felt as if I was in that moment clothed with the armour of divine might.' As he prepares to fire, Gilhaize feels that 'a glorious light shone around me' and is conscious that the ghosts of his own family are guiding him in his divinely sanctioned task. When he eventually manages to shoot Claverhouse and, at a stroke, changes the course of Scottish history, Gilhaize perceives 'a vision in the air as if all the angels of brightness, and the martyrs in their vestments of glory, were assembled on the walls and battlements of heaven to witness the event'. Providence then smiles upon Gilhaize again, as Claverhouse's officers fail to observe 'from what quarter the summoning bolt of justice came', and misdirect their return of fire, allowing the killer to escape unscathed, in body at least, for, mentally deranged, he has come to conflate his personal vendetta against the killers of his family and his historical status as God's chosen instrument for the liberation of Scotland: 'Thus was my avenging vow fulfilled – and thus was my native land delivered from bondage.'[30]

Literary critics have been disinclined to accept the straightforwardly heroic reading of the killing of Claverhouse, notwithstanding its obvious alignment with the broader thrust of the narrative as a whole. In her edition of the novel, Patricia Wilson argues that the reader, appreciating both Ringan's sense of his divinely appointed mission and the sufferings that have brought about his disengagement from reality, can at the point where he kills Claverhouse 'feel only compassion for Ringan's delusion, for we cannot regard the deed or its probable outcome as he does'.[31] Similarly, John MacQueen interprets Ringan as a 'predestinarian', who 'believes to obsession that he is singled out by a particular providence to play the role which he completes with the

[30]   John Galt, *Ringan Gilhaize, or the Covenanters*, ed. P. Wilson (Edinburgh, 1995), pp. 362, 367, 445–7.

[31]   P. Wilson, 'Introduction', ibid., p. xii. See also P. Wilson, 'Ringan Gilhaize: A Neglected Masterpiece?', in C.A. Whatley (ed.), *John Galt 1779–1979* (Edinburgh, 1979), esp. pp. 138–9.

assassination of Claverhouse after the victory of Killiecrankie'.[32] Douglas
Gifford, on the other hand, although he describes *Ringan Gilhaize* as 'the
dark and complex portrait of a "justified murderer"', whose 'destiny' is
to kill Claverhouse, is reluctant to foreclose upon the manifest ambiguities
of the novel. Indeed, Gifford is open to both a mythic and a subversive
reading of the novel, sensitive not only to the ways in which Gilhaize carries
a 'weight of historical responsibility' as the symbolic bearer of the scars of
religious persecution, but also to the final twist in which this saga of heroism
is ultimately deflated, for Gifford acknowledges the 'possibility, contained
in Ringan's Hebraic monologue and austere obsessive attitudes, that Galt's
deeper purpose is parodic, and that the novel ultimately satirizes the self-
deluding vengefulness of God's chosen.'[33]

Ambiguity, not least on the score of godly killing, also characterizes
James Hogg's curious reaction to *Old Mortality*. Hogg's initial response to
the calumnies detected in *Old Mortality* came in his novel *The Brownie of
Bodsbeck* (1818), a conventional depiction of Covenanting heroism and
suffering. However, this uncomplicated vindication of the Covenanters
was followed in 1824 by the highly unconventional *Private Memoirs and
Confessions of a Justified Sinner*, which used two very different narratives
of the same run of events – the autobiography of the justified sinner and a
commonsensical third-person account of the sinner's life by the purported
editor of the autobiography – to investigate the murky area where Calvinist
excess and an unbridled antinomianism appeared hard to distinguish.
These narratives tell a strange story, set in the Lowlands during the first
decade of the eighteenth century, of a hardline Calvinist, Robert Wringhim,
who ventures beyond the orthodox limits of Calvinism into murder and
other depravities, possibly under the influence of the Devil, who appears
to him in the guise of the mysterious figure Gil-Martin; however, if Satan
turns out to be a mere figment of Wringhim's overwrought Calvinist
imagination, then Wringhim's murderous career is not attributable to
diabolic powers, but is the product of a descent into madness, a descent
accelerated by an uncritical acceptance of the harsh logic of Calvinist
theology. The solution is left open, but en route the reader is alerted to the
possibility – at least – that godly killing is not only a form of false religion,
as an enlightened philosopher such as Hume would have read it, but worse
than enthusiasm, a form of diabolism. Hogg's achievement resides in the
tension that he establishes and perpetuates between an enlightened and
naturalistic interpretation of Wringhim as a madman and ideological

---

[32]   J. MacQueen, *The Rise of the Historical Novel* (Edinburgh, 1989), p. 133. See
also J. MacQueen, 'Ringan Gilhaize and Particular Providence', in Whatley (ed.), *Galt*, esp.
pp. 113–15.

[33]   D. Gifford, 'Myth, Parody and Dissociation: Scottish Fiction 1814–1914', in Gifford
(ed.), *History of Scottish Literature Vol. 3* (Aberdeen, 1987), p. 225.

fanatic and an equally persuasive supernaturalism that treats Wringhim, not unsympathetically, as a victim of genuine satanic temptation and, ultimately, demonic possession. These are the issues that catch the attention of Hogg's modern readership; however, his contemporaries, immersed in presbyterian culture, history and lore, and attuned to the debate triggered by *Old Mortality*, would have caught echoes of older debates about the legitimacy of godly assassination. After all, the murder of Sharp surfaces conspicuously in both *Old Mortality* and *Ringan Gilhaize*. When Wringhim describes his murder of the moderate clergyman, the Reverend Blanchard, whose Calvinism is lacking in antinomian rigour, as 'the great work of reformation by blood' and his own status as 'an assassin in the cause of Christ and his Church', Hogg seems to parody the theories of righteous judgement found in *Naphtali* and *A Hind Let Loose*.[34]

Notwithstanding the interventions of Galt and Hogg, an older tradition of presbyterian casuistry persisted. The Rev. Dr Robert Burns of Paisley in his four-volume annotated edition of Wodrow's *History*, published in 1828–30, steered a careful line between chiding Wodrow for 'stating that no party of Presbyterians approved of the deed' in 1679, and putting the counter-argument that 'the great body of the Presbyterians disapproved of the deed, and therefore it ought not to be brought as a stigma upon their cause'.[35] It did indeed remain a 'stigma'. In his *Life and Times of Archbishop Sharp* (1839), Thomas Stephen, the medical librarian at King's College London, a decidedly Anglican institution, claimed that the murder of Sharp was all the 'more disgraceful, inasmuch as it has been sedulously inculcated into many otherways good people, that this sacrilegious murder was a lawful deed, and just punishment'. Presbyterian equivocation – at best – over the murder was as bad as the killing itself. According to Stephen, a 'moral cloud' had hung over Scotland and its kirk for 'a century and a half' and was only now 'beginning to be dispelled'.[36] However, from the appearance of the presbyterian novels of the 1820s sectarian mudslinging and defensiveness constituted only one strand of the debate on assassinations. No longer did the security of the presbyterians depend on their disassociating themselves from the principles and practice of assassination, and the political legitimacy – or otherwise – of assassination yielded in large measure to a psychological exploration of fanaticism. Nevertheless both *Ringan Gilhaize* and the *Confessions of a Justified Sinner* presented their readers with a puzzle: just

---

[34]   James Hogg, *The Private Memoirs and Confessions of a Justified Sinner* (Oxford, 1995), pp. 139–40.

[35]   Robert Wodrow, *The History of the Sufferings of the Church of Scotland*, ed. Robert Burns (4 vols, Glasgow, 1828–30), vol. 3, p. 48 fn.

[36]   Thomas Stephen, *The Life and Times of Archbishop Sharp* (London, 1839), pp. 576–7.

how could one determine whether a supposedly righteous assassination was the direct consequence of an individual murderer's abnormality or was the result of some genuine supernatural intervention – whether benign or satanic – that guided the hand of the killer? Framed in these terms, the issue of godly assassination retained some of the distinctive features of presbyterian casuistry in the age of Wodrow, most notably the invocation of an interventionist Providence that served to downplay the role of human agency in the execution of righteous judgement. Buchanan lurks as a rather shadowy presence behind these debates. Later generations of Scots presbyterians knew him, of course, as an authority for tyrannicide, but their emphasis upon assassination as a kind of providential deliverance obscured the forthright humanism of Buchanan's legacy.

CHAPTER 14

George Buchanan and Revolution Principles, 1688–1788[*]

Caroline Erskine

In 1781, in an address to the Glasgow Literary Society, John Anderson, holder of the Chair of Natural Philosophy at the University of Glasgow and eventual founder of Anderson's Institution, proposed that a monument be built on Buchanan Street, by public subscription, to commemorate the life and works of George Buchanan. According to Anderson, Buchanan was a proponent of modern and rational ideas, and his renowned *De Iure Regni apud Scotos* 'anticipates the political Doctrines which have become so famous in this Island of late years'. Indeed, Buchanan might be seen as a prophet of the Revolution of 1688: 'To set aside the Monarch who misbehaves and to exalt another Heir of [the] Line; is no more than what was done at the last Revolution of the freest state that has ever existed.'[1] This monument was never built, but Anderson's proposal is suggestive of the trajectory of Buchanan's reputation in the eighteenth century.

For over a century after his death in 1582, George Buchanan's radical theory of resistance to tyranny was critical to the making of his reputation. In Scotland and in England, Buchanan's ideas were appropriated by Covenanters, parliamentarians, regicides, republicans and Whigs to justify resistance, while those who supported kings and their prerogatives branded him as a dangerous incendiary. He was flattered with citations by such intellectual giants of the seventeenth century as the Covenanter Samuel Rutherford, the regicide John Milton, and the Whig martyr of the Rye House Plot of 1683, Algernon Sidney.[2] English royalists during the Restoration, in attacking 'certain pernicious books and damnable

---

[*] I am grateful to Colin Kidd, James Coleman, John Coffey and Gordon Pentland for valuable discussions that contributed much to the ideas on which this chapter is based.

[1] John Anderson, 'Of the Propriety of Erecting an Obelisk in Honour of Buchanan: A Discourse read to the Literary Society in Glasgow College, November 1781', Anderson Collection, Strathclyde University Library Special Collections, MS 25, pp. 2–3.

[2] See Samuel Rutherford, *Lex, Rex: The Law and the Prince* (London 1644), pp. 60, 152, 265; John Milton, *The Tenure of Kings and Magistrates*, in M. Dzelzainis (ed.), *Political Writings* (Cambridge, 1991), pp. 23–5; Algernon Sidney, *Discourses Concerning Government* (Indianapolis, IN, 1990), pp. 292, 314–15, 546.

doctrines', in the Decree of the University of Oxford of 1683, similarly honoured Buchanan with condemnation in the strongest terms.[3]

From 1689, however, neither Scotland nor England was an arena of revolution, and this brought about a shift in Buchanan's reputation, albeit a slow and stuttering one. Owing largely to the efforts of admiring Whigs, Buchanan was reshaped as a hero of civil and religious liberty and gained entry into a pantheon of Scottish worthies. He was made compatible with British Revolution Principles and could be named as a prophet of the Glorious Revolution. In 1788, a particularly auspicious date, as the centenary of the Revolution, an obelisk to commemorate Buchanan was built in his birthplace, Killearn. And it, like Anderson's proposal of 1781, sought to associate Buchanan with the overthrow of the last Stuart king.

However, Buchanan's transition from fomenter of rebellion to libertarian hero was incomplete and insecure by 1788. The issue of resistance lost some of its sharp edge in the century from 1688, but it was not entirely blunted, and some contemporaries of the late eighteenth century overestimated the extent to which Buchanan could be named as an uncontentious libertarian icon. Those political reformers of the 1790s who made confident links between themselves and George Buchanan while defending themselves against charges of sedition made near-fatal mistakes.

A general historiographical consensus prevails affirming that in England the Revolution of 1688 was justified in insipid terms, with the Convention's fiction that James II had abdicated the throne. The Whigs were afraid that any suggestion that the people had resisted the tyrannical king, or that the will of the people had enthroned his replacements, might invite future challenges to the English constitution; therefore they played safe with tame rhetoric.[4] In Scotland the Claim of Right of April 1689 made the seemingly unembarrassed admission that, through his own actions, James VII 'Forefaulted' his right to the crown.[5] Superficially, at least, Scotland's Revolution Settlement appears to have been more radical than that of England, yet here too, qualifications are required. Bruce Lenman, for example, emphasizes the deficiencies of Whig argument in Scotland,

---

3   *Oxford Decree.*

4   John P. Kenyon, *Revolution Principles: The Politics of Party, 1689–1720* (Cambridge, 1977), p. 10. Mark Goldie, 'The Revolution of 1689 and the Structure of Political Argument', *Bulletin of Research in the Humanities*, 83 (1980): pp. 473–564, at pp. 489–90. For a recent dissenting opinion on this issue that argues that Whig thinking was less a cowardly compromise and more a flexible and successful response to Jacobite criticism, see J. Rudolph, *Revolution by Degrees: James Tyrrell and Whig Political Thought in the late Seventeenth Century* (Basingstoke, 2002), Introduction.

5   *The Declaration of the Estates of the Kingdom of Scotland, Containing the Claim of Right, and the Offer of the Crown to their Majesties, King William and Queen Mary* (Edinburgh, 1689), p. 4.

noting its antiquarian quality, a charge that can even be extended to the term 'forefaulted' as having feudal and conservative associations.[6]

Colin Kidd finds the newly ascendant presbyterian Church of Scotland sensitive to its heritage of Covenanting resistance, a heritage that disenfranchised episcopalians were keen to exploit for polemical gain.[7] In this context the legacy of George Buchanan was vigorously debated. Episcopalian polemicists did not treat Buchanan purely as a prophet of resistance, but rather undertook to paint a positive picture of John Knox and George Buchanan as representatives of the first Scottish Reformation of the sixteenth century. This, after all, was the Reformation that episcopalians wished to claim as their own, and they sought to marshal Knox and Buchanan on their side in order to attack the second Reformation, the Covenanting period of the seventeenth century.[8] In response, Whig presbyterian polemicists challenged the episcopalians' separation of the first and second Reformations. George Ridpath, for example, put forward an image of continuity, uniting Knox and Buchanan with presbyterians of the Jacobean era such as David Calderwood, and then with the Covenanters George Gillespie and Samuel Rutherford, in order to demonstrate the sustained achievement of presbyterian learning.[9]

The most emphatic apologist for the Covenanters in the first half of the eighteenth century was the church historian Robert Wodrow, whose *History of the Sufferings of the Church of Scotland*, published in 1721–22, sought to challenge the perception of seventeenth-century presbyterians as lawless rebels. Instead he presented the Covenanters as early warriors for Revolution Principles: 'We suffered the hardships I relate, for adhering to our Reformation blessings, and humbly claim the character of contending and suffering for revolution Principles, even before the revolution was brought about.'[10] However, the rehabilitation of the Covenanters as broadly acceptable Protestant heroes could not be made convincingly in mainstream Whig circles in the eighteenth century, and their reputation for

---

[6]   Bruce Lenman, 'The Poverty of Political Theory in the Scottish Revolution of 1688–90', in Lois Schwoerer (ed.), *The Revolution of 1688–89: Changing Perspectives* (Cambridge, 1992), pp. 245, 255.

[7]   Colin Kidd, *Subverting Scotland's Past: Scottish Whig Historians and the Creation of an Anglo-British Identity, 1689–c.1830* (Cambridge, 1993), p. 51.

[8]   [Alexander Monro], *The Spirit of Calumny and Slander ... Particularly addresss'd to Mr George Ridpath* (London, 1693), p. 8; [John Sage], *The Fundamental Charter of Presbytery, as it has been lately established in the Kingdom of Scotland* (London, 1697), pp. 8, 144, 217–18.

[9]   [George Ridpath], *An Answer to the Scotch Presbyterian Eloquence* (London, 1693), p. 47.

[10]   Robert Wodrow, 'Dedication to the King', *The History of the Sufferings of the Church of Scotland from the Restoration to the Revolution*, ed. Robert Burns (2 vols, Glasgow, 1828–30), vol. 1, p. xxxv.

rebellious antinomianism would persist. Things might have been different, however, for Buchanan. The strong ideological link that presbyterians had forged between the first and second Reformations could be broken in the eighteenth century, as episcopalians were already seeking to do. For Buchanan, iconic status beckoned.

In 1749 John Love wrote *A Vindication of Mr George Buchanan* as a foray into the ongoing debate over the virtue of Mary Queen of Scots in which the defenders of Mary sought to discredit her detractor Buchanan. More interesting than the text itself is Love's preface, dedicating his production to the Revolution Club of Edinburgh. He cast Buchanan as a founder of Revolution Principles: 'His famous Dialogue, *De jure Regni apud Scotos*, contains the most solid Principles of Government, founded on Reason, the Nature of human Societies, Justice, and the Constitution of the Kingdom, according to which the nation proceeded at the late Happy Revolution.'[11] Buchanan, in the eyes of this worshipful Whig, was a thoroughly safe, rational and reasonable political theorist. This sort of bland praise is an indicator of the development of Buchanan's iconic status. The image of Buchanan as a Protestant hero was becoming stronger than the substance of his writings. As with British Revolution Principles, so with the mutating reputation of George Buchanan, the thorny question of resistance could safely be ignored.

The enemies of Whiggism also made connections between Buchanan and Revolution Principles, as they sought to demonize both. The Jacobite antiquarian Father Thomas Innes attacked Buchanan's reputation as a historian in his *Critical Essay on the Ancient Inhabitants of the Northern Parts of Britain* of 1729. He rightly demolished Buchanan's claim that the first king of Scots had been enthroned in 330 BCE (a claim that had allowed him to embellish numerous examples of resistance against tyrannical kings), and lopped forty spurious monarchs from the royal genealogy.[12] However, Innes recognized that his minutely detailed antiquarian researches would be as a pinprick on the mighty reputation of Buchanan the historian, poet, playwright, political theorist and polemical detractor of Mary Queen of Scots. He complained of Buchanan's stature in a letter to the Old Pretender in 1729, charging that his principles, 'joined to the fanatical spirit of the time', had led the execution of the Pretender's grandfather, Charles I, and the deposition of his father, James VII & II. Innes complained, 'since the *Revolution*, these wretched libels of *Buchanan* are become as classic authors'.[13]

---

[11]   [John Love], *A Vindication of Mr George Buchanan* (Edinburgh, 1749), pp. iv–v.

[12]   William Ferguson, *The Identity of the Scottish Nation: An Historic Quest* (Edinburgh, 1998), pp. 189–91.

[13]   Thomas Innes, 'Copy of Mr. Thomas Innes' Letter to the King', in *The Miscellany of the Spalding Club II* (Aberdeen, 1842), p. 355.

Both John Love and Thomas Innes undoubtedly exaggerated the influence of Buchanan's ideas upon the political landscape of the eighteenth century. The publishing of his works in this period acts as a reminder of the polymathic nature of his output: Buchanan's corpus of work was not universally controversial. His two most regularly reissued works of the eighteenth century were probably the politically urgent *Rerum Scoticarum Historia* and the non-controversial and ecumenical Psalm Paraphrases.[14] The publication of Buchanan's *Opera Omnia*, undertaken by the Jacobite episcopalian Thomas Ruddiman and his publisher Robert Freebairn in 1715, was also intended to score both partisan and non-partisan points: in some respects they sought to attack Buchanan's Whig reputation, but in others they wished to cultivate admiration for a talented Scot, a national hero.[15]

There is more to this than simple rhetorical connections between George Buchanan, the Revolution of 1688, and those who supported or opposed it. Central to this eighteenth-century context is the question of how liberty was understood in Scotland and England. As the risk of Stuart restoration faded and the centenary of the Revolution approached, it can be questioned how far understandings of liberty moved away from the negative fear of 'popery and arbitrary government' towards a more positive and enlarged view of 'civil and religious liberty'. The latter can be seen as a vague and widely acceptable definition of British liberty, rooted in Revolution Principles, that claimed Magna Carta as its ancestor, that privileged moderation rather than resistance, that was tolerant, and that celebrated the limited monarchy that had been preserved in 1688. This was a view of British liberty shaved of the excesses that too great an enthusiasm for liberty might engender.

However, the rhetoric of civil and religious liberty was Janus faced, capable of progressive and retrogressive uses. In the second half of the eighteenth century it could be deployed by those who sought to emphasize their loyalty to the Hanoverian state, by English Protestant dissenters such

---

[14] Durkan's *Buchanan Bibliography* terminates in 1725, but its coverage of the relative popularity of different texts for republication is broadly representative of the eighteenth century as a whole. Later noteworthy examples are as follows: *De Iure Regni* published in Latin in Glasgow in 1750 and in English in London in 1799. *History of Scotland* published in Latin in Edinburgh in 1727 and Aberdeen in 1762, and in English in London in 1722 and 1733, Edinburgh in 1762 and 1766, and London in 1799. Psalms reissued in at least the following years: Edinburgh 1725, 1732, 1737, 1772; London 1775. In addition, a myriad of editions of individual and collected poems appeared in the eighteenth century.

[15] John Robertson, *The Scottish Enlightenment and the Militia Issue* (Edinburgh, 1985), p. 51; Kidd, *Subverting Scotland's Past*, p. 92; Colin Kidd, 'The Ideological Significance of Scottish Jacobite Latinity', in J. Black and J. Gregory (eds), *Culture, Politics and Society in Britain, 1660–1800* (Manchester, 1991), pp. 110–30; see also Esther Mijers, Chapter 12 above.

as Joseph Priestley, or by the Moderate party of the Church of Scotland,
led by William Robertson. As was to become typical of the new strain
of civil and religious liberty, Priestley praised the British constitution
as the best in the world, but suggested it might have minor defects that
ought to be repaired, with the civil disabilities imposed upon Catholics
and Protestant dissenters principal among them.[16] Similarly, Robertson
took a principled but highly unpopular stand in favour of Catholic Relief
in 1779.[17] According to his *History of Scotland*, published in 1759, civil
and religious liberty had tentatively begun to blossom in the era of the
Scottish Reformation, but their progress was retarded in the seventeenth
century, 'a situation no less fatal to the liberty than to the taste and genius
of the nation'.[18] The bicentenary of the Scottish Reformation in 1760 was
barely noticed,[19] but the centenary of the Revolution of 1688 would be a
different matter, and Robertson celebrated with hyperbolic rhetoric the
accelerations of the progress of liberty that Scotland had experienced in
1688 and 1707. In 1689, said Robertson, 'The Sceptre was placed in the
hands of Sovereigns who had no title to sway it, but what they derived from
the people'. Anyone who studied the British constitution might admire it
as 'the most perfect production of political wisdom' and recommend it 'as
a model for the imitation of mankind'.[20]

Alternatively, there were many, particularly in Scotland, who regarded
civil and religious liberty and the celebration of 1688 merely as a new
expression of the old loathing of popery and arbitrary government. This
backward-looking strand is particularly to be seen among the successors
of the Covenanters in eighteenth-century Scotland, such as Seceders and
Reformed Presbyterians. These sects found it impossible to reconcile
themselves to a British constitution that they regarded as uncovenanted,
erastian and prelatical. It is likely that the author of an anonymous tract
of 1768 entitled *An Essay on Civil and Religious Liberty* falls under this
grouping. This pamphlet represented the era of the Covenanters as the
most 'noble stand made for civil and religious liberty'. Its author did not
heap generous praise upon the British constitution, instead complaining
that a 'Jacobite and Popish faction' prevailed during the reign of Queen
Anne and imposed on Scottish presbyterians the 'accursed yoke of

---

[16]   Joseph Priestley, *An Essay on the First Principles of Government, and on the Nature of Political, Civil, and Religious Liberty* (London, 1771), pp. 130–33, 250–51.

[17]   William Robertson, 'Speech on Roman Catholic Relief', in *Miscellaneous Works and Commentaries*, ed. J. Smitten (London, 1996), pp. 144, 152, 157.

[18]   William Robertson, *The History of Scotland during the reigns of Queen Mary and of King James VI* (2 vols, London, 1759), vol. 2, p. 254.

[19]   J.H.S. Burleigh, 'The Scottish Reformation as seen in 1660 and 1760', *Records of the Scottish Church History Society*, 13 (1957–59): pp. 241–56, at p. 250.

[20]   Robertson, 'Sermon on the Centenary of the Glorious Revolution', in *Miscellaneous Works*, ed. Smitten, pp. 178, 183.

patronage'. This had led to many evils, particularly the ascendancy of the Moderate party under William Robertson, which had reconciled itself to patronage and approved of the type of enlightened minister often chosen by lay patrons.[21]

It has been argued that Robertson's views of civil and religious liberty, far from being progressive, should be seen as an example of vulgar Whiggism, a crude form of Whig polemic that was vehemently anti-Catholic, anti-tyranny and anti-Stuart, that defended the Glorious Revolution, and regarded the British constitution as near perfect.[22] This is a persuasive argument: undoubtedly some of Robertson's hyperbolic encomiums to the Revolution and the British constitution do smack of vulgar Whiggism. However, in comparison to the thoroughly backward-looking rhetoric of the eighteenth-century Covenanters, Robertson's views on civil and religious liberty can be seen as progressive. This broadly based understanding of British liberty was progressive in that it would continue into the era of the French Revolution and the nineteenth century. It was progressive in that it would give the reputation of George Buchanan a future in a way that the Covenanting tradition could not. Ultimately, the tradition of civil and religious liberty would even bestow respectability upon the reputations of certain seventeenth-century Covenanters, something that, again, their own narrow tradition could not do.

'Civil and religious liberty', then, was one of the slogans of 1788, which is in itself an interesting point at which to take the political temperature of Britain. On 30 January the royal family solemnly trooped to Westminster Abbey to observe the anniversary of the execution of Charles I and heard a sermon based on that classic text of the debate over resistance to tyrants, Romans 13.[23] Later they would discover that on the same day the Young Pretender, Charles Edward Stuart, had died in Rome. The stage was set for commemoration of the centenary of the Revolution that had excluded the male Stuart line from the thrones of Scotland and England, a line that was now almost extinct. The year 1788 was a unique moment for appreciation of the British constitution. A year earlier the infant republic of America had unveiled its new rational constitution. And a year later the French Revolution would erupt. As Colin Kidd suggests, 1788 stands as a brief moment of self-expression for Whigs before the outbreak of the French

---

[21] *An Essay on Civil and Religious Liberty* (Glasgow, 1768), pp. 19, 21.
[22] Richard B. Sher, '1688 and 1788: William Robertson on Revolution in Britain and France', in Paul Dukes and John Dunkley (eds), *Culture and Revolution* (London, 1999), pp. 98–109, at p. 101.
[23] *The Times*, 31 January 1788, p. 2.

Revolution and its escalation a few years later made any radical rhetoric appear dangerously imprudent.[24]

In June 1788 the foundation stone of the Buchanan monument in Killearn was laid by the minister of the parish, Reverend James Graham.[25] It appears that the monument was largely a local project paid for by local gentlemen, although the *Glasgow Mercury* stated, somewhat more expansively, that gentlemen 'particularly in and about the city of Glasgow' had made an important contribution.[26] Perhaps some of John Anderson's inspiration for Glasgow found its way to Killearn. Reverend Graham stated later that the monument was modelled on an obelisk built in 1736 in Ulster to commemorate the Battle of the Boyne, and certainly the two monuments were very similar.[27] This cemented the link between Buchanan and the Revolution that took place over a century after his death.

Then, in November 1788, came the opportunity to commemorate the centenary of the Revolution, an opportunity that was grasped with varying degrees of enthusiasm by political and sectarian groups in Scotland and England. The illness of King George III and the fears that a regency government would be required, with the risk of upsetting the constitutional balance between crown and parliament, may have impacted upon the rhetoric of the commemorations.[28] In London the Revolution Society met on 4 November 1788. Its members stated their purpose: to be 'of service in preserving and disseminating the principles of Civil and Religious Liberty'.[29] They stated their principles, 'that the Abuse of Power Justifies Resistance'.[30] They then drank forty-one toasts to a selection of

---

[24]   Notably, William Robertson's family suppressed his unpublished sermon on the centenary of the Glorious Revolution because its triumphalist Whiggish tone could have been construed as dangerously radical in the aftermath of the French Revolution. Colin Kidd, 'The Kirk, the French Revolution, and the Burden of Scottish Whiggery', in Nigel Aston (ed.), *Religious Change in Europe, 1650–1914* (Oxford, 1997), pp. 213–34, at pp. 223–5.

[25]   H. Scott, *Fasti Ecclesiae Scoticanae* (11 vols, Edinburgh, 1915–81), vol. 3, p. 349.

[26]   *Glasgow Mercury*, 2 July 1788. The entry for Killearn in the first *Statistical Account* was not written by the parish minister, Rev. Graham, but by Rev. David Ure, a minister from Glasgow. J. Sinclair, *The Statistical Account of Scotland 1791–99*, ed. D.J. Withrington and I.R. Grant (19 vols, Wakefield, 1978), vol. 9, p. 383.

[27]   Rev. Graham did write the entry for Killearn in the *New Statistical Account*: see *The New Statistical Account of Scotland* (15 vols, Edinburgh, 1845), vol. 8, p. 66; James Howley, *The Follies and Garden Buildings of Ireland* (New Haven, CT, 1993), p. 15.

[28]   For a full discussion of the English context of the commemoration of the Revolution of 1688, see Tamara Hunt, *Defining John Bull: Caricature, Politics and National Identity in Late Georgian England* (Aldershot, 2003), p. 56; Nicholas Rogers, *Crowds, Culture and Politics in Georgian Britain* (Oxford, 1998), pp. 177–84; and Kathleen Wilson, 'Inventing Revolution: 1688 and Eighteenth-century Popular Politics', *Journal of British Studies*, 28 (1989): pp. 349–86.

[29]   *An Abstract of the History and Proceedings of the Revolution Society in London* (1789), p. 7.

[30]   Ibid., p. 14–15.

heroes that suggested they had a very clear view of who their political ancestors were: John Hampden, Lord Russell, Algernon Sidney, Andrew Marvell, John Milton and John Locke.

This commemoration was the work in particular of Protestant dissenters who associated the Revolution of 1688 with the extension of liberty of conscience – but not full civil liberty – and hoped for the repeal of the Test Act. Dissenting centenary sermons, however, unlike secular celebrations, tended to be couched in moderate terms. Robert Stevenson put forward a strong case for rights of resistance, but with caveats circumscribing action by the common people, and gave thanks for the Toleration Act without demanding relief from civil penalties.[31] Caleb Evans cited John Locke approvingly and referred to 'virtuous resistance of tyrannical encroachments', but he did not specify who had undertaken, or who had the right to undertake, such action, suggesting that he also wished to avoid accusations of leaning towards popular democracy, regarding Providence as an altogether safer explanation for the Revolution.[32] Newspaper coverage of the anniversary suggests that many commemorations took place across England, with *The Times* suggesting that 'all ranks of people' had been involved, even, it was claimed, Roman Catholics.[33]

In Scotland the established church had proclaimed the anniversary to be a day of national thanksgiving, in memory of Britain's deliverance 'from civil and religious oppression', and with thanks due to a 'special interposition of Divine Providence'.[34] Ministers dutifully preached sermons emphasizing the benefits that the Revolution Settlement had bestowed, not upon Scotland, but upon *Britain*, and explained the Revolution in terms that were, if anything, even more conservative than those used in its immediate aftermath. John Robertson, in a sermon entitled *Britain the Chosen Nation*, emphasized that the Revolution was a gift of Providence, and enjoined his

---

[31]   Robert Stevenson, *The Principles of the Revolution Asserted and Vindicated, and its Advantages Stated* (London, 1788), esp. pp. 21–5.

[32]   Caleb Evans, *British Freedom Realized. A Sermon, Preached at Broadmead, Bristol, November 5, 1788* (Bristol, n.d.), pp. 11, 14–15; quotation at p. 13. For an altogether milder Dissenting sermon that emphasized the contribution of the House of Lords as well as the House of Commons to the British constitution, see William Wood, *Two Sermons, Preached at Mill-Chapel, in Leeds, on the Celebration of the Hundredth Anniversary of the Happy Revolution* (Leeds, 1788). The political character of these dissenting sermons comes across more strongly when compared to Anglican productions such as that by the antiquary Samuel Pegge, who dedicated his centenary sermon to the Duke of Devonshire and heaped praise upon his ancestor and other aristocrats who brought about the Revolution. Samuel Pegge, *A Sermon Preached at Whittington in the County of Derby, on the Grand Jubilee, or Centenary Commemoration of the Glorious Revolution* (Chesterfield, 1788).

[33]   *The Times*, 7 November 1788, p. 2. See also *The Times*, 5 November 1788, p. 2; *The Times*, 21 November 1788, p. 4.

[34]   'Proclamation of the General Assembly', *Secular Anniversary of the Revolution* (Glasgow, 1788), p. 1.

listeners to obedience to their government, lest God should withdraw his benevolence from an ungrateful nation.[35] A number of ministers of the established church took a strongly British approach to their thanksgiving, citing Magna Carta, discussing the reign of Elizabeth, the defeat of the Spanish Armada, and England's troubles of the seventeenth century.[36]

Scottish churchmen, it seems, were uncomfortable with ascribing their principles of civil and religious liberty to a pantheon of Scottish heroes. Protestant worthies such as John Knox, George Buchanan and the Covenanters were almost entirely absent from the rhetoric of the centenary commemorations. If anything, the message coming from Church of Scotland pulpits was that of a subverted pantheon, a rogues' gallery of a backward nation. Alexander Ranken said 'Scotland was almost perpetually distracted with civil and foreign wars. The names of Bruce and Baliol, of Queen Mary and John Knox are sufficient to recal [sic] to our memory the turbulence, the political weakness, and slow improvement of that kingdom.'[37] Only England and later Britain, he implied, had offered Scotland progress in civil and religious liberty.

Secular celebrations in Scotland also had a strongly British tinge. One pamphlet, entitled the *Secular Anniversary of the Revolution*, in a vein similar to the toasts drunk in London, lauded Lord Russell and Algernon Sidney, the Whig martyrs of the Rye House Plot, and those executed following the Monmouth Rebellion. This pamphlet had a song appended to the end of it, to be sung to the tune of *Rule Britannia*, itself an ode to Britain written by the Lowland Scot James Thomson. This new version, entitled *Hymn to Liberty or Political Freedom*, took first a Scottish then a British angle, first praising 'native valour' and 'the patriot sword', 'A Bruce has reign'd, a Wallace bled'. This language is striking given that Robert Burns's composition of *Scots Wha Hae* lay five years in the future at this time. But a later verse about the Revolution of 1688 and the coming of William was strongly British in its orientation: 'By each true Briton wish'd he came, While Tyranny confounded stood.'[38] Allusions to Scotland and Britain were cyclical, but the British emphasis won out overall.

A valuable counterpoint to the tame rhetoric of most Scottish commemorations of the centenary can be found in the sermons and

---

[35]   John Robertson, *Britain the Chosen Nation, A Thanksgiving Sermon Preached, November 5ᵗʰ, 1788* (Kilmarnock, 1788), p. 18.

[36]   Henry Hunter, *The Universal and Everlasting Dominion of God* (London, 1788), p. 31; James Playfair, *A Sermon on the Centennial Day of the Revolution in Great Britain* (Dundee, 1788), p. 13; Alexander Ranken, *A Discourse on the Advantages of the Revolution of 1688* (Glasgow, 1788), pp. 10, 14, 16–19; Robert Small, *A Sermon on the Blessings of the Revolution of 1688, preached at Dundee* (Edinburgh, 1792), pp. 38–9.

[37]   Ranken, *Discourse on the Advantages of the Revolution*, p. 14.

[38]   *Secular Anniversary of the Revolution*, pp. 6–7.

publications of the heirs of the Covenanters in eighteenth-century Scotland. The Seceders were splintered in two camps, Burghers and Antiburghers, of which the latter were the more theologically conservative.[39] Buchanan could hold only limited appeal for these sects who placed their emphasis on the second Scottish Reformation, the age of the Covenants – Covenants that they believed should continue to be upheld. The first Reformation, the age of Knox and Buchanan, held less appeal, not least because while the first Reformation was an era of victory and success, the Covenanting mind preferred to concentrate on periods of struggle and persecution. Earlier outpourings by adherents of these sects give an indication of their narrow pantheon of heroes. A Cloud of Witnesses and John Howie's Scots Worthies are well-known martyrologies that focus most particularly on the Covenanting period, more narrowly on the Covenanters of the Restoration and, narrower still, on the Cameronian martyrs of the 1680s.[40]

The Burgher minister John Peddie gave a sermon on the centenary of the Revolution that walked a tightrope between conservatism and careful criticism of the present constitution. He placed heavy emphasis on Providence, but John Knox was also named as an agent of God's Reformation in Scotland. Peddie praised the constitution of Britain that allowed his congregation to separate from the Church of Scotland over the issue of lay patronage, but he also emphasized the malcontents of Scotland's post-Revolution religious settlement, singling out patronage for criticism.[41]

Even more strongly worded was the contribution to the centenary debate made by Archibald Bruce, an Antiburgher both theologically conservative and politically radical. Protestants ought not to celebrate idolatrous 'feast days', or discuss political matters in their church assemblies, he argued. He was vehemently opposed to the celebration of a revolution that he

---

[39]   For deeper analysis than space permits here of the intellectual backgrounds of Reformed Presbyterians and Seceders, see Colin Kidd, 'Conditional Britons: The Scots Covenanting Tradition and the Eighteenth-century British State', English Historical Review, 107 (2002): pp. 1147–76.

[40]   A Cloud of Witnesses, first published in 1714, reached fifteen editions by 1814 and included the letters and speeches of the principal martyrs such as Donald Cargill and Richard Cameron, along with a list of the humble presbyterians of south-west Scotland who died during the persecution. A Cloud of Witnesses for the Royal Prerogatives of Jesus Christ, ed. Rev. J.H. Thomson (Edinburgh, 1871). John Howie's Biographica Scoticana, first published in 1775, focused heavily on the Covenanting heroes of the second Reformation, including Cameron and Cargill, but also devoted some space to heroes of the first Reformation with biographical accounts of John Knox, George Wishart and George Buchanan. John Howie, The Scots Worthies: Containing a Brief Historical Account of the Most Eminent Noblemen, Gentlemen, Ministers, and Others, who Testified or Suffered for the Cause of Reformation in Scotland (Glasgow, 1846).

[41]   James Peddie, The Revolution the Work of God and a Cause of Joy (Edinburgh, 1789), pp. 7, 66. See also John McKerrow, History of the Secession Church (Edinburgh, 1845), pp. 566–7.

regarded as incomplete and uncovenanted and attacked the established church for its proclamation of a day of thanksgiving, a measure he viewed as a sycophantic gesture to the imperfect British constitution. While deliverance from civil and religious tyranny was of course something to be grateful for, it should be remembered that the greatest purity and perfection of Scottish Protestantism was reached in the seventeenth century and had since declined. Presbyterians should not celebrate while further reformation was urgently required. Yet, Bruce argued, it was a sad sign of the times that this purity, and those Covenanters who struggled so ardently to maintain it against oppression, were not objects of admiration but had instead, since 1689, been 'stigmatised as rebels'.[42] In short, only Burghers were willing to uphold Scotland's *Reformation* principles as an acceptable and praiseworthy contribution to civil and religious liberty. Ministers of the established church preferred to avoid allusions to Scotland's pre-Revolution Protestant tradition because it was too radical, while Antiburghers criticized the present context as not radical enough.

In Scotland, then, the formulation of a pantheon of libertarian heroes was more problematic than in England or in Britain as a whole; and in each of these contexts it was radicals from outwith the established religious traditions who were most comfortable venerating historical heroes. The English pantheon, particularly as conceived in strongly Whiggish and dissenting circles, had coalesced quite some time before 1788. Lord Cobham's building programme to commemorate his heroes at Stowe can be seen as a particularly early example, begun in the 1730s and including busts of King Alfred, Queen Elizabeth, William Shakespeare, Walter Raleigh, John Hampden, John Milton, Isaac Newton and William of Orange.[43] In the mid-eighteenth century the Whig publisher Thomas Hollis named his landholdings after his political heroes, including the Englishmen John Milton, Algernon Sidney, John Locke and Andrew Marvell, and the Scot George Buchanan.[44]

At this point, the imagined quality of a pantheon of heroes must be emphasized, as having quite different qualities from the textual canons of which authors like Buchanan and Locke may be assumed to be members. Membership of a canon is associated with merit, on the uniqueness and interest and relevance of an author's ideas. A pantheon, in contrast, is

---

[42]   Calvianus Presbyter [Archibald Bruce], *Annus Secularis; or the British Jubilee* (Edinburgh, 1788), pp. 228–9. See also McKerrow, *History of the Secession Church*, pp. 344–5.

[43]   Christine Gerrard, *The Patriot Opposition to Walpole: Politics, Poetry, and National Myth, 1725–1742* (Oxford, 1994), p. 36; Mark Goldie, 'John Locke: Icon of Liberty', *History Today*, 54 (2004): pp. 33–4.

[44]   Annabel Patterson, *Early Modern Liberalism* (Cambridge, 1997), p. 37. I am grateful to John Coffey for suggesting this reference.

based on more grandiose but potentially less flattering foundations. It is based not on texts but on associations. In a pantheon of heroes, the members acquire an equal status that undermines their uniqueness. Yet their intrinsic meanings, the qualities that they have displayed in order to gain their place, are assumed to be the same. Whigs like Cobham and Hollis admired the objects of their commemoration not just for their ideas, but for the collective values that arose from assembling them.

The middle of the eighteenth century also witnessed the beginnings of a British pantheon of heroes, which, although primarily construed in literary terms, drew strong connections between *belles-lettres* and commitment to liberty. In three biographical collections of the 1760s and 1770s Buchanan's life and works were discussed alongside those of other sixteenth-century Protestant luminaries such as John Knox, William Shakespeare, William Camden, Philip Sidney and John Foxe. Each author emphasized similar aspects of the narrative of Buchanan's life, for example his relatively humble origins, and his delicate constitution that made him unsuitable for a military career. All praised his Latin style in the highest terms, and the educational value of his plays in particular, but were more cautious in their estimations of his political theory and treatment of Mary Queen of Scots.[45]

Such biographical collections had a clear didactic intent, to bring examples of virtue and fortitude to the attention of readers. This was also an avowed aim of the Buchanan monument built at Killearn, and Richard Finlay finds the same intent in Scottish admiration of such heroes as William Wallace and Robert Burns in the nineteenth century.[46] In the late eighteenth century, however, the consolidation of a Scottish pantheon was in its infancy. In 1788 even Robert Bruce, as the examples above highlight, could be revered or suppressed depending on the needs of the context: he could be praised as a representative of Scottish military vigour, or deplored as a symbol of Scottish backwardness. Enlightened historians such as

---

[45] [Joseph Towers], *British Biography; or, An Accurate and Impartial Account of the Lives and Writings of Eminent Persons, In Great Britain and Ireland* (10 vols, London, 1767), vol. 3, pp. 55–64; T. Mortimer, *The British Plutarch, containing the Lives of the most Eminent Statesmen, Patriots, Divines, Warriors, Philosophers, Poets, and Artists of Great Britain and Ireland* (6 vols, London, 1776), vol. 2, pp. 252–62; John Berkenhout, *Biographia Literaria; or a Biographical History of Literature: Containing the Lives of English, Scottish and Irish Authors* (London, 1777), vol. 1, pp. 342–6. Each of these short biographies of Buchanan drew to a considerable extent on Dr George Mackenzie's account, although each also made an effort to temper his rabidly episcopalian, Jacobite and pro-Marian prejudices in their assessments of Buchanan. George Mackenzie M.D., *The Lives and Characters of the Most Eminent Writers of the Scots Nation* (3 vols, Edinburgh, 1722), vol. 3, pp. 156–86.

[46] Reverend Ure suggested that the Killearn monument was built in order that, 'The living may reap advantage from the dead. Emulation is thereby excited, and the active powers of the mind stimulated by an ardour to excel in whatever is praiseworthy': *Statistical Account*, vol. 9, p. 383. Richard J. Finlay, 'Heroes, Myths and Anniversaries in Modern Scotland', *Scottish Affairs*, 18 (1997): pp. 108–25, at p. 109.

David Hume and William Robertson can be credited with contributing to this trend: they saw in Scottish history only examples of backwardness and looked to English history for lessons on liberty and progress.[47]

The 1790s were instrumental in altering perceptions of Scottish history and Scottish heroes. The unsettling effects of the French Revolution, with its slide towards atheistic republicanism, and the experience of the Revolutionary and Napoleonic Wars had a considerable impact on the formation of a Scottish pantheon of civil and religious liberty. Early in this revolutionary decade, two Scottish reformers on trial for sedition and speaking in their own defence named their heroes of Scottish history, and named Buchanan among them.[48] Both of them, Thomas Muir and William Skirving, were convicted and transported to Australia. Thomas Muir was on trial for various reformist activities, but the case against him focused particularly on the fact that at a British Convention of radicals in 1792 he had read out an Address from the United Irishmen, one section of which had said of Scotland:

> We rejoice that you do not consider yourselves as merged and melted down into another Country, but that in this great National Question you are still Scotland – the Land where Buchanan wrote, and Fletcher spoke, and Wallace fought.[49]

The prosecution's use of this Address from the United Irishmen is particularly interesting, as it opens up questions about how radical Buchanan was perceived to be in the context of the late eighteenth century. Buchanan's name did not feature in the selected excerpts of the Address read out by the prosecution, even though these were necessarily the most incriminating parts. Does this suggest that Buchanan's name had lost the radical associations of the previous two centuries?

The prosecution rather placed their emphasis on a disembodied section of this sentence that read, 'You are still Scotland', and attempted to suggest that the United Irishmen were urging Scots to support the dissolution of the Union.[50] Ironically, then, the completion of the sentence with the names of Buchanan, Fletcher and Wallace made the meaning more moderate. Or, to put it another way, the removal of these names gave it a more incriminating

---

[47]   J.G.A. Pocock, 'The Limits and Divisions of British History: In Search of the Unknown Subject', *American Historical Review*, 87 (1982): pp. 311–36, at p. 313.

[48]   For a full discussion of the context of the trials of the Scottish reformers to which this analysis is heavily indebted, see E.W. McFarland, *Ireland and Scotland in the Age of Revolution: Planting the Green Bough* (Edinburgh, 1994).

[49]   'Address from the Society of United Irishmen in Dublin', in ibid., p. 248.

[50]   Ibid.; 'The Trial of Thomas Muir', in T.J. Howell (ed.), *A Complete Collection of State Trials and Proceedings for High Treason* (34 vols, London, 1817), vol. 23, col. 124–6.

and damaging meaning. The Scottish legal establishment clearly regarded the ahistorical radicalism of the French Revolution as a more effective means of blackening the reformers than any association with the moorings of Scottish history.

This Irish allusion to a pantheon of Scottish heroes, Thomas Muir argued, had no particular radical signification, but was simply intended to illustrate the 'former lustre' of the independent kingdom of Scotland.[51] Indeed, it is tempting to agree with his explanation. This triumvirate of Wallace, Buchanan and Fletcher evoked three men who had written or fought in defence of freedom; however, these were very different forms of freedom, spaced several centuries apart, and it would be difficult to construe these as particularly democratic, or suited to the radical context of the 1790s.

William Skirving, at his trial in Edinburgh in January 1794, chose, somewhat misguidedly, to assert his innocence by reading aloud excerpts from the writings of David Erskine, 11th Earl of Buchan. He apparently believed that sharing opinions with a man of this station, 'in the higher spheres of life', was a mark of moderation.[52] However, Buchan was something of a radical himself: a supporter of the American and French Revolutions, he was regarded by his peers as a maverick, as Liam McIlvanney has shown.[53] Skirving nonetheless advanced Buchan (and indeed Buchanan) as a paragon of moderation. He read out the Earl's words, that Scottish history had been 'determined, and fixed by multiplied instances of changing the order of succession, and attainting their sovereigns for treason against the rights of the people'. Skirving then quoted the Earl's opinion of Buchanan: 'It is to Scotland and a Scotchman that the world is indebted for the establishment of the philosophical and logical principles of a free constitution.'[54] Buchan had argued, and Skirving evidently agreed with him, that George Buchanan should be admired as a Scottish hero.

It is significant that Muir and Skirving called upon the name and spirit of George Buchanan in defending themselves in court. Buchanan's aristocratic civic humanism cannot be seen as a direct influence on the reforming ideologies of the 1790s, and as Gordon Pentland notes, Buchanan's name and ideas did not feature in the discussions at the

---

[51] Ibid., vol. 23, col. 225.

[52] 'The Trial of William Skirving', in Howell (ed.), *State Trials*, vol. 23, col. 571.

[53] Liam McIlvanney, *Burns the Radical: Poetry and Politics in Late Eighteenth-century Scotland* (East Linton, 2002), p. 56.

[54] 'The Trial of William Skirving', in Howell (ed.), *State Trials*, vol. 23, col. 573; D. Stewart Erskine, Earl of Buchan, *Essays on the Lives and Writings of Fletcher of Saltoun and the Poet Thomson* (London, 1792), p. 33.

Convention that preceded the prosecutions.[55] Rather, Muir and Skirving's naming of Buchanan called upon his symbolic and rhetorical potential, as they sought to use their day in court to produce 'their own counter-discourse and counter-theatre'.[56] Muir and Skirving used the name of Buchanan just as the lawyer Thomas Erskine used the name of John Locke in his successful defence of the reformer Thomas Hardy in his trial for treason in London 1794.[57] Names such as Buchanan and Locke represented the accumulated political wisdom of centuries, and Muir and Skirving must have regarded them as safe to invoke because they were the antithesis of the French revolutionary radicalism that sought to jettison past wisdom and begin a new constitution with a clean slate. In making use of historical figures in these terms, then, it is likely that Muir and Skirving were doing more than just declaring an attachment to a set of political principles. By dropping names such as Buchanan's they hoped to produce positive associations in the minds of their hearers. In this sense, this name dropping does not constitute a canon of texts or theories, but a pantheon of heroes.

As a member of a developing Scottish pantheon of civil and religious liberty, then, Buchanan was judged less by his texts and he was understood – or misunderstood – in terms of the needs of particular contexts. The Earl of Buchan compared Buchanan to 'the morning star, to announce the approach of philosophical day', and called him 'the father of whiggery'.[58] Contributors to the radical journal *The Bee* also praised Buchanan in similarly high but undiscriminating terms. One contributor used 'Philo Buchananus' as his pseudonym.[59] Buchanan was further described as 'a herald of civil and religious liberty'.[60] Such hyperbolic praise, often vague and undiscriminating, displayed engagement not with Buchanan's ideas, but with what he had come to stand for. Such examples are not intended to criticize the uses that contemporaries of the eighteenth century made of Buchanan, but should rather highlight their creativity, and the flexibility that they were able to find and exploit in the name of George Buchanan.

---

[55]   Gordon Pentland, 'Patriotism, Universalism and the Scottish Conventions, 1792–1794', *History*, 89 (2004): pp. 340–60, at p. 346.

[56]   Michael T. Davis, 'Prosecution and Radical Discourse during the 1790s: The Case of the Scottish Sedition Trials', *International Journal of the Sociology of Law*, 33 (2005): pp. 148–58, at p. 153.

[57]   Mark Goldie, 'Introduction', in Goldie (ed.) *The Reception of Locke's Politics* (6 vols, London, 1999), vol. 1, p. xvii.

[58]   Buchan, *Essays on Fletcher and Thomson*, pp. xxi, 33. William Skirving also quoted this last expression of praise in his trial for sedition.

[59]   *The Bee*, 9 (1792): p. 330.

[60]   'Some Remarks on the Literary Character of George Buchanan', *The Bee*, 5 (1791): p. 232.

Commentators such as Thomas Muir and contributors to *The Bee* are, of course, hardly representative of political discourse in the late eighteenth century. Yet they illustrate the direction in which Buchanan's reputation was moving. When the threat from France and the climate of paranoid loyalism retreated, many of the most negative and controversial aspects of Buchanan's reputation were washed away. What remained above the high water line was Buchanan's status as a member of the Scottish pantheon of civil and religious liberty, a perception that privileged his Protestantism, his literary talents, and a cautious endorsement of his political theory.

To conclude, the second half of the eighteenth century witnessed the consolidation of inoffensive formulations like 'Revolution Principles' and 'civil and religious liberty', and the plucking of names from history to uphold these founding values of Britain. It has been argued that the development of this tame political culture marked an important turning point in the reputation of George Buchanan, a shift from radical and regicidal associations towards acceptance as a libertarian hero. The formation of this pantheon had been tentatively underway before 1788, and it faltered under the shifting political orthodoxies of the 1790s. However, by 1815, there was broad acceptance of a group of heroes that could safely be admired, and Buchanan was one of them.

In Scotland the development of a pantheon of libertarian heroes was difficult, partly owing to fears that nationalistic sentiments were out of place in a unionist culture, and partly owing to the difficulties of marketing the Covenanting tradition. Scotland's martyrs of the Restoration period were not charmingly maverick aristocratic radicals like Algernon Sidney. Covenanting field preachers such as Richard Cameron and Donald Cargill were radicals who were also religious fanatics, and it would be impossible, at that time, to fit them into the moderate British mould. In 1788 ecclesiastical celebrations dominated by the established churches of Britain sought to neutralize any radical potential that the Revolution of 1688, or the Restoration period that preceded it, might have had. While English Protestant Dissenters and Scottish Burgher Seceders praised the constitution that tolerated their beliefs, only the Antiburghers were willing to criticize the Revolution Settlement and unreservedly praise the radical presbyterian tradition that had preceded it.

The Covenanting tradition was a dead end in Buchanan's reputation, but broader fame as a libertarian hero beckoned, and in 1788 he was honoured as an object of pride for the whole Scottish nation with the building of the Killearn monument. Depoliticized and increasingly irrelevant as a political theorist, Buchanan had become more usable for his name than for his ideas, and praise of him tended to be undiscriminating and flexible. The Covenanters, in contrast, remained beyond the pale of the pantheon of civil and religious liberty until around the middle of the nineteenth century.

The extended pantheon came by this time to include such names as William Wallace and Robert Bruce, their acceptance guaranteed by centuries of reprints of Barbour's *Bruce* and Blind Hary's *Wallace*, and more recently bolstered by the poetry of Robert Burns; John Knox and George Buchanan, heroes of the first Reformation; James Guthrie and Alexander Peden, to name but two heroes of the second Reformation; Andrew Fletcher of Saltoun, incorruptible Whig; and Robert Burns and Thomas Muir of more recent memory.[61] All members of the pantheon, regardless of their historical context, their aims or their understanding of liberty, attained a degree of equality and could be linked together flexibly. As the mutating reputation of George Buchanan shows, however, the pantheon of Scottish heroes has been, and remains, a construct, dependent on a degree of distortion and the decontextualization of historical figures.

---

[61]   For a revealing insight into the composition of the pantheon by the mid-nineteenth century, see Charles Rogers, *Stirling: The Battle Ground of Civil and Religious Liberty* (London, 1857). Rogers was a cultural nationalist who agitated for the building of the Wallace Monument at Stirling, and who was a biographer of significant Scots including William Wallace, the reformer George Wishart, John Knox and Robert Burns.

Index

St Andrews Studies in Reformation History

The Shaping of a Community: The Rise and Reformation of the English Parish c. 1400–1560
Beat Kümin

Seminary or University? The Genevan Academy and Reformed Higher Education, 1560–1620
Karin Maag

Marian Protestantism: Six Studies
Andrew Pettegree

Protestant History and Identity in Sixteenth-Century Europe
(2 volumes) edited by Bruce Gordon

Antifraternalism and Anticlericalism in the German Reformation: Johann Eberlin von Günzburg and the Campaign against the Friars
Geoffrey Dipple

Reformations Old and New: Essays on the Socio-Economic Impact of Religious Change c. 1470–1630
edited by Beat Kümin

Piety and the People: Religious Printing in French, 1511–1551
Francis M. Higman

The Reformation in Eastern and Central Europe
edited by Karin Maag

John Foxe and the English Reformation
edited by David Loades

The Reformation and the Book
Jean-François Gilmont, edited and translated by Karin Maag

The Magnificent Ride: The First Reformation in Hussite Bohemia
Thomas A. Fudge

*Hatred in Print: Catholic Propaganda and Protestant Identity
during the French Wars of Religion*
Luc Racaut

Penitence, Preaching and the Coming of the Reformation
Anne T. Thayer

*Huguenot Heartland:
Montauban and Southern French Calvinism
during the French Wars of Religion*
Philip Conner

Charity and Lay Piety in Reformation London, 1500–1620
Claire S. Schen

*The British Union: A Critical Edition and Translation of
David Hume of Godscroft's De Unione Insulae Britannicae*
edited by Paul J. McGinnis and Arthur H. Williamson

*Reforming the Scottish Church:
John Winram (c. 1492–1582) and the Example of Fife*
Linda J. Dunbar

*Cultures of Communication from Reformation to Enlightenment:
Constructing Publics in the Early Modern German Lands*
James Van Horn Melton

*Sebastian Castellio, 1515-1563:
Humanist and Defender of Religious Toleration in a Confessional Age*
Hans R. Guggisberg, translated and edited by Bruce Gordon

*The Front-Runner of the Catholic Reformation:
The Life and Works of Johann von Staupitz*
Franz Posset

*The Correspondence of Reginald Pole:
Volume 2. A Calendar, 1547–1554: A Power in Rome*
Thomas F. Mayer

William of Orange and the Revolt of the Netherlands, 1572–1584
K.W. Swart, translated by J.C. Grayson

The Italian Reformers and the Zurich Church, c.1540–1620
Mark Taplin

Humanism and Calvinism
Andrew Melville and the Universities of Scotland, 1560–1625
Steven J. Reid

The Senses and the English Reformation
Matthew Milner

Early French Reform
The Theology and Spirituality of Guillaume Farel
Jason Zuidema and Theodore Van Raalte

Catholic and Protestant Translations of the Imitatio Christi, *1425–1650*
Maximilian von Habsburg

Getting Along?
Religious Identities and Confessional Relations in Early Modern England
–Essays in Honour of Professor W.J. Sheils
Edited by Nadine Lewycky and Adam Morton

From Priest's Whore to Pastor's Wife
Clerical Marriage and the Process of Reform in the
Early German Reformation
Marjorie Elizabeth Plummer